CASEWORK
A Psychosocial Therapy

Second Edition

CASEWORK
A Psychosocial Therapy

by

FLORENCE HOLLIS

Columbia University School of Social Work

with Preface to the First Edition by

Charlotte Towle

Random House New York

Now there are four chief obstacles in grasping
truth which hinder every man, however learned,
and scarcely allow anyone a clear title to learning,
namely,
submission to faulty and unworthy authority,
influence of custom,
popular prejudice,
concealment of our own ignorance accompanied
by an ostentacious display of our knowledge.

—Friar Roger Bacon, *Opus Majus*
(translated by Robert Belle Burke)

The publisher would like to offer acknowledgment to the Family Service Association of America for permission to use Tables 1, 2, and 3, and Figures 1, 2, 3, and 4, which are from Florence Hollis, *A Typology of Casework Treatment*, 1967 and 1968, and Table 4, which is from Edward Mullen, "Casework Communication," *Social Casework*, 49 (November 1968).

ISBN: 0-394-31379-8

Library of Congress Catalog Card Number: 70-168588

Typography by J. M. Wall

Manufactured in the United States of America

Second Edition
9 8 7 6 5 4

Preface to the First Edition

Without benefit of an author's Preface, which traditionally has served to reveal the author, the readers of this book will see Florence Hollis as a full-fledged social worker in action as educator and as casework practitioner.* Having thoroughly integrated her professional experience, she functions freely in both roles. Master of her subject, she is also perceptive of the integrative task confronting the reader, as she shows not only in her steadfast concern to convey methods of thinking in the content of the rich knowledge she imparts, but also in her concern to clarify, to point out what is merely speculative, and to provide evidence to support assertions. Her understanding is evident in her rare ability to involve the reader in the feeling, thinking, and doing which she not only is portraying but in which she herself is engaged as she envisages casework practice.

To an exceptional degree Miss Hollis dares to teach the hows of practice, the specific technical means which workers have used, or conceivably might use, with specific individuals in specific situations. In so doing she upholds the principle of individualization through imaginative consideration of possible and probable variables. Although she does not need to fear the stigma of technicianship, she misses this pitfall by a wide margin. The whats and hows of casework which she leads the reader to consider are rooted in basic principles of practice, which are steadfastly oriented to the whys implicit in individualization of persons in relation to time, place, other persons, and social circumstances. This work therefore has a dimension far beyond that of a textbook.

The author's use of the direct influence implicit in instruction sustains rather than devitalizes reflective thinking. Thus Miss Hollis, in her role as educator, adapts technical measures which she and her associates have formulated for use in casework prac-

---

* For the traditional purpose of the preface see *Famous Prefaces* (The Harvard Classics, Volume 39: Introductory Note, p. 3).

tice, on the assumption that one fosters rational behavior through providing the means to think rather than through "thinking for" —a weakness in many an author's approach to his readers, even as in many a caseworker's approach to his clients.

I welcome the author's abundant use of case citations. Technical means establish the validity of diagnostic thinking and treatment choices. With exceptions, in social work writing we have been more free in our use of case material to demonstrate what was done and why it was done than how it was done. Many factors doubtless have operated in our withdrawal from delineation of specific means. Among them one reason perhaps has been the unfortunate circumstance that, through removal from practice, some of us who write have not been sufficiently secure to risk facing or exposing our technical measures. There has also been a fear of technicianship, with its use of stereotypes rather than differential application of methods. The reflective consideration of possible "hows" should ease rather than heighten our fear.

This book will make an outstanding contribution to those who come to grips with what the author as educator teaches of psychosocial study, diagnosis, and treatment. Notably in two chapters on treatment, one on objectives, and one on procedures, Miss Hollis differentiates casework objectives and procedures from those in other kinds of therapy, but she does not divorce the two; in fact, casework help may bulwark other kinds of therapy. This is in contrast to the theory and practice of many social workers, who have disentangled therapy, casework, and relief-giving out of a concern to develop social work as a profession in its own right, distinct from psychiatry. Such a separation also has been justified, often in the light of reality pressures, as a necessary means of bringing the demands of practice within the scope of agency function and resources. The limitation in this has been the tendency to think categorically about the values of method, rather than about its appropriateness for the client.

The relationship among study, diagnosis, and treatment is demonstrated in the cases discussed in the chapter entitled "Three Variations in Treatment Emphasis" in which cases demonstrate the relationship between them. They are models of brief but comprehensive case summarization, with fine-point appraisal of movement in treatment, appropriate modification of diagnosis, and well-developed assessment of the factors operating in the treatment outcome. The author emphasizes that these cases are offered not as proof of theories or results but rather as demonstrations of the relationship among psychosocial study, diagnosis, and treatment. They were selected because the individuals involved were markedly similar, but their problems and social situations called for variation in treatment. They thus demonstrate the need for individualization within categories at a time when there has been a trend toward short cuts in diagnosis and in case analysis as a means to the formulation of principles of practice.

Certainly a profession does not come of age until it develops its own theory. The oversimplification at the root of shoddy practice is more likely to occur through the annexation of theory from other disciplines. Unassimilated, such borrowings may become cliches and easy generalizations which lend themselves to indiscriminate, patchy, or blanket use. Miss Hollis warns against oversimplification as "one of the worst traps into which a worker can fall." She herself clarifies without simplification by providing the wherewithal for coping with complexity. Her use of case materials has obvious value for teachers, supervisors, practitioners, and students. One must not overlook its value also for consultants in other disciplines—psychiatrists, psychoanalysts, psychologists and social scientists—from whom social caseworkers have derived formulations which, despite their value, have sometimes operated against differential thinking to raise the question: diagnosis and treatment of whom—this person or a type, this person or a disease entity, this specific social situation or a comparable one commonly encountered? Assumption of responsibility for engaging our consultants to think with us rather than for us may be facilitated not only through our grasp of case analysis but also through sharing our thinking with them.

This book is a timely contribution to the current interprofessional scene. Among the professions directly concerned with human welfare this is a period of synthesis. Cross-fertilization has been an integrative force in providing a common conceptual framework to serve as a means to communication and collaboration among the segments within social work and among disciplines formerly incompatible in their thinking. It has served to produce common principles of practice and some valid overlapping in practice. Inevitably, however, it has also brought invalid fusions which have fostered coalescence rather than integration. Within social work this synthesis has been expressed in the generic movement, a sound development when it has not surpassed the limits of what can be integrated, and also in an amalgamation rather than in a nice articulation of professional functions. In many multidisciplinary settings, the primary function of each profession in a clinical team has been subordinated or even defaced as social workers, psychologists, and psychiatrists have become psychotherapists operating with negligible difference from one another, and the psychiatrist has become more consultant, supervisor, and teacher than practitioner of his specialty. The pervasive influence of this abortive development on social work practice beyond clinic walls is progressively being corrected by a counter-movement instigated largely by social workers, which gives hope that in synthesizing we will not in the long run become synthetic. Miss Hollis's work heightens this hope, for it forthrightly establishes what social casework is and what it is not in all its helping measures.

Despite the headway made by the counter-movement, the coalescence of the several professions engaged in psychotherapy has fathered a new movement for the establishment of a "profession of psychotherapy," in which the basic education of the several disciplines involved would be merged to produce a unified profession.* An argument in favor of such a step is that the "dead wood" for psychotherapy in each profession's basic education could be sloughed off. This raises many questions, of which the most important are: Would there not be heavy losses to those served and those serving? Should not each profession retain responsibility for its therapy and therefore for its basic training? A well-reasoned answer to these questions as they bear upon social casework is to be found in Miss Hollis's conception of social

---

* One step in this direction has been taken in a conference on "An Ideal Training Program for Psychotherapists" held at Gould House, Ardsley-on-Hudson, New York, March 21–24, 1963, under the auspices of New York University and with the support of the Aaron E. Norman Fund. Representatives of the fields of clinical psychology, social work, psychiatry and psychoanalysis attended. A continuing committee was formed to consider the issues opened at this conference.

casework as an organic whole, in which treatment is a blend of the diagnostically determined technical procedures. Therapy in the sense of consideration of "dynamic and genetic intrapsychic factors" cannot be set apart from other measures which may support the client or which are indicated in the light of changing responses and goals. Generic casework principles still persist. A social worker may need to use all that he knows of social casework in the conduct of psychosocial therapy.

Now that the cause of social work is fast becoming a world cause, the community's expectations of it, as well as social work's expectations of itself, have mounted. The push for growth has stimulated, on the one hand, a quest for the new and much experimentation in an endeavor to expand the ways and means of social work. On the other hand, it has marshaled unconscious and conscious concern to synthesize as a means to the preservation of integrity. Periods of synthesis, in that they bring about new integrations which determine future developments, call for judicious extensions and discards, as Miss Hollis is aware. She perceptively has chosen to deal with a segment of casework practice because such a choice permits concentration upon basic well-established methodology, rather than upon the exploration of new trends still in the early stages of experimentation and assimilation. In closing the introduction she states:

A clear understanding of fundamental principles is never more needed than when theory is being expanded and choices must be made between what is to be retained and what discarded of both the new and the old. It is therefore perhaps especially timely for caseworkers to formulate as clearly as possible the nature of their basic frame of reference. Treatment will become more effective only when what is potentially sound and useful in the new is admitted to the main body of principles whose value has already been demonstrated.

In these times of pressure for marked change, these lines place the author among those social workers who might be described as evolutionists rather than as revolutionists, and whose behavior might be characterized as more adaptive than defensive. Throughout this book she tends to deal with a part with reference to the whole, in fact, to maintain the intactness of a valued whole.

To this end she brings together what belongs together and excludes the discrepant, pending the establishment of its relevance. She contends against those dichotomies which have been erected as defenses against complexity or against that which is emotionally unacceptable. Her guides have much in common with those developed by other writers as social casework has shifted progressively from the simplicity of its early focus on problems to the complexity of person or persons in the matrix of agency and social situation. She goes beyond many authors in her fine-point orientation of diagnosis and treatment to personality dynamics in normal and pathological behavior, individual and group.

The author's propensity to conserve wholeness, in the process of integrating the new, or in reviving old discards which now have a new dimension through their growth or through the growth of social work in ability to use them, is shown in her union of the psychic and the social. In considering the implications of such a union for the relationship of psychiatry, social casework, and the social sciences, she contests social work's substitution of the social scientist for the psychoanalytic psychiatrist as a mentor. She asserts that "sociological data amplify the rich understanding of the internal dynamics of the personality developed by the Freudian school of thought; they do not replace it." In elaboration she decries the "either-or" trend represented by those who would explain human behavior primarily in interpersonal terms, omitting intrapsychic phenomena. She argues for the use of both. She shows acceptance of specific contributions of the sociologist, notably the role concept, with reservations, however, about precipitous annexation of theory, pending exploration. When one recalls that the early split between social work and the social scientists occurred largely around the issue of individualization versus categorization of people, one finds, now, that social casework is better able to generalize its experience. The author is not retreating, however, from the formulation and use of categories. She individualizes within categories and thus brings individualization and categorization together. She raises hope that we may now integrate the contribution of the social scientist and not repeat the past through erecting dichotomies.

Miss Hollis holds the past, present, and future of the client together in study, diagnosis, and treatment. Some social workers have simplified through centering on the present, trusting, first, that the discernible imprint of the past will serve as a reliable basis for inference, and second, that future difficulties may well be averted through meeting current needs and solving current problems. Miss Hollis, in contrast, while focusing on the present, draws on the past in understanding the client and, where indicated, helps him cope with the persistence of the past in the present. She is concerned to reckon with the client's future both through reflective consideration of his aspirations, goals and fears, and through helping him plan for the future whenever possible.

Miss Hollis brings the intellect and the emotions into a two-way relationship. The concept of man as a rational being dominated the caseworker's early thinking on this relationship; therefore intellect was expected not only to govern thinking and doing, but also to fashion it. The caseworker accordingly relied heavily on imparting information and on appealing to reason in effecting change in behavior. Psychological insight, however, brought a focus on the irrational self. It gave prominence to the point of view that feelings fashion thinking and prompt action. Therefore rational behavior was contingent on a change in feeling. The treatment sequence began with understanding and modifying feeling, after which change in thinking and doing would follow almost automatically. If it did not, it was because the client was resistant to change or for some reason inaccessible to help. Perception of the fact that what a man knows and what he thinks may be the source of his feeling again reversed the sequence. But progressively the "either-or" sequence has given way to one in which the two conceptions interplay. The saying, "As a man thinketh in his heart, so is he" has become a generic concept in social work; without reference to a school of thought, in fact, it is central in the philosophy of social work. But a philosophy and technical procedures which make it come alive in practice have not readily been attained.

This philosophy was beautifully expressed by Jessie Taft in a paper entitled, "Living and Feeling," written in 1933 and recently reissued.* It has been variously stated and restated in the

---

* Jessie Taft, *Therapist and Social Work Educator.* Edited by Virginia P. Robinson (Philadelphia: University of Pennsylvania Press, 1962).

literature throughout the years, notably encapsulated long ago by Gordon Hamilton in the comment, "Casework lies midway between therapy and education," and developed further by other writers on casework.* It has been reflected in accounts of desirable practice, but it is my impression that it has not pervasively influenced practice. There is still evidence that heavy reliance on modifying feeling without reference to the part played by distorted thinking out of ignorance or error persists. We have had valid fear of intellectualization, out of past lack of skill in imparting knowledge and in helping individuals think—in short, out of lack of facility in our use of educational method. It is probable also that our identification with the psychoanalytic therapist's methods has impeded acceptance of our re-educative role. An outstanding contribution of Miss Hollis's book is the place given to a rational approach in which knowledge is imparted and thinking anew is engaged through reflective discussion. Miss Hollis formulates this approach as a major technical procedure of central importance when it is combined with other procedures which make it something more than the worker's intellectualization.

Finally, the author's organization and evaluation of technical procedures conserves the wholeness of social casework. Continuity, sequence, and integration of the parts emerges chapter by chapter and the wholeness is seen clearly in the summarization in the last chapter. The procedures are not arranged in a hierarchy of values; for example, insight therapy is not more valued than environmental modification. The author comments, "One technique is of no more value than another." The value lies in the blending of the procedures, in the matching and timing of them to the client's needs and abilities and in the skill with which any procedure is used. A decisive demand is that they support one another. The part played by the casework relationship and the worker's understanding of the unconscious in the conduct of all

---

* See Helen H. Perlman, *Social Casework: A Problem Solving Process* (Chicago: University of Chicago Press, 1957). See also Charlotte Towle, *Common Human Needs* (Washington, D.C.: Federal Security Agency, 1945; and New York: National Association of Social Workers, 1954), and *The Learner in Education for the Professions* (Chicago: University of Chicago Press, 1954).

the procedures is well developed in two chapters and recaptured in the summarization in the final chapter, as well as in the presentation of case examples throughout the book.

Among the types of procedure by which change can be wrought in the client's social effectiveness, the place the author gives to direct influence and to reflective discussion of the person-situation configuration affirms a trend which I, among others, have welcomed. As one member of what has seemed to be a minority group in the recent past, I have held steadfastly to these procedures as being the very stuff of social casework. I have decried the evisceration implied in the past depreciation and even discard of these procedures. Miss Hollis has restored these discards not only in reviving these aspects of early practice, but in making them an integral part of psychologically oriented casework.

In relation to the reflective discussion of the person-situation configuration, my role as educator has convinced me that, just as what we have learned in casework has been used adaptively in education, so what we have learned as educators may be used adaptively to a greater extent than formerly in casework. It is to be hoped that the imprint of the social worker's own educational experience may lay the groundwork for this and become influential in begetting his professional identity. When one recalls that a primary aim of social casework is to help clients become more rational social beings, one firmly supports Miss Hollis's emphasis on this procedure, for she would have us relate to the client's rational self and thereby affirm this potential. It is only as we treat man as rational that he may become more so.

In this work Miss Hollis has not only delineated the relationship between the social and psychological components of casework therapy, but has also shown the line between psychoanalysis or psychoanalytic therapy on the one hand, and the practice of the social worker as caseworker or therapist on the other. In doing so, she has carried forward the work of others. We will be in a better position to appraise new directions in casework practice, and to define and clarify issues, as this work excites controversy. It is less important that we all think alike than that we know our likenesses and differences, so that we can speak intelligibly from group to group, within social work and within the inter-

professional scene.   In serving this purpose the book will meet
an urgent need.

Charlotte Towle

September 1963
School of Social Service Administration
The University of Chicago

Acknowledgments

The writing of acknowledgments for a book is a happy moment for its author. The work is done and the book is safely in the hands of the printer, finished but still protected for a brief interlude from the friendly but nonetheless critical scrutiny it must soon undergo.

This book was written with the generous help of many colleagues to whom I am deeply grateful. First of all the caseworkers who were willing for their work to be studied: protection of the anonymity of their clients who appear in the book prevents my mentioning them by name, but I do want here to express my gratitude to them and to the agencies which generously allowed me to read and use data from their records. The agencies which contributed to the development of the book include:

The Community Service Society, New York, New York
The Family Service of Greater Boston, Boston, Massachusetts
The Family Service Society, Hartford, Connecticut
The Jewish Board of Guardians, New York, New York
The Judge Baker Guidance Center, Boston, Massachusetts
The Massachusetts General Hospital, Boston, Massachusetts

These agencies are in no sense to be held responsible for the content of the book, but I trust that their staffs will feel that my use of their work has lead to formulations which ring true in the light of their own professional experience.

In writing Chapters 5–11 on the classification of treatment procedures, I have drawn upon work done under grant number OM-513 of the National Institute of Mental Health. Chapter 10 reports the findings of further research completed several years after the publication of the first edition of this book. This further study was made possible by a continuation of grant OM-513. I am indeed grateful for this support.

A number of colleagues have given many hours of their time to reading and criticizing the manuscript in its several drafts.

Nothing is more important in the final stages of a book than for the author to be able to profit by the frank and discerning criticism of trusted colleagues. This preliminary putting of one's ideas to the test brings to light discrepancies between the intent and the actuality of communications, adds valuable ideas, and serves to protect the final readers from notions that cannot stand up to criticism or that are so poorly formulated that they do not deserve to see the light of day.

My first reader, the friend and colleague who has so generously shared her professional wisdom throughout the years, is Rosemary Reynolds. Others to whom I wish to express my appreciation are Lucille Austin, Esther Clemence, Jeanette Regensburg, Ruth Schwarz, Ann Shyne, Isabel Stamm, and Dr. George Wiedeman. To these I now add Rosalind Miller who read and made valuable suggestions concerning the new chapter 11.

I should like to mention too that the beginnings of this book included early conversations with Florence Day and Annette Garrett. They both wanted the book to be written and contributed to that initial impetus which sets a study going. In addition, Annette Garrett helped in the location of suitable agencies from which to request material. It has been a great pleasure also to have had Charlotte Towle consent to write the preface and to have her express her response to the book in such generous terms.

In writing the second edition I am indebted to many additional colleagues. First, to the doctoral students who worked on the typology, most of whom are themselves now engaged in social work education. Yetta Appel, Francis Turner, and Fil Verdiani carried major responsibility for testing the reliability of the typology of casework communications. Francis Turner's doctoral dissertation was the first in which the typology was used. Yetta Appel undertook background research which contributed to the formulations and methodology. Others who worked on the material from time to time in its early stages included Ben Avis Orcutt and William Reid. A number of students in Master's programs at both the Smith College and the Columbia University schools of social work also gave valuable help through their use of the typology in their Master's theses.

Later Shirley Ehrenkranz in her doctoral study of communications in joint husband-wife interviews tested the adaptability of the typology to such interviews and developed new categories. Edward Mullen in his dissertation adapted the typology to use with tapes and added to our knowledge of a number of factors influencing the distribution of communication procedures.

It was a pleasure to be able to enlist Isabel Stamm for the writing of her excellent chapter on family therapy which will orient the reader to the major current trends in this form of casework treatment.

In no small measure this second edition is the product of work done in recent years by casework teachers of both class and field who are members of the faculty of the Columbia University School of Social Work. This has been a fruitful colleague relationship in which ideas and teaching material have been generously shared. Issues have been debated; new ideas have been contributed; impetus has been given to the wish to develop a reformulation of psychosocial casework that would both preserve fundamental principles and integrate emerging ideas of demonstrated significance. The book makes no pretense, however, of representing group opinion. Heaven forbid that a faculty should arrive at such unanimity of thought that any one member of it could speak for the whole on a subject as broad as casework!

Master's and doctoral students too have contributed greatly to this second edition. Seeking, challenging, restless, determined to do things better than we have done, they force us constantly to reexamine our knowledge, reexpress it in convincing terms, modify it, augment it with the constant flow of new experience and new ideas that they so eagerly grasp in their urgent quest for answers. Without apology for my own generation of caseworkers, I respect and value the contributions of these younger colleagues too and fervently hope they do indeed push forward our knowledge of how to overcome our ever more pressing human dilemmas.

The second edition has again drawn upon the generosity of my friend Rosemary Reynolds. Not only has she given weeks of her time to helping to develop the extensive additions of recent writings to the bibliographical notes and to revising the index, but again, as in the first edition, she has shared her professional knowledge, acted as critical reader, and given constant encouragement to the undertaking. I am most grateful to her.

And finally, my thanks go also to the secretaries who in successive stages struggled with the manuscript and to the editors who with enthusiasm and tact sharpened words and syntax for more telling communication.

Florence Hollis

New York City
November 1971

Contents

Part Two

TREATMENT: AN ANALYSIS OF PROCEDURES

Part One

THE THEORETICAL
FRAMEWORK

1 | ⲁ Developing Practice

Casework is on the move! Treatment methods—or methods of intervention—developed experimentally in the fifties have matured into accepted procedures widely used by caseworkers in the seventies. Family group treatment and joint interviewing of several members of a family have established their value. Planned short-term work, including crisis treatment, is in extensive use. Where used appropriately it can often bring relief more quickly and sometimes more effectively than "open-ended" procedures. It enables more individuals and families to be served without long periods of waiting for help to become available. The effects of living chronically without adequate income for decent food, clothing, and housing are far better recognized than they were in the fifties. Many stereotypes about the "culture of poverty" have been exploded. The rich variations to be found among similar economic and racial or ethnic groups are emerging from the distorting generalizations that marked early efforts to understand cultural differences.[1] Black society and its aspirations are better understood. Simplistic explanations have yielded to a recognition of the interplay of multiple factors in shaping both the individual and his dilemmas, an interplay with direct implications for the casework process.

In many disciplines the approach to knowledge known as systems theory has proved to be a useful tool for helping the mind to deal with the complexities of modern knowledge. Psychosocial casework has found this mode of thought most congenial for dealing conceptually with the multiplicity of psychological, familial, and social forces at work in the human situation. The importance of the social environment and of agency operations has long been recognized by caseworkers,[2] but a reaffirmation of their importance as parts of the total system and hence of the caseworker's responsibility for modifying them emerged in the sixties.

The point of view reflected in this book is that this developing body of knowledge and practice represents a healthy growth and extension of the knowledge and practice of the fifties. The psychosocial approach to casework is an open system of thought that provides a wide framework for the incorporation of the developments of the sixties.[3] These extensions of the caseworker's range of knowledge and practice create a large learning task for all practitioners and especially for student caseworkers. Very little that the worker knew and used in the late fifties has become obsolete. Instead, the knowledge base has been expanded, built upon, enriched, so that there is more to learn and a wider range of approaches to master before the worker finds his own treatment emphases and preferences for specialization in practice.

The primary concern of this book is to analyze a particular segment of casework practice—the treatment of individuals experiencing problems in their interpersonal relationships. Marital, individual, and parent-child adjustment problems of clients in family service agencies, child guidance clinics, psychiatric clinics and mental hygiene centers serving either children or adults are focused upon in order to contribute to the improvement of the quality of casework treatment offered such clients. In analyzing the dynamics of the treatment procedures we have endeavored to clarify the underlying principles so that the reader will understand the essentials of this type of treatment and thereby enhance his own treatment skill.

Treatment of interpersonal adjustment problems does not constitute a separate form of casework but is rather one of many different clusters of casework procedures within the general matrix of therapeutic and interventive processes that constitute the broad field of casework. When the problem is chiefly one of disturbed relationships, certain procedures of treatment necessarily receive greater emphasis; if we were discussing problems due primarily to reality pressures, other procedures would be stressed. Nevertheless, in analyzing a particular treatment approach, we are inevitably also discussing general casework principles. The part cannot be isolated from the whole. All the work presented lies within the general scope of casework, and the principles involved are expressed in terms of their general applicability.

Many terms are currently used in referring to the casework process—"treatment," "the helping process," "intervention," "therapy," "service." Each has its own claim to appropriateness, for casework is a very broad field. Sometimes the client is emotionally or psychologically disturbed or distressed, or he needs help in the further development of his ego adaptive capacities. Where this is so, the term "therapy" is fitting. At other times, when the emphasis is on meeting practical needs or intervening in the environment, the term "therapy" is not descriptive and broader ones such as "intervention," "the helping process," or "casework service," are better. The term "treatment" is also general and broad enough to cover a wide range of casework activities, as anyone who takes the trouble to consult a good dictionary can easily learn. Some social workers dislike this term because to them it implies "sickness" and seems to put the blame for any distress or dilemma upon the client rather than on social conditions. When the term "treatment" is used in this book it distinctly does not carry any such connotation. It is often the *situation*—the environment—that must be treated—modified, changed. The term "psychosocial therapy" in the title of this book is used to focus attention on the fact that when casework is therapeutic it is not just *psycho*therapy but rather is strongly social as well as psychological in its approach.

This second edition has been expanded to include a more extensive discussion of the ways in which the caseworker intervenes in the client's immediate environment in order to reduce pressures or bring resources and opportunities within his reach. In 1962, when this book was first written, most work with the client was done through individual interviews. Joint interviews of married couples and family interviewing were then referred to by the author as "promising new trends" not covered by the data upon which the book was based. It is now widely recognized that interviewing couples together and families as a whole is a powerful tool for developing understanding of intrafamilial relationships and bringing change in these relationships. Sometimes the entire contact consists of such interviews. More commonly in casework both individual interviewing and group interviewing are used in the same family, each form of work having its own purpose and value. Chapter 12, in which this type of interviewing is given particular attention, has therefore been added in the present edition.

The new classification of casework treatment procedures introduced in the first edition was at that time based on what Norman Polansky has called "practice wisdom." It was then in the process of being studied by the author and other researchers with the help of a grant from the National Institute of Mental Health. This study and related research have substantiated the basic soundness of the classification. The typology has also subsequently been used as a tool in a number of studies examining the nature of casework practice. In Chapter 10 this research is discussed.

Communication theory is the latest arrival among the new sets of concepts brought to the fore in recent years, and it is increasingly being drawn upon. The attention it attracts to the importance of nonverbal and paraverbal communication and to the "slippage" in communication that occurs when the symbols of any type of communication are not given the same meaning by individuals who are attempting to communicate is of particular value. Many concepts from general systems theory are highly compatible with the concepts of psychosocial casework. As early as 1941 Gordon Hamilton[4] in a major paper used the term "organismic" to characterize the psychosocial approach and referred to its use by Henry A. Murray in his *Explorations in Personality*. Murray in describing an organism said: "The organism is from the beginning a whole, from which the parts are derived by self-differentiation. The whole and its parts are mutually related; the whole being as essential to an understanding of the parts as the parts are to an understanding of the whole."[5] He also referred to a human being as adapting, integrating, and differentiating "within a changing environmental matrix." Systems theory adds to this early conception the transactional concept of the relationships between the individual and his environment. These and other systems concepts have been found extremely useful in clarifying aspects of the person-situation gestalt so central to the psychosocial approach.

There are currently many new emphases in the field of case-work, as there are also in the entire range of social work. For casework, at least, these developments are evolutionary rather than revolutionary in nature. There is undoubtedly value in the renewed concern for the total family, the bringing of fathers into treatment, the increased use of the home visit, especially for diagnostic purposes. Of great importance also is the wider and more sophisticated use of the knowledge that the social sciences are acquiring of ethnic, class, and regional factors in personality and social adjustment; of role behavior; of various aspects of group behavior, especially as seen in institutional life; and of social interaction, family structure, and other related matters. The use of the group as a means of treatment by caseworkers has been steadily growing in importance over the last two decades and has created much common ground between casework and group work. Crisis treatment, planned short-term treatment, problems of service delivery, means of more effectively reaching low in-come groups are among the subjects currently being given high priority as areas of study.

Fundamental to an understanding of the new developments and their many variations and adaptations is a foundation in the basic knowledge and theory from which they derive. The task of evaluating these new emphases and enlarging the knowledge and understanding of the caseworker so that he can use them in his own practice when appropriate may seem formidable. It is made somewhat easier, however, because these new trends represent additions to already well-established casework treatment methods rather than anything in essence diametrically opposed to them. Rather than tearing down an erroneous or grossly inadequate frame of reference, the task is one of filling in parts of the frame-work that had perhaps been underemphasized or even unexplored, although they were theoretically provided for in the overall scheme.

We shall therefore begin by attempting to clarify the nature of the interaction between inner psychological and outer social components in the individual's development and functioning. The theoretical framework of casework already embraces both

these components, providing a meeting ground for psychodynamic theory and theories dealing with the impact upon man of
his social environment.

A clear understanding of fundamental principles is never more
needed than when theory is being expanded and choices must be
made between what is to be retained and what discarded of both
the new and the old. It is, therefore, perhaps especially timely
for caseworkers to formulate as clearly as possible the nature of
their basic frame of reference. Treatment will become more
effective only when what is potentially sound and useful in the
new is admitted to the main body of principles whose value has
already been demonstrated. Knowledge-building should be a
cooperative enterprise in which one reformulates, refines, and
adds to existing knowledge and theory, accrediting the value of
what has gone before in the certain realization that in due time
others will have their turn at reshaping what now seems so clear
to us.

NOTES

1. See Hylan Lewis, *Culture, Class and Poverty* (Washington, D.C.: Cross
   Tell, 1967), pp. 37, 43–49, and Hyman Rodman, "The Lower Class
   Value Stretch," in Louis A. Ferman, ed., *Poverty in America* (Ann
   Arbor, Mich.: University of Michigan Press, 1965), pp. 270–284.

2. Note especially Charlotte Towle, "Social Casework in Modern Society"
   and "Social Work: Cause and Function," in Helen H. Perlman, ed.,
   Helping: Charlotte Towle on Social Work and Social Casework
   (Chicago: University of Chicago Press, 1969), pp. 97–119.

3. For a similar view see Lydia Rapoport, "Social Casework: An Appraisal and an Affirmation," *Smith College Studies in Social Work*, 39
   (June 1969), 213–235.

4. Gordon Hamilton, "The Underlying Philosophy of Social Casework,"
   Family, 23 (July 1941), 139–148.

5. Henry A. Murray, *Explorations in Personality* (New York: Oxford
   University Press, 1938), pp. 38–39.

2 | Personality, Social Functioning, and the Casework Method

Casework has always been a psychosocial treatment method. It recognizes the interplay of both internal psychological and external social causes of dysfunctioning and endeavors to enable the individual to meet his needs more fully and to function more adequately in his social relationships. Throughout its history it has drawn continuously from other scientific fields as they uncovered data and developed theory that promised to throw light upon either the psychological or the social side of human problems.

CASEWORK, PSYCHIATRY, AND SOCIAL SCIENCE

Today casework finds its own characteristic psychosocial approach gaining recognition in two closely related fields—psychiatry and the social sciences. Psychiatrists have long worked in close collaboration with social workers in psychiatric clinics, child guidance clinics, and family service agencies, and the two professions have greatly influenced each other. Less extensively, individual psychiatrists and analysts have collaborated with individual social scientists in bringing clinical practice and personality theory into a closer relationship with academic psychology and sociology. As a result, psychiatry has gained additional impetus toward understanding the social component in human ills, and the social sciences are increasingly interested in the interaction between characteristics of the social structure and the psychology of the individual as determinants of behavior.[1] This heightened understanding is now bringing the social sciences and social work closer to each other, with the prospect of further mutual influence and gain.

Central to casework is the notion of "the-person-in-his-situation"[2] as a threefold configuration consisting of the person, the situation, and the interaction between them. The terms "internal pressure" and "external pressure" are often used to describe forces within the individual and forces within the environment as they impinge upon or interact with each other. External pressure is sometimes referred to as *press* and internal pressure as *stress*.

Casework recognizes this interaction as highly complex. It is not by any means a billiard-ball type of action and reaction between man and his environment, for the external press is immediately modified by the way in which the individual perceives it. Depending upon his nature, upon his need or internal stress, the individual will react to his perception of the press in his own peculiar way. Furthermore, since the term "situation" most often implies a human situation—family, friends, employer, teacher, and so on—the situation is as complicated as the "person" who confronts it. When the person reacts to the external press, this reaction in turn becomes a press upon some other human being, who then responds with his own set of perceptions and needs. Hence understanding of the person-in-his-situation requires varying degrees of understanding of the psychology of all the people involved in the gestalt. For the situation is never just one person but rather a multiplicity of persons (to the sociologist, a *role network*) having varying degrees of importance in the life of the client.

Concepts from Systems Theory

The whole gestalt can well be regarded as a system, and many concepts from general systems theory are useful in describing characteristics of the various systems involved in the person-in-his-situation constellation.[3] We know that the individual is in constant interaction—or transaction—with other members of his immediate family; with other relatives; with a network of friends and acquaintances, including neighbors; with an employment system if he works; and so on through all his social relationships. Through his wife and children he may be in either direct or indirect interaction with other systems, especially the school system. The unit of attention in casework becomes those systems that appear to be of salient importance to the problem for which the individual has sought help or to others that later become the focus of treatment.

A primary characteristic of any system is that all parts of a system are in transaction, so that whatever affects one part of the system affects all parts to some degree. If a child in a family becomes seriously ill, this is certain to affect the father to some degree, whether because of his concern over the child, because of his direct involvement in the child's care, or because of the time or attention his wife must devote to the child. This in turn may influence many other systems in which he is involved, such as the extended family system and the employment system. He may be unable to make his weekly visit to his elderly mother, thus not only disappointing her but also interfering with plans that his sister, with whom his mother lives, may have had for much needed time freed by his visit. The disruption may also cause him to be irritable at work, which may contribute to increased tensions between himself and his foreman or his fellow workers. When two systems are in interaction because they have a common member, occurrences in one system will, to a greater or lesser degree, affect the other system. This is sometimes referred to as *input* from one system to another. If the child's illness continues, there may well be a series of repetitions of this kind of input from the original nuclear family system to the extended family and employment systems. Depending upon the importance of the part played by the father, both of these systems may be seriously disrupted in their functioning by the changes in his behavior.

Another characteristic of interacting or transacting systems is the constant *feedback* among systems. The father's sister may begin to put pressure on him to resume his regular visits, which in turn may cause tension between him and his wife. His foreman may be critical; if he talks about this to his wife this may worry her; her consequent tension may be increased to the point that she is irritable with the other children. This may lead to changes in their work at school, another system in which they are involved. The school problem may then increase the stress felt by both father and mother, adding to the tension between them and increasing the father's difficulty in performing normally at work.

Thus the feedback from other systems intensifies the tension in the family and causes other family members to behave differently in still other systems of which they are a part. Obviously the possible chain of events is endless, and the individual who is being influenced by many forces at the same time has to arrive at some resolution within himself that ultimately determines how he will act.

This resolution within himself is by no means entirely accounted for by the various pressures to which he is exposed. Again, this is not a billiard-ball type of reaction between the individual and his environment. Such an analogue would overlook the nature of the individuals who make up any social system.

When one individual says or does something to another, the second person's response is seldom simple and direct. Many other influences enter into his reaction. First, the action is filtered through his perceptive faculties, which may distort what actually happened. Then the perception is worked upon by other ego and superego processes. The ego may react according to its notions about the other person's intent, about the reasons behind his action. The reaction will be influenced by the mood of the recipient, the other pressures he is under at the time, his general feelings toward the first person. Inevitably it will also depend upon various aspects of his total personality: the quality of his capacity for relationships with others, the intensity of various drives and needs, his standards and ideals for his behavior, the capacity of his ego for impulse control, his ability to express his feelings adequately, the ways in which his ego defends him against anxiety, and so on. The personality is also a system with various and sometimes conflicting forces within itself, and every action, every response is shaped both by these internal forces and by the presses and gratifications (either experienced or anticipated) from others with whom the individual is in interaction or transaction.

Influence of Reference Groups

One dimension of the person-in-his-situation that social scientists particularly have illuminated is the way in which an individual's beliefs, values, and expectations are influenced by the beliefs, values, and expectations characteristic of others of his ethnic background, class, and nationality—in other words, the importance of his reference groups.[4] Freud long ago sketched some of the mechanisms by which such influence takes place, as for example identification and superego and ego-ideal formation. Sociological study of different ethnic groups and social classes has increased our knowledge of the varying content of these beliefs, values, and expectations. It has also emphasized the extent to which these forces continue to influence individual psychology long after the formative years in which the main tendencies of the personality take form.

Sociology has also developed insights into the influence of social role upon behavior.[5] Role expectations held by an individual are the product not only of his culture but also of the customs of his immediate family and often of exposure to other groups and cultures that attract him. All these social groups will strongly influence both his own expectations of and for himself and his expectations of others. Consequently his evaluations of the actions of others and his reactions to them will be markedly affected by this factor.

These sociological data amplify the rich understanding of the internal dynamics of the personality developed by the Freudian school of thought; they do not replace it. Freud's discoveries concerning the libidinal and aggressive drives and their stages of maturation, the effect of infantile thought processes on the child's perception and understanding of the world, the influence of early relationships within the immediate family, and the profound effect of all of these as they continue, through their persistence in the unconscious, to influence later thought processes and emotions, remain basic to the understanding of the individual. To this must be added the later work of Freud and the work of many others on the development and qualities of the ego. Casework will drastically impoverish itself if it contents itself with accepting explanations of human behavior that rely only upon interpersonal phenomena, omitting those key intrapsychic factors that from the start influence the child's perception of and reaction to his interpersonal experiences. On the other hand it can be greatly enriched if an understanding of interpersonal behavior and of group influences is added to knowledge of the inner life of the child and the adult.

THE BASIC VALUES OF CASEWORK

Casework is characterized also by its direct concern for the well-being of the individual. It is not primarily an organ of social control, designed to bring the individual into conformity with society and thus rid society of the social hazard presented by the discontented, unsatisfied, rebellious individual. On the contrary, casework came into being as a response to the needs of human beings for protection against social and natural deprivations and catastrophes. Historically it represents a turning away from the laissez-faire doctrines that followed the unhappy combination of Malthusian thinking with Darwin's emphasis on the development of strength through the survival of the fittest. From its inception casework has stressed the value of the individual, and for the past forty years, at least, has constantly emphasized the right of each man to live in his own unique way, provided he does not infringe unduly upon the rights of others.[6] This emphasis upon the innate worth of the individual is an extremely important, fundamental characteristic of casework. It is the ingredient that makes it possible to establish the relationship of trust that is so essential for effective treatment. From it grow the two essential characteristics of the caseworker's attitude toward his client; first, *acceptance* and second, respect for the client's right to make his own decisions—often referred to as *self-determination*.

By acceptance we mean the maintaining of an attitude of warm good will toward the client, whether or not his way of behaving is socially acceptable and whether or not it is to the worker's personal liking. It is true that we cannot always live up to this ideal in actual practice, but the more we do so the more possibility there is that the goals of casework will be accomplished. Acceptance must not be confused with refraining from evaluating the appropriateness or usefulness of the client's ways of functioning. But such evaluation is of little use if it is accompanied by feelings of condemnation or hostility toward the client.

Self-determination is perhaps not too felicitous a term; it is too absolute in its implications. What is really meant by this concept is that self-direction, the right to make his own choices, is a highly valued attribute of the individual. The more he can make his own decisions and direct his own life the better, and the less the caseworker tries to take over these responsibilities the better. No one in this world can continually do exactly as he wants, but he can make his own decisions about how to find his way among the limitations and opportunities presented by external reality.

In order to make sound decisions the client sometimes simply needs better information; at other times he needs help from the caseworker in understanding various aspects of his dilemma. Not infrequently the client's ego is to varying degrees impaired in its capacity for accurate perception or judgment, or its functioning is distorted by the operation of mechanisms of defense so that the problem becomes one of helping him to develop greater capacity for decision making. The objective of such work is to increase his ability to make his own decisions, not to make them for him. In extreme situations, where there is danger of real harm to others or to the client himself, or where the client is incapable of carrying this responsibility, the caseworker must take over and make decisions for him. But he does so only where the necessity for such action is clear.

A belief in the value of self-determination does not mean that the caseworker plays a passive role with his clients. On the contrary, he promotes changes in the client's functioning that he believes will enable the client to meet his needs more effectively. But the means the worker chooses to bring about change must ever be consistent with the goal of increasing the client's capacity for self-direction. Thus the relationship is consistently an honest one, the worker showing respect for the wishes of the client and sometimes offering suggestions and advice, not, however, as directives but as opinions that the client is free to accept or reject. Whenever possible—and this is most of the time—the client is helped to think things through for himself, to correct his own misconceptions, and to accept the maximum responsibility of which he is capable for formulating his own ideas. Where more active guidance is needed either because the client lacks knowledge, as is sometimes true in child-rearing problems, or because he is limited by the extent of his education or his intellectual capacity, more active guidance may need to be given. But even in these circumstances every effort is made to promote his ability to direct himself. Strong emphasis is placed on techniques for drawing out the client's own reasoning capacities.

PERSONALITY AND SOCIAL FUNCTIONING

In this book we will consider casework procedures as they are used to bring about change in the individual's social functioning and particularly in his interpersonal relationships. As we noted in Chapter 1, this is not the whole of casework, but it is an extremely important part of the whole and is carried on by all caseworkers under whatever auspices they work. Although the data on which this book is based derive from family, medical, and psychiatric settings, the principles presented hold for casework in any setting in which interpersonal relationships are a treatment concern.

The Social Environment

Before we can comprehend the dynamics of this type of casework treatment, however, we must have a clear picture of what the caseworker understands by personality and its social functioning. Social functioning represents the interplay between the two major variables—the social environment and the individual—each of which, in its turn, is a composite of various forces. The environment offers opportunities and gratifications, frustrations and deprivations. It consists not only of concrete realities—such as the availability of food, clothing, shelter, medical care, employment opportunities, physical safety, recreational opportunities, educational opportunities—but also of sociopsychological realities expressed through interpersonal relationships. For human beings need social relationships as much as they need food and shelter. We know that a baby can die because he is deprived of mothering.[7] An individual must rely on the environment to provide him with opportunities for social relationships of all sorts—parents, brothers and sisters, extended family relationships, marriage partners, friends, acquaintances. The quality of these relationships is to no small degree determined by forces independent of the individual's own efforts and choices. Although the qualities of "other people" exert particular force in childhood family relationships, in varying measure they exercise a potent influence upon adult relationships too.

Socially determined psychological realities also exert profound pressures, particularly in the areas of values and perceptions. Ethnic, class, regional, and role factors influence standards of behavior, aspirations, and perceptions of others and of self. At first these influences are transmitted primarily through the parents, later through other social relationships. The total environment, then, as experienced by any individual, is a complex set of interacting forces impinging upon him simultaneously from many different directions and interacting with an equally complex set of forces within his own personality.[8]

The Individual: The Contribution of Freudian Theory

Most caseworkers have found in the work of Freud and his followers[9] a valuable frame of reference for the understanding of the individual.* In recent years attention has been given particularly to the understanding of the ego as developed by such psychoanalytic theorists as Anna Freud, Hartman, Kris, Erikson, Rapaport, and White.[10] Without attempting a detailed review of Freudian theory, I should like to comment on certain features of importance for understanding its use in casework.[11]

First, Freudian theory assumes that the individual from birth onward is characterized by certain sets of drives, libidinal and aggressive in nature. These vary in both absolute and relative strength in different individuals and constitute a continuing and

---

* A divergent point of view is held by the functional school of social work, which bases its work in part upon the writings of Otto Rank. Karen Horney and Harry Stack Sullivan have also contributed insights to current casework practice and are considered of paramount importance by some caseworkers. The behavioral modification school of thought opposes all dynamic personality theories, including those of both Freud and Rank.

unique demand upon the environment. Moreover, the personality
from birth onward includes a set of adaptive qualities, known in
composite as the *ego*. These qualities also vary in strength and
quality in different individuals. The personality proceeds in its
development under two major influences: internal biologically determined stages of maturation in both the drives and the ego, and
interaction between the individual and his environment. Under
these combined influences the drives change their form of demand
and expression during the familiar oral, anal, oedipal, and genital
stages of growth; the ego moves from primary to secondary
modes of thought, develops its superego formation, builds its
mechanisms of defense, adapts its perceptions and judgments to
reality, and strengthens its capacities for direction and control.
The libidinal drive proceeds from its early narcissistic stage, forming first oral dependent relationships, then moving to adult object
relationships. Sexual feelings develop and are gradually sorted
out for their special function in the range of libidinal feelings:
love, affection, and less intense positive responses. The aggressive
drives differentiate into hostility and constructive aggression har-
nessed to the job of mastering the environment and the self.[12]
Erikson describes this maturation process as the achievement of
basic trust, autonomy, and initiative.[13]

Because Freud elaborated more upon the needs and responses
of the individual than upon the impact of the environment, it has
become popular to regard Freudian theory as a theory of the instincts or a biological theory and to accuse it of disregarding
environmental influences. But the truth is that Freud strongly
emphasized the influence of both intra- and extrafamilial life experiences. Indeed, one of his major departures from predecessors
such as Janet and Charcot, who regarded neurosis as a manifesta-
tion of constitutional weakness, was to see neurosis in terms of human relationships. The person with a hysterical paralysis, for
example, is using this symptom to protect himself from something
he fears in his relationships with other people. Although Freudian
theory sees neurosis as a way of resolving conflicts among inner
drives, the superego, and the ego, it also recognizes that such conflicts themselves emerge from the interactions between the child
and his parents or other parent figures. Freud's theory definitely
rests upon social interaction as well as upon intrapsychic factors;

it is therefore harmonious with the long-standing psychosocial orientation of casework and can be part of a total frame of reference that includes whatever data the social sciences can provide to illuminate the nature of the environment and the social forces with which the individual interacts.

This dual orientation lends itself very well to the systematizing of casework findings. Since the caseworker's laboratory is the common everyday world, he has had ample opportunity to observe the interplay between inner and outer forces. He has repeatedly seen people change for better and for worse under the impact of both benign and traumatic environments. He has observed people of diverse classes, ethnic origins, and regions and is well aware that adult behavior varies not only from group to group according to group norms but also within each group in accordance with the individual personality differences and life experiences of its members. Because traditionally the caseworker has dealt with family units, he is particularly aware of the interplay among family members and of the profound influence of parents as well as other members of the family upon the development of the child's personality.

On the other hand Freudian theory stoutly maintains that man is not the mere product of his environment, clay upon which social influences leave their imprint. It insists, and rightly, that the individual makes his own demands upon his environment. This assertion of the individual's role in shaping his interaction with his environment carries with it the corollary implication that even if it were possible to provide exactly the same environment for two different babies the resultant adult personalities would differ.

The foregoing may seem highly theoretical, but it has major practical implications. It shifts emphasis from manipulation of the environment and a conditioning type of approach to emphasis upon *interaction*, particularly upon the individual's part in that interaction. In cases of marital adjustment it guards the worker against seeing the partner to whom he is talking as merely the victim in the relationship. In parent-child disorders it leads to a balanced examination both of what the parent is doing to the child and of what the child is doing to and demanding of the parent. In general, it leads to the assumption that the individual himself can almost always do something about his problem and that the worker's task is to increase his capacity to do so. This by no means, however, precludes recognition of realistic environmental pressures where they exist, nor does it deny the responsibility of the caseworker to ameliorate such pressures.

Interactions Between Individual and Environment

As noted earlier, the individual does not react to his environment as it exists but rather as he sees it, and a host of internal factors influence his perceptions. Among these are the primitive thought processes that distort the world of early childhood. Wishes are embued with magical power. Hence when the child wishes that a parent or brother or sister should get hurt, he may feel that he has actually caused any mishap that subsequently occurs, and therefore fear retaliation. When someone close to him has died, he may regard this as an act of purposeful abandonment and resent it accordingly. He cannot always distinguish his own thoughts and feelings from the thoughts and feelings of others: when he is angry he believes others are angry at him. Contradictory ideas exist side by side in his mind and he has no need to reconcile them. When he is crossed, his anger is not tempered by the good things he has experienced from the same source that now frustrates him. He generalizes indiscriminately, often expecting all grown-up men to be like father, all women like mother. His misperceptions cause him to react in a way that actually affects the response of his environment to him. Hence he is already to a degree creating his own environment.

These early distortions would not be quite so serious a matter if childish things were always left behind, but unfortunately the adult to a greater or lesser extent continues these infantile thought processes. They become an important ingredient in certain ego defense mechanisms. In the mechanism known as *projection* the individual will confuse his own thoughts and feelings with those of others. In *transference* he will either generalize indiscriminately or actually confuse one person with another because of superficial similarities. In *isolation* he will separate parts of his experience so that matters that are actually interrelated appear not to affect one another.[14] He will often fail to correct misapprehensions about his environment although contrary evidence is readily at hand.

Indeed, the individual's whole perception of the world around him is a combination in varying degrees of what is actually there and what he expects to find. We often do not see what we do not look for, but we create for ourselves what we seek to find. The person who anticipates that someone else will be hostile may read into the other person's behavior belligerent meanings whether or not they actually exist, and by his own responses may very well give rise to hostility in the other person. In so doing, he has to a high degree created his own environment—a form of the self-fulfilling prophecy.

Such misperceptions are not entirely a matter of individual psychology. A child learns that a radiator is hot not only by direct experience but also by being told so by a person whose words he trusts; and if he trusts another person, he will believe a false statement as readily as a true one. Indeed, if it is "everybody" who holds something to be true, it becomes extremely difficult for even the good adult mind to have a contrary opinion. How many generations saw sails disappearing over the horizon and continued to believe the world was flat? Belief is often so strong that the believer is cut off from even the opportunity of testing it. Race stereotypes are a cardinal example. Not only do whites have many misperceptions about blacks but blacks also have them about whites. Similarly, the "generation gap" is based to no small degree on stereotypes that often cause people on both sides of the magic dividing line to react according to distorted beliefs and misunderstandings rather than realities. Conflict caused by realistic competition of interests between different economic or cultural classes and groups is compounded by misinformation and distortions, sometimes newly created and sometimes handed down from one generation to another. The element of expectation that is part of one's perception of his environment is a joint product of actual experience, individual distortion growing out of faulty thought processes, ideas incorporated from the idiosyncrasies of close associates, and ideas learned by personal contact but actually the product of group opinion—class, ethnic, regional, occupational, religious, political, and so on. Certain ideas are commonly held in the Middle West but not in the East, in the North but not in the South, in cities but not in rural areas, in the Soviet Union but not in the United States, among white-collar workers but not among industrial workers, among women but not among men, in poverty-stricken city areas but not in suburbia, and so on.

Role expectation is a form of group opinion especially significant for social work.[15] Specific ways of behaving are commonly accepted as appropriate or necessary for the individual in certain areas of functioning—for example, as parent, as husband or wife, as employer—and he is perceived in terms of the way his role performance conforms to the norms held by his group. For instance, a man's perception of whether or not his wife loves him depends upon quite different cues in different groups. In some cultures the wife's housekeeping tasks are deemed so important that the husband would see her subordination of them to interest in a job as personal neglect and evidence of lack of love. This perception would be reinforced by the opinions of his friends, before whom he would be disgraced. Similarly, a parent's view of his child depends very greatly upon the extent to which the child behaves according to group-influenced expectations.

The client will also have certain expectations of how the caseworker will act, and these will vary according to his personal and social experience. If the worker is to convey the same impression of good will, objectivity, and competence to clients of varying life experience he will need to be aware of their preconceptions and of the different interpretations they will make of his actions. He will need to be more "friendly" with some, more "professional" with others. With the "hard-to-reach," much generous "doing for" may be necessary to overcome the stereotype of the caseworker as an interfering, hostile do-gooder. When we think of the person-situation gestalt as a social system this factor of faulty perception by the ego is seen as a major component in faulty communication among different members of a family or of any other social system. Preconceptions can cause people not to listen to each other at all or actually to hear something different from what has been said. Distortions in the way intonation is heard make great differences in interpretation of meaning. Internal elaborations and attributions of intent by the receiver can cause endless misunderstanding. With nonverbal communication the opportunity for distortion is even greater.[16]

Most communication takes place through symbols—both verbal and nonverbal. This creates another wide-open opportunity for distortion. For accurate communication, symbols must be commonly understood by sender and receiver. The meaning of gestures, posture, intonation, and even words of the same language differ markedly among people of different educational backgrounds, different social classes, and different ethnic groups. Symbols of courtesy and discourtesy that are so basic to interpersonal relationships are particularly vulnerable to such misinterpretation.

Caseworkers must not only become familiar with the varying meaning assigned to symbols by different client groups and individuals but must also be alert to the signs that such misinterpretations exist even when the specific nature of a misunderstanding is not known. Thus alerted, the caseworker can easily explore with the clients the possibility that this has occurred.

Inaccurate perception can extend toward the self as well as toward others. An important component in the way we regard ourselves is the way in which other people regard us. A child who is constantly told he is stupid often believes this himself, whether or not it is true. A boy who is labeled a delinquent because he truants from school may begin to classify himself as a delinquent and start to associate with boys who are delinquent or think of themselves as such, and in the end he may actually become delinquent. This particular mechanism has a circular effect. When an individual feels himself an outcast for any reason, he begins to distort his perception of how other people react to him. Even when their behavior toward him does not fit his stereotype of rejection, he reacts as if it did and uses this belief to reinforce his picture of himself—a vicious circle, indeed.

CAUSES OF INTERPERSONAL ADJUSTMENT PROBLEMS

Clients come for casework treatment because there has been a breakdown in their social adjustment. This breakdown has three possible interacting sources: (1) infantile needs and drives left over from childhood that cause the individual to make inappropriate demands upon his adult world; (2) a current life situation that exerts excessive pressure upon him; and (3) faulty ego and superego functioning. The degree to which each of these is present varies with different people. Sometimes all three are contributing to the client's dilemma.

Persisting infantile needs and drives may lead to exaggerated narcissistic needs, excessive dependence or hostility, fixations on early family figures, fear of separation (with resulting anxiety or timidity, which makes the individual require excessive protection and prevents him from assuming adult responsibilities), and abnormalities in the expression of sexual and aggressive drives. Although it is sometimes possible for people to find social situations in which such abnormal needs can be gratified, for the most part this does not occur. The individual is then left with a constant sense of frustration and characteristically behaves in a way that creates antagonism in his social environment and cuts him off from gratifications he might otherwise receive.

Common among current life pressures are those of economic deprivation, lack of opportunity for employment, marginal working conditions, poor housing and neighborhood conditions, substandard educational opportunities, racial and ethnic hostility, illness, and loss of love by death or separation. To these must be added innumerable individual life experiences that arouse anger-provoking frustration or feelings of inadequacy or guilt. They may occur in family relationships, when the needs of one individual conflict in a major way with those of another. They may occur when employment and living conditions are realistically very frustrating and pressing, even though not substandard. And they may occur when general social conditions, such as racial discrimination, create constant environmental pressure of major proportions.

Faulty ego functioning includes distorted perception of either the outside world or the self, poor judgment, insufficient ability to control impulses or to direct behavior, poor reality testing, and inappropriate uses of the ego defenses. Faulty superego functioning may be of several kinds. Sometimes the superego is so primitive that the individual has not incorporated much in the way of standards at all. He just doesn't care about "right and wrong." More frequently, he does care but his standards and self-requirements are too high, too low, or otherwise out of harmony with his environment. Faulty ego and superego functioning adds substantially to the environmental pressures felt by the individual. If he misperceives pressures, the stress actually experienced in response to his distorted version of reality may be more severe than would have been appropriate to the actual life pressures. Such faulty functioning may also lead him to behave in such a way that he deprives himself of satisfactions he might otherwise have, creates guilt-arousing situations, exposes himself unnecessarily to situations in which he is inadequate, and surrounds himself with people who confirm his childish distortions of the world, thus reinforcing his tendency to faulty functioning. It is in reducing the extent of this secondary elaboration that the caseworker can be particularly helpful. Freed from some of these self-created pressures, the individual may be able to find in his life sufficient satisfaction of his basic needs to maintain a fairly comfortable equilibrium even though many childish needs and reactions remain untouched.

REDUCING ENVIRONMENTAL PRESS

When a major part of the cause of the client's discomfort is in the environment, it is sometimes possible for the caseworker to modify the pressure directly. Many governmental programs are set up to alleviate financial need. A caseworker who is a staff member of such a program can provide funds directly to the client. Often workers in other agencies intervene on behalf of the client who is experiencing difficulty in establishing his eligibility in such programs. Other life pressures can be overcome by such direct services as obtaining medical care during illness, placing the homeless or neglected child in an adoptive or foster home, locating better housing, opening up educational and recreational opportunities. Attitudes of other individuals who are creating difficulties for the client can sometimes be modified by casework contact; when such modification is required, environmental manipulation itself becomes psychological in nature. Some of the services mentioned—child placement is a prime example—can be extremely complicated in the treatment required. Environmental services rarely stand alone. They are usually accompanied by work directly with the client in which his reactions become the focus of attention. The public assistance client may not understand or respond realistically to the eligibility process. The hospital patient may be unwilling to undergo the recommended medical procedures. The child may not be ready to use the educational or recreational services that have been opened up. Much preparation involving both the resource and the client may be required before environmental pressure can be relieved.

Often, instead of meeting the need directly, it is advisable to help the client bring about a change in the situation himself. The caseworker's effort is then directed toward telling the client about possible opportunities, helping him decide whether or not he wants to use them and, if so, how to go about using them. It is preferable that a client do his own manipulation of the environment, if he can effectively do so.

Environmental changes brought about solely for the purpose of removing unusual pressures or deficiencies need not involve an effort to change the individual himself. He may function more comfortably as a result of such change, but his inner balance may remain the same.

TREATMENT OF INTERNAL FACTORS THROUGH
ENVIRONMENTAL WORK

To whatever extent the major causative factors in the client's problem lie either in too great a residue of infantile desires and needs or in faulty ego and superego functioning, change in the person himself becomes a potential goal of treatment. Such treatment may attempt to bring about either lasting changes in the client's personality or way of functioning or temporary adjustments of behavior during a period of stress.

Environmental change can sometimes become the means through which changes in personality are brought about. With children especially, lasting personality change occurs rather readily in response to environmental change, and this is the predominant method of casework treatment used with children. We try either to bring about changes in the parents' attitudes and behavior or to make substitute arrangements through which the child is provided with a better milieu than that of his natural home. For many years foster-home care has generally been considered the preferred plan unless adoption is possible; institutional care is sometimes more appropriate for children whose first placement occurs in adolescence and for children who need special treatment or are too disturbed to function in the ordinary community. Day-care centers are important resources for children who can remain at home except during their parents' work hours. Recently there has been experimentation with small-group homes and with day foster homes and other innovations.

Major personality changes in the child—particularly the young child—can often be brought about by these various forms of substitute parental care. Less profound changes are promoted by modifications in the school environment or by the provision of recreational and other group experiences such as camping, bringing a "big brother" into the situation, and so on. Because the child's personality is still so fluid, environmental changes profoundly affect his view of the world, the extent to which infantile strivings remain a part of his adult personality, his identifications, his ability to bear frustration, and in general the quality of his ego functioning. When such changes are impossible or are not sufficiently effective, direct casework with the child will either accompany environmental modification or become the major form of treatment.

With adults, the chances of bringing about personality change through environmental means are considerably narrowed. A radical change in environment will sometimes bring about a genuine personality change, as, for example, when a particularly fortunate choice of marriage partner leads to a long period of satisfying living that seems to undo the effects of earlier misfortune and brings about a real reorientation to life, or when events of traumatic proportions cause lasting regression in adult personality patterns. Sometimes the constant repetition of small traumata can have a cumulative effect of similar proportions. It is rarely possible, however, to arrange favorable environmental experiences of proportions sufficient to bring about significant personality changes in the adult. Changes in behavior, yes, but changes built into the personality, hardly ever. For example, a woman may become less tense, less hostile, and more able to give love to her children when she is working outside the home and having others care for her children during the day than when she devotes her own full time to their care. If the caseworker helps her to recognize this and to arrange her life so that she can take a job, there may be marked improvement in her functioning. It should be noted, however, that a change in personality is not necessarily involved. Rather, the client has wisely provided herself with a set of circumstances within which she can use her current adaptive patterns to better advantage. If for some reason she has to give up her work, her functioning in relation to her children and her husband may again deteriorate. In many instances, however, such a change in functioning alone is an entirely appropriate treatment aim. Indeed, looked at as a way of providing the client's children with a better emotional environment, it may be the means for bringing about substantial changes in *their* personalities.

DIRECT WORK WITH THE INDIVIDUAL

Intrapsychic factors causing personal difficulties for adults are usually modified primarily through work with the individual directed toward modification of the dysfunctioning aspect of the personality. (This approach is also used with children, but usually in combination with whatever environmental changes can be achieved.) Casework uses for this purpose current reactions and behavior and memories that are either immediately accessible to consciousness or else suppressed, unverbalized or uncomprehended, but not repressed or so remote from consciousness that only such means as free association, hypnosis, or therapy under drugs can bring them to the surface.*

To understand how work with this part of the personality can be effective, we must appreciate the extent to which the personality system is a balance of forces. One way of conceptualizing

* See Chapter 11 for full discussion of this point.

these forces is the Freudian "structural approach" in which the terms "id," "ego," and "superego" are used to describe the major components of the personality. Each of these components consists of a set of subcomponents. There are many different drives for the id; the ego functions in many different ways; many different standards and goals constitute the superego. These components have the potential for sound functioning or for dysfunctioning in terms of an individual's interaction with others. Each part of the personality system has a measure of both potentials. On one side are the immature or unusual needs and drives, the view of the world distorted by early childhood experiences, and infantile modes of thought. On the other are (1) more mature needs and drives that can be harmonious with the needs of others and (2) those aspects of the ego and superego that exert a pull toward personally and socially realistic functioning. The latter include the ability to make accurate appraisals of others, of the self, and of the external world, and responses likely to bring gratifications to the individual, to contribute to meeting the needs of those he associates with, and to contribute to the harmonious functioning of the social systems of which he is a part.

When certain inner drives push the individual toward socially unwise or self-destructive behavior, the healthy part of the ego says "No." When the irrational part of the ego distorts reality by projection or magical beliefs or when other unconscious or primitive thought processes cause distortions, the healthy part of the ego corrects this and keeps the irrational tendencies in check. It is often nip and tuck as to which side will win, depending upon the relative strength the two sets of forces can bring to bear in any particular situation. "If she had said just one more thing, I would have thrown the hammer at her. . . ." That is, "If I had been just a little more angry, nothing my ego was telling me would have been enough to keep me in control. . . ."

An interesting aspect of this balance of forces is that while the decision to act may hang upon a hair's weight of difference either in the opposing intrapsychic forces or in the nature and force of the pressure from the rest of the interpersonal system, the action that this slight difference triggers may be of major proportions and have extensive consequences. A series of such transactions can combine to make a pattern of considerable strength and significance. It is not alone the strength of a drive, such as a tremendously strong impulse or the degree of a tendency toward distortion, that determines whether an action is to be taken, for these may be opposed by an equally strong counterforce, in the form of capacity for reality testing and ability to control impulses. Insofar as the opposing strengths are almost equally balanced, a relatively small amount of improvement in ego functioning may be enough to enable the individual to make significant changes in his total social functioning. This is one of the answers to the oft-repeated question: "If the infantile demands and distortions are not modified, how can there be any real change?" The demands and distortions may remain untouched, but the person may handle them differently in interpersonal relationships if his ego is functioning better.

It is also important to remember that all formative influences do not occur in infancy, nor are they all unconscious. If unresolved oedipal rivalries have made a daughter see her mother as hostile, the daughter's feeling may be reinforced by experiencing actual hostility from her mother in the later years of growth, or it may be somewhat lessened by experiences of a contrary nature. In the latter instance, not only is the original tendency not reinforced but the ego is given a means by which to counteract the effect of the original distortion. In the former instance, when the mother's later behavior reinforces the daughter's belief that enmity must exist between them—a belief that may affect her attitude toward other women—there are several possible modes of attack that do not involve an effort to uncover and correct the original infantile content.

In one approach, the client is encouraged to ventilate her feelings about the events she spontaneously remembers or can recall with the help of "eductive" interviewing techniques. For a person who has not previously been able to express her anger toward her mother this in itself may have a useful cathartic effect, reducing the amount of suppressed hostility pressing for displacement on current female figures in the client's life. If there has been guilt over the angry feelings, the worker's acceptance of these feelings as warranted may reduce the guilt and subsequent need to use defenses such as hostility, projection, or turning against the self. If the anger has been displaced on a female child or on other adult women, it may be possible to enable the client to recognize and to stop behavior that provokes counterhostility and is thus causing her to experience constant repetitions of her original unhappy experience with a woman.

Another approach is to provide the client with an opportunity for a corrective relationship. By allowing a relationship to develop in which the client regards the worker as a mother figure, it may be possible to counteract the earlier bad mother-daughter experience by enabling the client to see through the new experience that the characteristics of her mother that caused her unhappiness are peculiar to her mother and not general characteristics of all women. This may also tend to undo some of the attitudes about herself, sex, marriage, child raising, and so on, that she acquired in her early relationship with her mother.

Another alternative is to enable the client to review her conscious and preconscious or near-conscious early memories of her experiences with her mother. By seeing their effects on her personality and current reactions to life she may free herself to a degree from these childhood and adolescent reinforcements of her oedipal distortions and, in turn, reduce the degree of distortion with which her adult ego must now deal. Along with this reduction of the force of her childhood experiences, she may be helped to recognize her tendency to carry over feelings from her childhood to her current relationships and may learn to improve these relationships by careful testing of her own reactions against the realities of other people's behavior.

None of these procedures will have touched directly the infantile core of the client's trouble. She will still have in her unconscious whatever hostilities and distortion tendencies and whatever component of infantile oedipal rivalry were there before the treatment. But the effect of some of the later childhood experiences that reinforced the earlier ones will have been reduced, the ego will have been strengthened in its efforts to correct and control destructive behavior, and the tendency to create repetitive hostile life experiences will have been lessened. Such changes in the balance of forces within the individual may well bring about marked improvement in functioning and constitute an internalized change in adaptive patterns.

All these approaches are built upon the assumption that even in adulthood the ego is open to influence and capable of growth and change. In systems terms, the assumption is that personality comprises an "open system," one that constantly changes in response to exchanges with the outside world, including situational changes that can be brought about by the caseworker and interaction with the worker in the process of treatment. They are also built upon the assumption that the individual is constantly evolving, that there is some individual initiative within each person, unique to himself, which acts upon others as well as receives from others. Some central core influences the receptivity to the outside, even the reaching out for it, and the selective use of what others, including the caseworker, offer.

DIRECTIVE VS. COGNITIVE THERAPIES

Casework is a form of treatment that relies heavily upon cognitive measures and makes use of directive techniques like suggestion, advice, and persuasion only when diagnosis indicates that the client is unlikely to respond to measures that rely upon his own active thinking. This may be the case when he is so overwhelmed by pressing happenings in his life—sickness, death, desertion—that he is unable to make use of his usual reflective powers, or when he is severely handicapped in doing so, as with some individuals suffering from severe character disorders or borderline psychosis, or recovering from a period of mental illness.

In truly directive therapies the therapist prefers to take a very active part in advising the client, relying primarily upon the weight of his "professional authority" and upon the positive transference to modify the client's, or patient's, responses. Casework differs markedly from such therapies. It never uses directive procedures in isolation from cognitive measures and employs them only when the client is not ready or able to use reflective procedures. Even in the case of the very severely disturbed or inadequate person, with whom methods of "direct influence" may need to play a relatively large part in treatment, such methods would never, in casework, constitute the sole ingredient. Students sometimes ask whether there is not an incompatibility between the employment of directive procedures to even this limited degree and the principle of self-determination. But they fail to see that self-determination is not an absolute value. Whereas it requires that every effort be made to increase the client's capacity for self-direction, it also recognizes that clients vary in this capacity and that a limited amount of directiveness in treatment is sometimes advisable.*

Some writers recognize only two ways of influencing behavior: one characterized by the bringing of unconscious factors under the control of the ego, the other by methods that rest essentially on the therapist's authority and the influence of the transference. Certain writers, such as Eissler,[17] condescendingly refer to the second type of treatment as "magic" and consider it to be mainly manipulative and to bring only unstable changes in functioning, because—as they maintain—such changes are not truly built into the personality but remain a reflection of the continuing relationship with the therapist.

The first method referred to, psychoanalysis, attempts to modify infantile drive derivatives and needs that have partly become unconscious, cause intrapsychic conflict in the individual, and interfere with the adaptive functioning of the ego and superego. By inducing a strongly regressive transference in the patient, it enables his adult ego to relive and reevaluate early life experiences so that infantile attachments and fantasies can truly be relinquished and infantile misconceptions corrected. But as Grete Bibring[18] has so clearly pointed out, psychoanalysis, in addition to enabling the ego to assume control over unconscious factors, also makes use of "techniques of influence" such as those that Eissler ascribes to his second category and considers a form of magic. Psychoanalysis does in many instances bring about profound changes in personality. These changes often give promise of being permanent, though they are not necessarily so.

In casework we find a kind of treatment of which Eissler does not take note. It is clearly not psychoanalysis, but neither is it mainly manipulative. Like analysis it sometimes uses techniques of influence, and it does so to a greater degree than is true in analysis. It is, however, by no means primarily a directive ther-

---

* See Chapter 6, page 102, for further discussion of this point.

apy, relying on the worker's professional authority to persuade the client to change his behavior in a given direction. Rather it seeks to engage the client's *ego*—his capacity to think, to reflect, to understand—in a reevaluation of himself-in-his-situation. It engages the client as fully as possible in his own treatment, endeavoring not only to preserve but to enhance his reliance upon himself and the extent to which he is able to guide his actions by realistic understanding.

In addition to improvement in external functioning, such treatment often brings about such internalized modifications as improvement of the ego's perception and reality testing ability, shifts in the use of defenses, changes in the demands—or in the reaction to the demands—of the superego, lasting reductions in the strength of destructive character traits such as chronic latent hostility and dependence, relinquishing of parental ties, and maturation in the instinctual life. Such shifts are built into the personality and enable the individual to function better even when he is confronted by circumstances identical or essentially similar to those under which his functioning was previously impaired. Such changes can be expected to continue after treatment has ended.

In summary, then, when casework is employed to help the client achieve better social functioning, it becomes a form of psychosocial therapy. It relies mainly on cognitive procedures closely allied to psychoanalytic techniques, augmented by methods of direct influence and by direct efforts to bring about environmental changes when diagnosis indicates that these will be more effective. Focus is always upon the person-situation gestalt, which is seen as an interacting balance of forces between the needs of the person and the influence upon him of the environment. Individual functioning is the end result of a complicated interaction between complementary parts of the personality highly susceptible to outside influences. In psychosocial therapy influence is brought to bear on either the environment or the personality or both. When it is directed toward the personality, it can reduce the force of destructive trends in the individual by decreasing the force of earlier life experiences and by increasing the capacity of the ego and superego to handle current life experiences more realistically.

NOTES

1. For discussions of this, see Talcott Parsons, "Psychoanalysis and the Social Structure," in *Essays in Sociological Theory* (Glencoe, Ill.: Free Press, 1954); Geza Roheim, *Psychoanalysis and Anthropology: Culture, Personality and the Unconscious* (New York: International Universities Press, 1950); and Ludwig von Bertalanffy, "General System Theory and Psychiatry," in Silvano Arieti, ed., *American Handbook of Psychiatry*, vol. 3 (New York: Basic Books, 1966), pp. 705–772.

2. Gordon Hamilton and many other writers have stressed this point of view. See her *Theory and Practice of Social Work*, rev. ed., (New York: Columbia University Press, 1951).

3. Ludwig von Bertalanffy, *General Systems Theory: Foundations, Development, Application* (New York: George Braziller, 1968), is a basic reference on systems theory; William Gray, Frederick J. Duhl, and Nicholas D. Rizzo, eds., *General Systems Theory and Psychiatry* (Boston: Little, Brown & Co., 1969), is also useful as a general reference; Werner A. Lutz, in his *Concepts and Principles Underlying Social Casework Practice* (Washington, D.C.: National Association of Social Workers, Medical Social Work Section, 1956), first introduced the systems theory approach to casework; articles from casework, psychiatry, and psychology are increasingly recognizing its usefulness; for example, see: Gordon Allport, "The Open System in Personality Theory," *Journal of Abnormal and Social Psychology*, 61 (November 1960), 301–310; Ludwig von Bertalanffy, "General System Theory and Psychiatry," in Arieti, ed., *op. cit.*, pp. 705–721; William Gordon, "Basic Constructs for an Integrative and Generative Conception of Social Work," in Gordon Hearn, ed., *The General Systems Approach: Contributions toward a Holistic Conception of Social Work* (New York: Council on Social Work Education, 1969); Lynn Hoffman and Lorence Long, "A Systems Dilemma," *Family Process*, 8 (September 1969), 211–234.

4. Florence Kluckhohn's work in this area has been of special interest to social workers. See Florence Kluckhohn, "Variations in the Basic Values of Family Systems," *Social Casework*, 39 (February–March 1958), 63–72; and Florence Kluckhohn and John P. Spiegel, *Integration and Conflict in Family Behavior*, Group for the Advancement of Psychiatry Report No. 27 (New York: Group for the Advancement of Psychiatry, 1954). More recently values of both white and

black low-income families have received much attention; of interest are: Jessie Bernard, *Marriage and Family Among Negroes* (Englewood Cliffs, N.J.: Prentice-Hall, 1966); Hylan Lewis, *Culture, Class and Poverty* (Washington, D.C.: Cross Tell, 1967); Sylvia R. McMillan, "Aspirations of Low-income Mothers," *Journal of Marriage and the Family*, 29 (May 1967), 282–287; Salvador Minuchin, *Families of the Slums* (New York: Basic Books, 1967).

5. Bruce Biddle and Edwin J. Thomas, *Role Theory: Concepts and Research* (New York: John Wiley & Sons, 1966); Neal Gross, Ward S. Mason, and Alexander McEachern, *Explorations in Role Analysis: Studies of the School Superintendency Role* (New York: John Wiley & Sons, 1958); and Helen H. Perlman, *Persona: Social Role and Personality* (Chicago: University of Chicago Press, 1968), are excellent sources for understanding role concepts. For illustrations of their use in treatment see: John Ballweg, "Resolution of Conjugal Role Adjustment After Retirement," *Journal of Marriage and the Family*, 29 (May 1967), 277–281; Catherine M. Bittermann, "The Multimarriage Family," *Social Casework*, 49 (April 1968), 218–221; Alexander B. Taylor, "Role Perception, Empathy and Marriage Adjustment," *Sociology and Social Research*, 52 (October 1967), 22–34; Barbara K. Varley, "The Use of Role Theory in the Treatment of Disturbed Adolescents," *Social Casework*, 49 (June 1968), 362–366; Irving Weisman, "Offender Status, Role Behavior, and Treatment Considerations," *Social Casework*, 48 (July 1967), 422–425.

6. For a fuller discussion of casework values, see Herbert Bisno, *The Philosophy of Social Work* (Washington, D.C.: Public Affairs Press, 1952). Also see the author's "Principles and Assumptions Underlying Casework Practice," *Social Work* (London), 12 (1955), 41–55; Harriett Bartlett, *The Common Base of Social Work Practice* (New York: National Association of Social Workers, 1970), pp. 63–69; William Gordon, "Knowledge and Value: Their Distinction and Relationship in Clarifying Social Work Practice," *Social Work*, 10 (July 1965), 32–35; and Katherine Kendall, ed., *Social Work Values in an Age of Discontent* (New York: Council on Social Work Education, 1970).

7. For comprehensive review of the findings concerning the effects of maternal deprivation, see John Bowlby, *Maternal Care and Mental Health*, 2nd ed., World Health Organization Monograph Series No. 2 (Geneva: World Health Organization, 1952); and Mary D. Ainsworth, "The Effects of Maternal Deprivation: A Review of Findings and Controversy in the Context of Research Strategy," in *Deprivation of Maternal Care: A Reassessment of Its Effects* (Geneva: World Health Organization, 1962).

8. A rich literature has developed in recent years pertinent to the social worker's understanding of the nature of the social component in the person-situation interaction. The following, in addition to items cited elsewhere, are among the useful readings: Andrew Billingsley, *Black*

Families in White America (Englewood Cliffs, N.J.: Prentice-Hall, 1968); Jerome Cohen, "Social Work and the Culture of Poverty," *Social Work*, 9 (January 1964), 3–11; Bruce and Barbara Dohrenwend, *Social Status and Psychological Disorder* (New York: John Wiley & Sons, 1969); Louis A. Ferman, ed., *Poverty in America*, rev. ed., (Ann Arbor: University of Michigan Press, 1968); Alejandro Garcia, "The Chicano and Social Work," *Social Casework*, 52 (May 1971), 274–278; Paul and Lois Glasser, eds., *Families in Crisis* (New York: Harper & Row, 1970); Elizabeth Herzog, "Is there a Breakdown of the Negro Family?" *Social Work*, 11 (January 1966), 3–10; Florence Hollis, "Casework and Social Class," *Social Casework*, 46 (October 1965), 463–471; Camille Jeffers, *Living Poor* (Ann Arbor, Mich.: Ann Arbor Publishers, 1967); Mirra Komarovsky, with Jane Phillips, *Blue-Collar Marriage* (New York: Random House, 1964); Maurine LaBarre, "The Strengths of the Self-Supporting Poor," *Social Casework*, 49 (October 1968), 459–466; Hylan Lewis, "Child Rearing Among Low-Income Families," in Louis A. Ferman, ed., *Poverty in America* (Ann Arbor: University of Michigan Press, 1965), pp. 342–353; Elliot Liebow, *Tally's Corner* (Boston: Little, Brown & Co., 1967); S. M. Miller, "The American Lower Class: A Typological Approach," *Social Research*, 31 (1964), 1–22; Eleanor Pavenstedt, ed., *The Drifters: Children of Disorganized Lower-Class Families* (Boston: Little, Brown & Co., 1967); Norman A. Polansky, "Powerlessness among Rural Appalachian Youth," *Rural Sociology*, 34 (June 1969), 219–222; Frank Riessman, Jerome Cohen, and Arthur Pearl, eds., *Mental Health of the Poor* (New York: Free Press, 1964); *Social Casework*, 51 (May 1970), the entire issue on Black experience by Black authors; Edwin J. Thomas, ed., *Behavioral Science for Social Workers* (New York: Free Press, 1967); Francis J. Turner, "Ethnic Difference and Client Performance," *Social Service Review*, 44 (March 1970), 1–10; Eileen Younghusband, "Intercultural Aspects of Social Work," *Journal of Education for Social Work*, 2 (Spring 1966), 59–65.

9. For comments on this, see Annette Garrett, "Modern Casework: The Contributions of Ego Psychology," in Howard J. Parad, ed., *Ego Psychology and Dynamic Casework* (New York: Family Service Association of America, 1958), pp. 38–52; Gordon Hamilton, "A Theory of Personality: Freud's Contribution to Social Work," in Parad, ed., *op. cit.*, pp. 11–37; Eleanor B. Weisberger, "The Current Usefulness of Psychoanalytic Theory to Casework," *Smith College Studies in Social Work*, 37 (February 1967), 106–118.

10. See Anna Freud, *The Ego and the Mechanisms of Defense* (New York: International Universities Press, 1946); Heinz Hartmann, *Ego Psychology and the Problem of Adaptation* (New York: International Universities Press, 1958); Heinz Hartmann, Ernst Kris, and R. Loewenstein, "Comments on the Formation of Psychic Structure," in Ruth S. Eissler et al., eds., *The Psychoanalytic Study of the Child*, vol. 2 (New York: International Universities Press, 1946), pp. 11–38; Ernst

Kris, "Notes on the Development and on Some Current Problems of Psychoanalytic Child Psychology," in Ruth S. Eissler et al., eds., *The Psychoanalytic Study of the Child*, vol. 5 (New York: International Universities Press, 1950), pp. 24–46; Erik Erikson, *Identity and the Life Cycle* (New York: International Universities Press, 1959); David Rapaport, *Organization and Pathology of Thought* (New York: Columbia University Press, 1951); Robert W. White, *Ego and Reality in Psychoanalytic Theory* (New York: International Universities Press, 1963). For a general discussion of the "structural theory" see: Jacob Arlow and Charles Brenner, *Psychoanalytic Concepts and the Structural Theory* (New York: International Universities Press, 1964), pp. 103–113. For casework use of "ego psychology" see: Parad, ed., *op. cit.*; Howard J. Parad and R. Miller, eds., *Ego-Oriented Casework: Problems and Perspectives* (New York: Family Service Association of America, 1963); and Isabel Stamm, "Ego Psychology in the Emerging Theoretical Base of Casework," in A. J. Kahn, ed., *Issues in American Social Work* (New York: Columbia University Press, 1959), pp. 80–109.

11. Charles Brenner, *An Elementary Textbook of Psychoanalysis* (Garden City, N.Y.: Doubleday, Anchor Books, 1955), and Norman Cameron, *Personality Development and Psychopathology* (Boston: Houghton Mifflin, 1963), are useful texts on Freudian concepts of personality and psychopathology.

12. Ways of thinking and feeling characteristic of the young child are vividly portrayed in the studies of Jean Piaget and Susan Isaacs. See especially Jean Piaget, *The Child's Conception of the World* (New York: Harcourt, Brace & Co., 1929), and Susan Isaacs, *Social Development in Young Children* (New York: Harcourt, Brace & Co., 1937). For less detailed but useful descriptions see: Erik Erikson, *Childhood and Society* (New York: W. W. Norton and Co., 1950); and Selma Fraiberg, *The Magic Years* (New York: Charles Scribner's Sons, 1959); John Flavell, *The Developmental Psychology of Jean Piaget* (Princeton, N.J.: Van Nostrand, 1963), deals with Piaget's work as a whole.

13. Erikson, *Identity and the Life Cycle, op. cit.*, p. 54.

14. For a full and clear discussion of these and other mechanisms of defense, see Anna Freud, *The Ego and the Mechanisms of Defense* (New York: International Universities Press, 1946).

15. See note 5.

16. The importance of the subject of communication is receiving increasing recognition by caseworkers. Lottie Marcus in Chapter 1 of "The Effect of Extralinguistic Phenomena on the Judgment of Anxiety" (doctoral dissertation, Columbia University School of Social Work, 1969), surveys the pertinent literature and provides an excellent bibliography. Other references of value are: Starkey Duncan, "Nonverbal Communication," *Psychological Bulletin*, 72 (1969), 118–137;

Norman A. Polansky, *Ego Psychology and Communication* (New York: Atherton Press, 1971); Brett A. Seabury, "Arrangement of Physical Space in Social Work Settings," *Social Work*, 16 (October 1971), 43–49.

17. Kurt R. Eissler, "The Chicago Institute of Psychoanalysis and the Sixth Period of Development of Psychoanalytic Technique," *Journal of General Psychology*, 42 (1950), 118 ff.

18. Grete L. Bibring discusses "manipulation" as a technique of both casework and psychoanalysis in "Psychiatry and Social Work," *Journal of Social Casework*, 28 (June 1947), 203–211, and in "Psychiatric Principles in Casework," *Journal of Social Casework*, 30 (June 1949), 230–235.

3 | *Some Examples of Casework in Practice*

Before we proceed with further discussion of theory, some case illustrations may be of value in demonstrating the use in actual practice of the concepts presented in the introductory chapter. The case of Mr. and Mrs. Ryman,* for example, is of particular interest because the problems in social functioning encountered by this couple reflect all three types of causation described in Chapter 2 and the dynamics of the treatment process by which they were enabled to achieve better functioning demonstrate clearly many of the points made there.

NEGATIVE COMPLEMENTARITY IN A MARRIAGE

Mrs. Ryman, the wife of a successful young executive, was on the point of leaving her "impossible" husband when she came to the family service agency. There were violent quarrels in which he swore at her abusively. He was jealous of their children, particularly of nine-year-old Alice, born while he was overseas; he was critical and hostile toward her and favored the second daughter, two years younger. Mrs. Ryman felt that she received no love from her husband. She objected to sexual relations with him and wanted either to separate from him or to continue in a purely practical living arrangement that would provide financial support for herself and the children. She desired no companionship with her husband and wanted to exclude him from the upbringing of the children, since she considered this a woman's

---

* All case material in this book is disguised and fictitious names are used throughout.

job and also thought his influence on the children was harmful. In this view she was reinforced by her mother's attitude that it was hopeless to try to improve her relationship with her husband.

The current situational pressures on Mrs. Ryman are obvious. She was receiving very little love from her husband; instead, he was verbally abusive to her. He was also handling the children badly, creating problems with which she was left to deal. Her mother's attitude pushed her farther in the direction of quarreling with her husband, rather than of trying to improve their relationship.

What infantile needs did Mrs. Ryman bring to her situation from her childhood? When she was two or three years old, her father left her mother. Eventually he divorced her, but for a number of years he was in and out of the house, remaining an extremely attractive figure to the daughter, but also a deserting one. She was his favorite child. When she was seven her mother remarried, but this marriage also ended in separation when the child was thirteen or fourteen. She remembers her stepfather as violently hostile. Her mother hated men and inculcated this hatred in her daughter.

As a result of her early life, Mrs. Ryman carried over into adulthood a number of childish needs and reactions that caused her to make unusual demands on her adult world. She was partially frigid, fearful of sex, guilty on the few occasions when she allowed herself to enjoy it, and prudish in her refusal to participate in anything but the most conservative form of sex relationship, wanting for herself a husband who had little or no sex interest himself. She was overly devoted to her mother and so dependent upon her approval that she allowed her to continue to guide her adult life. Lacking other love gratification, she became overly possessive of her children, excluding her husband from participation in their upbringing. She also brought into adulthood excessive hostility to men, a hostility displaced from her feelings toward her two fathers and reinforced by her mother's attitude.

There was also faulty ego functioning in her evaluation of her husband, whom she could not see as the fundamentally loving person he was. Because of her earlier experiences Mrs. Ryman anticipated hostility and desertion on his part, and was unable to believe that he really loved her and wanted to find ways of improving their relationship. In actuality, in the early years of their marriage, Mr. Ryman was devoted to his wife, hoping to be able to "awaken" her. But when he returned from overseas service, he found her so preoccupied with the children that she had little interest in him and resisted sex relations. A number of times he lost his temper with her and with the older child, and from that point on she became increasingly cold, withdrawn, and hostile despite all his warm efforts to make amends.

Because of her distorted attitude toward men, Mrs. Ryman now saw her husband as the bad father her mother had pictured and she had experienced in childhood. Indeed, her husband's absence during the war must have encouraged displacement of the feelings she had had toward her deserting father. It was impossible for her to understand or sympathize with her husband's needs. Instead, she deprived and belittled him in a way that brought to the fore immaturities in his own personality. Thus, because of her own personality impairment, Mrs. Ryman had created for herself a hostile, attacking husband out of a fundamentally loving one and had deprived herself of the love she could have had because of her own inability to receive it. The interplay between intrapsychic and interpersonal factors is abundantly clear.

Looking at the problem from Mr. Ryman's side, what do we see? He was somewhat overattached to his mother, although not in a truly neurotic way, with correspondingly excessive needs for mothering from his wife, and with some adolescentlike insecurities about his masculinity. Late in treatment, he recalled his hurt and anger when an older sister who had been very much of a mother to him had turned her affections to a younger brother born when he was seven. At the beginning of his marriage, nevertheless, he appeared to have been a fairly mature young man, with a normal capacity for love and free of marked neurotic traits.

Upon his return from military service, however, he met what was essentially a traumatic situation. As noted in the preceding chapter, we tend to think of a trauma as a sudden dramatic event, but in actuality the repeated shock of lesser events can have an effect comparable in its proportions to a single major blow. Although Mr. Ryman came gradually to realize his wife's consistently unyielding hostility, this realization was, in effect, a trauma for him. For a long time he denied the severity of her reaction, alternately trying in every way he knew to recapture their earlier relationship and responding with fury when his efforts were frustrated.

As he became lonelier and more frustrated and angry, regression set in; his need for the sort of love he had had from his mother and sister increased. He responded with the jealousy he had felt for his brother, displacing his anger from his brother to his older child, who seemed to have stolen his place. His adolescentlike doubts about his own virility were also rearoused now that he seemed unable to awaken response in his wife. Earlier guilt feelings about sex, not quite outgrown, reasserted themselves, and he began to feel that some of his less conventional sex desires might be wrong and were contributing to his troubles. In his need to defend himself against these anxieties, he became at times short-tempered, unreasonable, and sharply attacking. He saw his wife as hostile and destructive, and lost to a large degree his former ability to understand her needs.

Three interacting sets of forces, then, had combined to create their present dilemma for the Rymans: infantile needs and weaknesses in libidinal functioning deriving from childhood, current life deprivations and pressures, and nonadaptive ego functioning that united with the childish drive remnants to create additional environmental hazards.

Mr. and Mrs. Ryman began treatment simultaneously, each coming for weekly interviews. At the beginning they had different workers; later, Mrs. Ryman at her own request transferred to her husband's caseworker. (Were the case being handled today essentially the same content would have to be covered, but the same caseworker would probably see both partners from the beginning and would hold joint interviews as well as individual ones. The extent to which joint or individual interviews predominated would have depended upon the needs of the clients and the worker's preference for one type or the other.)

At first Mr. Ryman needed to talk in detail about his wife's cold and hostile behavior, but he immediately followed this up by talking about his own angry reactions and his guilt about his inability to control himself. The caseworker was able to reduce some of his tension by showing sympathetic understanding of his frustrations and of his unhappiness about them. This laid the groundwork for his later ability to work on the shortcomings in his own responses. The caseworker did not give false reassurance about his inability to control his anger, but instead agreed without condemnation that it was a problem for him and worked against his own expressed desires for his family.

In this atmosphere Mr. Ryman became increasingly able to describe the details of interaction between himself, his wife, and his children. As he recounted incidents involving the children, he became more aware of the effect of his angry spells on them, both in confusing and frightening them and in alienating them from him. He also began to see that much of his anger toward Alice was really intended for his wife and that he was using the child to hurt Mrs. Ryman. This realization made it more possible for him to control his outbursts against Alice. But his wife, unfortunately, did not show any appreciation of his efforts to change, nor did she respond any more generously to his need for love.

As Mr. Ryman's description of his wife's treatment of him increased in freedom and vehemence, he suddenly saw that he felt she was taking away his masculinity and was trying to destroy him. It was apparent to the worker that this in turn aroused his doubts about himself and that he defended himself against his self-doubts by a show of masculine aggression punctuated with crude and abusive language. At this point the worker's assessment of the family interaction was that Mrs. Ryman's attacks on her husband were not primarily reactive to initial hostility on his part. Rather they constituted a realistic pressure upon Mr. Ryman activated by her own distorted preconceptions about men. Since it was not yet possible to bring about a change in Mrs. Ryman, the worker attempted to strengthen in two directions Mr. Ryman's ability to withstand his wife's continuing hostility. The dynamics of one approach rested on the relationship between the client and therapist. Wherever possible the worker conveyed to Mr. Ryman her own view of him as an adequate male; she expressed directly her opinion that his sexual desires were normal, as they were. The worker's continued acceptance of the healthiness of Mr. Ryman's desires and the naturalness of his anger made it possible for him to begin to regain his self-confidence and opened the way for his trying to understand his wife. This made possible a second approach—that of helping him to understand his wife. He was increasingly able to see that his wife had great anxiety about sex. He reviewed the early life experiences that had brought about the sex inhibitions that she could not control. The more he saw the problem in her, the less anxious he became about himself. He was freed to understand and appreciate her unhappiness and to see more fully the way in which his angry behavior had increased her fears. As he became more able to place the responsibility for their sexual problem on his wife, where, in this case, it really belonged, Mr. Ryman was in large measure relieved of his own reawakened doubts about himself and his sexual needs and competence. This in turn removed a large part of his need to become hostile toward his wife.

The balance of forces within his personality was now shifted sufficiently to enable him gradually to acquire control of his own reactions. When he did become angry he was repeatedly able to trace his anger to its current source in the frustrating sexual situation and keep it where it belonged—as he said, "in the bedroom"—instead of allowing it to spill over to do harm in other areas of his family life where it did not belong; he could also keep himself from acts of retaliation that worsened rather than improved his situation. Thus the area of social disturbance was greatly narrowed.

Toward the end of treatment, as Mrs. Ryman also began to change, Mr. Ryman showed sympathetic understanding of her problems and tried to help her to become less fearful in their sexual relationship. He also examined more fully his jealousy of his children and came to see its similarity to his childhood reactions to his sister; this in turn gave him greater motivation for controlling his responses and keeping them from doing harm to the children.

The treatment of Mr. Ryman touched only briefly on the childish components in his adult personality; it was concerned primarily with strengthening the healthy part of his ego in order to enable it to deal better with frustrations. His perception of himself as a healthy male was shored up, and he was enabled to see the realities of his situation more clearly, thereby ridding himself of harmful distortions. He was also helped to understand the interaction between himself and his family and the effects his

own responses were having on them. Perceiving and compre-
hending the situation more clearly, he was better able to judge
the direction he wanted his affairs to take and to control his own
responses in a way more likely to bring his goal about.

The initial period of work with Mrs. Ryman was not fruitful.
Her repeated and extensive expressions of anger at her husband
brought her little relief. She was completely unwilling to examine her own reactions to their relationship or accept even a
modicum of responsibility for their troubles. She was aware of
the effect on their marriage of her lack of participation in their
sex life and developed superficial understanding of the fact that
the cause of her fears lay in her own childhood, in the absence of
her father and in her mother's insistence that she see all men as
bad. But instead of trying to free herself from these influences,
she used them as an excuse and demanded that her husband adjust
to her inhibitions.

The next step in treatment, which occurred after Mrs. Ryman
began seeing the same worker as her husband, became one of
helping Mrs. Ryman recognize that despite her husband's use of
treatment to improve his behavior toward her, she still wanted to
hold on to her grudges and refused to change her side of the
relationship. The worker did not express criticism of Mrs.
Ryman for this nor did she urge her to change, but rather limited
herself to pointing out that there would be no purpose in setting
up interviews if Mrs. Ryman really was satisfied to continue the
status quo.

Gradually Mrs. Ryman acknowledged that she was fighting a
battle from her past; she accepted the worker's comment that in
so doing she was making trouble for herself as well as for her
husband and volunteered that she played favorites with the children, preferring Alice, the child toward whom her husband was
hostile. As Mrs. Ryman began to consider her mistakes, the
worker kept the treatment oriented to Mrs. Ryman's own well-
being, so that the client would see the need for change not as a
dutiful adaptation to her husband but as a way of better achieving
her own deepest wishes for herself and her children.

As Mrs. Ryman began to recognize instances in which she had
distorted her husband's actions, assuming hostility when none
existed, she was able to see that she had not been trying to

understand him. She began to correct her distortions and to look more realistically at Mr. Ryman, as well as at her own tendency to blame him at times when she herself was at fault. The beginnings of a better relationship with her husband brought feelings of disloyalty to her mother to the fore. As she recognized these feelings her adult judgment gradually took hold and another obstacle to better adjustment lost some of its power. For the first time she began to talk about the positive elements in her marriage. She saw that she had been shutting her husband out of the lives of her children and began to handle herself differently in that triangular relationship. At this point in her adjustment her discussion of their sexual difficulties took on a different quality; she conceded that the problem was really hers and that she ought to try to get over it. For the first time she could truly understand her husband's feelings of rejection. Her attitude toward his sexual advances now changed, even though she was not yet comfortable in her own sexual responses.

In analyzing the case of Mrs. Ryman, we see again that treatment enabled the client's ego to take control over a larger part of her personality. First, submerged feelings and wishes were brought clearly within the ego's perception. Then the realities and consequences of behavior to which the individual was previously blind emerged. As with Mr. Ryman, the direct influence of the worker, in the nature of a corrective experience in the treatment relationship, was also of great importance. The therapist conveyed her own belief that Mrs. Ryman had a right to grow up and enjoy her marriage and that men were not by nature hostile and disloyal but rather capable of providing comfort and happiness to a woman.

Whether continued casework treatment would have brought about further improvement is not known, for at this point the couple had to leave the country because of Mr. Ryman's business. The total relationship between Mr. and Mrs. Ryman was markedly improved; the outright battles were a thing of the past, the children were no longer pawns in the marital struggle, and an atmosphere of true warmth had begun to emerge in the family.

A SUPEREGO DISTURBANCE

Casework treatment is "thematic." It does not attempt to deal thoroughly with all aspects of the client's adjustment or personality; rather, it studies the current adjustment and life history of the individual to ascertain where his functioning is inadequate and causes discomfort and what particular facets of his personality that need strengthening might be susceptible to change by casework methods. Certain social themes and certain psychological themes appear repetitively in interviews, their choice being determined partly by client interest and partly by conscious focusing on the part of the worker.

Work with Jean Emerson, for instance, viewed from the psychological side, concentrated on superego inadequacies. Viewed socially, it focused on her relationships with her friends and on her effort to find close relationships that would be both deeply satisfying and in harmony with the demands of her social environment.

In discussing changes in the superego, we must distinguish sharply between *structure* and *content*. Normally, a child learns very early in life that there is such a thing as right and wrong and acquires the desire to do "right" things and avoid doing "wrong" things in order both to please his parents and to avoid punishment. If this basic structure is absent or seriously defective in the adult, it is very difficult to bring change. Fortunately, the basic structure is usually present, but the content—the pattern of what is believed right and what is believed wrong—is unrealistic. Sometimes it is consistently too high in the standard it requires, sometimes too low. At other times it is inconsistent, with contrary patterns or with lacunae, as Adelaide Johnson[1] has called them, curious blank spots where otherwise mature individuals seem to lack socially acceptable standards. It is this area of content that is amenable to casework influence.

Jean Emerson, a young woman in her early twenties, came to the agency to seek help in freeing herself from a group of young people with whom she had been associating. They were engaging in various forms of socially borderline behavior including petty stealing. Jean had been in revolt against conventional behavior for many years, but her friends' activities had begun to dissatisfy and frighten her. She was in conflict both about what she thought she ought to do and what she wanted to do.

Jean's early life history embodied three factors often associated with later superego disturbance. In the first place, her mother had used overly severe physical punishment as a form of discipline, setting up a rebellion against the very standards she was trying to inculcate. In the second place, the mother constantly warned against certain forms of forbidden behavior, as though she anticipated that her daughter would be unable to refrain from indulging in them. As Adelaide Johnson and others have pointed out, a child's ability to discipline his own impulses is greatly aided by a belief on the part of his parents that he will be good most of the time. The parent who constantly warns the child against misbehavior, as Jean's mother did, is actually dangling a temptation before him—an excellent example of the "double bind" so well described by Bateson and Jackson.[2] In the third place, Mrs. Emerson's own superego was defective. She was extremely impulsive and inconsistent in behavior. Since the child learns more rapidly from what the parent does than from what he says, Jean was influenced by her mother's unsound example.

Jean's father appears to have had a much more stable superego than her mother, but he was a weaker person and so was unable to make his influence felt as strongly as that of his wife. Nevertheless, he did contribute a positive element to Jean's development, which she became more able to use as she responded to treatment.

Work with Jean combined a corrective relationship experience with discussions of current realities designed to strengthen the ego in its perception, judgment, and ability to control. This strengthening in turn brought about changes in the content of the superego. Because of the nature of the transference, Jean identified with the worker and accepted some of her values. In addition, Jean's own increasingly realistic ego began to build up values of a more socially useful type, which gradually became part of her ideal for herself.

To begin with, the worker showed interest in Jean, understanding of her plight, and appreciation of her conflict about it; but she carefully refrained from falling into the trap of immediately aligning herself with Jean's impulsive move toward a more conventional life. To have plunged immediately into approving and implementing her initial impulse would have been to overlook Jean's ambivalence, to mobilize her resistance to change, and to provide her with an opportunity once again to act out the old mother-daughter drama, with the worker cast in the role of the strict, punitive, and distrustful mother. Even if ways could have been found to avoid this latter pitfall, had the worker moved too quickly in getting Jean away from her companions she would have run the risk of sacrificing the long-range goal of enabling her to build a new set of life objectives that would become a lasting part of her personality.

The worker therefore used early interviews to encourage Jean to look at her proposed move from all angles, to face the loss of friendships that would be involved, and to air her fears of not being able to find new ones. The worker made it clear that she was ready to help work out plans for such a move if and when Jean really decided to make it, but did not try to rush the decision. She assumed throughout, as was diagnostically indicated, that Jean was capable of deciding for herself what was wise and unwise activity and that she both desired and was capable of finding for herself a way of life in which she could be relatively at peace with the world as well as with herself.

As Jean became more certain of her resolve, the worker showed her agreement with it and tacitly implied she would be able to carry it through. When the decision was finally made, she gave help in the form of suggestions about practical steps to take. When Jean moved to a new location the worker showed pleasure, but gentle pleasure geared to the client's own satisfaction in her accomplishments.

During the inevitable period of loneliness before Jean could find new friendships, the worker's friendly interest in her everyday life became an emotional crutch to tide her over until real life experiences could again meet her needs. She and the worker discussed her new acquaintances, including Jean's ways of reacting to them and her distorted evaluation of their attitudes toward her. They went into details of how she handled herself on her job. The worker shared her own interests in movies and popular music, so that Jean saw her as a person who thought it was good to have fun and who knew something of a young person's world. As Jean's growing interest in dating and eventual marriage aroused her interest in homemaking skills, the worker brought her recipes and even helped her in sewing a dress. As the worker gradually gained her trust and admiration, Jean began to identify with the worker and incorporate some of her values.

Although there was a minimum of active direction on the worker's part, as the relationship between her and Jean grew stronger she was able to be more direct in expressing opinions when these were called for, thus providing Jean with guides for behavior that she had not had earlier in her life. As Jean herself put it toward the end of treatment, "When you are told you are a bum all your life, you begin to believe it"; and she particularly stressed the value of the worker's "believing" in her. At the same time she said she was glad the caseworker had not "indulged" her, referring to the fact that the worker had gradually cut through her self-deceptions and rationalizations, enabling her ego to make its decisions on the basis of facts rather than of self-coddling distortions.

Here again, as in the case of the Rymans, the early formative experiences in the client's life were touched on but by no means thoroughly explored. The main dynamics of treatment lay in strengthening the more accessible parts of the personality in ways that would enable them to counterbalance the early traumata.

The effect of the client-worker relationship was by no means the only dynamic in treatment, but it played a larger part in this case than it did in the work with the Rymans. There has been a tendency to belittle so-called transference cures. Some distrust of such cures is well based. When nothing more is done than to use suggestion as a way of directly removing symptomatic behavior, it is extremely likely that a new form of symptom will arise, and not infrequently a more harmful symptom than the one originally chosen by the client. If, however, the transference is used to remove or lessen the effect of factors *causative* to the maladjustment, it is an entirely different situation.

This principle may be seen in the work with Jean. Had the worker used her influence directly to induce her client to move to a different neighborhood, to give up certain friends, and to make certain other friendships, this would have been "symptomatic" treatment. The improvement would then very likely have been only temporary, because the forces originally at work would have pushed the client in the direction of repetitive behavior and she would have chosen acquaintances similar to the friends she had just relinquished. Instead, the worker-client relationship was used to counteract the self-image and values derived from earlier life experiences that were basic to later social adjustment.

Two additional factors would seem to influence the endurance of transference improvement. One, of course, is the length of time the transference itself remains alive. If the treatment has ended by mutual consent and with the positive transference elements in ascendancy, if dependence has been lessened before the close of treatment to a point where the client has confidence in his ability to maintain his improvement alone, and if the negative feelings inevitable in separation have been foreseen and worked through before ending the treatment, the effects of the transference may continue to be helpful for indefinite periods of time.

A second important factor is the extent to which improved life conditions achieved through the behavior changes originating in transference reinforce the effect of transference itself. If the experience of living confirms the wisdom of ways of behavior promoted by the therapist through the medium of transference, the client may gradually be led to integrate the new ways into his ego structure, independently of their original transference source. This element was important in the case of Jean Emerson.

UNDERSTANDING EARLY LIFE EXPERIENCES

Sometimes early life material assumes major importance in developing a client's understanding of current reactions. This was true in the case of Mr. Fuller, who was having difficulty in two areas—his work and his relationship with his son. These became the social themes around which treatment revolved; but it soon became apparent that they were in large part a reflection of problems that had their roots in neurotic personality characteristics. Mr. Fuller's feelings toward his father and the subsequent displacement of these feelings in his current work and family relationships thus became the psychological themes of treatment, with the emphasis more upon self-understanding than was true in Jean Emerson's case.

Mr. Fuller complained to the therapist at length about his employer's immoderate demands, spoke of his wife's impatience with his investing too much of himself in his job, and gave innumerable instances of his boss's stupidity and unreasonableness and of arguments in which Mr. Fuller was repeatedly able to come out on top. When the worker asked why he worked so hard for a man he disliked, Mr. Fuller said he thought the cause lay in the ideas about work that his father had inculcated in him. He described his father as a perfectionist demanding high performance of his son, who had worked for him during his adolescence. He told of his consequent fear of criticism, and his efforts to avoid it by requiring more than adequate performance of himself on a job. At the same time, he expressed great anger at his boss for his unjustified criticisms. As a result of this discussion, Mr. Fuller began to think more objectively about his father's standards and ideals and to realize that he as an adult could set more realistic rules for himself.

Despite this new awareness, his troubles with his employer and his complaints continued unchanged. The worker indicated that she accepted the fact that this was a difficult reality situation and that his boss was unreasonable, but she added that there were certain factors about his response to the situation that needed further exploration and study. Why should Mr. Fuller tire himself out working overtime with no extra pay to do a better job for a boss he didn't like? Mr. Fuller was quick to see the illogic of his own behavior and was astonished at his own foolishness, when in reality he could easily make his boss hire additional help. Spurred on by this, he admitted his feelings of inadequacy and his need to show that he was really much better than the boss, that he was, in fact, a superman.

This admission led to further discussion of his father's attitudes, and for the first time real ambivalence began to come through. Mr. Fuller would swing from describing his father's great strength and intelligence to belittling him as a vocational failure and a man who thought he ruled his family but was actually under his wife's domination. He told of his father's disparaging treatment of him, of his dominating him and his refusal to try ideas the son had about improving the family business. Finally he burst out that "he adored the old man in many ways yet sometimes he hated him with every fiber in his body." Subsequently, Mr. Fuller saw the repetitive nature of his relationship with his employer as a displacement from his father. His belligerent behavior with his boss was in part a living out of suppressed and repressed anger at his father and in part an attempt to prove to himself that he was an ideal, loving son by carrying out his father's mandate to be a perfect, or superperfect, workman. He became able to handle his work life more realistically, and in time he changed to a more remunerative and less demanding job.

Several processes were at work in bringing about this change. First came the step of convincing Mr. Fuller that his current behavior was irrational. Sometimes such a realization in itself is enough to enable a person to modify his reactions; but in cases where such modification does not occur, motivation has nevertheless been created for the client to pursue the matter further. A second factor was Mr. Fuller's recognition of the displacement from father to employer. Often a client is well aware of hostile feelings toward parents and blind only to the fact of displacement; but in more complicated situations, as with Mr. Fuller, the feelings are themselves half-concealed. A third factor, then, became the bringing to light of the strength of Mr. Fuller's anger at his father. The most important fourth factor was the worker's acceptance of that anger and the consequent reduction in Mr. Fuller's guilt about it.

Viewed in the framework of Freudian theory, this case is one of classical oedipal reactions. Mr. Fuller had recalled events in his adolescence that reflected and reinforced unresolved infantile rivalries with his father. Other material in the record substantiates this, but at no point did the therapist get into these underlying, unconscious reactions. The strength of the total oedipal component in Mr. Fuller's problem was, however, reduced in several ways: the reinforcement of the original experiences occurring in adolescence was greatly lessened; when he became less hostilely provocative toward "father persons," he no longer evoked responses that seemed to confirm his original distortions concerning men in authority; and some of the feelings of anger and fear were drained off as in his conscious mind the father became a less powerful figure. This decreased his guilt and the need for destructive, defensive behavior.

Very little, if any, of the material that came through in this instance had probably been unconscious; rather it seemed to be preconscious in nature. Occasionally, a very limited amount of unconscious data does come through in casework, and this is well illustrated in the theme of Mr. Fuller's complicated relationship with his son. Mr. Fuller was very eager for his son to be an aggressive, masculine little boy, for, he said, he himself had been weak and delicate as a child. Yet there were situations in which he was extremely overprotective of the boy, as, for example, his insistence that Edward hold on to his hand when they were together on city streets. Once in discussing this, Mr. Fuller suddenly called Edward "Lester." By following up this slip, the worker learned that Lester was a younger brother who, at the age of six, had run into the street in the path of an automobile and been killed. The accident occurred just a few months after Mr. Fuller's father's death, when Mr. Fuller, then eighteen, had been delegated, as the oldest son, to take over his father's responsibilities in the family. As he told about the details of his brother's death, he described himself as so shocked that he fainted when he had to identify his brother's body in the morgue; but at the same time he had not cried and had been surprisingly unfeeling about his mother's grief. As he spoke, however, he suddenly began to cry violently and had considerable difficulty in regaining control. Mr. Fuller very easily made the connection to his present overprotectiveness with Edward.

Although Mr. Fuller had never forgotten the facts of this event, he had in large measure repressed the affect. Its release probably reduced the extent to which the occurrence controlled Mr. Fuller's behavior. Awareness of the transference from brother to son also provided him with a means of combating it.

It seems likely that despite his denials he did have irrational unconscious feelings of guilt about the accident, and the worker may have reduced these to a slight degree by her own acceptance of the fact that he was not at fault. Had his overprotectiveness continued, it might have been advisable to relieve his possible guilt feelings by bringing them to light.

Note that in both these instances of exploration of childhood material a principle of economy was followed. The caseworker pursued a theme only as far as seemed necessary to bring improvement in the social adaptation of the client. In the first instance, emphasis was upon modifying the hostilities and consequent fears that Mr. Fuller carried over from his childhood experiences with his father to adult life, where their inappropriateness created problems in his work. His adult ego was helped to become aware of these early feelings and to recognize their continued existence and destructive expression in his current life. In the second instance, recovery of the feelings about his brother's death and recognition of the effect his concern about his brother had on his relationship with his son enabled him to overcome the inconsistencies in his handling of the child. The balance between the adaptive forces of his ego and the drive toward behavior motivated by unresolved earlier life problems was tipped in favor of the adult ego. The reduction in the force of these childhood remnants was sufficient to enable the adaptive forces to achieve improved functioning both in his work life and in his relationship with his son.

NOTES

1. Adelaide M. Johnson, "Sanctions for Superego Lacunae of Adolescents," in Kurt R. Eissler, ed., *Searchlights on Delinquency* (New York: International Universities Press, 1949), pp. 225–244.
2. Gregory Bateson, Don D. Jackson, Jay Haley, and John Weakland, "Toward a Theory of Schizophrenia," *Behavioral Science*, 1 (1956), 251–264; and Don D. Jackson, ed., *Communication, Family and Marriage: Human Communication*, vol. 1 (Palo Alto, Calif.: Science and Behavior Books, 1968).

4 | Classifications of Casework Treatment

Logic might dictate that we move into detailed discussion of the casework process by way of chapters on psychosocial study, diagnosis, treatment planning, and treatment procedures. But in order to understand what information we should seek in the psychosocial study and what type of diagnosis will be useful in treatment planning, we first need further understanding of the nature of treatment itself as it has evolved in casework.

Every treatment step is a goal-directed procedure and seeks to bring into action various dynamics to bring about its intended effect. Suppose our client is a widow who is afraid of an operation partly because she is too sick to work out plans for the care of her children during her absence from home, partly because she is going to a strange doctor and is uncertain about the outcome of the operation, and partly because unconsciously she fears punishment for her hostile attitudes toward her mother, who had a similar illness and became a permanent cripple following an operation that the client erroneously assumes was similar to the one she is about to undergo. Many different dynamics can be employed to reduce this woman's anxiety.

One alternative is the environmental one of providing for the care of the children during her absence. This can have a double effect: it will relieve her of that part of her anxiety that is caused by realistic concern for the welfare of her children; and it will demonstrate to her that others care for her welfare and are ready to come to her assistance when she is weak and unable to manage her own affairs. We know that in serious illness regression may lead to a state of intense dependence. It is extremely important at such a time for the patient to feel that someone with strength will take care of him. The way in which plans for the children are made will also be of importance. If relatives or friends toward whom the patient has warm feelings can care for them, so much the better. If agency care must be sought, the degree of relief from anxiety felt by the patient will vary with the amount of confidence she has in the good will and competence of the caseworker who makes this arrangement. Every effort should therefore be made to establish a strong, positive relationship with the patient.

A second possible mode of help consists of getting the client to air her anxieties and reassuring her about them insofar as this is realistic. The worker can encourage her to express her fears about the operation and show understanding of her anxiety, indicating that it is a natural reaction, not a sign of childishness on her part. Not infrequently, he may also be able to reassure her that the doctors are interested in her and are skillful. If the operation is not a dangerous one, this reality can also be used to allay fears once they have been adequately expressed. The patient's response to this approach will depend very largely upon the extent of her confidence in the worker.

A third way of reducing the anxiety would be to help the patient understand more fully the facts about the operation itself. Arrangement could be made for her to talk in detail with the doctor. Subsequently, she might again go over the facts with the caseworker, clarifying her understanding of what the doctor had told her.

A fourth alternative, to be undertaken only if it is both necessary and feasible, would be to help her gain understanding of the relationship between her feelings about her mother and her mother's illness and her current reactions to her own illness.

These procedures all have a common aim—to reduce anxiety—but the dynamics involved in each are different. In one instance one of the stimuli for the anxiety is removed by environmental measures; in another, reassurance is given—a procedure that depends for its effectiveness upon the client's confidence in the worker; in the third, the patient uses her reasoning powers to help her understand her situation more realistically; and in the fourth, she applies these reasoning powers toward an understanding of early developmental factors that affect her current reactions.

EARLY AND CURRENT CLASSIFICATIONS

There have been many classifications of casework treatment methods. Mary Richmond made only the very simple distinction between "direct" and "indirect" treatment. By the former she meant those processes that take place directly between the client and the worker—the "influence of mind upon mind"—and by the latter, changes that the worker brings about in the client's human and physical environment.[1] Porter Lee made essentially the same distinction in his reference to "executive" and "leadership" forms of treatment, as did Gordon Hamilton in her early writings.[2] In 1947 Grete Bibring,[3] a psychoanalyst who had worked closely with caseworkers for a number of years in Boston, mentioned five groups of technical procedures used by all types of therapists, including caseworkers. These were suggestion, emotional relief, immediate influence (or manipulation), clarification, and interpretation. It was her impression that interpretation was used sparingly in casework, and chiefly in dealing with preconscious rather than unconscious material, but she did not altogether rule out interpretation of unconscious material. Her major distinction was between interpretation, which she characterized as having as its goal insight development (the principal objective of psychoanalysis), and the other techniques, for which insight development was not a goal.

Bibring's classification represented a distinct elaboration of the earlier direct treatment method and reflected the influence of psychoanalysis in enriching the caseworker's understanding of the ways in which psychological forces can be used in treatment. Suggestion, emotional relief, and manipulation, though not recognized in these terms, were undoubtedly a part of early casework methodology, as was also a technique not specifically designated by Bibring—that of helping the client to reason his way through to a favorable solution of his problems. Clarification in the sense of helping the client to separate objective reality from his own distortions of the external world was, like insight development, the result of the incorporation of analytic concepts and played little part in casework until the 1930's and 1940's.

Also in 1947 the present writer suggested another classification of treatment methods.[4] These were environmental modification (corresponding to the earlier indirect method) and psychological support, clarification, and insight development (representing subdivisions of direct treatment). This classification and Bibring's were similar in that both attempted to group techniques according to the psychological dynamics by which they operated. Bibring's suggestion, emotional relief, and manipulation corresponded to different aspects of the Hollis psychological support; insight development was the same in the two classifications. But Hollis used clarification in a broader sense than did Bibring, covering by that term the general encouragement of a reasoning approach to problems as well as the separation of objective reality from distortions of external events—actually two different processes, which experience indicates are better understood as distinct categories.

In 1948 Lucille Austin suggested a somewhat different type of classification,[5] directed primarily toward separating clusters of techniques not by their dynamics but by their use in the pursuit of a predominant treatment goal. "Social therapy" she described as consisting primarily of "the use of techniques designed to influence positively various factors in the environment and of the effective use of social resources." In pursuit of this aim, psychological support and a rational approach to reality problems would complement the Richmond indirect treatment techniques. When, on the other hand, the aim was primarily that of modifying the client's behavior, Austin suggested the term "psychotherapy" to describe the treatment techniques and proposed three subdivisions of this method. At the two extremes she placed *supportive therapy* and *insight therapy*, and she designated an intermediate form *experiential therapy*.

Supportive therapy, as the name indicates, relies heavily on the techniques of psychological support but may often include Richmond's indirect methods and a rational approach to reality problems. The aim of this form of treatment is the prevention of further breakdown in clients whose egos are weak and who may be particularly vulnerable to further breakdown under pressure. Austin described insight therapy as having the aim of achieving a change in the ego by developing the patient's insight into his difficulties and increasing the ability of the ego to deal with them through the emotional experience in the transference situation. Emphasis was placed upon the use of interpretive techniques to lead the client to greater awareness of his feelings and of the unconscious motivations that underlie his reactions. It was expected that relevant childhood memories would be recalled and blocking emotions discharged. The transference would be used to help the client understand how his irrational impulses arose and their inappropriateness in the present situation. In addition, there would be selected use of other direct and indirect techniques. Experiential therapy is in part a blending of supportive and insight therapy, with the central focus on the development and use of the relationship as a corrective emotional experience. Sometimes the techniques emphasized in supportive therapy are stressed and sometimes those more characteristic of insight therapy; however, dynamic rather than genetic interpretations are emphasized.

Austin recognized that although her supportive treatment was designed primarily to maintain present strengths, psychological improvement often occurred. "As anxiety diminishes the ego gains strength to handle immediate situations, and the experience of more adequate functioning becomes itself a growth process." Similarly, in the experiential form of treatment, although Austin at one point maintains that "in this group change represents primarily better adaptations within the existing personality structure," she goes on to say that "in certain cases maturation already under way is carried through to completion." She further maintains that the objectives of experiential treatment "are mainly loosening restrictive ties to figures in the past, redirecting emotional energies, and promoting growth through increased satisfactions in living."[6]

In 1953 a committee of the Family Service Association of America published a report[7] based in part on the reading of a series of cases in family service agencies. This report proposed a new classification of casework treatment. Type A, or "supportive casework," was designated as "treatment aimed at maintaining adaptive patterns," and Type B as "treatment aimed at modification of adaptive patterns." The first type of treatment was described as resting upon the use of such techniques as "manipulation of the environment, reassurance, persuasion, direct advice and guidance, suggestion, logical discussion, exercise of professional authority and immediate influence."[8]   The second was characterized mainly by its use of the technique of clarification.   The committee also reported that it had decided not to include a category corresponding to the insight development or insight therapy included in preceding classifications because it found that this type of treatment was used in very few agencies.

Five years later, in 1958, this classification was further developed by a committee of the Community Service Society of New York.   Their document, *Method and Process in Social Casework*,[9] describes in more detail the techniques used in the "supportive treatment method" and the "modifying treatment method."   This report also recognizes clarification as the predominant technique in the second method.   It sees this technique as being used to increase consistently "the client's awareness and understanding of the use, meaning, and effect of disabling patterns of response, eventually including the pathological use of a defense mechanism."   Its description of the process includes "enabling the client to see and understand the conscious and preconscious dissatisfactions and gratifications in his responses to selected aspects of his life's situation" and "encouraging the client to recognize the connection between incidents in his remembered past and his current attitudes and behavior, and the inappropriate influence of the past on the present."

These two reports played an important part in clarifying several issues concerning casework treatment.   Their specificity was a distinct improvement over earlier efforts.   Three issues were identified and spelled out in a way that led to further study: (1) To what extent is "insight therapy" undertaken by caseworkers?   (2) Are changes in adaptive patterns dependent upon the use of clarification as a predominant treatment technique? (3) Is casework correctly conceptualized as a dichotomous process having two distinct treatment modes, one in which clarification is the predominant technique and one in which this technique is either absent or plays a minor role?

PERSONALITY CHANGES AND TREATMENT TECHNIQUES

The first of these issues to be examined systematically was that of the relationship between changes in adaptive patterns and treatment method. Sidney Berkowitz,[10] in a paper given at the National Conference of Social Work in the spring of 1955, took the position that adaptive patterns can be modified through a process of ego influence with little or no reference to—or clarification of—the relation of the past to the present. Subsequently, study of a series of cases led this writer ·to the same conclusion.

To understand this question we need to consider what is meant by a change in adaptive patterns. What is the distinction between a change in adaptive patterns and an improvement in social functioning without modification of habitual patterns of behavior? A change in adaptive patterns is one that is internalized, built into the personality. It results in an improvement in functioning that cannot be accounted for by improved circumstances, the passing of a crisis, or the influence of the worker during the period of treatment; rather, it constitutes a change in the client's way of functioning that will enable him to respond differently even when his external situation has not changed and when the worker is not part of his current life. He will have learned to act differently and will respond to the same or similar life events more appropriately than he did before treatment.

Improvement in functioning *without* a change in adaptive patterns might be said to occur in situations such as the following. A man has been quarreling with his wife because of anxiety about his business. In discussions with the worker, he comes to understand the cause of his irritability, transfers to another position in which he is under less pressure, and subsequently is more even-tempered at home. A widow who is depressed because of the loss of her husband is therefore unable to care adequately for her children. She is helped during this period of grief, and as the grief subsides, is able to function normally again in relation to the children. A structural iron worker loses a leg in an accident and is told he will no longer be able to continue in his line of work. He loses interest in life, does not try to obtain a prosthesis, and retreats to dependent, whining, childlike behavior, to the despair of his formerly dependent wife. After a good deal of skillful work, including some development of understanding of his current responses, he regains his former stability and finds a new work adjustment. In none of these cases have new adaptive patterns necessarily been established.

Such improvements in functioning often occur in response to supportive treatment methods and constitute a very important type of recovery from a period of strain or disaster that might otherwise result in permanent impairment of functioning. But can the other type of improved functioning, that which does rest upon modification of habitual patterns of behavior, be brought about without treatment in which clarification is the predominant technique?

In actuality, it is not hard to find cases in which such modification does appear to have taken place entirely or in large part in response to supportive treatment methods. Brief sketches of a series of cases will illustrate the point.

Mrs. Knight, an exceedingly immature young woman still in her teens, was married to a man old enough to be her father. At first he thoroughly enjoyed her childish dependence, but soon he became irritated by her inability to manage his home and be an adequate mother to the two children of his former marriage. Mrs. Knight sought help "in growing up" from the caseworker. The approach was one of guidance and support, with reliance on elements in the relationship, on considerable logical discussion, on extensive use of a visiting homemaker and of a nurse who educated the client in matters concerning her own and the children's health. With the ego strengthened by increased knowledge and skill, the psychosocial maturation that had been arrested when Mrs. Knight was overwhelmed by demands beyond her ability to meet began again to take place, with marked improvement in her functioning as a wife and mother. There was every reason to believe that the improvement in adaptive patterns would be lasting.

Mr. Graham wavered between compulsive and impulsive behavior when he came to the agency. He was in trouble because of debts, excessive drinking, and instability in his relationships with women. The worker became the good, kind, but gently firm parent and used "logical discussion" to guide the client away from the impulsive patterns through which he made so much trouble for himself and others. The client's dependency led him to want to please and imitate the worker. The experience of greater satisfactions when ego controls over impulsive behavior were strengthened reinforced new adaptive patterns.

Mrs. Landers, the mother of five children, was driven by a strong need to succeed, which showed itself in the form of perfectionistic demands upon the children and excessive self-criticism when difficulties arose in her own relationship with them. The worker became the "good mother" and on the basis of this relationship was able to help Mrs. Landers to handle the children more realistically and to reduce the severity of the demands of her superego upon the children and upon herself. Mrs. Landers became able to set up more lenient goals for her family and to see at a number of points that she was overreacting in holding herself so completely responsible for their behavior. Once again, a nurse was used for discussion of health problems; better housing plans were worked out; camp opportunities were provided for the children. Mrs. Landers learned new ways of handling her children and incorporated less demanding standards for herself and her family.

These three cases illustrate change in adaptive patterns with *no* use of clarification. In the following three situations clarification was used in a very limited way in relation to certain themes of adjustment, but it was not a predominant technique and much change occurred along lines not touched by clarifying methods.

In Chapter 3 we discussed the work with Jean Emerson, in which clarification was used only around the theme of Jean's distorted evaluation of the attitudes her new friends had toward her. In a number of equally important areas change was sought and achieved without the use of clarification. Jean was helped to develop a socially realistic superego and the ability to function well and with satisfaction in her work and her human relationships. Such new adaptive patterns can become so incorporated into the personality that these gains become a permanent part of functioning.

Mr. Ingersol, a married man of thirty-five, was repeatedly in trouble because of impulsive behavior at work and with his wife. Periodic drinking complicated the problem. The aim of treatment was to help him control his impulsiveness and his drinking. For a long time Mr. Ingersol denied that his drinking was a problem and that his own behavior contributed to his quarrels with his wife. After treatment had advanced to a point where Mr. Ingersol trusted the caseworker, it was possible again and again to get him to go over the details of what happened between himself and his wife when he had been drinking excessively, to recall exactly how many drinks he had had and exactly what he did and said during the course of an evening. He gradually came to see that after a certain number of drinks he said things he would not otherwise have said and that his behavior on such occasions precipitated certain responses from his wife she would not otherwise have given. When he became able to admit to himself that his drinking really did cause trouble, he began to make a real effort to control it and actually succeeded in reducing it to a marked extent. A pattern of greater ego control was established, not by bringing suppressed material to consciousness or by seeking causative understanding of his drinking beyond current provocations, but by the effect of close examination of present realities.

Another factor at work in Mr. Ingersol's progress was the client-worker relationship itself. Mr. Ingersol was a dependent person who had greatly admired his father. He developed similar feelings toward his caseworker, whom he wanted to please as he had wanted to please his father. The worker used this dynamic, giving Mr. Ingersol credit and appreciation when he showed understanding of the effects of his behavior patterns and when he tried to modify them. His efforts to change were further fortified by the satisfaction he secured during periods of better relationship with his wife.

Logical discussion, advice, approval, and encouragement were all used in the effort to enable him to improve the quality and strength of his ego controls. At several points clarification was also used, but it was by no means the predominant technique. Considerable improvement in adaptive patterns seems to have occurred in this case although one could not be wholly optimistic about the permanence of the new patterns Mr. Ingersol had actually incorporated.

Susan Masters, a young woman in her late twenties, suffered from a character disorder that expressed itself chiefly in her social relationships. Although she thought she wanted to marry, she dated only men whom for one reason or another she could not marry. She had become a strict adherent of an ascetic philosophy that cut her off from many normal social pleasures. Exaggerated residual childish fantasies of omnipotence led her to undertake unrealistic educational plans. She complicated her social relationships by overreacting to slights, trying to use avoidance to solve difficulties that she created for herself, and seeking to gain satisfaction by creating competition among her friends. Because it was feared that Susan might be too disturbed to use clarification, it was at first decided to work through a supportive relationship and logical discussion of her way of handling her social situation. This method brought marked improvement in a number of areas.

In one area, however, clarification in the Bibring sense of the word was used, even though treatment did not include relating the current patterns to causative influences in the past. This was in Susan's use of the defense of avoidance. She often fancied that she had been slighted, and she handled difficulties that arose in her social relationships by avoiding discussing them with the people involved, instead of trying to straighten them out. Again and again the worker went over the details of what happened with her friends, had her repeat exactly what they said and did, and helped her to reexamine these current realities in the light of whether she really had been slighted or whether there might not be some other explanation of events. The worker also reviewed with her the possibility of other ways to straighten out these difficulties, helping her to see that she was making the situation worse by avoiding direct discussion with her friends. Current realities rather than hidden influences were discussed, and causative understanding was not pursued. With this help, however, Susan's ability to evaluate reality happenings improved, and she modified her pattern of avoidance.

Although there was very little modification of her fear of relationships with men, Susan became more realistic in her educational plans, less sensitive to slights, and more able to handle troubles with her friends in a straightforward way instead of by avoidance; she managed, moreover, to free herself from the more excessive features of her philosophical beliefs. In other words, there was great improvement in the quality of her ego functioning and some modification of her destructive use of defenses, all but one aspect of this occurring in response to techniques classified as supportive.

In each of these six cases, then, changes in adaptive patterns have occurred in response to supportive techniques. There seems to be reason to believe that the response to treatment is more fluid than the proposed dichotomizing hypothesis maintains. Apparently, there are many ways to bring about changes in adaptive patterns.

DIVERSE APPROACHES

What are some of these ways? There is first the basic personality change, often called "structural change" in psychoanalytic terminology, which occurs when some of the decisive formative experiences of life are reached with treatment and undergo reevaluation. This process involves bringing to consciousness and understanding material that was previously unconscious or repressed, such as memories, thoughts, or fantasies representing infantile destructive and sexual impulses and wishes, and reactions and distortions growing out of very early life experiences. Clearly, caseworkers do not attempt to achieve this type of change.

It was earlier pointed out, however, that irrational and inappropriate responses are also often based on *preconscious* influences, on events that at most have been *suppressed* rather than repressed and hence can be brought to the surface of the mind by the type of interviewing techniques used in casework. Indeed many early influences are not even suppressed. Sometimes they are well remembered but the client needs to recognize the connection between these childhood experiences and his current responses in order to see their irrationality. Experiences of adolescence and early adulthood may also be of great importance. The ego defenses in particular often operate on a preconscious level. Not infrequently a person can become aware of and will modify defense patterns when he sees their irrationality or their harmfulness without needing to look back to factors that influenced the development of such patterns. That is, the dynamic may be understood independently of origins. Recognizing the influence of early life experiences and becoming aware of defenses are both forms of clarification and constitute a second way in which adaptational patterns can be modified.

A third way of bringing about changes in adaptive patterns consists of helping the individual to deal more effectively with current life relationships and problems. Better understanding of other people, thoughtfulness about the effects of his own ways of relating to others, fuller awareness of his own feelings and actions and of the effect of others on him, will lead first to better functioning in the immediate current life, or at least a sector of current life. As individual incidents pile up, the adaptive patterns themselves may be modified, even though they have not been discussed as such. This form of change parallels natural life experience. Without the help of any type of therapy the relatively healthy individual repeatedly learns from his own experiences as he seeks to develop more effective ways of mastering the vicissitudes of life. A similar process occurs in treatment, but the individual's efforts need to be augmented by professional help.

Adaptive patterns also change in the context of a strong positive relationship to another person who is accorded a leadership or pattern-setting role in some area of living. In such a relationship the individual either identifies with the worker and imitates him, or ascribes to his values, accepts his assessment, or follows his suggestions and advice. The "corrective relationship" described by Austin as an important aspect of "experiential" treatment can bring change in this fourth way. Again treatment parallels a process common in natural life experience.

A fifth way in which adaptive patterns can change is in response to more favorable life experiences. As noted earlier, these are relatively easy to arrange for children but more difficult to create for adults. Nevertheless this can occasionally be done, especially in the income, employment, and educational spheres.

A sixth way in which personality change comes about is through the positive reinforcement that results from more effective and satisfying functioning. Sometimes this reinforcement is in the form of verbal or nonverbal communications from the worker. More often it arises in subsequent life experiences. When temporary change in functioning is rewarded by positive experiences in interpersonal relationships or in other important areas of functioning such as work, a powerful incentive is given to continue the new ways until they constitute a new adaptive pattern.

Several of these ways of bringing about change usually occur together in work with one individual or family. Treatment is actually a blend of many influences that in combination are designed to bring about more effective and satisfying functioning. Insofar as this is a correct formulation it suggests a negative answer to the question of whether casework is best conceptualized as a dichotomous process with two treatment modes. Rather we must seek a more fluid model that will readily permit us to think in terms of a blend of procedures flexibly adapted to the needs of the individual or family members.

NOTES

1. Mary E. Richmond, *What is Social Casework? An Introductory Description* (New York: Russell Sage Foundation, 1922), p. 102.

2. Gordon Hamilton, "Basic Concepts in Social Casework," *The Family*, 18 (July 1937), 147–156. Other references of interest are: Virginia P. Robinson, "An Analysis of Processes in the Records of Family Case Working Agencies," *The Family*, 2 (July 1921), 101–106; and *Social Casework, Generic and Specific: An Outline. A Report of the Milford Conference* (New York: American Association of Social Workers, 1929).

3. Grete L. Bibring, "Psychiatry and Social Work," *Journal of Social Casework*, 28 (June 1947), 203–211.

4. Florence Hollis, *Casework in Marital Disharmony* (doctoral dissertation, Bryn Mawr College, 1947); microfilmed (Ann Arbor, Mich:

University Microfilms, 1951). Also available in "The Techniques of Casework," *Journal of Social Casework*, 30 (June 1949), 235–244.

5. Lucille N. Austin, "Trends in Differential Treatment in Social Casework," *Journal of Social Casework*, 29 (June 1948), 203–211.

6. In a later article, "Qualifications for Psychotherapists, Social Caseworkers," *American Journal of Orthopsychiatry*, 26 (1956), 47–57, Austin suggests giving up the term "insight therapy" as an inaccurate designation, since insight is a quality or experience that may result from different procedures.

7. *Scope and Methods of the Family Service Agency*, Report of the Committee on Methods and Scope (New York: Family Service Association of America, 1953).

8. *Ibid.*, p. 19.

9. See *Method and Process in Social Casework, Report of a Staff Committee, Community Service Society of New York* (New York: Family Service Association of America, 1958).

10. Sidney Berkowitz was the first writer to raise questions about this issue. See his "Some Specific Techniques of Psychosocial Diagnosis and Treatment in Family Casework," *Social Casework*, 36 (November 1955), 399–406.

5 | *A Classification Based on Dynamic Considerations*

In the previous chapter we suggested that a more fluid model of treatment in casework was needed in order to express the concept of a blend of procedures rather than a dichotomy. In this chapter a typology designed to meet this need will be examined. When work on this typology was begun some years ago, it was soon discovered that it is no simple matter to formulate a logical and useful classification of casework treatment, especially if this formulation is to be rich enough in its dimensions to make conceptually worthwhile distinctions and yet not so elaborate as to be impractical.

But why, in any case, do we want a treatment classification? What purpose will it serve? Will it merely enable us to describe casework in an orderly way in writing and teaching? This is one important use of classification; the very need for such clarity constitutes a strong impetus toward classification. Agencies also feel a need for a systematic way of grouping cases for reports of accountability, work distribution, evaluation, and the like. More fundamental, however, is the necessity of classification for the study of casework itself. In order to use casework effectively we must ask ourselves for what sort of personality or problem is a particular treatment method or technique appropriate? What is the result of using this or that technique under such and such circumstances? What alternative means are available to the end we have in mind? Under what circumstances is one means more likely to serve the purpose than another?

Before we can answer these questions, the numerous variables involved must be separated. At the very least we will need to find some way of identifying and classifying not only treatment procedures but also personality characteristics, types of problems and situational factors, outcomes, and relationships among these variables. It is particularly important that the aim of treatment and the methods used be examined as separate variables. Only by so doing can we hope to test the relationship of one to the other and examine the conditions under which specific techniques can lead to specific results.

A FALSE START

A first objective, then, was to develop a classification of treatment techniques or procedures independent both of the type of ultimate modification sought and of the type of client for whom it might be of value. In my own first efforts to do this some years ago, while still enmeshed in the then current dichotomous mode of thought, I pursued the idea that the most important distinction between treatment modes was that of the type of psychological content discussed.[1] One form of treatment would deal only with material that could readily become fully conscious while the other would include exploration of suppressed preconscious material and other preconscious content equally capable of arousing anxiety. It was hypothesized that the latter treatment would be used only with clients who could bear the anxiety aroused by such treatment, with comparative immunity to the hazards of immobilization, development of more severe symptomatology, excessive regression, or acting out. Such clients would be people suffering from only a mild degree of neurosis and would not include psychotics, severe neurotics, or, because of insufficient motivation, clients with character disorders.

Subsequently a small exploratory study was undertaken to see whether this distinction was a valid one and also to examine further the relationship of treatment procedures to diagnosis. Twenty-five cases drawn from six agencies representing family service agencies, child guidance clinics, and psychiatric clinics in four different communities were explored. Limited as this study was, it was nevertheless extremely fruitful in pointing up the problems involved in classification and in providing material for experimentation with a series of classifications, each successively introducing modifications designed to meet the shortcomings of its predecessor.

Each agency was asked to submit examples both of supportive treatment and of treatment in which the technique of clarification was used, including an example of a case representing the greatest depth in treatment carried on in the agency. It was assumed that "supportive" cases would fall in the first group and "clarification" cases in the second. It was disconcerting to discover that workers differed enormously in their interpretation of this request. Cases of a type considered clarification by one worker would actually involve less use of the technique of clarification than cases classified as supportive by another worker. Troublesome as this confusion was, it led to the very useful observation that there was no sharp dividing line between supportive and clarification cases. In actual practice there appeared to be a continuum, beginning with cases in which no clarification whatsoever was used, going on to those in which snatches of it were used only from time to time, proceeding to others where it played a considerable part in treatment. Furthermore, it also became clear that in most cases treatment moved through phases in which the balance between supportive work and clarification was constantly changing. This pointed in the direction of seeking a classification that would permit us to study the blending of different techniques as they are used over a period of time within a particular case, rather than one that classified a case in terms of an arbitrary degree of clarification.*

When the twenty-five cases were examined to test my own hypothesis that supportive techniques did not deal with suppressed preconscious material, it became apparent that my suggestion for distinguishing between categories was one of those nice logical pieces of theory that are attractive for their simplicity but have little relationship to things as they are. To my chagrin it became clear that in a number of cases suppressed and other submerged material with anxiety-arousing potential came through in response to supportive techniques and played an important part in treatment in cases where clarification was pur-

---

* It is interesting that as far back as 1949, Annette Garrett, in reaction to the classifications then being devised, made essentially the same point in conversation with the author. She objected strongly to setting off insight development as a special method and maintained that in varying degrees insight development took place in a large range of cases.

posely avoided. A closer inspection of supportive treatment then led me to realize that this category is far more complicated than had generally been supposed and embraced a variety of widely different techniques. Reassurance and advice-giving, to name only two of these, are utterly different techniques, suitable under different circumstances and leading to quite different results, despite the fact that they are sometimes appropriately used with the same individual. Clarification too, when looked at closely, can be subdivided into several processes. A dichotomous classification, then, would seem to be too "global." Each category embraces a number of different techniques, thus obscuring differentiations that may be of crucial significance. Finer distinctions were evidently required if we were to understand the nature of casework procedures, their potentialities, and effects.

BASIC CONSIDERATIONS

With these observations in mind, a series of cases drawn from the original twenty-five was used as the raw material for a new classification. The material was selected for its clarity of dictation and for the variety of treatment methods it represented when viewed globally. The material was examined line by line in an effort to characterize each recorded happening in each interview. Various groupings of techniques were tried in an effort to arrive at meaningful and essential distinctions between different processes. The tackling of each new case became a testing of the system worked out on previous cases and frequently involved modifications in the system to accommodate the new material. The classification that resulted from this process has been experimented with and studied in a number of recent and continuing research projects.*

* I was fortunate in being able to enlist the interest of three groups of students—one at the Smith College School for Social Work,[2] two at the New York School of Social Work (now the Columbia University School of Social Work)[3]—in applying the new system to the classification of techniques in three series of interviews. Their findings became the basis for subsequent revisions of the typology and in general indicated that the main outlines of the classification are applicable and potentially useful. Also of great value was the work of Francis J. Turner, a doctoral

For this study, we wanted to devise a classification that would allow us to follow the flow of each interview and that could be used either in informal analysis or more rigorous research. The rationale of a classification must be related to the uses to which it will be put. This requires that the logic of the classification be related to the logic of the questions to be answered. Some of the possible uses of a classification of this kind have already been indicated. It must help us to examine the dynamics of treatment, to answer such questions as: In what way does a given procedure affect a client? What are the relationships of client personality factors to choice of treatment method? What is the relationship between problem and treatment steps? What factors in the client's response in a particular interview indicate the advisability of using a particular procedure? What procedures in early interviews are most likely to encourage the client to remain in treatment? And so on.

For such purposes it seemed best to base the classification on a set of hypotheses about the *dynamics of treatment,* that is, the *means* by which the treatment step or procedure is in general expected to produce its effect. In other words, the *type* of final change desired, and the *outcome* of treatment, are not the basis for the classification. As was pointed out in an earlier chapter in illustration of the different ways in which anxiety can be reduced, a given result can be achieved by a variety of procedures, ranging from direct reassurance to full understanding of the intrapsychic cause of the anxiety. However, under different circumstances and with different individuals one approach will be more effective than another. This question of which means is most useful under different conditions is central to any study seeking to understand and improve casework methodology and is therefore a particularly useful central dimension for a classification of casework

---

student at the New York School of Social Work, who experimented with the classification as a research instrument in his dissertation, "Social Work Treatment and Value Differences: An Exploration of Value Differences and Specific Use of Casework Techniques with Clients from Three Ethnic Groups Receiving Treatment in Family Agencies."[4] The latter study was supported in part by a grant from the National Institute of Mental Health, which also made possible further work to examine the usefulness of the classification for research purposes. This latter work and a number of subsequent studies will be discussed in the next chapter.

procedures. The term "dynamics of treatment" is used to indicate that the classification revolves around the nature of the "change component" that the procedure is generally designed to bring into action.

The classification also distinguishes sharply between the means employed and its actual effect. For example, the caseworker's expression of interest in and appreciation of a client's situation or feelings is generally thought to promote the client's perception of the worker as someone who is interested in him and capable of understanding him, and to strengthen his feeling that here is someone who will help or take care of him. By this means, it is hoped, his anxiety will be lessened and, consequently, his functioning will be improved. A paranoid person, however, may interpret this same response on the caseworker's part as a kind of magic mind reading, an effort to bring him under some obscure influence, and the technique will not have the desired effect. Nevertheless, in the typology proposed, the worker's technique would be classified as a "sustaining procedure," the term used for this type of potentially reassuring technique. Such a separation of the means employed from the outcome puts us in a position to examine the actual effect of a treatment step, to study the circumstances under which it does not have the desired effect, and thereafter to use it more appropriately; or, if we find it rarely has the effect we theoretically thought it should have, we are in a position to correct our theory.

A classification of this sort is not static: it can be modified as research and study constantly correct and expand our theories and can also lend itself well to expansion as new techniques are developed. At the same time, if required, it can be held static throughout a study or series of studies in which it is used.

THE MAIN DIVISIONS OF THE CLASSIFICATION

With these preliminaries, we may proceed to a brief description of the classification that has evolved from the studies described above. Detailed discussion of the specific technical procedures included under the main divisions of the classification will be found in later chapters. The major dimensions of the

classification will be presented in this chapter, together with
specific illustrations used only to clarify the meaning of the main
categories; we will thus be able to discuss certain general theoretical questions before going extensively into details of techniques.

For the moment, let us set aside the question of treatment
through the environment—Richmond's indirect treatment—and
deal only with those procedures that take place between the
worker and the client himself—Richmond's direct treatment.
Several clients within a given family, of course, may be receiving
casework treatment at the same time.

When working directly with the client, the caseworker uses six
major groups of techniques, which are all part of a communication
process taking place between client and worker. These six
groupings constitute a classification of communications according
to the dynamic they seek to evoke. The first two of these derive
their force or influence from the relationship that exists between
client and worker, from the way in which the client regards the
worker and the degree of influence which he accords the worker
or permits him to have in his life. The fourth, fifth, and sixth
groups rest primarily upon various kinds of reflective consideration promoted within the client. The third, drawing its strength
from ventilation, lies midway between.

The first group of procedures deal with *sustainment.* They
include such activities on the worker's part as demonstration of
interest, desire to help, understanding, expressions of confidence
in the client's abilities or competence, and reassurance concerning matters about which the client has anxiety and guilt.

Sustaining techniques are used in varying degrees in all cases.
Much of this type of communication takes place through nonverbal or paraverbal means—nods, smiles, an attentive posture,
murmurings. In the early interviews, no matter what else is
done, the worker usually tries, by giving the client a sympathetic
hearing and by other sustaining techniques, to lessen his anxiety
and give him the feeling that he is in a place where help will be
forthcoming. Subsequently, cases vary in the extent to which
sustaining techniques are needed, with fluctuations from time to
time in the same case.

The second group of procedures deal with *direct influence.*
These include a range of techniques among which suggestion

and advice are most frequently used. They involve in one form or another the expression of the worker's opinion about the kind of action a client should take.

Procedures of direct influence are far less universally used than sustaining techniques, but, particularly in their more subtle forms, they constitute a recognized part of casework treatment. One usually finds that where these procedures are being extensively used, there is also emphasis upon sustainment. Their effectiveness depends to a high degree upon the existence of a strong positive relationship between client and worker, which in turn is promoted by sustaining procedures.

The third group deals with *exploration, description,* and *ventilation.* It consists of communications designed to draw out descriptive and explanatory material from the client and to encourage him to pour out in the interview pent-up feelings and emotionally charged memories. Often there is relief from tension just in this outpouring. Quite frequently the relief obtained by verbalization is supported by sustaining procedures that further reduce the accompanying anxiety or guilt. At other times the content of the ventilating process is picked up for the purpose of promoting reflective consideration of it.

When we turn to techniques that rely upon the client's actively thinking about various aspects of his problem, it becomes more difficult to know where to draw the line between one kind of content and another. After experimentation with a number of groupings of these techniques, the one presented here was chosen because it seemed capable of illuminating many of the processes that unfold in treatment practice.

The fourth grouping consists of communications designed to encourage reflective consideration of the person-situation configuration. It is designated *person-situation reflection.* This broad category can be subdivided according to another dimension, that of the type of change in understanding toward which the communication is directed. The area of change may be: (1) the client's perception or understanding of others, of his health, or of any aspect of the outside world; (2) his understanding of his own behavior in terms of its actual or potential outcome or effect on others or on himself; (3) his awareness of the *nature* of his own behavior; (4) his awareness of causative aspects of his own behavior when these lie in the interactions between himself and others; and (5) his evaluation of himself or of some aspect of his behavior (in the sense of his self-image, his concepts of right or wrong, his principles, his values, or his preferences).

Note that in the first of these subdivisions attention is directed outward, in the second it is partly outward and partly inward, and in the last three it is directed inward to some aspect of the person's own feelings, thoughts, or actions, that is, toward a form of self-understanding that depends entirely upon reflection about specific interactions and reactions in the person-situation gestalt.

It is impossible to imagine a case in which most of these types of person-situation reflection would not at some time be used. The type of problem brought by the client is one of the important determinants of where the emphasis will be. The more realistic and external the problem, the greater the likelihood that interviews will emphasize procedures from the first two subdivisions; the greater the subjective involvement in the problem, the more likely it is that they will draw upon the third, fourth, and fifth subdivisions. These procedures of person-situation reflection are combined to varying degrees with sustaining techniques and may be accompanied to some degree by direct influence. They are techniques that are also always an important part of the treatment process when other types of reflective consideration are in action.

The fifth main treatment category also relies upon reflective discussion. It consists of procedures for encouraging the client to think about the psychological patterns involved in his behavior and the dynamics of these patterns and tendencies. This category can be referred to as *pattern-dynamic reflection.* The client is helped to reflect upon some of the internal reasons for his responses and actions. He is encouraged to look at the dynamics of his behavior by studying the relationship between one aspect of his behavior and another. He goes beyond thinking about a specific distortion of reality or inappropriate reaction toward consideration of the operations of the intrapsychic component itself.

The sixth treatment category, also a type of reflective discussion, includes procedures for encouraging the client to think about the development of his psychological patterns or tendencies —again, a subjective area. This is designated *developmental reflection.* Here, the client is helped to deal with early life experiences that are important because, although they occurred in the past, they have been internalized to such a degree that they are now part of his responses to current situations. As in pattern-dynamic reflection, treatment revolves around consideration of the relationship of one facet of behavior, one reaction to experience, to another; this time, however, in historical terms.

The search to understand the dynamics of adaptational patterns or of their development always rests upon a firm base of other procedures. There is always a great deal of prior explanation and usually ventilation and a great deal of person-situation type of reflection before consideration can be given to dynamic and developmental aspects. And, certainly, sustainment in one form or another is always a treatment ingredient.

ENVIRONMENTAL TREATMENT

Not since Mary Richmond's time have we given the same quality of attention to indirect as to direct work. This neglect has tended to downgrade environmental treatment in the worker's mind, as though it were something one learned to do with one's left hand, something unworthy of serious analysis. We have furthermore tended to think of direct work as psychological and indirect as nonpsychological, or "social." This is an absolutely false assumption. Environmental work also takes place with people and through psychological means. We cannot physically make a landlord, teacher, or anyone else do something for the benefit of our client. We have to talk with him about it, and in the process we must use psychological procedures of one sort or another. Broadening our view of casework in this way may help us to narrow the distance that seems so often to separate direct from indirect work.

Recognition of the extent to which environmental deficiencies contribute to the woes of individuals and families has led to increased attention in recent years to the importance of environmental or milieu work. One can think in terms of treatment *through* the environment and of treatment *of* the environment. The former makes use of resources and opportunities that exist or are potentially available for the benefit of the client in his total situation. The latter deals with modifications that are needed in his situation in order to lessen pressures or increase opportunities and gratifications. A clear example of treatment through the environment would be a worker's enlisting the help of a warm and friendly relative to provide companionship and practical assistance for a woman experiencing postoperative depression. Treatment of the environment is illustrated by a worker's intervening to bring change in a situation where a child is badly placed in a school system or a landlord is failing to make necessary repairs.

There are three general ways of looking at and classifying environmental work, each of which has its values and uses. First, it is sometimes useful to organize one's thinking about milieu work in terms of the *type of resource* one is trying to employ. A primary source of such help is the employing social agency itself. One thinks immediately of the child-placing agency where the worker is himself responsible for making resources of the agency available, such as foster homes and adoptive homes. Closely related is the employing agency or institution in which social work is not the sponsoring profession but is one of several services offered—for example, a hospital with a social service department. Here the worker is identified in the client's mind with the medical care and is in a good position to influence certain aspects of the medical service but naturally not to the same extent as in the agency administered by social workers.

A third type of resource is the social agency of which the worker is *not* a staff member. A fourth type consists of agencies employing social workers but administered by other professions and of which the worker is not a staff member. A fifth type is the agency that is administered by other professions and that does not employ any social workers.

Two additional types of environmental resources involve two sets of *individuals* in the milieu: (1) those who have an "instrumental" or task-oriented relationship to the client, such as employers and landlords, and (2) those who have an "expressive" or feeling-oriented relationship, such as relatives, friends, neighbors. Many differences exist in milieu work depending upon which of these seven types of situational contacts is involved. These will be discussed in Chapter 9.

One can also analyze environmental or milieu work from the viewpoint of the *type of communications* used. All milieu work takes place through some form of communication, regardless of whether it is verbal. Indeed, paraverbal and nonverbal communication is often of great importance. The type of classification presented in the preceding section on communications between worker and client is also of value in studying communications between worker and collateral. (*Collateral* is a term commonly used in casework to refer to contacts with individuals other than the client.) Environmental treatment makes use of the first four groups of procedures described for direct work with the client but does not use the fifth and sixth. One does not discuss with any collateral, be it a teacher, doctor, landlord, friend, or relative, the dynamics of his attitudes or behavior, or its development. It is only when the relative or sometimes the friend enters treatment himself that this type of reflection would become appropriate. On the other hand, each of the other four types of communication procedure *is* used in environmental work. There are times when the techniques of sustainment are important in building the relationship necessary to involve the collateral constructively—or less destructively—in the client's affairs. One does sometimes use direct influence—suggestion or advice. Exploration, description, and ventilation are of great importance. Indeed, encouragement of ventilation is often the key to a relationship that will permit cooperative work. The fourth group of procedures, person-situation reflection, almost always occurs in collateral work as the worker describes or explains a client and his needs. Through such discussion the worker hopes to modify or enlarge the collateral's understanding of the client and his needs or to work with the collateral in seeking to understand the client and how to help him. These four categories can be very useful in analyzing samples of work with collaterals. Reasons for the success or failure of efforts to help the client through his milieu can often be located by so doing.

Environmental work can also be classified by *type of role*— that is in terms of the *role* a worker may be assuming when he is working with a collateral individual or an agency. First of all, he may be the *provider* of a resource. This is true when he is the vehicle through which his own agency's services are given. Second, he may be the *locator* of a resource, as when he seeks and finds a resource that gives promise of meeting his client's need. Third, his role may be that of *interpreter* of the client's need to a collateral. Fourth, in more difficult situations he may become a *mediator* for the client with an unresponsive or poorly functioning collateral. Finally, in extreme situations, where an agency is clearly failing to carry its responsibilities or an individual is violating the client's rights, the worker may need to carry out a role characterized by *aggressive intervention*. We are giving increasing recognition to the importance of the two latter roles as we come to realize the extent to which clients do not receive services for which they are eligible—especially public assistance, health care, housing, appropriate educational resources. The term "advocacy" is now being used to describe activities through which the worker strives to secure for clients services to which he is entitled but which he is unjustly denied and is not able to secure by his own efforts.

In summary, then, this chapter offers a new classification of casework treatment procedures. It starts with the Richmond suggestion of separating casework into direct work with the client and indirect work with the environment on his behalf, and then goes on to pick up the component parts of more recent classifications, arriving at a new arrangement that uses as its logical foundation the major dynamics employed by modern casework in its effort to promote improvement in the client's functioning. Accordingly, six categories of direct treatment and three types of classification of environmental treatment are delineated. The six categories of client-worker communications are:

A. Sustainment
B. Direct influence
C. Exploration, description, ventilation
D. Person-situation reflection (discussion of the current or recent situation, client responses to it, and their interaction)
E. Pattern-dynamic reflection (discussion of the dynamics of response patterns or tendencies)

F. Developmental reflection (discussion of developmental aspects of response patterns or tendencies)

The types of environmental treatment are:
1. Type of resource
2. Type of communication (parallel to the first four client-worker categories)
3. Type of role

According to this system, the treatment of any case as a whole is seen as a constantly changing blend of some or all of these treatment procedures.[5] The nature of the blend will vary with the needs of the case and with the nature of the client's personality, his problem, and a number of other variables.

Chapter 10 will describe research that has been subsequently carried on concerning the first half of this typology, the classification of communication between client and worker. That chapter will report upon (1) research that has been carried on to further develop the classification and to study its reliability and (2) research in which this classification and another related one were used and which produced significant findings.[6] Before turning to this research, however, the next four chapters will describe and discuss in detail the use of the six sets of client-worker procedures and the three types of classification of environmental procedures.

NOTES

1. Unpublished paper given at the 1956 Biennial Meeting of the Family Service Association of America.
2. Teresa P. Domanski, Marion M. Johns, and Margaret A. G. Manly, "An Investigation of a Scheme for the Classification of Casework Treatment Activities" (master's thesis, Smith College School for Social Work, Northampton, Mass., 1960).
3. Jacqueline Betz, Phyllis Hartmann, Arlene Jaroslaw, Sheila Levine, Dena Schein, Gordon Smith, and Barbara Zeiss, "A Study of the Usefulness and Reliability of the Hollis Treatment Classification Scheme: A Continuation of Previous Research in this Area" (master's thesis, Columbia University School of Social Work, New York, 1961); and Marianne Buchenhorner, Robert Howell, Minna Koenigsberg, and Helen

Sloss, "The Use of Content Analysis to Compare Three Types of Casework Recording" (master's thesis, Columbia University School of Social Work, New York, 1966).

4. Francis J. Turner, "Social Work Treatment and Value Differences" (doctoral dissertation, Columbia University School of Social Work, New York, 1963).

5. Studies by Edward Mullen, Helen Pinkus, William Reid, and Ann Shyne bring them to similar conclusions. See Mullen's "Casework Communication," *Social Casework*, 49 (November 1968), 546–551; Pinkus's "Casework Techniques Related to Selected Characteristics of Clients and Workers" (doctoral dissertation, Columbia University School of Social Work, New York, 1968); Reid and Shyne's *Brief and Extended Casework* (New York: Columbia University Press, 1969), p. 89.

6. Students considering experimenting with the usefulness of this classification as a research instrument will be interested to know that for the last four client-worker categories it is of value to use a parallel classification of the client's activities. This matches almost point by point the worker's activities; for example, the client "discusses reflectively" this or that. It is important, however, to be as discriminating as possible as to whether the client is actively thinking about something or, on the contrary, merely describing it. Client content involving description without reflection is grouped with exploration-description-ventilation. For further details see Chapter 10.

Part Two

TREATMENT: AN ANALYSIS OF PROCEDURES

6 | *Sustainment, Direct Influence, and Ventilation*

Having discussed the skeletal outline of a new classification of casework treatment, we shall try in this and the following chapter to put flesh on its bare bones.

SUSTAINMENT

Sustaining procedures are perhaps the most basic and essential of all casework activities, for without them it would be extremely difficult even to explore the nature of the client's difficulties. It is well known that when a person must seek help from someone else, he undergoes discomfort and anxiety. He is admitting to himself as well as to others that he is unable to handle his own affairs. He is uncertain that he wants to reveal himself and his affairs to another person. Has he come to the right place and person? What will the caseworker think of him? Will the worker try to get him to do something he does not want to do? Is the worker competent? Will he be truly interested and ready to help? We know that the client will give more complete and less distorted information if his initial tension is relieved and he feels safe enough to discuss his situation frankly. The greater the degree of initial anxiety, the more important sustaining techniques become.

In problems that involve interpersonal adjustment, the anxiety typically continues, although with variations in level, throughout the whole period of treatment. Often the anxiety is itself one of the main problems in the individual's adjustment. Sometimes it is a general sense of incompetence or of inability to carry on life's activities adequately; sometimes it is acute concern about some external situation by which the client is confronted—an operation, a new and challenging job, a set of examinations; it may be a traumatic threat, such as the possible breakup of a marriage; sometimes it is fear of inner impulses, aggressive or sexual; and very frequently it is fear of the superego or conscience, expressing itself as a sense of guilt.

In general it can be said that the greater the client's anxiety either initially or during the course of treatment, the more need there will be for the use of sustaining techniques. Chief among these is interested, sympathetic listening, which conveys to the client the worker's concern for his well-being. This skill comes naturally to most caseworkers, for it is an interest in people and their affairs that has brought them into social work in the first place. Nevertheless, workers do vary in their receptiveness and in their ways of showing it. Receptiveness can be indicated by a subtle set of techniques, often not adequately recorded, for the necessary attitude is often expressed more in the worker's bodily behavior than in his words. Facial expression, tone of voice, even his way of sitting as he listens, convey the worker's interest as much as his choice of words does. The client is not seeking avid curiosity or oversolicitude on the worker's part, but neither does he want cold detachment.[1] An attitude of interest is essential throughout treatment. Special pains must be taken to communicate it to the client whenever his anxiety is high unless, as we shall see later, there is some special therapeutic reason for allowing tension to remain unrelieved.

A sustaining procedure that goes beyond expressing the basic attitude of interest and concern is that of conveying acceptance to the client. Despite the fact that the concept of acceptance has been emphasized in casework for many years,[2] it is still often misunderstood. It has to do with the worker's attitude—and hence communications—when the client is feeling guilty or for some reason unworthy of the worker's liking or respect. It is sometimes mistakenly assumed that the worker must be without an opinion about the rightness or wrongness, the advisability or inadvisability, of the client's activities. This would be impossible even if it were desirable—unless the worker were either an imbecile or a psychopath! It is true that the therapeutic attitude requires broad understanding of the validity of different values for people of different ethnic, religious, and class backgrounds.

Furthermore individuals within all groups vary markedly from each other. The worker must see clearly that there are good reasons for such variations and that within broad limits many value questions are matters of individual preference; he must recognize where his own values are individual, too, and not necessarily better than those of the people with whom he is working. Although all this is true and basic to the concept of acceptance, it by no means covers all of it. Acceptance means that whether the worker approves or disapproves of what the client has told about himself, he continues to feel and convey a positive, understanding attitude toward the client. It is actually possible for the worker to communicate this attitude even while he expresses his opinion that the client was wrong in his action. Acceptance is not an expression of opinion about an act but an expression of continued good will toward the perpetrator of the act.[3]

A further step in the sustaining process consists of actual reassurance about the client's feelings of guilt and anxiety. For instance, a mother who has great difficulty in recognizing feelings of hostility may in the course of treatment become aware of considerable anger toward her child. The worker may seek to reassure her by expressing understanding of the feeling and recognition of the provocation. This technique must be used with delicacy and discrimination. Yielding to the temptation to overuse reassurance in an attempt to build up a relationship or because the worker himself cannot endure the client's anxiety may merely leave the client with the feeling that the worker does not fully comprehend the reasons for his guilt or anxiety, or that the worker himself is deficient in moral discrimination and therefore not a person whose judgment matters. Moreover, when the client is ready to explore the reasons for his actions, the worker must be particularly careful not to give reassurance so readily that the client is made completely comfortable and feels no need to seek reasons for troublesome behavior.

In the illustration just presented, for example, it was important to reassure the mother at first because she had unusually high guilt and could acknowledge her feelings only with great reluctance. But after a period of the client's increased ability to talk about her angry feelings toward her child, the worker no longer needed to be reassuring; instead, she agreed that the feelings were unusually strong, and shifting to techniques for developing understanding, suggested seeking out some of the causes for this excessive irritation.

The worker must be even more careful in using techniques of reassurance when anxiety takes the form of fear of the external world or of internal drives that the client feels he may be unable to control. Such reassurance must be justified by reality, or the client will almost always sense falseness and at best get only temporary comfort. It certainly does no good to tell the patient he need not fear an exploratory operation that he already knows may reveal the presence of cancer. It would be more helpful to provide him with opportunities for expressing his anxiety and at least gaining relief through the process of ventilation. If the client is panicky about the operation, the worker's calm consideration of its possible outcomes will in itself be a reassuring process. Often the client is overreacting, either anticipating certain discovery of cancer when this possibility is not realistically justified, or ignoring the possibility of medical help for the condition even though it might be found to be malignant. Here reflective discussion combined with reassurance may clarify the realities of the patient's condition by bringing to his attention the possible positive outcome of the operation and the fact that cure may be possible even if cancer is found. If the worker already has the confidence of the client, he may provide further reassurance of the sustaining type by expressing his confidence in the doctors, when this is justified, thus increasing the client's trust in them and correspondingly lessening his anxiety.

When the individual is afraid of his own drives, reassurance that he can control them is sometimes helpful, but only if the worker has a factual basis for believing that the client is able to control his destructive impulses and wants to do so. Usually such reassurance accompanies one form or another of reflective discussion. Sometimes the worker refers to similar situations in which the client has been able to control himself. Sometimes the worker goes into the dynamics of behavior, pointing out that an acknowledged impulse can be more easily negated than a hidden one; or he may go into some of the unrealistic factors contributing to the drive. Occasionally the ego's desire to control has to be reinforced by looking at effects and alternatives. All these approaches can be strengthened by concurrent sustaining communications that convey the worker's understanding and acceptance of the drive, even when the effort is to dissuade the client from unwise actions.

It is important to recognize that anxiety can be lessened by many different techniques. For example, the achievement of even a small area of self-understanding may remove the cause of guilt feelings or modify a distortion that has been causing anxiety. In sustaining work, however, the relief comes not from self-understanding but because the worker in whom the client has placed confidence has said in effect that it is not necessary to be so worried. The dynamic is not one of reasoning but of faith dependent upon the client's confidence in the worker's knowledge and good will.

A similar process takes place when the worker expresses confidence in a client's abilities, recognizes his achievement, shows pleasure in his successes, and so on. Encouragement is especially important in work with children and is also effective with adults who customarily lack self-confidence, are faced with especially difficult tasks, or are going through a period of anxiety in which their normal self-confidence is weakened. The worker must take special care, however, to discriminate between honest appreciation and false praise or flattery. The very fact that people are insecure often makes them extremely sensitive to hollow insincerity, and their confidence in the worker will evaporate if they once suspect his encouraging comments are merely a technique meant to inject courage into their personalities.

Above all, when expressing confidence in the client's ability to handle some task or situation, the worker must not only be realistic in his estimation of the client's capacity but must also be sensitive to the client's own conception of his abilities. Too-ready reassurance, even when realistically justified, causes the client to bottle up his anxiety, which may then reappear in full force at the very moment he most needs whatever self-confidence he possesses. If the lack of self-confidence is very great, initial ventilation may be called for, followed by whatever help the client is able to assimilate from rational consideration of the situation of which he is so fearful.

One other caution concerning procedures of encouragement. They inevitably arouse in the client a feeling that he should live up to the worker's expectations. Particularly if there is a possibility that the client will fail, it is important to deal in advance with the anxiety that this may create by making it clear that the worker will not be upset by failure, will continue his interest and confidence in the client, and will help him to deal with his disappointment and to find another solution. In other words, the other sustaining techniques of acceptance and reassurance must often go hand in hand with encouragement.[4]

At times the client's need for sustainment is so great that it can only be met by actual "gifts of love." We are most familiar with the use of such techniques with children who, it has long been recognized, need concrete evidence of the worker's good will. Small gifts have always been part of the worker's way of building up a positive relationship with children, especially young children. It is also customary for the worker to express his liking or fondness for them directly and, with small children, to convey it physically, by holding a child on his lap, putting his arm protectively around an upset youngster, and the like.

A comparable process is sometimes needed with adults. In recent years the literature on the "hard to reach" has emphasized the importance of winning the client's confidence partly by doing concrete things for his benefit,[5] such as working out difficult situations with a landlord or with the department of welfare, arranging for camp for the children, taking the children to busy clinics when the mother cannot do this herself, or even providing money for various household needs. Although these services are given in their own right because of actual need, they often go beyond services that would be given routinely and are definitely understood as such by the client.

Sometimes when the contact has usually been in the office, the "gift" is a visit to the client in his home in a period of stress; sometimes it is the arranging of an extra interview or even merely the giving of extra time in a regular interview. Sometimes it is securing information or making a phone call. Whenever the worker's action is designed in part to convey to the client his concern for him and desire to help, it represents this form of sustaining work. This approach is particularly appropriate when the client is distrustful of the worker or is in a state of anxiety, in which he needs the care of a "good mother." Again, it would not be the only procedure employed, but it might either accompany or be a necessary prelude to other techniques. In work with adults, such concrete demonstrations are not universally needed and in any case must be used with great discrimination based on sound diagnostic thinking; they should not grow out of the worker's enjoyment of the client's gratitude or out of the worker's need to encourage a dependent relationship.

As noted earlier much sustainment is given by paraverbal and nonverbal means. Workers do not listen to clients impassively. Rather there is often a series of sympathetic "umms," facial and bodily expression of complete listening, facial changes and gestures that respond to, and sometimes mirror, what the client is saying or feeling. Brief verbal comments such as "yes," "I know," "I see," and repetition of the last word or two of a client's sentence are all used to show continuing attentiveness. Workers differ in their own expressiveness. Through the use of one-way viewing screens, film, and video tapes we are now in a position to study this illusive quality and its bearing upon successful work. It has also been noted in coding interviews that workers differ in the extent to which they insert sustaining words, phrases, and clauses into their reflective communications when there is the possibility that these communications may arouse anxiety.

A special problem arises with sustaining procedures in joint or family interviews. Comments that could easily be made in an individual interview have to be seen in the light of the effect they will have on other clients who will also hear them. Sympathy with the hurt feelings of one marital partner may convey disapproval to the other who caused the suffering. Or sustainment of one person may arouse the jealousy of another. This factor probably accounts for the findings of a study by Ehrenkranz[6] who in a content analysis comparing individual and joint interviews in marital counseling cases found significantly less sustainment when husband and wife were seen together than when seen separately.

DIRECT INFLUENCE

The second set of procedures, those designated direct influence, includes the various ways in which the worker tries to promote a specific kind of behavior on the client's part, such as dealing more advantageously with an employer, consulting a doctor, going through with a medical recommendation, handling the children in a certain way.[7] For many years this type of activity has been suspect in casework. In the days of innocence, when workers were universally thought to be wiser and better informed than clients, advice was one of the "visitor's" chief stocks in trade. Through bitter experience caseworkers gradually learned that the wife who took the worker's advice and separated from her alcoholic husband more often than not took him back again, despite her fear of the visitor's disapproval; that the mother who let herself be guided by the visitor's child-rearing theories somehow managed to demonstrate that they did not work with her Johnnie; and that the housewife who let herself be taught how to make up a set of budget envelopes did not simultaneously learn how to keep her fingers out of the wrong envelope when the installment man came to the door. Out of such experiences came considerable healthy reluctance about telling the client how to run his life. To a certain extent the official position of casework on this matter has often been more extreme than actual practice. Workers have probably intuitively recognized that there continues to be some need for guidance of at least some clients. Studies indicate that this need is probably inversely related to education.

Now, however, it is recognized that to use the client's trust in the worker as a vehicle for influencing his behavior is sometimes a very useful form of treatment, but three main safeguards must be observed. First, the worker must be reasonably sure that he knows enough about what is best for the client. Especially on important decisions, the worker rarely knows enough to justify influencing him. Application of this test will go far in cutting down the temptation to give advice unwisely. For instance, in a decision to break up a marriage, a third person cannot sufficiently appreciate the subjective feelings and needs involved to weigh them adequately along with the objective realities that seem, perhaps all too obviously, to point toward the wisdom of separation. The worker is better advised to use reflective discussion to try to help the client arrive at his own realization of both subjective and objective factors in his situation and to enable him to come to a wise decision for himself. Only then may there be reason for the worker's reinforcing the client's decision by expressing his agreement, but even this amount of influence must be used sparingly.

A second safeguard is to be quite sure that the need for advice rests in the client and not in the worker. This is a matter of self-examination for the worker. It is so tempting to tell people what to do; one feels so good to be called upon for professional advice! All the negative connotations of the word "authority" can be removed simply by putting "professional" in front of it and thereby transforming "authoritativeness" into "strength the client can lean on." That there is such a thing as professional authority is not to be denied, and under certain circumstances it can be put to very good use. However, the need to see oneself as an authority is not sufficient reason for invoking that role.

The third safeguard is to induce the client, whenever possible, to think things through for himself. Clients often seduce the worker into thinking advice is necessary when it is not. Some people like to be told what to do because passivity or dependence interfere with their ability to think things out for themselves and later, if things go wrong, they can always blame someone else. Anxious people, people with little self-confidence, childish people who want very much to please others often ask for more direction than they really need. In casework we have found that the more people can do things for themselves, the more *self*-directive they can be, the more likely they are to continue functioning successfully after the end of treatment. Therefore, techniques of influence should be subordinated to the various types of procedures for developing understanding.

In spite of these forewarnings, there are many situations in which techniques of influence are appropriate. This is particularly true in matters of child rearing, on which the worker, because of his expert knowledge, is able to give the client good advice. Often the client is not yet ready to think things through for himself, or strong cultural differences in his expectations of the worker may lead him to interpret the worker's refusal to give him direction as a sign of disinterest or incompetence. While the worker does not need to comply with a client's expectations throughout the whole of treatment, it is often important to do so at the beginning.

The very anxious or depressed client is also sometimes in need of direction, and it may be appropriate for the worker to provide it in the initial contact or throughout a period of crisis, gradually supplanting it, as the client's self-confidence grows, by methods that rest on understanding. Infantile personalities, too, are often not capable of complete self-direction and need at least a measure of guidance from the workers,[8] as may also people whose sense of reality is weak, such as ambulatory schizophrenics or borderline psychotics.[9] As long as the worker is philosophically committed to the value of self-direction, reasonably conscious of his own reactions to the client's need for dependence, and alert to every possibility of encouraging his client to think for himself, he will make wise use of procedures of influence.

As one works with these procedures, one discovers that they actually constitute a range of processes that form a continuum of degrees of directiveness. In the middle of the continuum one may place the giving of advice—definitely stating an opinion or taking a stand concerning actions the worker thinks the client should take. He may point out to a child's mother that Mary knows her way to school, is careful about crossing streets, and will have more chance to play with other children if her mother does not accompany her. Or he may comment to a man who is hesitating to ask for a seemingly deserved raise that several other men in his office have been given a raise and that the only way to find out if he can get one is to ask for it.

A less forceful way of presenting these same ideas might be for the worker to make a suggestion. He might comment to Mary's mother that it is only two blocks to the school and perhaps Mary is now able to walk this distance alone. Or he might wonder whether the second client has thought about asking the boss for a raise. The solution is raised in the client's mind in a way that conveys the worker's inclination toward it, but leaves the client with the alternative of rejecting the idea without feeling that he is going contrary to the worker's definite opinion. This form of suggestion must be distinguished clearly from suggestions of explanations or of lines of thought that are an inherent part of reflective processes. In direct influence the suggestion has to do with promoting a definite step or action on the client's part.

A still milder form of influence is that of simply underlining, giving emphasis to, a course of action the client himself is already contemplating. A mother thinks it might be a good idea to let six-year-old Mary walk to school alone; the worker agrees it would be worth trying. Or the client says he is thinking of asking the boss for a raise, and the worker nods approvingly. Even if the client eventually decides against the step, there is very little likelihood that he will feel he has gone against the worker's opinion, for it was his own idea in the first place. If he does go ahead with it and it works, he takes the credit for himself; if it fails, the edge is taken off the failure, since the worker also made the mistake of thinking it would work.

Toward the other end of the continuum is urging or insisting, putting a certain forcefulness behind the advice that is offered. The worker tells the mother that it is *essential* for her to take Mary to school, even though the child is frightened. Such pressure is often necessary in treatment of a true school phobia when the mother's own need to keep the child close to her is contributing to the difficulty, and the child herself cannot be properly treated unless she is put under considerable pressure to attend school despite her fears. Treatment of the child cannot wait upon a slow change in the mother's attitude, which might take months to bring about, for in the interim school problems will have been added to the initial phobia to such a degree that a permanent learning problem may ensue.[10]

Or the worker might tell the client he thinks it would be *very unwise* for him to ask for a raise when he is on such bad terms with his boss, that such an action might very well result in his being fired. When there is a possibility of severe consequences of an impulsive, ill-considered action, or when sufficient time is not available to help the client think a matter through rationally, such active persuasion may be worth trying. Sometimes it saves the client from unfortunate consequences. But if the client does not take the advice and suffers the predicted result, the worker must by all means avoid anything that can be construed as an "I told you so" attitude. Properly handled, with the client able to express his disappointment and to feel that the worker, too, regrets his disappointment, the failure may open the way to reflective consideration of what was involved and possibly ward off its repetition.

Most extreme of all the directive techniques is actual intervention in the client's life by such measures as removing a child from a home in which he is subjected to cruelty or to a high degree of neglect, or taking a psychotic client to the receiving ward of a hospital. Such forceful interventions must rest on two conditions: first, the worker must be fully convinced that the step is factually justified and not motivated by some overreaction on his own part; second, he must have thorough knowledge of the community resources involved in the action he has initiated and of the extent to which they will support it, for if it falls through he may well have lost his own contact with his client and made the situation worse. In the first illustration given, the worker must know the conditions under which a court would uphold his action in custody proceedings; in the second he must have sound clinical knowledge of the probable nature of the client's illness and of the procedures of the hospital to which he is to be taken. In both instances the action must be carried out with great skill. Firmness and kindness are needed. The probability of the client's acceding to the action with a minimum of resistance and disturbance is enhanced if in the first instance the worker is devoid of punitive motivation and in the second has his own anxiety sufficiently under control so that the client does not sense it. In both instances it is important for the worker to feel sufficiently confident of his ability to carry through the action that the client will sense this strength and therefore reject the temptation to test it.

Certain general rules can be laid down for the use of direct influence in casework. The first is that it should be used only in conjunction with procedures for developing understanding. In general, it is preferable to develop understanding, in which case the worker's influence is used only to support the client's own conclusions rather than to initiate them. The second rule is that preference should be given to the most gentle form of influence that can be successfully employed. Only the beginner or the clumsy worker makes major use of advice. The skillful practitioner finds ways of stirring his clients to thoughtfulness, for the most part simply by making a suggestion, or better still, by merely reinforcing the client's own ideas. Only in exceptional cases does he employ much advice, and urging or insisting is rarer still. Forceful intervention, except in direct work with children, is limited to protective work, where it is necessary to safeguard the welfare either of the client or of other people who may be harmed by him.[11]

Among the types of clients who typically seek a great deal of advice are compulsive people.[12] Because they are usually very ambivalent, having a hard time making up their own minds, they consequently find an initial relief in being told what to do. Moreover, they are also usually dependent and have very strong superegos, so that they are very anxious to please people whom they regard as authorities. Asking for advice, in other words, is one way of showing that one is indeed a very good little boy or girl.

Because of the anxiety involved and the fact that the asked-for guidance becomes a gift (in the sustaining sense) that helps to build up a positive relationship, it sometimes is wise, especially in the early stages, to accede to the compulsive client's request. It is particularly important, however, to use the milder degrees of influence whenever possible. Direct advice should be given tentatively, the worker offering it as something the client might like to try or as something that is often found helpful. Since the negativism of compulsive people sometimes leads them to ask for direction for the unconscious purpose of proving it will not work, this kind of qualifying comment will temper their need to show the advice is poor. If, on the other hand, they are truly trying to please the worker by following the advice, the tentative way in which it is offered will provide them with an anxiety-relieving excuse if they should fail.

It is obvious that a close relationship exists between sustaining techniques and direct influence. The latter techniques, except for intervention, are effective only in proportion to the client's trust in the worker. The client will come to the worker with certain preconceptions growing out of past experience with, or knowledge of, other social workers. Also, certain expectations are inherent in the worker's position—that is, they are *ascribed* to anyone functioning in this particular role. Immediately upon contact, the worker should begin to *achieve* the repute of a person to be trusted by virtue of his own ways of acting with the client. The client's trust in the worker will be made up mainly of two components—respect for the worker's competence and belief in his good will.[13] The latter is built up largely through sustaining processes.

Both direct influence and sustainment draw upon the client's dependence on the worker, a fact that must be kept in mind both in using these techniques and subsequently in helping the client regain or strengthen his ability to be self-reliant. How can we justify the use of dependence in treatment while at the same time emphasizing the importance of the client's self-determination? Some years ago the author suggested that "self-determination" was an unfortunate choice of words, implying as it does an oversimplified notion of autonomy and self-sufficiency.[14] "Self-direction" is perhaps a more accurate term, denoting not absolute independence but rather the capacity to guide oneself through the maze of interactions that make up the pattern of life. The worker seeks to enable the client to increase this capacity. It is generally recognized that self-determination is a relative, not absolute, value. If the client is endangering others or himself, this value must be superseded by another, namely, the worker's responsibility to prevent suffering; hence, the necessity for protective work. Most workers are ready to acknowledge this limitation to the client's right of self-direction but some flounder in another dilemma. What justification is there, they ask, for influencing the client at all? How can *you* have goals for treatment? Aren't goals the client's business?

My answer is that, except for procedures of intervention, the worker does not influence the client without his assent. He may have his goals for him, but the client makes them his own only to the extent that he is willing to accord the worker a place of influence in his life. Sometimes the client accepts the goals implicitly, sometimes explicitly, but insofar as possible with clear awareness of what they are. Anyone who deals with people inevitably influences them in one way or another, and whether he is conscious of it or not, he has a goal for his work. If one of the worker's primary values is the maximizing of the client's capacity for self-direction, he will relate his methods to that end. Again and again his choice of means will lead him toward the development of understanding. But he will also see that some clients are not ready to select their goals unaided, and that almost all clients require a degree of temporary dependence as a necessary bridge across which the processes of treatment move. The worker will acknowledge and grant this need, but he must be ever careful that the bridge of dependence he provides is no stronger than necessary for the work to be accomplished.

EXPLORATION-DESCRIPTION-VENTILATION

The third major division of the typology includes two related but different concepts: exploration-description and ventilation. To describe is simply to give the facts as one sees them. To ventilate is to bring out feelings associated with the facts. Exploration-description is a part of psychosocial study—an effort to secure from the client his description of himself and his situation and the interactions that are part of his dilemma. It occurs not only in the beginning interviews when the initial picture is emerging but also in each subsequent interview as the most recent events are gone over and bring to mind other connected events. It usually happens, however, that these factual descriptions are not neutral or emotionless. The client frequently experiences and sometimes expresses strong feelings as he reviews the facts as he sees them. The distinction between experiencing and expressing feeling is an important one and is the chief reason that exploration-description and ventilation are placed together. Clients often experience feelings, even strongly, without showing them. Less strong feelings, especially, are often not overtly expressed. The worker therefore needs to be alert throughout the exploration-description process for unexpressed feelings and respond in a way that would be therapeutic if the expected feeling did exist.

Often the worker encourages the client to ventilate feelings that have been restrained or suppressed. This expression— whether spontaneous or encouraged—can in itself bring relief. Verbalization is an important way of reducing feeling. Feelings of anger and hatred are especially likely to lose some of their intensity if they can be given adequate verbal expression. Guilt feelings are more complicated. Alleviation of these requires more than mere expression, although expression may be an important first step. It is the worker's attitude toward the guilt that is of primary importance. If the guilt is an appropriate response to events in the client's life the worker's continued acceptance of him after the guilt has been felt—whether put into words or not—is of high therapeutic value. Ventilation in this case should be followed by sustainment. An accepting gesture is sometimes enough. Expressing sympathy with the feeling of guilt sometimes helps: "Yes, it is hard to find you have been wrong." "We all do things sometimes that we later wish we hadn't." "Yes, I know, it's awfully hard to face it." Guilt feelings may also be inappropriate: a person may blame himself for too much, for too long, or for no reason. Ventilation then can be followed by either sustainment or reflective discussion of these overreactions in an effort to help the client assess his feelings more realistically.

This is not to say that guilt should always be relieved. Guilt is sometimes a healthy and realistic reaction. When this is so it should be accepted as such. It can reinforce the building of sound ego controls. It can mark the growth of understanding of others and concern for them. It can be an incentive to acts of restitution that heal torn relationships as well as restore feelings of self-worth.

Feelings of anxiety also can be relieved by being shared with a worker who is not himself anxious and who can help the client find a way of dealing with the cause of his anxiety once it is expressed. Here again ventilation is followed by sustainment or reflection or both. Often the worker's realistic confidence that the client has the strength to bear his anxiety and find ways of reducing it is an important contributing factor to his being able to do so. The pain of grief and sorrow also ebbs somewhat when the feelings are shared with a person who understands and cares. On the other hand, joyous emotions are enhanced when expressed to an appreciative listener.

Although a certain amount of emotional release is of value in all cases, there are some circumstances under which it should be held in check. Occasionally so much anxiety or other emotion is ventilated that it actually seems to be feeding on itself. Talking does not bring the client relief and a reduction of feeling but engrosses him more deeply in it. Under these circumstances, the expression of emotion is not helpful and the worker should not encourage it to continue but rather should turn the client's attention either to less emotionally laden content or to the question of what can be done to modify the situation or the feelings about which the client has been talking. The worker may even have to say quite directly that it does not seem to help to go over these matters and that it might be better to try not to dwell on them so constantly. Occasionally, especially with the psychotic or near-psychotic, ventilation may lead to the production of increasingly bizarre material or become an incentive to irrational action. Such a circumstance certainly needs to be foreseen and avoided.

Occasionally the worker may realize that the client is deriving marked gratification from talking freely about himself and seems to be making no effort to use the interviews to move toward any improvement in himself or his situation. This sometimes represents a passive type of self-pity, an effort to enlist the worker's sympathy. At other times the client's complaints seem to be only an excuse for not doing anything for himself and a way of putting all the blame for his troubles on others. Occasionally, the talking provides him with sexual or masochistic satisfaction. Gratification of any of these types is of no value in helping the client to better his plight and should not be continued once it becomes clear that this is the prevailing mood. Sometimes, too, clients who seek gratification in these ways are people who cannot be helped by casework. Care should be taken, however, to move away from this type of communication in a constructive rather than a destructive way. Often the reason for discouraging it can be explained directly to the client, thus leading him into a discussion of this aspect of his resistance. But to do so success-fully, the worker must be free of the hostile countertransference reactions that are so easily aroused by clients who make use of ventilation primarily for self-gratification.

As in sustainment, there is a difference in the extent to which ventilation of certain types can be used in joint and individual interviews. Ehrenkranz found "conspicuously" less ventilation in the joint interviews in her comparative study.[15] She suggests that this may have been due to the workers' tendency to accen-tuate the positive when clients with marital problems were will-ing to have joint interviews. Hollis had a similar finding and re-ported that it was especially true in ventilation of feelings about others.[16] There was probably some restraint in expressing hostile feelings in the presence of the other person. Actually, the ex-pression of hostility in a joint interview can be a powerful therapeutic tool and is sometimes encouraged. This is particu-larly true if one partner has been unable to express such feelings to the other and is able to bring out his true feelings with the support of the worker. This expression can lead to more honest communication and prevent the bottling up of feelings that then either explode when the pressure becomes too great or find an outlet in devious and sometimes more harmful ways. Such ex-pression can also have a profound influence on a partner who has been unwittingly hurtful because he was unaware of his spouse's feelings.

The extent to which such ventilation can be encouraged or even permitted in joint interviews depends upon its effect on both partners. It should not be allowed to continue if it creates too much anxiety in either partner or leads to ever-increasing hostility and counterhostility instead of greater understanding or the emergence of positive feelings. This need for caution is no doubt another cause of the finding that there is quantitatively less ventilation in joint than in individual interviews. It is also the author's impression that if there were a measure of *intensity* of ventilation it would be found to be much higher in joint in-terviews. When ventilation of hostility appears not to be helpful this should be discussed with the clients. Sometimes it is best at such times to turn to individual interviews until a less destruc-tive stage of the relationship has been reached.

NOTES

1. For interesting discussions of this see Clare Britton, "Casework Techniques in Child Care Services," *Social Casework*, 36 (January 1955), 3–13; Jerome Frank, "The Role of Hope in Psychotherapy," *International Journal of Psychiatry*, 5 (May 1968), 394; and Elizabeth Salomon, "Humanistic Values and Social Casework," *Social Casework*, 48 (January 1967), 26–32.

2. The importance of this concept was emphasized in many articles during the thirties. See especially Annette Garrett, *Interviewing: Its Principles and Methods*, (New York: Family Service Association of America, 1942), pp. 22–24; Gordon Hamilton, "Basic Concepts in Social Casework," *The Family*, 18 (July 1937), 147–156; Fern Lowry, "Objectives in Social Case Work," *The Family*, 18 (December 1937) 263–268; Charlotte Towle, "Factors in Treatment," *Proceedings of the National Conference of Social Work, 1936*, (Chicago: University of Chicago Press, 1936), pp. 179–191; and Marian Wyman, "What Is Basic in Case Work Practice?" in *Proceedings of the National Conference of Social Work, 1938*, (Chicago: University of Chicago Press, 1939), pp. 179–191.

3. See Alice W. Rue, "The Casework Approach to Protective Work," *The Family*, 18 (December 1937), 277–282; and Dale Hardman, "The Matter of Trust," *Crime and Delinquency*, 15 (April 1969), 203–218.

4. See Grace K. Nicholls, "Treatment of a Disturbed Mother-Child Relationship: A Case Presentation," in Howard J. Parad, ed., *Ego Psychology and Dynamic Casework* (New York: Family Service Association of America, 1958), pp. 117–125; and L. P. Laing, "The Use of Reassurance in Psychotherapy," *Smith College Studies in Social Work*, 22 (February 1952), 75–90.

5. For discussion of work with "the hard to reach," see especially Alice Overton, "Serving Families Who Don't Want Help," *Social Casework*, 34 (July 1953), 304–309; Walter Haas, "Reaching Out—A Dynamic Concept in Casework," *Social Work*, 4 (July 1959), 41–45; and *Casework Notebook* (St. Paul, Minn.: Family Centered Project Greater St. Paul, Community Chests and Councils, 1957), and Charles King, "Family Therapy with the Deprived Family," *Social Casework*, 48 (April 1967), 203–208.

6. Shirley M. Ehrenkranz, "A Study of Joint Interviewing in the Treatment of Marital Problems," *Social Casework*, 48 (October 1967), 500.

7. For an interesting study of one of these procedures, see Ruth T. Koehler, "The Use of Advice in Casework," *Smith College Studies in Social Work*, 23 (February 1953), 151–165; also Lynn and Lorence Long, "A Systems Dilemma," *Family Process*, 8 (September 1969), 211–234.

8. For illustrations see Katherine Baldwin, "Crisis-Focused Casework in a Child Guidance Clinic," *Social Casework*, 49 (January 1968), 28–34; Ethel Panter, "Ego-Building Procedures that Foster Social Function-

ing," *Social Casework*, 48 (March 1967), 139–145; Frances Scherz, "Treatment of Acting-out Character Disorders in a Marital Problem," in *Casework Papers, 1956*, (New York: Family Service Association of America, 1956), and Irving Weisman, "Offender Status, Role Behavior, and Treatment Considerations," *Social Casework*, 48 (July 1967), 422–425.

9. See Margaret M. Heyman, "Some Methods in Direct Casework Treatment of the Schizophrenic," *Journal of Psychiatric Social Work*, 19 (Summer 1949), 18–24.

10. As suggested by Emanuel Klein in "The Reluctance to Go to School," in Ruth S. Eissler et al., eds., *The Psychoanalytic Study of the Child*, vol. 1 (New York: International Universities Press, 1945), pp. 263–279. Also see Edwin Thomas, "Selected Sociobehavioral Techniques and Principles: An Approach to Interpersonal Helping," *Social Work*, 13 (January 1968), 12–26; and *The Sociobehavioral Approach and Application to Social Work* (New York: Council on Social Work Education, 1967). There is considerable evidence that conditioning, essentially a form of direct influence, can be effective in removing phobic symptoms.

11. Some general considerations involved in the use of authority of all degrees are well presented in Elliot Studt's "An Outline for Study of Social Authority Factors in Casework," *Social Casework*, 35 (June 1954), 231–238; see also Robert Foren and Bailey Royston, *Authority in Social Casework* (New York: Pergamon Press, 1968); Dale Hardman, "The Matter of Trust," *Crime and Delinquency*, 15 (April 1969), 203–218.

12. This is discussed by Sid Hirsohn in his "Casework with the Compulsive Mother," *Social Casework*, 32 (June 1951), 254–261. See also Catherine Bittermann, "Marital Adjustment Patterns of Clients with Compulsive Character Disorders: Implications for Treatment," *Social Casework*, 47 (November 1966), 575–582.

13. This question has been studied by Norman A. Polansky and his associates. See Norman A. Polansky and Jacob Kounin, "Clients' Reactions to Initial Interviews: A Field Study," *Human Relations*, 9 (1956), 237–264; and Jacob Kounin et al., "Experimental Studies of Clients' Reactions to Initial Interviews," *Human Relations*, 9 (1956), 265–293. See also Frank, *op. cit.*

14. Florence Hollis, "Principles and Assumptions Underlying Casework Practice," *Social Work* (London), 12 (1955), 41–55.

15. See Ehrenkranz, *op. cit.*

16. Florence Hollis, *A Typology of Casework Treatment* (New York: Family Service Association of America, 1968), p. 33.

7 | Reflective Discussion of the Person-Situation Configuration

Casework places great emphasis on drawing the client into reflective consideration of his situation and of his own functioning within it. In Chapter 5 we suggested the usefulness of three major divisions in work of this kind: person-situation reflection, in which consideration is given to the nature of the client's situation, his responses to it, and the interaction of situation and responses; pattern-dynamic reflection, in which response patterns or tendencies are considered; and developmental reflection, in which attention is centered on developmental factors in these patterns. The first category, the subject of this chapter, is a form of treatment universally used in casework. The worker always tries to help the client arrive at some measure of increased understanding, no matter how much reflective discussion may need to be buttressed by sustaining, directive, or ventilating work.[1] Because of the tendency for a number of years to emphasize either supportive casework or work leading to clarification or insight development, the type of reflective discussion that leads to an understanding that is neither clarification nor insight was lost sight of and not given the thorough study or accreditation it deserves. And yet this technique comprises a rich store of useful procedures fundamental to casework practice.

Person-situation reflection deals primarily with current and recent events. It is distinguished from developmental reflection by the fact that the latter is concerned with early life experiences, those that occur during the period when the individual would normally be living with his parents, the years of growth to adulthood. Pertinent material located in time between the beginning of adulthood and the present is also considered as part of person-situation reflection.

As indicated earlier, it is possible to break this category into five subdivisions: the client's consideration of others, the situation, or his physical health; his consideration of his own actions in terms of outcome, effects on self or others, or alternatives; his consideration of the nature of his acts, thoughts, and feelings; his consideration of the external provocation or stimulus or the immediate inner reasons for his reactions and responses; and his consideration of his own acts, feelings, and thoughts from an evaluative stance.

THE SITUATION: PEOPLE, CONDITIONS, HEALTH

The first of these subdivisions has to do with the client's thinking about his situation, a form of reflection that might be called *extroreflection*. Here we are dealing partly with perception and partly with a question of knowledge. So often people see only a distorted or one-sided picture of the reality before them, either because they see or hear what they anticipate or because their feelings lead them actually to ignore or blot out important aspects of a situation. The father who is convinced that his son is stupid like his own older brother may remember or stress only those subjects or activities in which his son has failed, but may without noticing it reveal to the worker areas in which the son's learning has been unimpeded. The worker's first approach would usually be to call the father's attention to events that show the other side of the boy's capacities. In this sort of situation workers often err by rushing into a discussion of the distortion itself—in this case the displacement from brother to son—instead of seeing whether, when the client's attention is called to the reality picture, he is able by this procedure alone to modify his earlier misconceptions. It is only by testing the client's capacity to do this that one can measure the force of his need to distort.

There is a rule of parsimony in treatment as well as in science. If a person is able, with a little help, to perceive more realistically, it is not necessary to pursue the whys and wherefores of his previous failure to do so. If, on the other hand, the distortion does not yield to a look at the facts, the diagnostic information and material that this preliminary effort has provided can later be used to draw the client's attention to the discrepancy between reality and his view of it. For instance, the worker might say, "Have you noticed, Mr. Dawson, that even when Frank came home with a B+ in history you found it hard to believe he was doing better? . . . I wonder what makes it so hard for you to have confidence in him." Or, "It's hard for you to believe Frank really got that B+, isn't it?" A perceptive client will often accept the cue and go on himself to talk about the things that complicate his feelings toward the child. Another will need more prompting from the worker in order for treatment to move on from this first type of understanding to an effort to arrive at dynamic or developmental understanding.

A person's lack of understanding may be due not so much to distortion of, or blindness to, the facts as to actual lack of knowledge about normal reactions. Parents, unaware of the universal turmoil of adolescence, the need to assert independence that so often shows itself in negativism, the seeking for peer approval—which today is taking the form, among other things, of flamboyant dress and renaissance hairstyles—mistake normal and healthy reactions for the alienation of the hippie. In so doing they may actually drive their children toward the very associations they fear. I do not mean to imply that casework (any more than any other profession) holds the magic key to the current turmoil of youth. Much of the turmoil has to do with grave problems of our total society for which we all bear responsibility. But nothing is to be gained by the parent's misconstruing normal development as incipient loss of a child and overreacting in a way that drives the child away at the very moment when communication most needs to be kept open. More understanding can lead to more patience, which in turn furthers the chance of greater exchange of ideas between generations. This implies neither supine parental abnegation of adult thinking about wise and unwise activities nor evasion of parental control when reality demands it and the power of control exists. But it does mean that the parent can be helped to see his child more realistically and in better perspective, thereby coming to understand more fully what the son or daughter is experiencing and to what inner needs and outer pressures he or she is responding. The parent then is certainly in a better position to help rather than hurt his child.

Harmful responses can also be due to commonly held prejudices and fears. A mother, for instance, may accept a child's report of being threatened by a child of another race without inquiring for details of what actually happened to see whether the child might have misinterpreted or exaggerated the event or whether the child might himself have provoked the incident. The caseworker, first demonstrating appreciation of the mother's concern, can go on to raise questions about what happened. This not only clarifies the reality for the mother but indirectly demonstrates the way in which the mother could have handled the situation. For the mother too needs first to comfort her son but then to help him to see whether his report of what happened was entirely accurate. If it was, then thought needs to be given to next steps—the second form of person-situation activity. What can the mother help the child to do? What can the mother herself do? If the report is not accurate, the mother can help her child not only because she enables him to see this particular episode more realistically but because this constitutes a step in the process of strengthening his ego's ability to assess reality.

Lack of imagination about another person's feelings or behavior or failure to identify with the feelings of another also may generate hostility between people. The husband intent on his own successful legal career fails to see that his college-trained wife is frustrated by household tasks and does not do them well because they do not seem to call on any of the knowledge she acquired in her college major in philosophy. Nor does it occur to him that since she really is inept at physical work, she needs some household help in caring for their three very young children, despite the fact that he has bought her expensive modern equipment. One man in such a situation had actually concluded that his wife was stupid because he did not realize the extent to which her feelings of frustration and anger were hindering her from learning new household skills. He was not incapable of understanding his wife's reactions when he was helped to do so—that is, to perceive her more accurately and fully—but without help, he was becoming constantly more irritated and more scornful of her capacities—the very thing that drove her to distraction.

The very process of understanding another person more fully sets in motion a change in behavior. As we saw earlier, we do not respond to the actual situation, but rather to our perception of it. Thus, when a distorted perception is corrected, the response often corrects itself.

Joint and family interviews offer excellent opportunities for increased understanding of one person by another. People often reveal aspects of themselves in the relative safety of the treatment situation that they have not had the courage to show in the hostile or anxiety-ridden home situation. A worker can draw out a client's thoughts and feelings for the specific purpose of enabling another family member who is listening to understand the one who is speaking.

The process of understanding the external world takes place not only in relation to people but also in respect to life events. Clients sometimes need help in understanding a budget, a business or work situation, medical recommendations, or the implications of their own or someone else's physical condition.[2] The more fully they can comprehend these things, the more appropriately will they handle them. Reflective consideration is a more tedious process than the giving of advice, but it increases the client's competence in a way that advisory processes do not.

Several choices of technique are open to the worker in helping the client reflect upon his understanding of people and situations. Some workers like to explain things to their clients in a more or less didactic way; others are more skillful in leading people to think things through for themselves. Some workers might immediately explain the universality of sibling jealousy to a mother who does not understand the irritability of her three-year-old after the birth of a new baby. It is usually a better procedure to ask the mother if she has herself thought of any explanation for the older child's peevishness. If she has not, there is still the possibility of inquiring whether she thinks the arrival of the new baby might be making Jane feel left out. The more one can get clients to think for themselves, the more conviction they will have about the answers they find. Furthermore, their dependency on the worker will not be so greatly increased, and at the same time they will be helped to develop an ego skill that they can apply to other situations.

One form of reflective consideration of the situation is currently receiving more thought: that of telling the client about ways in which he can bring about changes in his situation through either legal or social action. As lawyers become more interested in the problems of poverty and social injustice, more resources become available for clients seeking legal help to meet some of their external problems, but they often do not know of these possibilities. Straight information by the worker can increase the client's awareness of the resources within his reach. Similarly, there are today many organizations and neighborhood groups in which families can participate in effective group action to bring about improvement in adverse social conditions. It is just as important for workers to be well informed about these resources as about those of health, education, employment, and recreation.

DECISIONS, CONSEQUENCES, AND ALTERNATIVES

The second type of reflection concerning the person-situation gestalt lies between extroreflection and intrareflection and partakes of both. It involves decisions and activities of the client and their effects in interaction with his environment. Over and over again the worker strives to help the client think about the effect of his own actions on others, or about their consequences for himself.[3] An action may be a matter of practical decision, such as the advantages and disadvantages of moving into a housing project, the advisability of changing from one job to another, or the wisdom of training for a particular vocation. Or it may be a decision about a medical problem, such as whether or not to undergo recommended surgery. Often it involves a complicated interpersonal decision, such as whether or not to separate from husband or wife, to adopt a child, or to place a child for adoption. In any of these instances, the client tries imaginatively to foresee the consequences of a plan for himself and for the other people whose lives are involved in his decision. The worker contributes to the reflective discussion by bringing the client's attention to aspects of the situation that he may have overlooked.

At other times it is not a direct decision but rather an understanding of the effects of the client's own behavior on someone else that is involved in the consideration. A mother may not realize that when she hits her fourteen-year-old son in front of his pals, she is compelling him to defy her in order to maintain the respect of his friends. A husband may not see that when he nags his wife about her figure, he is only making her more hungry for forbidden sweets.[4] A child may not realize that when he is a poor sport in losing games, his friends go to play with someone else.

Here as elsewhere, the best procedure for the worker is not to "explain" the relationship between behavior and consequences but rather to lead the client to see the sequence himself: "What did Mike do when you hit him in front of the other fellows?" "Does your wife eat less when you needle her about her weight?" "What happened just before Johnny left you to play with Bud?" Many times the client will draw his own correct conclusions once the effects of his behavior are brought to his attention. If he needs more help, the worker may go on with, "Do you suppose that . . ." or "Have you noticed that . . ." or "Often boys of this age. . . ." When a full explanation is really needed, the worker should give it but not until an effort has been made to see whether the client can arrive at conclusions on his own, so that he will at least gain experience in thinking in terms of consequences in general as well as some understanding of the particular matter under discussion.

Discussion of decisions and future action is often linked with situational understanding. Greater knowledge of another person or of resources at one's command is naturally followed by consideration of what to do in the light of this knowledge. "How can I talk with Ted about this?" "What should I say to Jean?" The worker could respond with advice, but it is usually more helpful to encourage the client to think the answer out for himself, since this will increase his capacity to respond to future situations on his own. Similarly, when the use of a resource is at issue the client should be led step by step to consider the advantages and disadvantages for himself rather than being advised to take one course or another.

INNER AWARENESS, RESPONSES, AND DISTORTIONS

The third subdivision of this type of treatment, which parallels the procedure of helping the client look outward with greater perceptive accuracy, has to do with increasing the client's *inner* awareness. These processes, which are forms of intrareflection, are sometimes regarded as very complicated, particularly when they involve awareness of so-called hidden feelings or reactions. There are many degrees of "hiddenness." The client may be perfectly aware of his reactions but afraid to speak of them because he is ashamed of them or fears ridicule or criticism. This may be the case, for example, with a mother who is fully aware of her anger toward one of her children but is ashamed to admit it, or with a woman who is afraid to tell the worker about a recent abortion. Or the client may have refrained from talking about his feelings because he has not recognized their significance or importance: a man may know he is ashamed of having had tuberculosis, but he never speaks of it to the worker because he does not realize the way in which it is relevant to his employment failures. Or the client may be truly unaware of his feelings because they are not part of his conscious thought: a mother may not even be aware, for example, of the strong feelings of hostility she is harboring toward her child.*

It is a great temptation when a worker can read a client's thoughts to do so out loud. There are occasions when this is necessary—either because the client is quite unable to bring his thoughts into the open but will be relieved if the worker does so for him, or because there is therapeutic justification for bringing them out even though this may make him uncomfortable. Far more often skill lies in finding ways of enabling the client to bring out the hidden material himself. Where full awareness is present, the client often does this without any specific prompting, as he becomes more secure with the worker in response to a sustaining approach. If, however, it is obvious to the worker that the client is struggling with the question of whether to

---

* We are talking here not of early *memories* but of reactions to current life. The uncovering of hidden early *memories* is part of the process of developmental understanding rather than of the current person-situation gestalt.

speak of something or not, the worker may want to handle this hesitation directly by commenting that he knows it is hard sometimes to speak freely but hopes, as the client becomes more comfortable, he will be able to do so. Or the worker may say, "I know it is hard to talk sometimes, but I can only help you with the things you can bring yourself to talk about." Or, "Can you tell me what it is that makes it so hard for you to talk about this?" Or, "I have a feeling that you may be afraid I will criticize you. Is there anything I've said that makes you feel this way?" Or, "I'm not here to criticize you but to help you." Sustaining comments are particularly useful in putting the client more at ease.

At other times, when the worker is fairly sure of what the client is withholding, he may be able to make comments that refer tangentially to the anticipated content, thus inviting the client to talk about it but still not facing him with it directly. It is possible, for instance, to give reassurance of acceptance in advance of the client's communication: "It isn't always possible, you know, to feel love for a difficult child." Or, "Sometimes mothers, even though they try not to, do dislike a child." Or, "Sometimes a person is so desperate about a pregnancy that they feel they have to do something about it." Often one can call the client's attention to discrepancies between fact and feeling, or overemphasis, or inconsistencies, as these may point toward important feelings. Sometimes this can be done merely by repeating the revealing statement in a questioning tone.

On the less frequent occasions when it is actually advisable to put the matter into words for the client, this can be done tentatively, making it possible for the client to maintain his defenses if he needs to do so and also safeguarding him from agreeing too readily to a possibly incorrect interpretation if the worker is not certain of his perception of the client's thinking. Occasionally, a direct, unqualified interpretation is helpful, but for this the worker should be very sure of his ground.

As in the simpler process of spontaneous ventilation, when feelings are brought to expression, the worker has several choices as to his next step. He may turn to sustaining procedures, trying immediately to allay the client's anxiety or guilt; he may seek to involve the client in further understanding of the dynamics or of developmental aspects of his reactions; or he may concentrate on the immediate consequences of these reactions in the client's current life.

Closely related to the process of helping a person become aware of feelings and thoughts is the process of encouraging him to recognize and consider inappropriate, unusual, or problem activities or reactions. The worker calls the client's attention to the fact that she has several times called Mary "Janet." Or he comments on the oddity that the client continuously works overtime without extra compensation for a boss he says he hates, despite the fact that he could easily get another job. This very important procedure is often neglected by inexperienced workers to whom speed seems more essential than safety. Again, the more the client can think for himself, the better. When his attention is called to irrational or unproductive behavior, if he is capable of so doing he is very likely to go on himself to consideration either of the consequences of his behavior or the reasons for it. The worker who omits this step and rushes on to an explanation or interpretation deprives the client of the chance to seek this out for himself. Furthermore, the risk of an inaccurate or inadequate explanation is always greater when the worker trusts his own insight instead of the client's.

Another form of intrareflection consists of the effort to understand the immediate causes of reactions—that is, the external provocations and internal thought processes that contribute to the reaction. A husband is helped to realize that his criticisms of his wife's cooking are always expressed on the days when she visits her mother, whom he dislikes. This type of causation lies in interactions with others, the client's response to provocations, his reasons for doing something when these lie either in "the outer" or in his own feeling about "the outer." The worker might ask: "Do you think that the difference in values between yourself and Jim is causing a lot of your discontent?" Or, "You have talked about how upset you were to lose the baby. Do you think this made you irritable with Ben?" Or, "Do you really think you stayed with your husband just because of the children?"

Still another type of intrareflection has to do with self-evaluation. This may be in the superego sense of right or wrong or in the sense of evaluative comments about the self-image, principles, values, and preferences expressed in terms of relative importance or value. A worker may comment: "Don't you think you are really expecting too much of yourself?" Or, "Which means more to you, success in this competitive job or a closer relationship with Betty?"

Another facet of this process comes into play when the worker helps a client to use external realities to correct a distorted self-image. A boy who is excessively fearful of a school test is reminded of his successes in previous tests. A girl who says she has no one to invite to a party when she has told the worker of many friends is asked to think over the many people she actually knows. This type of reflection is closely related to reflection that develops a better understanding of external realities; indeed the two processes often occur in rapid succession. But consideration of external reality here is for the purpose of enabling the client to become aware of dysfunctional aspects of his own behavior, not primarily to understand another person. It is inwardly not outwardly directed reflection.

For many people person-situation reflection will suffice. When further consideration is both necessary and advisable, understanding of dynamic or developmental factors may be brought into play in order to help a person recognize distorted perceptions and unwise responses. Preliminary attempts to use discussion of current reality can provide important diagnostic information and also serve as a base from which to proceed to thought about dynamic or developmental factors. As a transition, a worker may comment: "I wonder what makes it so hard for you to believe you can do well when you have such a good previous record?" Or, "Have you noticed how you persist in thinking your husband doesn't love you even when what he says doesn't necessarily add up to that?"

REACTIONS TO THE WORKER AND TO TREATMENT

An important aspect of person-situation reflection is the client's thinking about the worker in his treatment role and about his own reactions to the worker, to treatment, or to agency rules and requirements. At times this is a special form of the client's reflection about his situation, for the worker is one aspect of that situation. Just as the client may misperceive other aspects of his situation, so he may distort or fail to understand casework and the caseworker. Here, too, previous life experiences may lead him to imagine hostility where it does not exist, to anticipate criticism, to fear domination, or to expect inappropriate gratification of dependency wishes. Or the client may simply lack knowledge of the nature of the casework "situation."

There is a tendency to think that there is something mysterious about the casework relationship, something that makes it fragile and untouchable except by the very expert. In fact, it is no more complicated than—but just as complicated as—any other relationship. In the type of reflective discussion considered here, attitudes and responses to the caseworker are handled in the same way as other attitudes and responses. Where distortions or misunderstandings exist, the worker tries to straighten them out by demonstrating the realities of his behavior toward the client and the actual nature of treatment.[5] If the client accuses the worker of disinterest because he refuses to give him more time, the worker may explain that his time has to be scheduled, that it is not a matter of lack of interest and that they can go on with the same discussion in their next interview. If the client thinks the worker is angry, it is well to find out what he is basing this conclusion on. If he has misinterpreted a remark, the worker can indicate what he really meant and reassure the client that he is not angry. (This assumes that the worker is truly not angry. When, as occasionally happens, he *is* angry, the only way to handle it is to admit it and either explain why, or, when appropriate, apologize, or do both.) If the client expects advice and is disappointed at not getting it, a simple explanation of why the worker doesn't think it will help may clear the air. Clients do not need long and theoretical explanations of treatment processes, but when they ask for information or when misunderstandings arise, it is not only appropriate but necessary that they be told enough about the nature of casework to enable them to participate constructively in the process. Participation in treatment is a role to which they are unaccustomed and that they may need to have explicitly defined.

The client needs, furthermore, to express, and even at times to be helped to become aware of, his own reactions to the worker and the treatment process. In general, it is very important to encourage clients to express their feelings toward the worker. If they are angry at being kept waiting, their annoyance should be aired or at least acknowledged. If they are dissatisfied with treatment and think it is a waste of time to come for interviews, the dissatisfaction should be brought into the open so that the reasons for it can be discussed and misunderstandings straightened out. If they fantasy that the worker is interested in a personal relationship with them, this, too, must be brought into open expression. Details of how this is done, of course, are guided by the worker's diagnostic understanding, and timing needs to be carefully watched.

Difference in race may create a barrier to the development of a relationship of trust. This may be because of previous experience, prejudice, reluctance to turn to a representative of another race for help, or lack of knowledge on the worker's part that has led to misunderstanding or to actions that have unintentionally offended the client. The worker's first concern, of course, is to avoid such tension by being sufficiently sensitive to the likelihood of its occurrence as to guard against behavior that will either precipitate or aggravate it. This requires both knowledge of how a person of a different racial or ethnic background may react and sensitivity to beginning reactions indicating that offense has been given or is anticipated. If hostility exists or offense occurs—or is thought to exist or to have occurred—it is best to try to bring it into the open so that it can be discussed. More frequently than not, honest discussion combined with sincere good will at least alleviates the tension. The worker must be careful, however, especially in the present climate, not to assume that hostility exists where it does not and not to assume it is due to race, ethnic, or class differences when in reality it has a quite different source.

When clients come to an agency because someone else insists —a school principal, marital partner, or concerned person in the community—the worker can anticipate hostility and resistance. Although sustaining techniques are important, as noted earlier, reflective procedures cannot be dispensed with. The client must know why the worker is there and for what initial purpose. He must know that he will not be pushed around or manipulated. He must know that his resentment is both understood and respected and that the worker asks primarily for a chance to demonstrate his good will and potential helpfulness. The worker need not say this in so many words, but one way or another the substance of these communications must get across to the client, along with the opportunity for him to express his anger and fears about the intrusion.

Again, the more the client can say things for himself, the better. Explanations and interpretations should be used sparingly, and chiefly when the client is unable to speak for himself, yet seems ready for understanding. Sometimes acceptance or reassurance about content has to be given before the client can acknowledge his thought. When the client has expressed his reactions, the worker makes a choice of the type of treatment procedure with which to continue.

It is sometimes held that caseworkers should not bring the client's thoughts about them to the surface except in intensive psychological treatment. Nothing could be further from the truth! It is frequently necessary to do just this in the most matter-of-fact, practical work. All casework depends in part upon establishing and maintaining a sound relationship between client and worker. Obstacles to such a relationship can occur in any form of treatment and can best be removed by recognition and discussion. We discussed earlier the sustaining steps that must often be taken to convince the hard-to-reach client of the worker's good will. It is equally important in such cases to bring the client's distrust into the open so that misconceptions can be explored and, when possible, corrected. Hard-to-reach clients have often had very bad experiences with other social workers or with people whom they mistakenly thought to be social workers, or their neighbors or friends have had such experiences. It is natural that they should expect and fear similar treatment from the current worker. Realistic discussion can be a first step in opening up the possibility of a more constructive casework relationship.

It has taken a good many pages to describe the treatment processes involved in reflective discussion of the person-situation configuration. This is not inappropriate, however, for, as we have seen, the type of understanding examined here is a central part of casework treatment with all types of clients and problems.[6] In a great many cases, more extensive understanding is either unnecessary or inadvisable. Frequently, however, a limited use of techniques that promote dynamic or developmental understanding is added to the person-situation techniques, while occasionally treatment involves the extensive use of such techniques.

NOTES

1. See Rosemary Reynolds and Else Siegle, "A Study of Casework with Sado-Masochistic Marriage Partners," *Social Casework*, 40 (December 1959), 545–551, for discussion of the use of reflective or "logical" discussion along with other techniques. Sidney Berkowitz also implies the use of such techniques in his article "Some Specific Techniques of Psychosocial Diagnosis and Treatment in Family Casework," *Social Casework*, 36 (November 1955), 399–406, though it is not directly spelled out. Gordon Hamilton, in the revised edition of *Theory and Practice of Social Casework* (New York: Columbia University Press, 1951), p. 250, uses the term "counseling" to designate many of the techniques referred to in this chapter. William Reid and Ann Shyne refer to similar procedures in their terms "logical discussion," "identifying specific reactions," and "confrontation;" see *Brief and Extended Casework* (New York: Columbia University Press, 1969), pp. 70–72.

2. For an excellent discussion of the use of this procedure with schizophrenics, see Margaret M. Heyman, "Some Methods in Direct Casework Treatment of the Schizophrenic," *Journal of Psychiatric Social Work*, 19 (Summer 1949), 18–24. For use with parents faced with problems concerning their children see Katherine Baldwin, "Crisis-Focused Casework in a Child Guidance Clinic," *Social Casework*, 49 (January 1968), 28–34; Audrey T. McCollum, "Mothers' Preparation for their Children's Hospitalization," *Social Casework*, 48 (July 1967), 407–415. Louise Bandler also gives many illustrations of this form of reflective discussion from her work with extremely deprived families

in her chapter, "Casework—A Process of Socialization: Gains, Limitations, Conclusions," in Eleanor Pavenstedt, ed., *The Drifters: Children of Disorganized Lower-Class Families* (Boston: Little, Brown & Co., 1967).

3. For illustrations and further discussion, see Laura Farber, "Casework Treatment of Ambulatory Schizophrenics," *Social Casework*, 39 (January 1958), 9–17; Frances H. Scherz, "Treatment of Acting-out Character Disorders in a Marital Problem," *Casework Papers, 1956* (New York: Family Service Association of America, 1956); and Miriam T. Weisberg, "Early Treatment of Infidelity in the Neurotic Man," *Social Casework*, 51 (June 1970), 358–367.

4. Miriam Jolesch refers to this type of work in joint interviews with marital partners in her article "Casework Treatment of Young Married Couples," *Social Casework*, 43 (May 1962), 245–251. She advocates the use of individual interviews initially, with joint interviews introduced when the clients have gained enough self-understanding in individual interviews to be ready to examine their interactional patterns.

5. Good illustrations of this can be found especially in articles on work with schizophrenics, with the "hard-to-reach," and with other clients who have high resistance to accepting help. See Margene M. Shea, "Establishing Initial Relationships with Schizophrenic Patients," *Social Casework*, 37 (January 1956), 25–29; Alice Overton, "Serving Families Who Don't Want Help," *Social Casework*, 34 (July 1953), 304–309; *Casework Notebook* (St. Paul, Minn.: Family Centered Project, Greater St. Paul, Community Chests and Councils, 1957); H. Aronson and B. Overall, "Treatment Expectations of Patients in two Social Classes," *Social Work*, 11 (January 1966), 35–41; Celia Benny et al., "Clinical Complexities in Work Adjustment of Deprived Youth," *Social Casework*, 50 (June 1969), 330–336; Dale E. Hardman, "The Matter of Trust," *Crime and Delinquency*, 15 (April 1969), 203–218; I. E. Molyneux, "A Study of Resistance in the Casework Relationship," *The Social Worker*, 34 (November 1966), 217–223.

6. Additional illustrations can be found in Salvador Minuchin and M. Montalvo, "Technique for Working with Disorganized Low Socio-Economic Families," *American Journal of Orthopsychiatry*, 37 (October 1967), 880–887; Jeanette Oppenheimer, "Use of Crisis Intervention in Casework with the Cancer Patient and His Family," *Social Work*, 12 (April 1967), 44–52; Ethel Panter, "Ego-Building Procedures that Foster Social Functioning," *Social Casework*, 48 (March 1967), 139–145; Veon Smith and Dean Hepworth, "Marriage Counseling with One Partner: Rationale and Clinical Implications," *Social Casework*, 48 (June 1967), 352–359; Edna Wasser, "Family Casework Focus on the Older Person," *Social Casework*, 47 (July 1966), 423–431.

Reflective Consideration of Dynamic and Developmental Factors

The two remaining forms of reflective communication are those that seek to promote dynamic and developmental understanding. Intrapsychic forces of which a person is not fully aware may so strongly influence his behavior that he cannot perceive and act differently in response to person-situation reflection alone. It is sometimes helpful to turn such a person's attention briefly to the underlying dynamics of his personality or to early life experiences that are still unfavorably influencing his current adjustment. Often, but not always, both types of understanding can be developed.

DYNAMIC UNDERSTANDING

When we consider dynamic factors with the client, we are simply extending the process of intrareflection, helping him to pursue further some of the intrapsychic reasons for his feelings, attitudes, and ways of acting, to understand the influence of one characteristic of his personality upon another—in other words, how his thoughts and emotions work. Here we go beyond the understanding of single interactions or even a series of interactions in the person-situation gestalt to consideration of the intrapsychic pattern or tendency that contributes to the interaction. Often the client himself is aware—sometimes clearly and sometimes vaguely—of his unrealistic or inappropriate behavior. He himself may delve into the question of why without any prompting from the caseworker. At other times, the worker takes the first step by calling the inappropriateness or inconsistency to the client's attention: "Have you noticed that you don't have trouble in being firm with Paula but seem to be so afraid to be firm with Ed?"—to a mother who does not realize that her difficulty in disciplining her son springs from her desperate fear of losing his love. At this point the worker is moving beyond one interpersonal event to raise a question about a series of such events, a pattern. Presumably, individual instances of difficulty in showing appropriate firmness had been considered before but without enabling this mother to act more appropriately. The worker then invites the client to think about a general tendency. Recognition of the pattern can turn the client's attention to the question of why? The answer may lie in displacement from husband to son, in underlying hostility to her son, in greater desire for this child's love, in specific early life events—to name a few of the possibilities. Similarly, in another situation the worker says, "I wonder how it is that you can be so understanding of the children and yet seem unable to try to understand your husband"—to a woman who is ordinarily very perceptive of other people's feelings but does not want to lessen the conflict with her husband because she fears the sex relationships he would want to resume if they were on good terms. Or "What do you suppose makes you constantly insult people you say you want to be friends with?" —to a man who defends himself against his fear of rejection by first antagonizing others. Often the worker has already sensed what the underlying tendency is. Whenever possible, however, the worker encourages the client to seek the answer for himself rather than interpreting it for him.

Sometimes the client does not recognize problem behavior; in other words, it is ego-syntonic and must become ego-alien if he is to be motivated to try to understand and modify it. A mother who continually got into tempestuous fights at the table with her son saw her reactions only in terms of his slow and sloppy eating habits, which she felt made such scenes inevitable. After a substantial period of patient listening, reflective discussion, and suggestions, the worker responded to the heated description of a stormy session with the comment, "You are like two children battling each other, aren't you?" The remark obviously carried a value judgment, for adults do not consider it a compliment to be told that they are behaving childishly. It carried force with this client because a strong relationship had been established between her and her worker, which made her value the worker's good opinion. The fact that the worker rarely took a position of this sort gave it added significance. Sometimes the client, in response to such a stimulus, begins himself to think about reasons for his reactions; at other times, further comment is needed: "There seems to be something between you and George that we need to understand —what thoughts come to you about it?" In this situation the client went on first to the realization that she prolonged the scenes at table for the pleasure she derived from hitting her son and later to the discovery that she had identified her son with her husband and was taking out on him anger she did not dare to express directly to her husband.

A client will seek understanding of his thoughts or actions only when he feels some dissatisfaction with them, recognizes them as unprofitable or in some way inappropriate or ego-alien. Until this attitude exists, dynamic interpretations will fall on deaf ears. When it does exist or has been brought into being, the client will often be able to arrive at understanding with relatively little use of interpretation by the worker.

Almost any aspect of the personality that is either conscious or near-conscious may come under scrutiny in this type of procedure. Occasionally, unconscious matters may come through, but in general casework is not designed to uncover unconscious material.* A very common area in which understanding is sought is that of defensive behavior, such as avoidance, defensive hostility, and the various mechanisms of turning against the self, projection, intellectualization, rationalization, suppression, inhibition, and isolation. "Have you ever noticed that sometimes people get angry when they are scared?" "I wonder if you weren't pretty edgy about having that talk with your brother-in-law, and in a way hit out at him before he had a chance to hit you." "Have you noticed how often you go off into this kind of theoretical discussion when I'm trying to get you to think about your own feelings toward Mary?" "You know, it's good that you try to learn so much about children,

* See Chapter 11.

but sometimes I wonder if it isn't a way of avoiding letting yourself realize what strong feelings you have when Johnny acts this way." "Do you think your wife was really mad, or were you so angry yourself that you kind of expected she would be? What did she actually say at the beginning?" "Do you think that you are feeling depressed because you are really so mad at Fred but feel you can't let it out? Sometimes, you know, you can turn those angry feelings against yourself and then you feel depressed."

Initially, defense mechanisms often have to be explained to clients because they are not familiar with the way they work and cannot be expected to arrive at this kind of understanding entirely on their own. Subsequently, however, clients are frequently able to spot their own use of a particular defense. One of the goals of this type of treatment is to enable them to do this for themselves.

The greatest care is necessary in work with defenses, however, for they are self-protective mechanisms used by the personality to ward off anxiety. They should not be abruptly "broken through," but rather "worked through" when evaluation indicates that the individual is able to bear the anxiety involved. For the most part, interpretations should be made tentatively, and certainly in an atmosphere of acceptance, which often needs to be put into words.[1]

Important as defense mechanisms are, they are by no means the only part of the personality under scrutiny in the process of dynamic understanding. Often certain superego characteristics need to be thought about, especially the oversensitivity of the severe conscience. The client who is too hard on himself may be helped by knowing that he is suffering from his own self-criticism rather than from the too-high requirements of others. The person who feels deeply hurt by the discovery of imperfections in himself may be helped if he recognizes that the demand for perfection is a function of his own personality. "Have you noticed how upset you get whenever anyone makes the slightest criticism of your work?" "You hold very high standards for yourself, don't you?" "I think you are harder on yourself than anyone else would be."[2]

One of the hazards of helping a person to become aware of

superego severity is that the worker himself may appear to the client to be too lax in his standards. It is extremely important to avoid this; and great care must be taken not to seem to be sponsoring antisocial behavior. If the client does, nevertheless, react in this way, his reaction must be brought into the open and discussed, with the worker making it clear that he is not opposed to standards as such but to unrealistic or harmful severity of conscience.

In one of the cases read for the classification study the worker showed particular skill and adaptability to the client's needs in an instance of this sort. The client was the mother of a child who had been sent to the agency for treatment because of school failures inconsistent with his intelligence. She was a very religious woman who set extremely high standards for herself and who initially found treatment difficult because the need to recognize that she might be contributing to her son's troubles shattered her faith in herself as a good mother. Every attempt at developing her understanding was taken as a criticism from which she cringed. One of her underlying problems was her effort to suppress and inhibit all hostile impulses, and she felt extreme guilt over her failures to do so. When the worker tried to reduce her self-condemnation, she thought the worker was trying to undermine her faith and principles.

One day she brought a Bible to the interview, and seemed quite agitated. When the worker asked her gently if she had brought the Bible for a special reason, she opened it to the famous letter of Paul to the Corinthians on love, reading particularly the verse, "When I was a child, I spake as a child, I felt as a child, I thought as a child; now that I am a man I have put away childish things," and she cried as she finished it. The worker said it was a beautiful letter and asked if she had ever thought of why it was written. Did she think perhaps Paul might have observed that many people brought into adulthood feelings and thoughts from childhood? Perhaps he wished to counsel men to put away these feelings and behave like adults. No one could quarrel with the ideals of love, charity, and understanding. Religion and psychiatry have the same goals; the only question is how to achieve them.

As the client still seemed confused, the worker put her

thoughts in terms of gardening, a known interest of this client. "If you had a garden and weeds were choking out the good plants, you could cut off the tops of the weeds and the garden would look good, but the roots would still be there. Wouldn't it be better to pull out the roots? It would be harder but the results would be better. The same thing is true for human emotions. Many of us try to hide our difficulties and stamp them down, but this takes energy that could be used for better things. It seems worthwhile to try to uproot the difficulties. The only method I know for uprooting them is to understand and face things that are painful and intolerable. I'm not arguing against the goals of religion, but sometimes I question the way it goes about attaining them." The client was silent for several minutes, and then said she was greatly relieved and that she had had no idea the caseworker had such deep understanding of her feelings.

A similar difficulty can occur under almost opposite circumstances. The client whose control of his impulses is tenuous may have great anxiety about a possible breakthrough of his hostile or sexual impulses if he allows himself to become aware of his desires. With such clients it is extremely important for the worker to make clear the distinction between recognizing a desire or wish and carrying it out, and to make explicit his position that he is not trying to encourage the client to act out his impulses but rather to recognize them so that he can control them more effectively. If this type of approach is to be used, however, careful diagnosis must have indicated that the client will not be unable to control his impulses once he becomes aware of them.

Excessively strong needs of the personality—especially dependence and, sometimes, narcissism—must also sometimes be understood when they are causing trouble for the individual. Insight can also be gained into unrealistic beliefs or persistently distorted perceptions as they influence behavior in harmful ways. One man in the cases read for the classification study was unaware that his typing of women as inferior intellectually resulted in constant belittling behavior toward his wife, an intelligent college graduate who unfortunately already suffered from unrealistic feelings of inferiority.

An important step in the process of dynamic understanding is the client's bringing reason and judgment to bear upon the characteristic of his personality and its functioning that has been brought to his attention. It was not enough for the religious mother to see that she was trying to handle her anger by suppressing it; she had to be able to think about what she was doing, to bring her own judgment to bear upon it. She had to become convinced that her way of handling her feelings was unsound before she was ready to try to give it up.

The client's reactions to the worker are a fruitful source of dynamic understanding. As defense mechanisms or personality characteristics such as fear of criticism or excessive dependence come into play in the client-worker relationship, they can be used to enable the client to see the inner workings of his personality in action. He can then use this understanding to recognize similar dynamics operating in other life experiences.

Pattern-dynamic reflection is usually built upon previous consideration of the person-situation configuration. A few comments about the dynamics involved enables the client to understand his own patterns more fully. This in turn lessens the strength of some of the deterrents to realistic and appropriate perception and response. Discussion usually returns soon to the person-situation realm, where progress can be made in relating better to other people. Even in those cases where pattern-dynamic reflecting is a major component in treatment, discussion never rests for long exclusively in that realm. Often dynamic understanding is needed—or possible—only fleetingly in the course even of lengthy treatment. It is always accompanied by sustaining measures, and may at times be supplemented by procedures of direct influence. Dynamic understanding is frequently achieved without going into the development of the personality characteristic under discussion.

DEVELOPMENTAL UNDERSTANDING

Encouragement of reflection upon developmental material is usually undertaken in an episodic way in casework, certain themes being explored as it becomes apparent that factors in the client's development are blocking improvement in his current social adjustment. The procedure is used to help the client become aware of the way in which certain of his present personality characteristics have been shaped by his earlier life experiences, and sometimes to modify his reactions to these experiences. It is sometimes necessary because certain dysfunctional characteristics cannot be overcome except by insight into experiences that contributed to their formation. The term "contributed" is used advisedly because casework never reaches all the determinants of a given phase of behavior. The ability to reach early causative factors is a relative matter in any case. Even analysts readily acknowledge that, in addition to constitutional factors, early preverbal experiences that cannot be reached even by analysis are potent in preparing an initial "personality set" that profoundly influences the way later infantile and childhood experiences are received by the individual.[3]

In Chapter 2 we pointed out that the factor of reinforcement is extremely important in personality development. Harmful infantile experiences are sometimes overcome by health-inducing later ones, but often, unfortunately, events serve to confirm and reinforce the child's misconceptions or distorted generalizations. Reference has also been made to the balance of forces in the personality and to the way in which lessening the strength of damaging tendencies in the personality may enable healthier components to take the ascendancy in controlling and directing personality functioning. The purpose of encouraging the client to reflect upon his early life experiences is to bring about such a change in the personality. In general, casework does not attempt to reach unconscious infantile experiences but rather conscious or near-conscious later childhood and adolescent events, which can be considered genetic only in the sense that they are contributory developmental experiences.

The worker must not assume that every time a client talks about his past life the worker is engaging in the process of developing understanding of it. Most of the time this is not the case. Considerable exploration of the past is often part of the effort to arrive at diagnostic understanding, on the basis of which the worker may decide about the advisability of seeking to help the client arrive at an understanding of a particular segment of his development.   Second, a great deal of the client's talk about his past is for the purpose of catharsis.   He may get considerable relief from telling the worker about painful events in his life and from expressing anger or grief about them.   Third, the client very often brings in his past to justify his present feelings, attitudes, or behavior.   He is not really trying to gain understanding for himself but rather to explain to the worker why he reacts as he does and, often, why he feels that he is right, or at least should not be blamed, for so reacting; in other words, the past is used as a defense of a present position.   This type of defense is sometimes of great importance to the client, for it protects him from overly severe self-criticism; it should be handled with great care and not be thoughtlessly or prematurely stripped away.   Fourth, the client may talk about the past to evade thinking about the present.   And finally, the client sometimes has the impression that the past is what the worker is interested in, and he talks about it in order to please the worker.

There are other times, however, when the client can be helped greatly in understanding unhealthy and unprofitable ways of acting by coming to understand some of their historical sources.   Some clients quickly and spontaneously seek this kind of understanding.   Others need help from the caseworker before they are ready and *able* to do so.   (Apparent readiness needs to be carefully distinguished from real readiness.   The current sophistication about Freudian ideas makes intellectualization about childhood events a particularly popular form of defense.)

Sound movement into consideration of developmental factors follows much the same pattern as that just described for moving into the dynamics of psychological functioning.   The client's attention is drawn to inappropriate or inconsistent behavior. Sometimes he himself makes the choice of seeking further understanding, reacting in one way or the other to the worker's pointing up of his problem.   At other times the worker takes the lead in steering his thinking toward his earlier life.   "Have you had feelings like this before?"   "Does this make you think at all of similar things that have happened to you?"   Or, more specifically, to a mother who is very upset by her son's barely average school report: "How was it for *you* in school?"   Or to a man who is unduly upset in mentioning his brother's childhood failure in school: "You haven't told me much about your brother— what was he like?"[4] In these illustrations the worker first explores the past and gives opportunities for ventilation about it in areas that he would expect to be related to the client's present feelings or actions. The client may then spontaneously see connections or the worker may suggest them.

Often in previous general exploration of the client's earlier life, or as the client has talked about his childhood for other reasons, the worker will have obtained clues to areas in the client's life that may be of significance in understanding a particular reaction. These clues should certainly be used in guiding the client's associations. A woman who was unreasonably resentful of what seemed to her neglect by her husband had earlier mentioned to the worker that her father had paid very little attention to her as a child. When she complained at length about her husband's neglect of her, the worker responded by asking her more about her father. The client, simply by thinking of the two parallel situations in juxtaposition, saw the similarity and asked if she could be carrying some of her feeling toward her father over to her husband.

But sometimes the worker must make the connection. A mother was unreasonably angry with her adolescent daughter for borrowing her costume jewelry. The worker was already aware of this woman's deep hostility to her mother and suspected that it was being displaced on her daughter. She also knew that as an adolescent and later the client had been required to carry too much of the financial burden of the home, so that she had been deprived of many things she wanted. The worker ventured the comment, "I wonder if Joan's taking your things that way doesn't arouse the same feelings you had as a girl when your mother didn't let you get pretty things for yourself." This touched off an outburst of feeling about the client's deprived adolescence, followed by the realization that she had been taking out on her daughter the stored-up feelings of her own childhood.

Sometimes a client is fully aware of pertinent early experiences and little or no anxiety is involved in recalling them; the problem is simply to enable him to recognize the influence of past on present. At other times the early feelings or experiences are to a degree hidden from view, for reasons that directly parallel the reasons for hiding *current* feelings and reactions. There may be fear of criticism of things that are perfectly well remembered, or an event may not be regarded as significant or pertinent to the interview, or memories may have been suppressed or repressed because of their painfulness.

There are times when the recollection of an event and recognition of its influence in current life may not be enough. Rather, the past event itself may need to be thought about and reevaluated so that the feelings about it are modified. If a woman who is very resentful that her father did not provide adequately for his family can be helped to realize that his failure was due to a combination of illness and widespread national unemployment rather than to weakness of character or unwillingness to carry his family responsibilities, the amount of hostility she displaces upon her husband, a hard-working, conscientious individual who does not earn as much as she would like him to, may be substantially reduced. A woman who had felt that her parents discriminated against her by not letting her go to college was helped to recognize that she herself had not shown any interest in college. She thus saw that her parents might not have been discriminating against her but were perhaps unaware of her interest in further education. This recognition, in turn, not only led to a reduction of the client's hostility toward her parents and enabled her to have better current relationships with them, it also substantially reduced her feeling, which had carried over into all her adult relationships, that she was not loved and was somehow unworthy of love.

Before moving into the reevaluation process, it is often necessary to allow considerable ventilation of initial hostile feelings, partly because of the relief the client obtains from such an outpouring and from the worker's continued acceptance of him despite feelings about which he may feel quite guilty, but also because he will probably not be ready to reconsider his earlier relationships until he has had an opportunity for catharsis. If the worker attempts the reevaluation process prematurely, the client is apt to resent it, thinking that the worker is unsympathetic, is criticizing him, or is siding with the person toward whom he is hostile.

Obviously, reevaluation is useful only when the client has really misconstrued the earlier situation. Many times the early reality has in fact been extremely painful or even traumatic. Under such circumstances ventilation, plus sympathetic acceptance by the worker and realization of the way in which early events are unnecessarily influencing current life, is appropriate.

The relationship with the worker can also often be used as a source of developmental understanding. When the client is clearly reacting to the worker in terms of attitudes carried over from early life, the worker should, if consideration of these factors is deemed appropriate, help him to recognize what he is doing. "Do you think that you fear criticism from me as you did from your father?" "Do you see what you are doing? You are trying to get me to urge you to study just as your mother used to do. Then you will be angry at me for 'nagging,' just as you used to be angry at your mother." Interpretations like these would be appropriate only after the client has achieved some measure of understanding of his feelings toward his parents. Sometimes such transference interpretations are necessary to straighten out the relationship with the worker so that treatment can proceed. They are also of great value in helping the client become aware of similar transferred reactions in other parts of his current life. The client is, so to speak, caught in the act. The worker—assuming he has sufficient self-awareness to be conscious of his own part in the interplay—is observing the client's reaction directly in a controlled situation. He is in an excellent position to make an accurate, convincing interpretation.[5]

The same general principle holds here as in other kinds of understanding: the more the client can do for himself, the better. If he sees connections by himself or questions the accuracy of his understanding of earlier events, fine! Otherwise, the more the worker can limit himself to starting the client on an appropriate train of thought by a question, suggestion, or tentative comment, the better. Interpretations, when they are necessary, should be made tentatively, unless the worker is absolutely sure of their accuracy. In every form of understanding the worker should endeavor to minimize the client's dependence on him and encourage his ability to think for himself.[6] Flashes of work on developmental patterns occur in many cases that are mainly focused on the person-situation configuration, without a sustained effort to reach early material. Indeed, we may think of both dynamic and developmental procedures as aids for the purpose of proceeding with person-situation understanding where such understanding is temporarily blocked by intrapsychic influences. And as with reflection upon dynamic factors, episodes of thinking about developmental factors are followed in treatment by a return to the person-situation configuration as soon as the new understanding has cleared the way for better perception and handling of current affairs. Sustaining comments often help to provide the client with the necessary confidence in the worker's good will and competence. When anxiety mounts as a result of some of the memories, feelings, and connections that are uncovered, sustaining communications can help to carry the client through a difficult period of work.

The techniques discussed in this and the preceding chapter are closely related. The intrareflective procedures of the person-situation configuration can be skillfully used only when the worker has substantial psychological knowledge and insight. A recent study reported by Mullen and by Reid and Shyne has found that some workers avoid using either pattern-dynamic or developmental reflection even when it is appropriate to do so.[7] This would seem to represent a lack in either their training or their capacity for this kind of work. A caseworker who is engaged in treatment of disturbances in interpersonal relationships stands very much in need of the total repertory of casework procedures.

In order to promote consideration of dynamic or developmental matters as a major part of treatment, the worker must, in addition to being skilled in all the other casework processes, be thoroughly familiar with the workings of the personality—of unconscious as well as of conscious factors—and with the way in which the personality develops and early life events find continued expression in the adult personality. The worker must be particularly sensitive to the nuances of the client's feelings, have considerable security when dealing with anxiety, and be aware of and able to control the flow of his own reactions. He must also be free of the need to probe into his client's life to secure vicarious satisfaction either of his own curiosity or of his appetite for power, or for other narcissistic gratifications.

NOTES

1. Annette Garrett, in her article "The Worker-Client Relationship" in Howard J. Parad, ed., *Ego Psychology and Dynamic Casework* (New York: Family Service Association of America, 1958), pp. 53–54 and 59–60, discusses this point in her section on transference and interpretation.
2. See Lillian Kaplan and Jean B. Livermore, "Treatment of Two Patients with Punishing Super-Egos," *Journal of Social Casework*, 29 (October 1948), 310–316.
3. For elaboration of this point, see Phyllis Greenacre, ed., *Affective Disorders: A Psychoanalytic Contribution to Their Study* (New York: International Universities Press, 1953).
4. For illustrations, see Lucille N. Austin, "Diagnosis and Treatment of the Client with Anxiety Hysteria," in Parad, ed., *op. cit.*, and Hank Walzer, "Casework Treatment of the Depressed Parent," *Social Casework*, 42 (December 1961), 505–512.
5. See Andrew Watson, "Reality Testing and Transference in Psychotherapy," *Smith College Studies in Social Work*, 36 (June 1966), 191–209.
6. Very useful discussions of the timing and methods of interpretation are to be found in Ralph Ormsby, "Interpretations in Casework Therapy," *Journal of Social Casework*, 29 (April 1948), 135–141, and Rubin Blanck, "The Case for Individual Treatment," *Social Casework*, 47 (February 1965), 70–74. Also of interest are: Emanuel Hammer, ed., *Use of Interpretation in Treatment: Technique and Art* (New York: Grune & Stratton, 1968), and Jules Masserman, ed., *Depressions: Theories and Therapies* (New York: Grune & Stratton, 1970).
7. See Edward J. Mullen, "Differences in Worker Style in Casework," *Social Casework*, 50 (June 1969), 347–353, and William J. Reid and Ann W. Shyne, *Brief and Extended Casework* (New York: Columbia University Press, 1969), pp. 82–93.

9 | *Environmental Work*

So far we have been considering forms of communication between worker and client. More often than not this direct work with the client is accompanied by casework intervention in the situational part of the systems of which the client is a part. In the preceding chapter we saw that reflective discussion of dynamic and developmental factors is interwoven with all the other forms of client-worker communication. Cases vary: in some there is no work of this type, in others it occurs in a scattering of interviews, in still others it plays a major role. Similarly, some clients do not need environmental help, either because their problems do not involve the type of situational matters in which the worker can intervene or because they are able to act on their own behalf. At the other extreme are cases in which a major part of the work consists of bringing about environmental changes through communications between worker and collateral. Again the concept of a blend is useful. This type of procedure is intertwined with others. It also involves subtleties and complexities which must be understood if the work is to be carried on with skill.

As we have seen, milieu work can be viewed in at least three ways: in terms of the types of communication between worker and collateral, in terms of the type of resource involved, and in terms of the role or function that the worker is carrying. In Chapter 17 we will discuss considerations that influence the decision to intervene in the environment rather than to help the client himself to take the initiative in using environmental opportunities or bringing about desired changes in his situation. In this chapter we will explore the *nature* of this type of work.[1]

There has recently been a tendency in some quarters to act as if environmental work could be routinely delegated to paraprofessionals and especially indigenous paraprofessional staff members. It is true that such staff can be extremely helpful in this area. They can become experts on resources, on client's rights, on eligibility procedures. They can be forceful advocates. By demonstration they can teach the client himself to become more effective in his use of resources. Extensive in-service training added to natural aptitude is necessary, however, if they are to become skillful in differential communication in environmental work.[2]

Milieu work should be assigned to technicians selectively, with the graduate worker carrying responsibility not only for the general direction and coordination of the work but also for making collateral contacts himself when a high degree of differential interviewing skill is needed.

TYPES OF COMMUNICATION

It is important to emphasize that the first four sets of communication procedures—sustainment, direct influence, exploration-description-ventilation, and person-situation reflection—are just as germane to environmental work as they are to direct work with the client. There is an unfortunate tendency to think of work directed toward the individual's environment as "manipulation" and therefore rather different in nature from contacts with the client himself. Actually the contrary is true. The skills needed for bringing about changes in the environment on the client's behalf are in many respects identical to those employed in direct work with the client. The *extent* of the procedures differs, but the greater part of the *range* is common to both approaches.

It is a grave mistake to assume that environmental work is simple and does not involve an understanding of people similar to that required for direct work with clients. Many a failure in the effort to modify or use the environment is directly caused by this type of oversimplification. In work with collaterals, contact does have to be established, and sustaining procedures can be of great value. The client is not the only person who may be afraid of criticism: so may be the teacher, the public assistance worker, the nurse, the landlord. Their way of handling their feelings may be defensive hostility, which leads them to attack either the worker or the client. Often they too will respond better if the worker shows that he understands the problem they are up against and has not come to criticize, if they feel the worker is interested in their point of view and is willing to listen to the headaches the client has caused them. They, too, sometimes need encouragement concerning efforts they have already made to deal with the situation.

Procedures of direct influence also have a place in environmental work, particularly when the worker is trying to modify the way in which another person is acting toward his client. Reinforcement and suggestion play a large role in such activity, with advice sometimes of value, and insistence or even active intervention occasionally necessary. Ventilation is sometimes useful when the person being interviewed has a great deal of emotion about the client, or about the situation in which he and the client are involved. The landlord resolved to report to the police a boy who has broken a window may need to express a good deal of feeling about this and other misdeeds of the child-client before he is ready to consider a less punitive course of action. So, too, may the nurse or the teacher who has had to put up with an "acting-out" child or the landlord who sees the money he should have received as rent going into an Easter outfit. It goes without saying that intervention between a client and the natural consequences of "acting out" is itself a matter for careful diagnostic evaluation of all pertinent aspects of the client-situation system.

As in direct work, procedures for reflective discussion are of the greatest value with collaterals wherever they can be used, particularly in the process of helping one person to understand another. Often such understanding is brought about simply by telling the person about some aspects of the client and his life. At other times the worker may enter into the reflective process with the interviewee in much the same way as with a client, although the scope of the contact is more limited, indeed frequently to a single interview. Often worker and "collateral" are actually thinking together to arrive at a solution in which the interviewee is involved.

The worker is less likely in such contacts to use procedures that involve thinking about the *self*, although this, too, can occasionally take place. On the other hand, it is often necessary to straighten out the relationship between the caseworker and the "environmental" person. The worker's intent or attitudes may need to be clarified before effective work can proceed. Naturally the details of achieving this type of understanding vary with the context in which they are being applied. The worker is less likely to bring the interviewee's reactions into the open, but he must be all the more sensitive to them and skillful in finding tactful ways of conveying his own true attitudes and role to the interviewee.

All that has been said, then, about sustaining work, directive procedures, ventilation, and reflective discussion of the person-situation gestalt applies to work with people in the client's milieu as well as to contacts with the client himself—to indirect as well as direct treatment in the Mary Richmond sense. On the other hand, it is extremely unlikely that a collateral will become involved in discussion of dynamic or developmental aspects of his reactions. When a person in the client's milieu is sufficiently involved in his affairs to be willing to engage in the process of gaining self-understanding, the situation is one of interpersonal adjustment in which both individuals become clients.

TYPES OF RESOURCES

Moving from types of communication to variations in the type of resource or collateral that the worker is using or attempting to use, we arrive at a new set of considerations. Earlier, seven types of resources were distinguished.

Employing Social Agency

The first type is the social agency in which the caseworker is employed. Here the worker has a two-fold responsibility: first to use these services appropriately and skillfully, whatever they may be, and second to share responsibility for constant improvement in these resources. The foster home, for instance, is an agency resource that can be used on behalf of the client. No resource is more complicated and no resource requires more careful, thorough diagnostic assessment of the total child-parent-situation gestalt than that required in child placement, be it in a foster home or in an institution. Much thought has gone into the question of whether the foster parent is a client or a type of staff member. There is a third possibility. Is he not in many respects a type of resource? Certainly the first four types of casework communication are continuously used in work with foster parents. As in work with other resource people, the expertise of the foster parent must be respected. Even the new foster parent usually has skill in child rearing, though he is ignorant of the special complexities of caring for a *foster* child. The successful experienced foster parent has much to teach the caseworker new to the child-placement field, just as the successful experienced teacher knows far more about the child as a learner in the classroom than the caseworker does.

There is a cooperative quality in work with other experts that calls for delicate sensitivity to considerations of status if a good working relationship is to be achieved. The fact that the foster parent receives money from the agency is an important component in the total picture. Worker and foster parent are both parts of the same agency system, both subject to agency policies; they are allies in caring for the child, but they have different places in the hierarchy. The worker carries an authority that the foster parent does not have in that the worker's opinion carries great weight not only in the decision about the removal of particular children from the home but also in the decision of whether to use, or continue using, the home at all. All that the worker says and does then has special meaning for the foster parent because it occurs within this context. A feeling that suggestions must be taken may lead to resentment and pretense. It is especially important that an atmosphere be created in which the parent is free both to express opinions different from the worker's and to ventilate feelings about the children in his care. Since the foster mother especially has not only the family income at stake but also her self-esteem, which rests in large part upon her confidence in herself as a particularly good mother, sustainment can be of vital importance.

Sometimes, it is true, work with foster parents moves close to the client-worker pattern found in parent-child adjustment problems in the natural family. Even then, however, the parent's status as a resource, and hence a collateral, is still in existence. When the worker loses sight of this role, complications ensue.

The child-care agency is a particularly good example of the type of social agency in which the worker has major responsibility for influencing agency policy. The worker is in a key position to observe the effects of policy on both clients and foster or adoptive parents and should be thinking in terms of policy formulation as well as in terms of work with clients and substitute parents. Agencies can and often do provide effective channels for passing on the worker's observations and ideas so that policy can be a fluid instrument with wide room for change and experimentation rather than a set of relatively fixed administrative rulings. Experimentation with new ideas is essential if service is to be pertinent and effective.

The public assistance agency is difficult to classify as to type of resource. At present it is usually considered to be a social agency. Ideally, it should be a social agency. The extent to which this is an accurate designation, however, varies tremendously. In some communities social workers have considerable influence in policy making in these agencies. In many others control of policy is primarily in the hands of men whose prior experience has been in various types of business or public administration. Furthermore, basic policy is controlled to a high degree by law. Until the middle 1960s, very little progress in proportion to the enormity of the task was made in staffing agencies with graduate social workers. Even more recently, progress has been slow and punctuated by periods of regression. Hence, although these agencies are technically social agencies, in many ways they operate more like a business organization or utility in which a small proportion of staff positions are held by professionally trained social workers. The worker, then, in using the resources of his own agency is often in the difficult position of being the representative of an agency but in disagreement with many of its policies. Sometimes he can bring changes in these policies. He certainly has responsibility for doing everything within his power to improve services.

Actually, in some agencies there is considerable leeway in administrative policy and opportunity for constructive change in response to pressure at the caseworker and supervisory level.[3]

In many communities, however, some of the most socially undesirable policies persist, including extremely inadequate assistance grants and policies that not only discourage healthy social behavior but are destructive to individuals and families. The worker then faces many complications in bringing his agency's resources to his client. It is difficult enough when a policy that he knows is necessary and fair creates hardship for a client. Then the path is fairly clear—allow or even encourage the anger to be expressed, genuinely appreciate the hardship for the client, sometimes explain why the policy is necessary, and help him make the best possible adaptation to it. Under these circumstances there is no basic conflict about carrying out the policy. But when the policy is neither fair, wise, nor necessary, it is even more important for the client's anger to be expressed and for him to know that the worker recognizes the hardship and genuinely regrets it.

Four alternative courses are open to the worker. One is to express to the client his personal disagreement with the policy and perhaps tell of efforts that are being made to change it. At the same time he may help the client to decide whether alternatives to assistance from the agency are available and, if they are not and if no legitimate way around it can be found, help him to comply with agency policy.

The second course is for the worker to decide that he can no longer carry out policy with which he is in basic disagreement, and leave the agency. There are situations in which this action is justified, but it is not a truly satisfactory solution. If all workers who disagree with a bad policy leave the agency no one is left to fight for better ones. The worker who leaves is all too easily replaced by a worker without any social work education who will not find it so difficult to carry out destructive agency policies. This is not to say that every worker needs to feel duty-bound to stay forever in a poor agency. Eventually one justly may feel that one has fought long enough and someone else should take up the cudgels.

The third course is that taken by workers who stand strongly for better policy and stay within the system to work for it. In favorable situations they are able to bring about improvements in policy and its administration. They often have the power, especially at the supervisory and higher administrative levels, through flexibility and intelligent application of policy to modify its impact on the client considerably. They may be able to give some protection to clients; at the very least they can help keep things from getting worse. Workers who choose either the second or third courses can also work through channels external to the agency to bring about better legislation that can improve the whole system. The effort to bring such change has gone as far as court action by social work employees challenging the legality of extreme policies.

The fourth course is the most precarious one—that of staying in the agency but circumventing its policies. It usually carries no particular danger to the worker, for if he loses his job he can generally find another, and loss of his job is the worst that is likely to happen to him unless he engages in criminal misconduct. But this course of action does introduce all sorts of complications into the client-worker relationship in that it smacks of collusion and political favoritism. It gives substance to rumors about the need for "pull" in the agency, favoritism, and dishonesty among workers. It usually involves dishonesty in intrastaff relationships—often at several levels. If it is at all widespread, it supplies ammunition for the next politically motivated exposé, which may well result in a decrease of funds for all clients and stricter controls from above.

Soon we may well have a different type of public welfare system. But present indications are that even if whatever comes next is better than what we now have, it will still be far from perfect. If social workers are a part of such a new program the foregoing discussion will still be pertinent.

One aspect of the giving of resources in the public assistance agency has been clear in principle for decades. This is the connection between financial help and the client's acceptance of other casework services. Financial assistance is a right based on financial need. It should *never* be made contingent upon the acceptance of casework help. It should *never* be used as a weapon to coerce a client to do something unrelated to his basic eligibility, any more than one would refuse medical care to a sick person to force him to behave in one way or another that is unrelated to his medical care. Since the idea is widespread that workers do withhold financial assistance for such reasons, a worker in a public assistance agency must be sensitive to the possibility that the client believes this and take pains to make it clear that the client is free to reject his help and that doing so will not affect his eligibility for assistance.

The complete separation of casework help from responsibility for determining eligibility is currently being sought as a solution to this particular dilemma. The more income programs that can be put on some type of simple grant basis the better. But the programs currently being given serious consideration continue to involve procedures that would require complicated individual discriminations. Furthermore, while thousands of clients may eventually be placed under assistance programs with simple eligibility formulae such as those now in effect in the Old Age and Survivor's Insurance program, other thousands will inevitably be either insufficiently covered by these programs or involved in programs in which individual eligibility and amount of assistance is still to some degree a matter of administrative judgment. Therefore, if the client is not to be worse off than before, the eligibility process must not be turned over to clerks supervised by administrators whose only interest is economy. Frustrated as its position in public assistance has been, social work nevertheless has unquestionably given some measure of protection to the client and has represented his welfare as has no other profession or interested group. This influence must continue to be represented at least in administration and supervision if the client is not to be short-changed under any new system. Furthermore, families in poverty very much need the kind of help casework can give to deal with the many pressures of their lives. Casework is not the only kind of help they need, but it is one very important kind. Private agencies are not sufficiently financed to take on more than a very small part of this service. Along with new plans for financial assistance must come provision for casework service by an adequately trained staff operating under public auspices and publicly financed. Much creative and imaginative work is being done today by community groups of all sorts— some with social work participation, some in opposition to social work—in establishing valuable resources—job training, day care for children, drug addiction programs, community mental health centers, and many other useful programs. But these by no means cover the total need for service. A well-run, public family service program is vitally needed either as part of the agency administering financial assistance or under independent auspices but readily accessible to individuals and families that apply for or receive assistance.

Social Work Department of Agency Directed by Other Profession

The second type of resource is the department that employs the caseworker but is part of an organization primarily controlled by another profession—for example, a hospital or a school. In this situation, the caseworker offers the client a resource with which he is associated but that is not his primary responsibility. Other things being equal, he is in a less advantageous position than the predominant profession to bring change in the major agency service. At the same time, however, he is part of that service and therefore must do everything he can from his own observations of its effect on clients to contribute toward changes that will improve that service. The social worker in such settings must have thorough knowledge of the system within which he is working, its lines of responsibility, and its power structure. He must understand the "culture" of the other profession or professions with which he is dealing. He must have infinite tact, a high degree of self-confidence and confidence in his own profession, and the courage and zest to pursue his aims in spite of exasperating discouragements.[4] Usually progress in this situation is cumulative. The total position of the department is more important than any single decision. Once the competence and value of the department have been established and recognized the head of the service will be listened to and an attitude of mutual respect will permeate interrelationships.

Systems theory observations concerning the importance of the *point of maximum reverberation** are fully confirmed in the role played by key persons in the medical and nursing hierarchy. It is extremely important that pressure for change be exercised only after sound diagnostic assessment of the hospital or school system has been made. The most effective way for change to take place is for the department head to give courageous leadership to the staff, following through in pressing for needed changes. At the same time the staff needs to understand the complex forces within which change takes place in a large multiprofessional organization; sometimes an administrator cannot share with his staff all that is going on, including all the efforts he may be making, matters of timing, and all the sad, frustrating reasons for lack of progress. It is practically impossible to keep this sort of information confidential once it is shared, yet to divulge it may completely defeat the objectives in which all are interested. Change in a "host agency" calls for team play of the highest order, and nothing is more important in team play than mutual respect and trust.

Changes within the social work department itself have much in common with changes in the more autonomous social agency of the child welfare or family service type. Money is a factor in all agencies. The child welfare and family agencies must often seek the approval of a lay board or a community chest in much the same way that a department of an organization with a different primary function must secure approval of whatever intra-agency authority it is responsible to.

When we turn from the worker-agency relationship to the worker-client in this second type of resource, we find that the worker is seen by the client not only as a caseworker but also as representing the major functions of the hospital, school, or court. He therefore must deal with client reactions to these services, including their weaknesses. In this respect the same considerations hold as earlier discussed concerning the worker in the social agency.

---

* According to systems theory, change applied to part of a system will reverberate in a differential way throughout the system. A point of maximum reverberation is a point at which any change will cause great changes in the total system.

It is also one of the primary functions of a worker in an agency primarily under the auspices of another profession to facilitate the way in which his agency is being used as a resource by the client. He often interprets the agency services to the client. He helps the other professional to understand the needs of the client better. Because he sees the client from a different vantage point and within a different professional frame of reference from the doctor, teacher, or judge, he can contribute greatly to the quality of the other service. At times he may need to act as mediator between the service and the client and sometimes even as active advocate on the client's behalf. Doctors occasionally are reluctant to give adequate attention to certain patients because of their critical or hostile attitudes or their failure to understand or follow medical advice. The medical social worker often acts to remedy this situation. A teacher may take a dislike to a child. By acquainting her with the facts of the child's background the caseworker may be able to modify the teacher's reactions. Here again thorough understanding of the organization as a system and of the ways of working, patterns of thought, and values of the other profession is essential if either mediation or active advocacy is to be successful.

Institutional Resources Where Worker Is Not a Staff Member

The third and fourth types of resources are institutional resources that employ social workers but of which the worker is not himself a staff member. The third type consists of other social agencies. The fourth type consists of social work departments of which the worker is not a staff member in agencies that are directed by other professions. The third type includes not only casework agencies but also community centers where there are opportunities for group experiences, hobby development, recreation, and social action through groups. Organizations such as visiting homemakers, day-care centers, and employment counseling services also fall in this category when they are administered by social workers. When these same organizations are under the leadership or direction of other professionals but employ social workers, they fall into the fourth type of resource.

The worker who has had a sound social work education is familiar with what social agencies in most fields do. When he enters a new community, he should familiarize himself as quickly as possible with a wide range of agencies. Colleagues who have been in the community longer will be knowledgeable about such resources. Agencies often keep resource files. Common objectives, a common professional language and body of knowledge, and a common value system facilitate the use of such resources. But no profession is completely homogeneous. Within a range, values, objectives, language, and even knowledge differ. Idiosyncrasies exist within as well as among professions. Here too one must be sensitive to the reaction of the other worker within the other agency and use communication skills. Social workers are people too. They also have their off days, days when they are under pressure or upset about work or personal affairs and not operating in good style.

A further factor in work with another social agency is, of course, the policies and resources of that agency. Some of these are fixed, others are flexible. In milieu work it is often necessary for the caseworker to push toward the maximum extension of that flexibility. In so doing, if he has correctly assessed his client's need and interpreted it skillfully, his best ally should be his colleague in the other agency. Sometimes, too, the worker in the other agency is more familiar with other similar resources than is the first worker and therefore able to suggest alternatives when his own agency is unable to meet the need. There are times also when his greater experience with the type of problem experienced by the client leads him rightly to a different assessment of the client's need. Under these circumstances, conferences between workers are usually the best means for arriving at a reassessment.

In order to avoid either duplication of services or work at cross purposes in agencies administered by other groups or professions but employing social workers it is important to ascertain whether the client has already received casework service. If so, one works with the other worker if the case is active and through the social

work department if it is closed. In any case it is usually best to
consult someone in the social work department about the best
way of helping a client to straighten out any complications that
have arisen in his relationship with the organization. It is extremely useful to develop friendly colleague relationships with
workers in other agencies to facilitate this type of resource work.

Organizations Not Employing Social Workers

The fifth type of resource refers to a variety of agencies
and organizations not employing social workers. In such organizations one deals, of course, directly with individuals whose
point of view, experience, and reactions are relatively unknown.
The greater the worker's knowledge about the other organization or profession and the resources of the particular institution
the more likely he is to be able to help the client to make appropriate use of it. Much exploratory work may need to be
done before the proper help can be secured. Not only will the
client's time be wasted if he is sent to an inappropriate place, but
he may also be discouraged from trying further. It may be an
ego-debilitating experience. It may also reduce his confidence in
the worker's interest and competence and may have a negative
effect on simultaneous direct work with the client. Both phone
work and footwork may be necessary to prepare the way for
the client's own first contact. Ingenuity in locating appropriate
resources and skill in interesting other organizations in a client
are particularly valuable in milieu work using resources not connected with social work.

Task-Oriented Collaterals

We have already seen in the section on types of communication a number of illustrations of contacts with *individuals* on the
client's behalf. The last two types of resources both involve
individuals. The sixth type includes collaterals whose relationship with the client is *instrumental*, or task oriented, as with
employers or landlords. With these individuals the worker may
be seeking such opportunities as jobs or better housing for the

client, or he may be intervening on behalf of the client in a misunderstanding or a clash that is creating hardship for the client. In each of these cases the worker deals not with another profession or some type of service organization but rather with people who have their own interests at stake. They tend to be either indifferent to the client or hostile. In preparation for such contacts it is essential that the worker be sure of his facts or else be aware of the possibility that he does not have all the facts. Overidentification with the client is a frequent cause of failure in this type of contact. There is no sense in persuading an employer to make special plans to hire a client by giving a false picture of the client's abilities or readiness for work. It will only end in embitterment on both sides. When liabilities are acknowledged and sympathetically interpreted, the collateral makes his decision realistically in the light of his own attitude about the liabilities, his willingness to take a risk, and his assessment of how much damage may be done to his business if the liability cannot be overcome or contained. If the situation is such that the worker cannot be frank, it is better for the client to find his own job.

Similarly, when the worker is trying to modify the attitudes or actions of an instrumental collateral, he has to listen with an open mind to the collateral's side of the story. He must then judge whether to press for greater understanding of the client's point of view or perhaps to drain off some of the irritation and then work with the client to arrive at some mutual amelioration of the total situation.

Feeling-Oriented Collaterals

The seventh type of resource includes those individuals who have an "expressive," or feeling-oriented, relationship with the client. With these individuals the situation is quite different than that connected with instrumental collaterals, since an expressive relationship implies some investment in the client's welfare. This is true even when anger exists and the worker is intervening in the hope of improving their interaction. In such relationships anger itself is a sign of caring—of involvement. With caring, a new component enters. The relative or even friend feels that he knows the client better than the worker does—and indeed he may. If he feels he has a stake in the situation, he may want the worker to change the client rather than to respond positively himself to the worker's need for his help or the worker's efforts to induce him to modify his own relationship with the client. He may even be opposed to the worker's efforts.

Here we reach ground that is very close to work with the client himself. Sometimes, in fact, it turns into direct work in which the collateral becomes a second client either through individual interviews or by a shift to family or joint interviewing. Short of this, however, relatives and friends can become powerful allies in treatment. Sometimes it is sufficient to let them know they are needed. At other times work must be done to help them understand ways in which they can assist the client. Simply helping relatives and friends to see their importance to the client and the ways in which they can help often motivates them to offer opportunities and psychological support. They may need assurance that a little involvement in the client's troubles will not result in their being left with greater responsibility than they are either obligated to assume or want to assume. This is particularly true when the client is elderly or disabled. Needless to say, the question of whether to intervene directly with friends or relatives or to help the individual to approach them himself is a delicate one calling for careful assessment and discussion with the client.

Sometimes the worker uses friends and relatives to accomplish psychological objectives identical in nature with those sought in direct treatment. Relatives, friends, teachers, and doctors are sometimes in a far better position than the social worker to give sustaining help to a client. Often they do so spontaneously, but the caseworker can also motivate them to take this type of responsibility. Particularly with extremely anxious people, it is sometimes most helpful to enlist the interest of a friend or relative who likes the client and has a warm nature with a good deal of common sense and capacity for equanimity. It is surprising how often such people can be found if the worker is alert to the possibility and is not so tied to his desk that he never makes contact with them.

It is often true, too, that the worker is not the person in the best position to exercise direct influence in the client's life. A friend or relative, a club leader, doctor, clergyman, lawyer, or teacher often carries more influence with the client, is better qualified as an adviser in a particular area, and can be enlisted in the client's interest. Sometimes a visiting homemaker can take on an educational function that is in part advisory and in part a matter of increasing a woman's understanding of the practical problems of running a home. This was the key, for instance, to the resolution of a marital problem that was threatening to end in divorce for a very young, immature wife, whose failures in home management not only irritated her husband but also reinforced her emotional childishness, discouraging her from growing into a more adult role in any aspect of her marriage. The visiting homemaker's work went hand in hand with the direct efforts of the caseworker to help her to mature.

Similarly, people other than the worker, particularly other professionals, may be better able to help the client understand certain aspects of his situation. After the client has discussed a problem with the appropriate medical, religious, educational, or vocational expert, however, he may well need the caseworker's help in assimilating the information he has obtained and deciding upon his own course of action. Although it is true that the client can sometimes take full responsibility himself for such consultations and does not need help from the worker in arranging them, the consultations are often more productive when the worker has helped in the selection of the person to be consulted and can orient him in advance about the client and his problem.

TYPES OF ROLES

One further aspect of environmental work remains to be discussed, that of variations related to the role of the worker— provider, locater, or creator of a resource; interpreter; mediator; aggressive intervener. Obviously, a worker often carries more than one role simultaneously as he works on various aspects of his client's milieu. His role may shift rapidly and conflict between roles can exist. Each role has its own characteristics.

The worker is the *provider* of a resource when he gives the resource through his own agency. Many of the intricacies of this role have been discussed in the section on the social agency as a type of resource. From the point of view of his role, the worker represents the resource and the client reacts as though the worker were himself responsible for both the positive and negative features of the service given or withheld. This in turn can have positive or negative effects on concomitant direct work with the client. Thorough knowledge of agency policies, flexibility in their application, readiness to help the client decide whether he wants the resource or wants to qualify for it are all part of the administration of a resource. So also is working with the client's resentment and resistance when these occur. Direct and indirect work are here closely intertwined.

The role of *locater* of a resource is an extremely important one. Success in it depends not only on thorough knowledge of the local community but also on imaginative assessment of the client's need. The worker must display ingenuity in finding the resource in unexpected places and skill in interesting particular individuals in making special provisions for the client's special needs. Patience and much phone work and some footwork may be required.

Just beyond the locater role comes that of *creator* of a resource. The same qualities and activities are involved in this as in the more difficult of the examples of the locater role. Volunteers can often be interested in providing or arranging for various kinds of services when organized resources are not available or when normal resources do not offer quite what the client needs. Churches can sometimes be involved in such activity, as can "service oriented" clubs of various types. The wider the worker's network of associations in his community the more likely he is to be able to become a resource creator.

In the role of *interpreter* the worker is helping someone else to understand the client. The accuracy and completeness of his own understanding of the client is the obvious base line. As has been noted in the discussion of communication procedures with collaterals, it is essential that the worker be attuned also to the attitudes and feelings of the person to whom he is trying to explain the client. Much of the time this is no simple fact-giving process but rather an interactional one in which information and opinions are exchanged and feelings often come into play. The worker thus is often oriented to previously unknown aspects of his client's functioning that may be pertinent to his direct work with his client.

In helping another person to understand a client or feel differently toward him the preservation of confidentiality is important. The worker must be sure that the client is willing to have the contact made and for information to be shared. The information given should be only that which is pertinent to the objective of the interview. Particular care must be taken not to divulge inadvertently information that might create difficulty for the client. The nature of the communications is strongly influenced by the type of collateral to whom information is being given. Other things being equal, the worker can share more freely with a fellow social worker or with a member of another "helping" profession. Beyond this, special care must be taken to be guided not only by the collateral's personality and attitude toward the client but also by knowledge of the role he plays in the client's life and of ways in which his self-interest or other responsibilities may be involved. Occasionally, despite the greatest care, misuse is made of information or the client thinks that this has occurred, even if it has not. The worker should be alert to the possibility of this in interviews with the client and bring into the open any indications the client may give that the contact has misfired.

The next two roles to be discussed are those of *mediator* and *aggressive intervener*. They share some common features, since mediation and aggressive intervention are two aspects of case advocacy. Both go further than interpretation. Both assume some strain or conflict in the relationship between client and collateral. They differ, however, as to method. Mediation relies on the force of greater understanding of the client and of his needs and rights by the collateral. Aggressive intervention calls for the use of some type of force.[5] Mediation involves both direct and indirect casework. In this type of work with the collateral all that has been said about the role of interpreter holds for that of mediator—some of it with even greater force. Since this role occurs only when there is tension between a client and another individual or representative of an institution, there is often anger or at best irritation or annoyance. When an institution or agency of some sort is involved, there is usually defensiveness about a decision already made or action already taken. The possibility of client distortion or simply of misunderstanding or misinterpretation is high. The worker must be ready to listen to the other side and be able to withhold judgment. He must try to understand the collateral's point of view and sometimes modify his own. Mediation is a two-way street, and the worker's interview with the collateral may lead him to a new view of the client; he may feel that the client himself must alter his views if change in the interpersonal situation is to occur. On the other hand, if in the worker's opinion the client's position is well taken, the right moment and the right words need to be found to induce the collateral to reconsider his position or his view of the client. In terms of communication procedures this requires ventilation and person-situation reflection, with timing and tact of the utmost importance.

The recent growth in the problem of destructive activities especially by youths in their teens and young adults has greatly complicated the question of intervention on the client's behalf. On the one hand, fear and hysteria lead to unjustified punitiveness, to hasty accusations founded on little evidence, and to exaggerated fears concerning what in other times would be considered a "normal" degree of "acting up." On the other hand, the forms that youth aggression now takes are often truly dangerous, and individuals have a right to protect themselves and others in legitimate ways. The social worker is not a lawyer for the client and does not have the legally recognized responsibility to plead the client's case, right or wrong. The social worker is just as deeply concerned about the client's rights and his well-being as the lawyer, but his orientation and his responsibility are to the whole as well as to the part—to some degree to "the other" as well as to the client. Therefore the decision about intervention in this type of situation calls for careful evaluation of long-run as well as short-run effects. Either *over-* or *under-*protection can be unrealistic and lead to further aggressive activities that help neither client nor others.

There are times when it is clear that a client's rights are being ignored, denied, or abrogated and mediation has not been successful in attaining a correction of the injustice. Here the worker must turn to the second type of advocacy—aggressive intervention. He argues forcefully for the client, often goes beyond the collateral himself to his supervisor or a higher executive, and enlists the efforts of upper administrative levels of his own agency. He may use other community resources—individual or organizational—to bring pressure to bear in the client's favor. The growth of a group of lawyers particularly interested in protecting the rights of clients who are in poverty or subject to discrimination has provided a new and valuable resource upon which to call for case advocacy that goes beyond what the social worker himself can do.

When the worker moves from persuasion to a form of pressure or exercise of power, new considerations come into focus. The use of power inevitably arouses hostility and resistance. If the worker uses it and loses, the client may be worse off than before because of the counterhostility that has been generated. It is therefore a form of advocacy to be turned to only after other methods, including mediation, have failed, when one is quite sure that injustice is being done, and when the aggressive effort has some possibility of succeeding. When there is danger of backfire, the client should know this and decide himself whether he wants to take this risk, with the worker helping him to weigh the pros and cons realistically. The means that are taken will also affect the worker's total relationship with the client and other objectives the worker may have with his client, so these effects must also be taken into consideration.

Professional goals and ethics also are involved in the way in which aggressive intervention is carried on. The worker is still operating as a caseworker, and means that are in conflict with professional ethics are not justified by the ends they serve.[6] The interpreter and mediator roles stress the social worker's art of reconciliation, of bringing opposing interests into a cooperative relationship built on greater understanding. These are powerful tools. Aggressive intervention on the other hand is an approach of confrontation. It relies on force rather than on reconciliation. It, too, is powerful, but it is a two-edged sword that should be used with caution and with an effort to anticipate unintended consequences.

When the worker is employed by an agency the total system becomes pertinent to decisions about what means to use. Often a higher level within the worker's own agency can bring pressure more effectively than the worker himself or may even succeed through mediation so that aggressive intervention is not needed at all.

A distinction is commonly made between *case advocacy* and the more general *social action* or *social reform advocacy*. The former refers to the worker's efforts to remedy an immediate concrete injustice to which his individual client is being subjected. The latter refers to a more general attempt to bring about changes in policies or practices that adversely affect a whole group of clients or others in the community. In practice, the line between case advocacy and social action advocacy is sometimes blurred. This is particularly true in the "store front" type of local community operation that is set up in part to give individual service and in part to promote community activity in social improvement projects. While the same *agency* may operate on both levels, clients who need individual help beyond brief contacts should not be assigned to a worker who is at the same time involved directly with the client in general social action.

It often happens that when a client gains self-confidence, some freedom from his own pressing concerns, and greater knowledge of the effect of community conditions, he joins a group in the general community through which he can participate in social action. If he shows interest in this the worker frequently can help him locate appropriate groups to join just as he helps the client locate other resources. It is not wise to use the casework treatment relationship to *enlist* the client in causes, no matter how good those causes may be. To do so is similar in principle to steering him into the worker's own church or his own political party and carries all the same hazards of the client's feeling impelled to please the worker upon whom he is dependent for social or psychological help. The caseworker's role differs in this respect from that of the group worker or community organizer, whose recognized role is often this very activity and is sometimes an acknowledged reason for his contact with group members. With so much injustice prevailing today the need for social action advocacy is great. The caseworker has many avenues through which he should participate in bringing about social change. Often the agency of which he is a staff member is already engaged in social action within its area of competence and effectiveness. It may, then, be part of his regular work to participate in this action. The movement from case to cause is essential. By collecting information about injustice as it appears in individual cases, the worker can supply the data that can initiate the social advocacy and evidence by means of which change can be accomplished.[7] Agencies carry definite responsibility for providing ways in which such information can become effective. If the agency is not active in areas in which it could be effective the worker, as a staff member, can work toward interesting his agency in a social-action program. He also has his personal political life, his professional associations, and opportunities for common action with groups of colleagues.[8] Socially minded lawyers and social workers have also found recently that they have similar objectives and have worked collaboratively with great effectiveness. Participation in social advocacy of one type or another is a clear professional responsibility.

Viewing work with collaterals from the three vantage points of communication procedures, type of resource or collateral, and role of the worker brings out the complexity of this type of work and highlights the breadth of skill necessary for successful environmental work. It is a part of the total treatment process in most cases, and in some it plays a decisive role. Any worker who is inept in applying his basic understanding and skills to work in the environment is seriously handicapped in his efforts to help clients with intra- or interpersonal problems.

NOTES

1. The following discuss various aspects of work on the situational component of the person-situation gestalt: Louise Bandler, "Casework—A Process of Socialization: Gains, Limitations, Conclusions," in Eleanor Pavenstedt, ed., *The Drifters: Children of Disorganized Lower-Class Families* (Boston: Little, Brown & Co., 1967); Celia Benny, "Casework and the Sheltered Workshop in Rehabilitation of the Mentally Ill," *Social Casework*, 41 (November 1960), 465–472; Berta Fantl, "Preventive Intervention," *Social Work*, 7 (July 1962), 41–47; Henry Freeman et al., "Can a Family Agency Be Relevant to the Inner Urban Scene?" *Social Casework*, 51 (January 1970), 12–21; Evelyn A. Lance, "Intensive Work with a Deprived Family," *Social Casework*, 50 (December 1969), 454–460; Margaret Milloy, "Casework with the Older Person and His Family," *Social Casework*, 45 (October 1964), 450–456; Bernard Neugebore, "Opportunity Centered Social Services," *Social Work*, 15 (April 1970), 47–52; William B. Neser and Eugene E. Tillock, "Special Problems Encountered in the Rehabilitation of Quadriplegic Patients," *Social Casework*, 43 (March 1962), 125–129; Arthur Pierson, "Social Work Techniques with the Poor," *Social Casework*, 51 (October 1970), 481–485; Lydia Rapoport, "Social Casework: An Appraisal and an Affirmation," *Smith College Studies in Social Work*, 39 (June 1969), 213–235; Lydia Rapoport and Kate Dorst, "Teamwork in a Rehabilitation Setting: A Case Illustration," *Social Casework*, 41 (June 1960), 291–297; Ben Schlesinger, ed., *The Multiproblem Family* (Toronto: University of Toronto Press, 1963); Max Siporin, "Social Treatment: A New-Old Helping Method," *Social Work*, 15 (July 1970), 13–25.

2. See Charles Grosser, "Local Residents as Mediators Between Middle-Class Professional Workers and Lower-Class Clients," *Social Service Review*, 40 (March 1966), 56–63; Francine Sobey, *The Non-Professional Revolution in Mental Health* (New York: Columbia University Press, 1970).

3. The following recent articles deal with the role of caseworkers in the public assistance agency: Daniel Knight, "New Directions for Public Welfare Caseworkers," *Public Welfare*, 27 (1969), 92–94; Ruth Pauley, "The Public Welfare Agency of the Future," *Social Casework*, 47 (May 1966), 286–292; Russell Smith, "In Defence of Public Welfare," *Social Work*, 11 (October 1966), 90–97; J. Thompson and D. Riley, "Use of Professionals in Public Welfare," *Social Work*, 11 (January 1966), 22–27; Harry Wasserman, "The Moral Posture of the Social Worker in a Public Agency," *Public Welfare*, 25 (1967), 38–44.

4. See William Brennan and Shanti Khinduka, "Role Discrepancies and Professional Socialization: The Case of the Juvenile Probation Officer," *Social Work*, 15 (April 1970), 87–94; Katherine and Marvin Olsen, "Role Expectations and Perceptions for Social Workers in Medical Settings," *Social Work*, 12 (July 1967) 70–78; Gerald M. Shattuck and John

M. Martin, "New Professional Work Roles and Their Integration into a Social Agency Structure," *Social Work,* 14 (July 1969), 13–20.

5. A controversial subject! See Irvin Epstein, "Social Workers and Social Action: Attitudes toward Social Action Strategies," *Social Work,* 13 (April 1968), 101–108; David Hunter, "Social Action to Influence Institutional Change," *Social Casework,* 51 (April 1970), 225–231; Robert H. MacRae, "Social Work and Social Action," *Social Service Review,* 40 (March 1966), 1–7; William Schwartz, "Private Troubles and Public Issues: One Social Work Job or Two?" in National Conference of Social Welfare, *Social Welfare Forum* (New York: Columbia University Press, 1969), pp. 22–43.

6. Gordon Hamilton discusses this in "The Role of Social Casework in Social Policy," *Social Casework,* 33 (October 1952), 315–324.

7. Alvin S. Schorr, "Editorial Page," *Social Work,* 11 (July 1966), 2; Robert Sunley, "Family Advocacy from Case to Cause," *Social Casework,* 51 (June 1970), 347–357; Charlotte Towle, "Social Work: Cause and Function," in Helen H. Perlman, ed., *Helping: Charlotte Towle on Social Work and Social Casework* (Chicago: University of Chicago Press, 1969), pp. 277–299.

8. National Association of Social Workers, *Ad hoc* Committee on Advocacy, "Champion of Social Victims," *Social Work,* 14 (April 1969), 16–22.

10 | Studying and Working with the Typology

Shortly after the typology of treatment communications described in preceding chapters was developed, the writer secured a grant from the National Institute of Mental Health* that made it possible to test the reliability of the typology and its suitability and usefulness for clarifying and studying the casework process. It was important first of all to use the proposed classification in an analysis of a large number of casework interviews to see whether, indeed, the communications that occurred could be fitted comfortably into the various categories as hypothesized. If it was found that this was possible, the reliability of the typology then had to be tested. That is, it was necessary to see to what extent independent coders classifying the same material would agree in assigning items to the same categories. If the reliability was found to be acceptable, it would then be possible to go on to use the typology to study aspects of the casework process itself. The classification was found to be both appropriate and reasonably reliable. Various substantive issues were then examined with the use of the typology by the writer and by other researchers. The general outlines of these studies—both examining the appropriateness and reliability of the classification and using it as a research tool—are the subject of this chapter.

RESEARCH METHODOLOGY

A series of studies was initially set up by the author using 123 interviews from 63 cases carried in 6 family service agencies. In all these cases the problem was one of marital adjustment. The

* Grant No. MH–00513, National Institute of Mental Health, U.S. Department of Health, Education, and Welfare.

sample was systematically selected at the point of case assignment, and it represented an unbiased cross-section of the work of the agencies. The workers ranged in experience from recent school of social work graduates to seasoned practitioners. Special rules were set up for detailed *process recording* to be completed within no more than two days after the interview.[1]

Process recording is a form of recording used for special purposes by caseworkers. In these studies an interview running from three-quarters of an hour to an hour was usually reported in approximately three pages of single-spaced typing. Obviously this was not verbatim reproduction but rather a detailed description of what transpired with considerable paraphrasing. Workers were asked to be particularly careful to separate the worker's contributions to the interview from those of the client. The excerpts from three of the interviews that are reproduced in Figures 1, 2, and 3 illustrate the kind of detail secured. Later studies using both tape recording and process recording indicate that some skewing of the material occurred in the process recording. Nevertheless, on the whole there was great similarity in the findings of the two kinds of recordings.

In the first of the studies operational definitions were developed for each category of the classification, ambiguities in the typology were cleared up, and where necessary, modifications were made in the original definitions and new categories were developed. Procedures were also worked out for coding in a way that would make it possible to handle the material quantitatively. This is not necessary for ordinary on-the-job use of the classification but is essential if it is to be used in research comparing groups of cases.

For the purposes of the studies it was decided to do line-by-line content analysis determining the proper coding by using the clause having its subject and predicate on the coded line.* Figures 1, 2, and 3 demonstrate the mechanics of the coding process. The capital letters, beginning with the first column, have the following meanings:

* For use in formal research, a Manual for Coding giving further details concerning units for either process or tape recordings should be secured from the author.

15 but her husband would want to go home every other weekend. He would
16 leave her with his mother and then he would go out for the entire
17 weekend. Sometimes she would visit her mother on Sunday. If
18 they went there he would behave but if he stayed with his parents,
19 he didn't. With some anger in her voice she told me they
20 had bought furniture three times since they are here. Each time
21 he would want to go back home to live and actually they moved
22 back three times. However, when they went down there they wouldn't
23 have anything. In fact, she said there were times when they
24 didn't have enough to eat. I wondered how he always managed to
25 get jobs. She said one time he worked in a filling station; an-
26 other time he helped a man build a garage. I wondered what he
27 does up here and she said he works for the D. Plant, and they
28 have taken him back each time that he returned. I said he must
29 be a good worker if they did this and she said he is and that is
30 the reason he has always gotten his job back. She said they
31 could have bought a home in the time they have been here if he
32 would only have stayed and acted like people should act. Now
33 he wants another baby. He told her when he came back last weekend
34 if she had another baby that would be all he wants. Their
35 youngest child is seven.
36   I asked how Mr. Z was with the children. She said he is real
37 good with them. Makes over them and does like any normal father.
38 She feels the marital problem is hard on the children. The one
39 girl has dropped in her grades in school and while she isn't
40 certain it is because of the trouble at home, Mrs. Z feels
41 there must be some connection. The older girl can cry but the

Figure 1. Record No. 18: Excerpt from a First Interview

U = Unclassified
A = Sustainment
B = Direct nifluence
C = Exploration-description-ventilation
D = Person-situation reflection
E = Pattern-dynamic reflection
F = Developmental reflection

The small letters indicate subdivisions of D called change objectives—i.e., the type of understanding by the client that is sought:

	U	A	B	C	D	E	F	a	b	c	d	e	f	g	
15				X											15
16				X											16
17				X											17
18				X											18
19				X											19
20				X											20
21				X											21
22				X											22
23				X											23
24				O											24
25				X											25
26				X											26
27				O X											27
28				X											28
29				O											29
30				X											30
31				X											31
32				X											32
33				X											33
34				X											34
35				X											35
36				O											36
37				X											37
38				X											38
39				X											39
40				X											40
41				X											41

a = of others or any aspect of the outside world or of the client's own physical health

b = of the effect or outcome of the client's own behavior

c = of the nature of the client's own behavior

d = of the provocation or current causation of his behavior

g = of evaluative aspects of his own behavior

Early in the formulation of the typology it became abundantly clear that one gets only a very partial picture of the nature of the casework treatment process and its dynamics if one pays attention only to the worker's remarks. Therefore both client

13 man should. I asked if she thought it was possible to force him
14 to marry her if he really did not want to, that many men do not
15 and of course many women do not care to marry either regardless
16 of pregnancy, by her own statements earlier his relatives tried
17 to influence him against marrying her, but he did anyway, and
18 from my impression of Mr. R. from the one interview, he did not
19 indicate any regrets about marrying her and does seem to care about
20 her. She answered that it is true, his uncles tried to persuade
21 him against marriage, but he could not have gotten away with it
22 anyway, because she was the "apple of my daddy's eye" and
23 her daddy made Mr. R. marry her, and Mr. R. knew her daddy would
24 not take any foolishness from him: Breaking down completely she
25 continued that she loved her daddy so much, and he her, and yet
26 she disgraced him and her mother, she disgraced her whole family,
27 when they had so much confidence in her and such high hopes for
28 her. They were shocked when she got pregnant and it was weeks
29 before they even spoke to her, and they forgave her but they have
30 not forgotten. I said it was rather cruel of them to stop speaking
31 to her for getting pregnant, but more importantly, since she
32 feels there is something to forgive she has not forgiven herself,
33 when everyone else has, and I thought perhaps her feeling against
34 herself for getting pregnant before marriage is causing her much
35 too much grief and other emotional problems, which is causing
36 herself and her whole family trouble. She continued crying, saying
37 "I know it is, I know it is, but I can't help it", to which I said
38 that we would continue to talk more about it and perhaps after
39 she will be able to feel differently about it. Eventually she
40 calmed down and meekly asked, "Do you really think I will?" to
41 which I said I thought she would if she really wanted to.

Figure 2. Record No. 27: Excerpt from a Third Interview

and worker communications are classified: x represents a client
communication, and o represents one by the worker.

The coded chart makes it easy to follow the flow of an interview. Did a worker's reflective comment induce a period of reflection on the client's part or did the client respond briefly and
return to explanations and ventilation? To what extent does the
client initiate reflective comments himself without needing stimu-

	U	A	B	C	D	E	F	a	b	c	d	e	f	g	
13					O			O							13
14					O			O							14
15					O			O							15
16					O			O							16
17					O			O							17
18					O			O							18
19					O			O							19
20					X			X							20
21					X			X							21
22					X			X							22
23					X			X							23
24					X			X							24
25					X			X		X					25
26					X									X	26
27					X									X	27
28				X											28
29				X											29
30		O													30
31		O													31
32					O									O	32
33					O									O	33
34						O									34
35						O									35
36					O				O						36
37					X	X				X					37
38			O												38
39		O													39
40					X										40
41		O													41

lation by the worker? The charts give the answer. Note how clearly the contrast between the three interview samples shows up. Both client and worker in the first case stick entirely to exploration-description-ventilation. In the second sample, communications are almost entirely in person-situation reflection, with the worker taking an active part in stimulating this and also offering sustainment. In the third interview, the worker's

1   I learned at this point that for five years during the marriage,
2 at the time when Mrs. Y. became involved with the other man, she had
3 worked as a doctor's assistant. Since then, she has on occasion done
4 fill in work for a doctor who has provided all kinds of free medical
5 services. This doctor recently called saying that one of his employees
6 was leaving, and asking if Mrs. Y. would work on Saturdays temporarily.
7 Her husband opposes this on the grounds that she should stay home
8 with the children. Mrs. Y. could not see this—he is at home on
9 Saturdays, can watch the children. Besides, they have their own
10 activities. She didn't see that it would hurt anyone for her to work
11 one day a week. I said perhaps her husband wants her to stay home
12 with him. She became a little thoughtful, saying that this might be
13 true, but when they are home together on Saturdays, he is out in the
14 barn working, she is running errands, etc., it is not that they are
15 sitting there kissing and holding hands.
16   At this, Mrs. Y. began to tell me that she is a very affectionate
17 person. But she can't show affection overtly to her children. This
18 sometimes bothers her—though she likes to cuddle "the baby in the
19 family." She guessed she felt this way about her oldest daughter
20 when she was born, but when the 2nd came along 2 years later she was so
21 overwhelmed with responsibility that she stopped being so affectionate.
22 She commented that neither of her parents had been people who were
23 affectionate with children. Maybe this explains the need she has for
24 affection. She commented here that her husband is not so affectionate
25 as she wished he was. When I asked about this, she said in some ways
26 they are very affectionate with each other, they always kiss hello
27 and goodby, she waves to him from the door, etc. Their friends
28 have commented on this. However, something is missing. I asked
29 her to think about what this was. She guessed she felt her husband's
30 affection was routine. She goes to him, hugs him, just on impulse,
31 but he never does this with her. I said this seemed to puzzle her,
32 and she believed it did. Went on to say that her husband doesn't like
33 her relationship with the children, her not being affectionate with
34 them. I said earlier she seemed to be connecting this with the fact
35 that her parents had not been affectionate with her. It might be
36 that because she hadn't received affection, it was hard to give it.
37 She couldn't understand this, though, because she can give it to her
38 husband. Maybe this seemed so important to him because his mother
39 was very affectionate with him. Even now, she kisses him when she
40 sees him. He has always been her favorite child. Perhaps he expects
41 that she be the same way with her children. She commented, as she

Figure 3. Record No. 34: Excerpt from a Second Interview

	U	A	B	C	D	E	F	a	b	c	d	g	
1	X												1
2				X									2
3				X									3
4				X									4
5				X									5
6				X									6
7				X									7
8				X									8
9				X									9
10				X									10
11					O			O					11
12					X			X					12
13					X			X					13
14					X			X					14
15	X												15
16					X					X			16
17					X					X			17
18					X					X			18
19					X					X			19
20					X						X		20
21					X						X		21
22							X						22
23							X						23
24					X					X			24
25					O					O			25
26					X					X			26
27					X					X			27
28					X					X			28
29					O X					O X			29
30					X					X			30
31					X O			X O					31
32				X	X			X					32
33				X									33
34							O						34
35							O						35
36							O						36
37							X						37
38					X			X					38
39					X			X					39
40					X			X					40
41					X			X					41
Total: X	2	0	0	11	21	0	3	9	0	10	2	0	X
O	0	0	0	0	4	0	3	2	0	2	0	0	O
T	2	0	0	11	25	0	6	11	0	12	2	0	T
	U	A	B	C	D	E	F	a	b	c	d	g	

comment initiates the switch from the client's exploration-description-ventilation to reflection but thereafter the worker is considerably less active than in the second excerpt.

When using the typology informally for study of one's own work or analysis of a single case, one can simply indicate the categories in pencil by code letter in the margins of the record. This can give a quick picture of the type of intervention the worker is using and the nature of the client's participation in the treatment process. One can quickly spot, for instance, whether client or worker is entirely involved in description and ventilation or engaged in reflection. Having made this objective observation, the worker is then prompted to consider its significance: Has he perhaps not been sufficiently active in stimulating the client to reflection? On the other hand, perhaps at that particular stage it is necessary and important for a great deal of ventilation to take place.

It is possible to observe whether sustaining comments seem to have enabled a client to talk more freely or think more actively, or if they have instead merely induced complacency or passivity. Analysis by the worker himself of a series of interviews with a number of clients will enable him to spot his own idiosyncrasies. Does he tend toward activity or toward passivity? Is he over-reassuring? How directive is he? In reflective communications procedures does he tend to stimulate the client to think or tend to give explanations and interpretations? To what extent are his procedures varied in accordance with the needs of different clients?

If one's main interest lies in studying what the worker is doing or in comparing one group of workers with another or even one worker with another, it may be sufficient to analyze worker comments alone. This is far less time-consuming, since the client usually talks at least three times as much as the worker.

RELIABILITY OF CLASSIFICATION

The next step in studying the typology was to test its reliability. For this purpose two reliability tests were run, using respectively 19 and 20 interviews. Each interview was coded

TABLE 1. Agreement Between
Judges as Measured by Spearman r

CATEGORY	CLIENT	WORKER
A	—	.83*
C	.82*	.87*
D	.76*	.75*
a	.70†	.70†
b	.45	.65†
c	.73*	.84*
d	.56	.30

* Significance level $\leq$ .001
† Significance level $\leq$ .005

line-by-line by two judges working independently. Agreement between judges was then measured by either the Spearman Rank Order Correlation Coefficient or the Fisher Exact Probability Test.* Tables 1 and 2 give the results of these agreement tests.

The figures in Table 1 represent the average of two reliability tests done in two successive years. The figures in Table 2 were obtained in the second of these tests. Work has been done subsequently to further define the weaker categories. These tables therefore represent a conservative estimate of the extent to which reliability can be secured.

In Table 1, the reliabilities shown for *b* are largely attributable to problems in deciding whether certain client statements should be considered as efforts to understand the other person, which is an *a* type of content, or instead, as efforts to understand the effects of the client's own actions on another person, which is a *b* content. As can be seen from details of Table 2, the reliability problem for Worker E is in part a statistical one caused by the small number of instances in combination with the skewed distribution. Although it was hoped that eventually all items could be brought up to a reliability score of .80, a score as high as .70 obviously represents a substantial improvement

---

* For discussion of the reasons for using these measurements see "A Typology of Casework Treatment," p. 11.

TABLE 2. Agreement Between Judges as Measured by Fisher Exact Probability Test

CATEGORY	AGREE		DIS-AGREE	SIG. LEVEL
	Present	Absent		
Client E	1	18	1	.10
F	5	13	2	.005
Worker B	4	11	5	.05
E	0	18	2	N.S.
F	2	16	2	.05

over judgments arrived at in a global way and is considered sufficient to warrant use of the typology in quantitative research.

A PROFILE OF COMMUNICATION DISTRIBUTION

The next study in which the classification was used produced a profile of the first five interviews in a series of cases of marital counseling. Seventy-five interviews were coded for this purpose by two independent judges. When there was disagreement between judges the material was reviewed by a third judge—the author—who entered a final rating in each instance. These codings, plus those in which the two original judges agreed, then became the basis for establishing a "profile" of the distribution of communications among the six major categories of procedures in the first five interviews of fifteen cases of marital counseling. It was predicted that communications (of both client and worker) would appear in the following order of frequency: first, exploration-description-ventilation (C); second, person-situation reflection (D); third, sustainment (A); fourth, developmental reflection (F); fifth and sixth, either pattern-dynamic reflection (E) or direct influence (B). It was also predicted that person-situation reflection would reach a maximum in the third interview and remain steady from then on and that pattern-dynamic reflection would be rare in the first and second interviews but more frequent in the third, fourth, and fifth. It was thought that early life reflection would be similar to pattern-dynamic re-

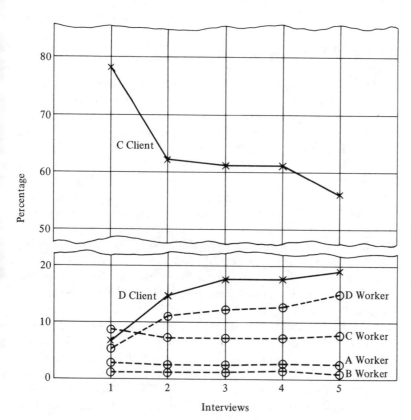

Figure 4. Client and Worker Communications by Major Category: Percentage of Total Interviews (15 Cases)

TABLE 3. Major Category Communications Expressed as Percentages of Total Communications (15 Cases)

CATEGORY	CLIENT COMMUNICATIONS					WORKER COMMUNICATIONS				
	Interview					Interview				
	1	2	3	4	5	1	2	3	4	5
A*	—	—	—	—	—	02.0	01.7	01.5	01.6	01.6
B*	—	.—	—	—	—	00.6	00.8	00.7	01.3	00.7
C	78.3	62.4	60.8	60.8	56.4	08.4	07.0	06.9	06.0	06.7
D	05.7	14.4	17.3	17.1	18.7	04.8	10.8	11.7	12.1	14.6
E	—	00.4	00.3	00.2	00.1	—	00.2	00.5	00.5	00.6
F	00.1	01.8	00.2	00.2	00.2	00.1	00.5	00.1	00.2	00.3
TOTAL	84.1	79.0	78.6	78.3	75.4	15.9	21.0	21.4	21.7	24.5

*Not applicable to client communications.

flection, though somewhat more frequent, and that direct influence would be rare throughout.

Table 3 and Figure 4 show the results of this analysis. Table 3 shows the average percentage for the fifteen cases of each major type of procedure found in each of the five successive interviews. Figure 4 shows this in graphic form for A, B, C, and D (E and F communications were so few they could not be charted).

One is at once struck by the extent to which client talk outweighs worker talk—three to five times as much, although the amount that the worker contributes increases as the interviews progress. This shift can be attributed to two major factors. First, the client's need to unburden himself and the worker's need to learn as much as possible about the situation combine to put the emphasis on ventilation-description-exploration in the first interview. Usually a brief inquiry from the worker suffices to touch off a fairly lengthy response from the client. Second, the worker's increased understanding of the situation, the client's desire for more definitive responses, and often his growing readiness for understanding lead to greater activity on the worker's part in subsequent interviews. Note that the proportion of both client and worker communications falling in reflective categories triples between the first and fifth interviews. Equally apparent is the important part played continuously by the client's descriptive communications and ventilation. A small part of this material relates to the client's early life, but predominantly it has to do with current and recent events.

Current person-situation reflection is clearly the second most important procedure. Sustainment, although quantitatively small, is remarkably steady throughout the five interviews. Direct influence, pattern-dynamic reflection, and developmental reflection are all rare, with pattern-dynamic reflection slightly more frequent than developmental reflection. The fact that direct influence, contrary to prediction, is somewhat more frequent than developmental or pattern-dynamic reflection is accounted for by the number of comments made by the worker concerning how to use the interviews themselves. That is, they pertain to the treatment process itself rather than advice about the client's decisions or actions in outside life. Further analysis indicated that an average of only 0.3 percent of the directive content was of the latter type over the five interviews. Both client and worker person-situation reflection take their main jump in the second interview and increase slowly thereafter. The amount of developmental and pattern-dynamic reflection is so small that changes from one interview to another cannot be considered sufficient to indicate trends.

But what of the individual cases within these groups? Do they tend to be very much alike, resembling the general profile, or is there considerable variation in the work done with different families and individuals even when they seek help for the same problem? Uniformity is not the rule. On the contrary, there is great variation. Analysis revealed that over the first five interviews, total person-situation reflection varied from an average of 9 percent per interview in one case to 48 percent per interview in another. Over the third, fourth, and fifth interviews, one-third of the cases had less than 20 percent of their content in this category, one-third had between 20 and 39 percent, one-third had 40 percent or over. Exploration-description-ventilation shows a negative correlation with person-situation reflection. Pattern-dynamic reflection varied from one case in which it did not appear in any interview to four cases in which it was touched on in three of the five interviews, although it never reached more than 4.2 percent of any one interview. Developmental reflection was absent in almost half the cases. Its maximum in a single interview was 9.4 percent. In a later study, Mullen also found great variation among different cases.[2]

This is as we should expect it to be, for many factors influence the development of treatment—the nature of the problems the client is dealing with, the qualities and abilities of the client, the worker's preferences and skills, the time available, and other variables.

COMPARISON OF DATA FROM SEVERAL STUDIES

It is of value to compare these findings with those of three other researchers who have conducted similar studies. Mullen,[3] who used the Hollis instrument in a study of taped interviews of marital and parent-child problems, included in his report a table combining four profiles: his own findings, the Hollis findings, the findings of a study by Reid, and one by Pinkus; the last two studies used the Reid-Shyne reformulation of the Community Service Society classification (see Table 4). Mullen was thoroughly familiar with both classifications and was able to work out approximate equivalents between the two typologies.*

In Table 4 worker communications only are used, and the percentages represent proportions of total worker communications rather than, as in the previous tables, proportions of the total of worker plus client communications. Note that in all four studies more than 80 percent of the worker's part in the interview is devoted to exploration-description-ventilation and person-situation reflection. Pattern-dynamic reflection (which Mullen terms personality reflection) is 5 percent or less, developmental reflection does not exceed 2 percent, direct influence is never more than 5.2 percent, and sustainment does not exceed 8.1 percent. As noted above, direct influence in the sense of advice or suggestions about matters outside the treatment situation itself is very small.

It is possible that more sustainment actually occurs in interviews than these studies reveal. Sustaining communications are very often of a nonverbal or paraverbal nature. Tape recordings do not reveal nonverbal communications at all, and the coding unit used did not provide for paraverbal phenomena from the tapes. Use of the typology on interviews recorded on video tape would probably reveal a far larger component of sustainment than has been noted in the studies so far reported. In the process recording such communications were coded if they were described in the recording. This may account for the higher figure in the Hollis study. It is doubtful, however, if more than a very small proportion of the nonverbal and paraverbal sustaining communications were actually recorded even in the process material.

Note that in the relative proportion of C and D material Mullen and Hollis find more D while Reid and Pinkus both find more C material. The writer is of the opinion that this is due to differences in the coding *units* used in the two systems. The units used by Reid and Pinkus did not give weighting to the length of

---

* This classification is described on pages 70–72 of the Reid-Shyne report (see note 11, Chapter 18, page 326).

TABLE 4. A Comparison of Four Process Studies

TREATMENT PROCEDURE[a]	PROPORTION OF WORKER COMMUNICATION			
	Mullen[b]	Hollis[c]	Reid-CSS[d]	Pinkus[e]
Sustainment (A)	.027	.081	.043	.050
Direct Influence (B)	.052	.036	.040	.015
Exploration-Description-Ventilation (C)	.368	.398	.463	.508
Person-Situation Reflection (D)	.459	.457	.354	.313
Personality Reflection (E)	.005	.013	.014	.050
Early Life Reflection (F)	.014	.015	.020	.016
Other[f]	.073	—	.066	.048
Total	.998	1.000	1.000	1.000

SOURCE: Edward J. Mullen, "Casework Communication," in *Social Casework*, 49 (November 1968), p. 551.
[a] Two classifications were used in these four studies, the Hollis and the Reid-CSS typologies. The figures are, therefore, approximations.
[b] Marital and parent-child problems. Hollis system. Continued-service client interviews one through fourteen. N = 87 taped interviews, 35 clients, 6 workers. See Edward J. Mullen, "Casework Treatment Procedures as a Function of Client Diagnostic Variables. A Study of Their Relationship in the Casework Interview" (doctoral dissertation, Columbia University School of Social Work, New York, 1968), p. 119.
[c] Marital problems. Hollis system. Client interviews one through five. N = 75 process (written) interviews, 15 clients, 11 workers. See Florence Hollis, "A Profile of Early Interviews in Marital Counseling," *Social Casework*, 49 (January 1968), 39. (The figures are the means of the five groups of interviews reported by Hollis.)
[d] Marital and parent-child problems. Reid-CSS system. Short-term and continued-service client interviews one through five. N = 121 taped interviews, 30 cases, 7 workers. See William J. Reid, "Characteristics of Casework Intervention," *Welfare in Review*, 5 (October 1967), 13–14.
[e] Psychiatric and family problems. Reid-CSS system. Primarily beyond client interview fifteen. N = 111 taped interviews, 59 workers. See Helen Pinkus, "Casework Techniques Related to Selected Characteristics of Clients and Workers" (doctoral dissertation, Columbia University School of Social Work, New York, 1968), p. 176.
[f] Technical and inaudible.

a communication, whereas the Hollis system did. Since C-type comments by the worker tend to be shorter than D-type comments, which often include explanations and interpretations, this technical difference would explain the lighter weighting given C and the heavier weighting given D by the Hollis system.

These then are the central tendencies, the picture one gets by averaging the work done over groups of cases. Exploration-description-ventilation and person-situation reflection are clearly the central procedures, with the other four in a peripheral role.

Two important features of these studies must be kept in mind. First, the first three studies summarized by Mullen consisted of cases in which only interpersonal adjustment problems were the focus of attention, while the fourth study was heavily weighted with such problems. In work with severely disorganized families, for instance, we should probably find more use of directive techniques and also more sustainment. Even so, the core treatment procedures would probably still be exploration-description-ventilation and person-situation reflection. Other types of problems might produce somewhat different profiles. Further studies are needed to test these assumptions.

Second, none of these studies included an analysis of environmental treatment. Undoubtedly some work with factors in the environment was going on in many of these cases, even though the type of dysfunction involved called mainly for direct work with the individual. In other types of cases, in which the problem lies more in the social system than in interpersonal relationships, environmental work might assume major proportions.

CONCLUSIONS: A PROFILE OF THE CASEWORK PROCESS

Research inevitably deals in such abstractions that one tends to lose sight of the meaning and significance of the findings. What do these studies tell us about casework? Are they harmonious with the position set forth earlier that casework often takes the form of a therapy through which we endeavor to bring about some change in personality, some strengthening in the ego's ability to carry out its functions of enabling the individual to live more productively, less abrasively, and with greater satisfaction?

The picture we get is of a reality-based treatment in which the individual is helped to learn about himself primarily by learning to understand what is going on in his current life. On the one hand it is a process of his trying to understand other people with whom he has meaningful relationships, elements in his practical life situation, sometimes his physical condition and medical care. On the other hand, and intertwined with this, he attempts to become more aware of his own reactions to specific people and in specific circumstances, more aware of what touches off certain kinds of reactions. Sometimes he evaluates his reactions; sometimes he looks at them in terms of their actual or possible consequences. In order to engage himself in these reflective processes he is encouraged to talk at length descriptively and often with emotion about himself, his associates, and his situation to a worker who listens with attention, understanding, and acceptance. The worker helps to focus the exploration-description-ventilation process on pertinent content, and through sustaining expressions he encourages the formation of the relationship of trust necessary for one person to use another's help. Directive techniques are used sparingly. Understanding of intrapsychic patterns and their development is by no means unimportant, although procedures dealing with them are sparingly used in most casework practice. Procedures of pattern-dynamic and developmental reflection are used in highly varying degree. In many cases they do not appear at all, in others occasionally, in some with fair regularity over a period of treatment. They always rely for much of their impact on substantial prior and subsequent work on understanding the current person-situation gestalt.

The picture is distinctly one of a blend of procedures with the admixture of those procedures leading to intrapsychic understanding following the pattern of a continuum rather than one that would indicate a dichotomous type of distribution.

This typology has now been used as a research instrument in a number of other studies, as can be seen from the following list.

Chamberlain, Edna. "Testing with a Treatment Typology."[4]
Ehrenkranz, Shirley M. "A Study of the Techniques and Procedures Used in Joint Interviewing in the Treatment of Marital Problems."[5]
Hollis, Florence. "Continuance and Discontinuance in Marital Counseling and Some Observations on Joint Interviews."[6]
Mullen, Edward J. "Casework Treatment Procedures as a Function of Client Diagnostic Variables."[7]
Orcutt, Ben Avis. "Process Analysis in the First Phase of Treatment"—a part of a larger study, *Casework with Wives of Alcoholics.*[8]
Turner, Francis J. "Social Work Treatment and Value Differences."[9]

Turner, Francis J. "Ethnic Difference and Client Performance."[10]

In each of these studies, groups of cases were compared in order to determine the extent to which procedures used in treatment vary in association with other variables. Each of the seven studies produced significant findings. Some of these findings support aspects of currently accepted theory. Some throw other aspects into question. Others that are primarily descriptive have brought previously unnoted or at least undemonstrated tendencies to light.

Much research lies ahead. The typology itself needs further development. It is clear that reflective communications of all types vary in the extent to which they either have a tendency to relieve anxiety and in general support the client or, on the other hand, tend to arouse anxiety. Since anxiety and confidence are both hypothesized to be important variables in treatment, it would be useful to find ways of classifying reflective communications along this dimension. Reflective communications also vary in the extent to which they are given in a directive or nondirective way. Indicators for this dimension must also be developed. Indices could be obtained by combining sustainment scores with anxiety relieving or supportive reflection scores and by combining scores of direct influence with directive reflection scores.

Work also needs to be done on the unit to be coded. The small units used, although good from the point of view of precision, are expensive to use because the coding becomes very time consuming. If a way can be found to code larger units reliably, the usefulness of the typology will be increased.

The value of the typology in environmental or milieu treatment has not as yet been examined at all, and of course this should be done.

As for substantive studies, the questions that need examination are myriad. To name a few: Are certain "worker styles" associated with higher effectiveness of treatment with certain types of problems or certain types of personality? What are the components of these styles? What are the emphases within them? How do such factors as socioeconomic class or education relate to treatment procedures? In another type of study one could take a series of person-situation reflection episodes or a series of pattern-dynamic or developmental episodes to examine what evidence there is that these did or did not affect the client's subsequent responses.

Caseworkers have long and inconclusively debated, on the basis of impressionistic data, many issues that would lend themselves to more rigorous study. To move ahead in such studies we must state our hypotheses in accurate terms based on the realities of casework practice, we must define our objectives far more precisely than heretofore, and we must continue to develop research instruments specifically designed for the examination and measurement of the phenomena to which they are to be applied.

NOTES

1. Readers interested in the full report of the research should turn to Florence Hollis, *A Typology of Casework Treatment*, (New York: Family Service Association of America, 1968).

2. Edward J. Mullen, "Casework Communication," *Social Casework*, 49 (November 1968), 546–551.

3. *Ibid.*

4. Edna Chamberlain, "Testing with a Treatment Typology," *Australian Journal of Social Work*, 22 (December 1969), 3–8.

5. Shirley Ehrenkranz, "A Study of the Techniques and Procedures Used in Joint Interviewing in the Treatment of Marital Problems" (doctoral dissertation, Columbia University School of Social Work, New York, 1967). Two articles based on the dissertation were published, "A Study of Joint Interviewing in the Treatment of Marital Problems," *Social Casework*, 48 (October and November 1967), 498–502 and 570–574.

6. Florence Hollis, "Continuance and Discontinuance in Marital Counseling and Some Observations on Joint Interviews," in Hollis, *op. cit.*, pp. 27–34.

7. Edward J. Mullen, "Casework Treatment Procedures as a Function of Client Diagnostic Variables" (doctoral dissertation, Columbia University School of Social Work, New York, 1968). Three articles based on the dissertation were published: "Casework Communication," *Social Casework*, 49 (November 1968), 546–551; "The Relation Between Diagnosis and Treatment in Casework," *Social Casework*, 50

(April 1969), 218–226; "Differences in Worker Style in Casework," *Social Casework*, 50 (June 1969) 347–353.

8. Ben Avis Orcutt, "Process Analysis in the First Phase of Treatment," in Pauline Cohen and Merton Krause, *Casework with Wives of Alcoholics* (New York: Family Service Association of America, 1971), pp. 147–164.

9. Francis Turner, "Social Work Treatment and Value Differences," (doctoral dissertation, Columbia University School of Social Work, New York, 1963). An article based on the dissertation: "A Comparison of Procedures in the Treatment of Clients with Two Different Value Orientations," *Social Casework*, 45 (May 1964), 273–277.

10. Francis Turner, "Ethnic Difference and Client Performance," *Social Service Review*, 44 (March 1970), 1–10.

11 | Casework and the Unconscious

We have referred several times to the tantalizing question of how much casework deals with unconscious material. The question has many aspects. The point of view that will be developed in this chapter holds that at the present time casework proper deals directly with various types of preconscious material but does not ordinarily attempt to bring unconscious material to consciousness. It is true that some caseworkers have in one way or another secured additional training that prepares them for exploring the unconscious and dealing with repressed material brought into consciousness. Occasionally agencies offer this kind of training to staff members; more often it is secured either in a psychoanalytically-oriented training institute or through arrangements for training with a private therapist. In some training centers, caseworkers who are themselves graduates of such courses are, along with psychiatrists and psychologists, teaching members of the staff. The individual caseworker is responsible for securing additional preparation for this type of work. It is not at present part of the curriculum of any school of social work known to the writer. Confusion about the role of unconscious material in casework is common chiefly because of lack of clarity about the wide range of preconscious content.

The caseworker certainly needs to know a great deal *about* the unconscious: its nature and the generally recognized ways in which it plays a part in the mental life and behavior of the individual. Such knowledge is essential both for diagnostic understanding and for treatment of problems of interpersonal adjustment,[1] for the unconscious as well as the conscious is always involved in such problems.

Furthermore, it is not in diagnosis alone that the worker touches the unconscious. Despite the fact that the caseworker does not try to *elicit* unconscious material, it is nevertheless invariably involved indirectly in treatment. The client's reaction to the worker is influenced by unconscious as well as by conscious factors. Whether or not transference reactions are brought into the open, they are operative and in turn are affected by the worker's behavior. Sustaining procedures often speak more to the unconscious than to the conscious. The client may not be able to tell you how he has come to trust the worker, but somehow something within him has said, "This one I can trust"— or "This one I can*not* trust." The unconscious often reveals itself by tone of voice or gesture, signs to which the worker must be attuned, for often he must recognize fear, hostility, and distrust before the client himself comes to know the meaning of his own feelings; or perhaps he must sense greatly feared positive feelings toward him, which the client may cover by outward hostility.

The worker's comments often are directed to the unconscious even though no unconscious material is openly discussed. One of the cases read for the study of classification offers a very interesting instance of the use of this procedure. The client involved was a woman with a very high degree of repressed infantile hostility. Unconsciously she still wanted to destroy anyone who thwarted her, but she was very much afraid of this primitive desire. She had covered it up with a cringing, whining, self-abasing personality and strongly overidentified with suffering in other people. Although her destructive impulses were well under control, her fear of hurting others was so strong that she constantly felt responsible for other people's suffering and overly responsible for the ills that befell her children. She had had an extremely traumatic childhood in which, during wartime, she had witnessed the destruction of members of her family, including a younger brother, at a time when infantile death wishes can be expected to be strong. The underlying problem in this client's case was thought to be too severe to respond to casework directed toward developmental understanding. But an effort was made to give her some relief from the constant guilt aroused by her unconscious wishes and her unconscious belief in their magical power.

The work was strongly sustaining, in the hope that a consistently giving and accepting relationship with the worker over a long period of time would to some degree counteract the effects of the client's early life, at least during a period in which her daughter could be given help to withstand her mother's negative influence on her growth. The sustaining process was combined with some directive work particularly concerned with handling the daughter, as much reflective consideration of the person-situation configuration as she was capable of, and a great deal of catharsis about both past and present. The client had a quick mind and a good sense of humor on which the worker capitalized. One day, the client was commiserating at length about the men who had been wounded and imprisoned in the war overseas. Her whole demeanor, as she spoke, implied that she felt responsible for their suffering. The worker, with a twinkle in her eye, said dryly that of course she would need to feel especially bad about this because she was there herself in the forces that attacked them. The spontaneous response—"No, I was not"—was followed by a slight rueful smile of recognition and a lightening of the whole tone of the interview. Subsequently, the phrase, "Like in the war, I suppose," could be counted on to interrupt similar self-castigating episodes. Later, in talks about her daughter, the client's childhood jealousy of her brother and consequent guilt over her harmful wishes toward him were discussed in terms of the mistake children make of thinking that their wishes will actually cause harm to happen. In none of these interviews was the client's own repressed hostility brought to the fore. Nevertheless, the worker had spoken, as it were, to the unconscious, and a shift seemed to occur in the client's unconscious belief that her own deadly wishes would cause her daughter to commit suicide.

This case, parenthetically, was a remarkable illustration of the way in which the unconscious can create its own environment. The client's daughter had somehow become aware of her mother's underlying fear and sensed that to threaten suicide was the most successful way both to hurt her mother and to express her own great hostility to her. The mother's unconscious behavior, by eliciting the daughter's threats, had created a situation which raised the possibility that she would once again feel responsible for the death of a child.

The technique of speaking to the unconscious is often used in work with adolescents or young adults of the same sex as the worker, where identification with the worker is encouraged in order to strengthen femininity or masculinity—in effect, to say to the client's unconscious, "You don't need to be afraid of growing up. It is good to want to be a sexually mature adult," and thus to counteract fears engendered in the unconscious by unloving or restrictive parents.[2]

UNCONSCIOUS OR PRECONSCIOUS?

The question in need of clarification, however, is the extent to which the caseworker takes responsibility for bringing unconscious material to consciousness. This is a controversial subject and one of considerable importance for casework, for it has implications both for the education of caseworkers and for professional responsibility. In discussing it, we are referring to work with adults, *not* to work with children. It is difficult enough to distinguish between unconscious and preconscious material in adults; with children the line between the two is almost impossible to draw.[3]

Much of the confusion on the issue stems from the fact that there are different formulations about the unconscious and the preconscious in psychoanalysis itself. Before going into these differences, it may be well to recall the kind of content that casework does reach. We have indicated that much of casework is concerned with thoughts that enter consciousness easily when the client's attention is turned to them. But we have also referred repeatedly to the client's discussing "hidden" feelings, vague and obscure thoughts and memories, of which he had not been aware. We have further noted that clients can become aware of defenses of which they were not previously conscious and that they can recall childhood experiences that they seemed to have forgotten. Certainly they often become aware of feelings and thoughts, especially ego-dystonic feelings and thoughts, that they not only had never before put into words but had never allowed themselves consciously to experience.

This area of hidden thoughts is neither freely accessible nor stubbornly inaccessible. In psychoanalysis it seems to constitute a no-man's land that is sometimes assigned to the unconscious and sometimes to the preconscious, so perhaps it is small wonder that caseworkers too are confused. Freud himself was none too consistent on the subject. For the most part he wrote as if he were restricting the preconscious to content that needs only "attention cathexis" to become conscious, that is, to thoughts that the individual can bring into consciousness merely by turning his attention to them—thoughts that are completely accessible. All else seemed to be considered part of the unconscious, held from consciousness by countercathexis, or by the "censor," which would not allow material that would be offensive to the other parts of the personality to emerge. Even in his 1915 article on the unconscious,[4] however, Freud was not entirely satisfied with this simple division of the sheep from the goats. "Study of the derivatives of the unconscious," he said, "will altogether disappoint our expectations of a schematically clear division of the one mental system from the other."[5] And further, "A very great part of the preconscious material *originates in the unconscious, has the characteristics of the unconscious and is subject to a censorship before it can pass into consciousness.* Another part of the preconscious can become conscious without any censorship."[6] The existence of a *"second censorship, located between the system's preconscious and conscious, is proved beyond question."*[7] Freud here seems to be referring to the very kind of content that emerges in response to casework techniques. Until comparatively recently, however, little attention has been paid in analytic literature to this notion of preconscious content that is not readily accessible. The tendency has been to consider such material as part of the unconscious, some of it at least being referred to as "derivative" unconscious material.

This tendency may have been due to the fact that *unconscious* was defined not only in terms of its inaccessibility but also by certain functional qualities. Unconscious content was said to operate by means of the *primary process,* conscious content by the *secondary process.* The primary process is characterized by mobility of the psychic energies, dominance of the pleasure principle and striving toward gratification discharge, absence of a time sense, the use of displacement and condensation in thinking, nonrecognition of contradictions, and so on. The secondary process is characterized by less mobility of the psychic energies, dominance of the reality principle and the capacity for delayed discharge, a sense of time, recognition of contradictions, and the preeminence of other logical modes of thought.

Meanwhile, however, there has been another tendency in analytic writings to distinguish between *unconscious* and *conscious* primarily in terms of relative accessibility. Kubie, for instance, limits the preconscious to "borderline processes of which we are unconscious but which can be made conscious relatively easily merely by taking thought."[8] E. Pumpian-Mindlin writes, "Preconscious material is that of which we may not be fully aware but which can be easily recalled. Unconscious material however consists of all that which not only can not be recalled 'at will' but also cannot be recovered except through special means, e.g., free association work in the analysis itself or spontaneously under unusual circumstances 'in a flash' so to speak."[9] The assumption is widely accepted that unconscious material is content that generally can be reached only by free association, hypnosis, or the use of drugs that suspend the operation of the repressing forces.

It seems to have been more or less taken for granted that the qualities of being ruled by the primary process and of being inaccessible usually occur together. Perhaps because their techniques have given analysts ready access to both preconscious and unconscious material, their attention has not been called until relatively recently to the theoretical question of whether a given piece of content emerged in response to free association or independently of it.

In the 1950s, with the growth of more concern about the nature of the ego—especially in the work of such theorists as Hartmann, Kris, Lowenstein, and Rapaport—interest turned to the preconscious. Kris comments on three problems that arise concerning the accessibility of preconscious material:

> First, not all preconscious processes reach consciousness with equal ease. Some can only be recaptured with considerable effort. What differences exist between the former and the latter?
>
> Second, preconscious mental processes are extremely different from each other both in content and in the kind of thought processes used;

they cover continua reaching from purposeful reflection to fantasy, and from logical formulation to dreamlike imagery. How can these differences be accounted for?

Third, when preconscious material emerges into consciousness the reaction varies greatly. The process may not be noticed—the usual reaction if the preconscious process is readily available to consciousness. But emergence into consciousness can be accompanied by strong emotional reactions. How may we account for these reactions?[10]

Kris then proceeds to say that there appear to be mobile energy discharges in such preconscious activities as daydreaming, that such dreams play the same role of wish fulfillment as night dreams, that they may be ruled by the pleasure principle and that they utilize nonlogical thought processes in much the same way as the unconscious. He goes on to point out that a good deal of creative thinking goes on without conscious awareness during the "elaboration phase," and when it emerges into consciousness may even appear to the individual as something that comes from without—inspiration. He draws attention also to "preconscious lapses" of memory—temporary withdrawals from consciousness of content that can later be recovered without special techniques.

Kris finally suggests that three conditions may exist for eliminating "the countercathexis between preconsciousness and consciousness": full cathexis of neutral energy, or attention; ego syntonicity in the intersystemic sense, or freedom from conflict between id and superego; and ego syntonicity in the intrasystemic sense, or harmony among the various ego functions.[11]

Rapaport, drawing upon the work of a number of other writers, goes even further, suggesting hierarchical series in which the various qualities of the primary and secondary processes exist in varying degrees. "Different degrees of difficulty are encountered in making various daydreams conscious, in holding on to them once they are conscious; this indicates that a countercathectic energy-distribution controls the transition from preconscious to conscious processes."[12] Again, "It is likely we deal here not with only two but with a whole hierarchy of such controlling energy-distributions. At any rate, it seems that consciousness is not an all-or-none proposition; rather there exists a continuous series of its forms."[13]

These writings provide a most useful theoretical explanation for the empirical findings of casework about the emergence of hidden material. The caseworker does not use free association, hypnosis, or drugs, but he does repeatedly have clients talk about matters of which they have not previously been aware and of which presumably they could not have become conscious without the intervention of the caseworker. Is it not possible that casework promotes the emergence of the less accessible part of the preconscious by meeting the three conditions laid down by Kris? Sometimes the worker merely increases the hypercathexis of this content by drawing the client's attention to it. At other times he increases its ego syntonicity through an accepting attitude and "eductive" interviewing methods, either reducing the conflict between the id and the superego by guilt-reducing comments, or else lessening the intra-ego conflict. For instance, he may explain that contrary emotions, such as love and hate, can exist side by side without the logical necessity for assuming that the presence of the one indicates that the other is not genuine.

Some years ago the author attempted to explain the basis for the emergence of hidden material in casework as follows:

The term "unconscious" refers to memories, thoughts, and fantasies which, upon entering consciousness, were so anxiety-creating that they were automatically repressed, and material of a similar or even greater anxiety-producing potential which was never even allowed to reach consciousness. These consist of memories, thoughts, and fantasies representing infantile destructive and sexual impulses and wishes, material concerning matters strongly prohibited or invoking punishment by parents especially in preschool years, later traumatic events, and derivatives so closely related to these matters that to recall them would involve danger of a break-through of the associated material. If casework deals with unconscious material at all it is only in a minor way with these derivatives.

The term "preconscious" covers a wide range of memories, thoughts, and fantasies. It includes, first, material that differs in no way from conscious material except that it is not at the moment the subject of attention. Second, it applies to material that has relatively little cathexis, either because it originated very long ago or was not very important to the person. Third, it refers to suppressed material—that is, ideas that were so anxiety-arousing that by more or less conscious choice or effort they were pushed out of consciousness. Fourth, it refers to material that has never been fully conscious but would arouse anxiety comparable to that of suppressed ideas if it entered consciousness. There is a vast amount of content in these last two types of preconscious material and it is primarily this content, I believe, that casework deals with in . . . developing self-awareness.[14]

The anxiety referred to is created by the intersystemic and intrasystemic conflicts noted by Kris. "Suppression" is a term analysts sometimes use for the force—the countercathexis—that operates between certain parts of the preconscious and the conscious. Casework experience, in other words, is consistent with the formulations of Kris and Rapaport, and greatly illuminated by them.

LEVELS OF CONSCIOUSNESS IN CASEWORK TREATMENT

There was a period in the late forties when many of us believed that casework in "insight development" had as its aim the bringing of true unconscious material to consciousness. I am inclined to think that for the most part we were confusing "unconscious" with "*not* conscious" and were actually dealing with preconscious suppressed material. The Family Service Association of America committee study of classification (referred to in Chapter 4) attempted to locate illustrations of cases of such "insight development" in a wide range of family service agencies but reported finding none. Frequent sampling by others and by the author of material from psychiatric and family agencies in which such cases might be expected to be found has confirmed the impression that very few cases in casework agencies uncover unconscious material in the strict sense of that term. In those few that do, there is almost always a special condition: either the worker is operating directly under psychoanalytic supervision and consulting regularly and frequently on the case, with help from the analyst on details of treatment, or he has secured special training in analytic therapy beyond his casework training. Occasionally a psychiatric agency offers direct psychoanalytic supervision to caseworkers. Some workers have associated themselves with analysts who "control" their work; others have gone through a definite course of training for this work, where such a course is available to nonmedically trained personnel. There is every reason to believe that caseworkers trained as psychoanalytic therapists (not to be confused with psychoanalysis proper) are competent. Indeed, a few caseworkers have gone on to become fully trained psychoanalysts.

It should be recognized, however, that casework training has not in itself prepared them to do either psychoanalytic therapy or psychoanalysis proper, although it may have given them an excellent base from which to proceed.[15] Certainly, a basic requirement for work with the unconscious would be a successful personal analysis. A personal analysis is not a requirement of casework training, but many caseworkers have of their own choice undertaken it. Caseworkers occasionally mistakenly believe that a personal analysis in itself qualifies them to do psychoanalytic therapy. The ordinary psychoanalysis is a therapeutic procedure designed to rid the patient of neurotic symptoms and character disturbances that are causing malfunctioning. It often achieves these goals, and with it a much-to-be-cherished maturing of the personality, but such success does not mean that the particular features essential for deeply probing therapeutic work have necessarily been achieved. Furthermore, analysis alone is not sufficient preparation for this type of work. Intensive study of the unconscious and of therapeutic procedures and close supervision by an analyst during a training period are minimum additional requirements of preparation for such work. Certainly even a moderately successful personal analysis is of professional value to the caseworker. It lessens hostilities and personality distortions that may interfere with realistic perception of the client and freedom to relate to his needs in a therapeutic way. It deepens the worker's understanding of the workings of the personality and of the unconscious. Yet despite the fact that it unquestionably adds to the therapeutic capabilities of anyone who undertakes it, the basic aptitude for therapeutic work varies so greatly that some workers who have not undergone analysis are superior to others who have had its benefits.

If the central focus of casework is conscious material and the various levels of preconscious material, by what means does the worker avoid going into deeper layers of the mind than he is prepared for? This becomes a real issue only in those types of treatment that involve pattern-dynamic or developmental content or promotion of self-awareness in the person-situation configuration. A first consideration in using these processes is a diagnostic one: How strong are the forces of repression and suppression in this person? If, as in psychosis, the repressing forces are weak and material that would normally be unconscious is already breaking through, the worker must be extremely careful not to set in motion a process that will accelerate the breakthrough. He can help the psychotic or near-psychotic client to understand matters of which he is already aware; such understanding can sometimes be very helpful in combination with constant effort to strengthen the client's relationship to reality and to bring about greater control of his id impulses. But in work with the psychotic, the caseworker should not become involved in the pursuit of hidden material, for such pursuit may lead to a breakthrough of unconscious matter with which the worker is not equipped to deal.[16] On the other hand, when such material is already in consciousness and the client refers to it a worker can sometimes use it to therapeutic advantage.

Except with psychotic or near-psychotic individuals, a worker does not need to be afraid of breaking into the unconscious as long as casework techniques are adhered to. Except where the ego is seriously impaired, the forces of repression provide a strong barrier to the unconscious. Casework customarily uses a number of procedures that tend to *avoid* overcoming repression. Most of these are well known. The once-a-week interview discourages too great intensity and regression in the transference and keeps the client's investment in introspection at a lower level than would more frequent interviews. The seating of the client face to face with the worker at a desk or table maximizes the reality elements in the relationship, rather than promoting extensive transference reactions. Although the worker often understands some of the unconscious significance of dreams and symbols, he interprets them in ways that refer to conscious and preconscious material rather than using them as means to beckon unconscious memories to the surface. Reporting of dreams is generally discouraged, although sometimes when the client does bring them in their manifest content can be profitably discussed.

An illustration of how dream content may be used without interpreting its unconscious significance to the client occurs in the following: A client dreamed that a man fell by her window, and that she then saw him smashed dead on the ground, with arms and legs cut off. The dead man got up and kissed her with "a kiss of death." The dream occurred during a period when the client was extremely angry at a man with whom she was living but who would not marry her. The dream so upset her that she had to go to sleep with one of her children because of an impulse to throw herself out the window. Much of the meaning of the dream was clear. The client wished that her lover would die, and in both the symbolism of the dream and afterward in reality, she wanted to kill herself as punishment for her wish. She was all the more frightened by the dream and by her own subsequent impulse because she came from a culture in which dreams were taken very seriously and were thought to portend the future. It was important to lessen both her continuing anxiety and the magical quality with which she invested dreams. The worker spoke of dreams as childlike wishes, and of the very good reasons the client had for feeling a great deal of anger toward her friend. She then explained how in dreams our minds operate like children's in thinking that a wish can actually take effect: hence the client's need to punish herself. She was able to relate this discussion to earlier discussions about the wishes of the client's small children, pointing out the naturalness of their sometimes wishing that certain people were dead, and then reacting with fear of punishment. The worker did not pursue the latent meaning of the dream by asking for associations or by commenting on the obvious symbolic significance of the man's passing her window and the cut-off arms and legs.

The use of "eductive" interviewing is perhaps the most important factor distinguishing casework methods from those designed to elicit unconscious mental content. This distinction is not always as clearly understood as it should be, but the difficulty is in part a semantic one. Caseworkers sometimes maintain that they do use free association because they encourage their clients to speak as freely as possible. Actually, by this they usually mean that they are giving their clients permission and encouragement to talk about whatever is troubling them. They are not making it a condition of treatment that the client tell them everything that comes into his mind. But it is precisely this condition that distinguishes free association. In free association the patient really is not free to select what he says; he is *bound* by the obligation to share all his thoughts. All patients at one time or another violate this rule, but when they do the content is brought all the more forcefully to their attention, and they return to it again and again until it has to be blurted out. Until it is, they know they are violating the fundamental analytic rule and feel guilt and embarrassment that only make more trouble for them.

The casework client, filled with hostility toward his worker, is under no obligation to say out loud the thought that crosses his mind—you look like Mrs. Astor's pet pony! The analytic patient is. The client does not feel forced to speak of matters of which he is deeply ashamed, nor is he required to produce seemingly irrelevant or nonsensical thoughts. The analytic patient must. *Permission* to speak freely and the *obligation* to say whatever comes to mind are very different things indeed. This voluntary selection of communications not only excludes from the casework interview the very leads that are nearest to the unconscious, but equally important, it also removes one of the dynamics that produces the regressive transference so important in analytic work. The patient who is under obligation to speak and does not do so feels like a disobedient child. If he speaks against his will, he still feels like a child who has been forced to do something unpleasant or to confess a fault or misdoing to a parent. This feeling promotes the regressive transference that helps the client to relive his early childhood and infantile years with the analyst and provokes the repressed memories of fantasies and experiences that have contributed to his illness. Casework does not seek to establish this type of transference.

CASEWORK AND OTHER PROFESSIONS PRACTICING
PSYCHOTHERAPY

This discussion leads naturally to the question of the relationship between casework and other professions practicing psychotherapy. It should be clear by now that there are fundamental differences between psychoanalysis and casework, despite the fact that modern casework draws upon psychoanalytic personality theory and has many principles in common with psychoanalysis. Similarly, casework also differs from those forms of treatment usually designated as psychoanalytic *therapy* or psychoanalytic psychotherapy.[17] These are forms of treatment that, although they do not attempt as complete an analysis of the unconscious as is characteristic of psychoanalysis itself, do explore unconscious material to varying degrees. The range of treatment among these therapies is great.[18] Some are close to full analysis while others, insofar as the extensiveness of their work in the unconscious is concerned, are close to casework. This group of therapies embraces many different points of view. It includes the work of Freudian-trained analysts with patients for whom full analytic exploration of the unconscious is either unnecessary or inadvisable; some of the treatment carried on by schools of thought such as Horney's, in which it is believed that it is unnecessary to go into infantile fantasy life as fully as Freudians do; and the work of therapists who are Freudian-oriented and have undergone some discipline in work with the unconscious but have not secured full analytic training.

The general term "psychotherapy" is sometimes used specifically to designate these various types of treatment. When so used to refer to treatment that relies upon the uncovering and understanding of previously unconscious material, it distinguishes these therapies from casework. In common parlance, however, the word is not so restricted. Both psychiatrists and psychologists commonly use it indiscriminately to refer to any type of psychological treatment carried on under their auspices. It is very important also to understand that psychiatry and psychoanalysis are by no means identical professions. Psychiatry diagnoses and treats various forms of mental disturbance according to the disciplines of a variety of schools of thought. Relatively speaking, only a very small number of psychiatrists have completed psychoanalytic training. American psychiatry was slower than casework to study and accept the Freudian point of view, and currently many psychiatrists use Freudian ideas only superficially, if at all. When conducted by such psychiatrists, treatment referred to as psychotherapy not only does not involve work with the unconscious but often is not even based upon understanding of the unconscious. On the other hand, there is a large group of psychiatrists who, like caseworkers, have found psychoanalytic theory extremely useful and have studied and used it in various ways in their treatment, but who also, like caseworkers, have not had specific training in the direct handling of unconscious material. Some of the work of this group is very close to casework in its general boundaries, although it usually does not include much if any work with the environment. There is also considerable variation among psychiatrists in the emphasis they place on directive versus cognitive techniques.

Among clinical psychologists—those psychologists most likely to be practicing psychotherapy—similar variations exist. Some have assimilated Freudian concepts in a fashion parallel to some of their psychiatric and casework colleagues. A larger group has tended toward eclecticism, with Freudian concepts contributing in varying degrees to the blend. Other psychologists follow Rogerian methods; others rely heavily on operant conditioning; and a very small group, mostly Europeans, are fully trained lay analysts.

When the term "psychotherapy" is used in a broad sense covering all these variations in treatment, it is obvious that it can equally well apply to casework when casework methods are brought to bear upon psychological problems[19]—as is usually the case when the overt problem is one of interpersonal adjustment. The writer's personal preference is for the term "psychosocial therapy" for this type of casework because this gives recognition to the social component of the caseworker's methodology. Psychiatry, clinical psychology, and casework are not identical professions. In addition to being a psychotherapist, the psychiatrist is a physician skilled in the use of drugs and other physical therapies, with more experience in differential diagnosis and with knowledge of somatic and neurological disorders outside the caseworker's area of training. The psychologist often has studied certain aspects of the human mind (such as intelligence and sensory perception), learning theory, comparative theory, and research methodology more intensively than the caseworker. The caseworker, on the other hand, has greater knowledge of family life, of social conditions, of community resources, of many of the concrete realities of life and often a greater awareness of class, racial, and ethnic factors. He also has thorough knowledge of social agency services. It is in their common knowledge of personality and psychotherapeutic techniques that the three disciplines overlap.

The caseworker should be oriented to these variations in treatment and function in the related professions both for the purposes of collaborative work and for referrals. When one is considering whether to refer a client from a caseworker to a psychiatrist for "psychotherapy," one needs to be informed both about the nature of the client's needs and about the kind of treatment that will be available. If referral is for the purpose of enabling the client to make use of deeper treatment than casework can offer, one must make sure that the psychiatrist to whom the referral is being made is actually offering this type of treatment. Obviously such treatment cannot be provided in a clinic offering fifteen-minute appointments once a month, or with a therapist whose competence does not include psychoanalytic psychotherapy.

This is not to say that one would not make referrals to a psychiatrist or clinic that does not offer some form of psychoanalytic therapy. Particularly in psychoses, psychosomatic illnesses, and some severe neuroses, a careful decision must be made as to whether treatment under medical rather than nonmedical auspices may not be more advisable. Some patients get more security from a medical doctor. For others, physical and psychological care must be so closely coordinated that simultaneous treatment under separate auspices is not advisable. For others, the risk of further breakdown may be so great that accessibility of hospital care is important and only treatment under medical supervision is advisable. And psychiatric care will enable still others to take advantage of the possibilities offered by modern psychopharmacology, especially the use of tranquilizing and energizing drugs.

Variations in psychiatric training are also important in choosing agency consultants and instructors for schools of social work. The caseworker who identifies himself in point of view with this book needs considerable knowledge of Freudian theory and draws upon Freudian treatment principles; the more thoroughly the consultant or instructor is trained in this point of view, the more helpful he will be. This is not to say that schools should not offer courses in comparative personality theory or should refrain from drawing upon other theories where appropriate. The writer does take the position, however, that there should be strong concentration in whatever point of view a school believes offers the greatest therapeutic potential. When education is for practice it is more useful for the student to know one point of view thoroughly than to have a smattering of many divergent approaches.

Casework is certainly not a "branch" of psychoanalysis. It has developed its own blend of treatment, resting in part on its own special knowledge, values, responsibilities, and place in society. It is responsible for deciding for itself what body of psychological knowledge and theory will best enable it to fulfill its purposes. When the choice falls, as it has in recent years for most of casework, upon psychoanalysis, it becomes the duty of caseworkers and consulting or teaching analysts to work out together what content will be of value for students and workers. In the end, casework must be responsible for itself.

NOTES

1. An excellent discussion of the worker's need to understand the unconscious is found in Ner Littner's "The Impact of the Client's Unconscious on the Caseworker's Reactions," in Howard J Parad, ed., *Ego Psychology and Dynamic Casework* (New York: Family Service Association of America, 1958), pp. 73–87.

2. An illustration of this procedure with adults can be found in Yonata Feldman, "A Casework Approach Toward Understanding Parents of Emotionally Disturbed Children," *Social Work*, 3 (July 1958), 23–29.

3. Jeanette Regensburg and Selma Fraiberg deal with this question in the pamphlet *Direct Casework with Children* (New York: Family Service Association of America, 1957). Fraiberg discusses specifically some differences between work with adults and with children, recommending substantial additional training for caseworkers doing "psychotherapy" with children. She uses the term "psychotherapy" in the restricted sense, which parallels the use of the term "psychoanalytic therapy" in this book. See her p. 21, and pp. 198–200 of this chapter.

4. Sigmund Freud, "The Unconscious" (1915), in *Collected Papers*, vol. 4 (London: Hogarth Press, 1949), pp. 98–136.

5. *Ibid.*, p. 122.

6. *Ibid.*, p. 124. Italics added.

7. *Ibid.*, p. 125. Italics added.

8. Lawrence S Kubie, "Problems and Techniques of Psychoanalytic Validation and Progress," in E. Pumpian-Mindlin, ed., *Psychoanalysis as Science* (New York: Basic Books, 1952), p. 91.

9. E. Pumpian-Mindlin, "The Position of Psychoanalysis in Relation to the Biological and Social Sciences," in Pumpian-Mindlin, ed., *op. cit.*, p. 146.

10. Ernst Kris, "On Preconscious Mental Processes," *Psychoanalytic Quarterly*, 19 (1950), 542.

11. *Ibid.*, p. 556.

12. David Rapaport, *Organization and Pathology of Thought* (New York: Columbia University Press, 1951), p. 718.

13. *Ibid.*, p. 719.

14. Florence Hollis, "Personality Diagnosis in Casework," in Parad, ed., *op. cit.*, p. 85.

15. For a similar point of view, see Lucille N. Austin, "Qualifications for Psychotherapists, Social Caseworkers," *American Journal of Orthopsychiatry*, 26 (1956), 47–57.

16. See Paul Federn, "Principles of Psychotherapy in Latent Schizophrenia," *American Journal of Orthopsychiatry*, 1 (April 1947), 129–144, and "Psychoanalysis of Psychoses," *Psychiatric Quarterly*, 17 (1943), 3–19, 246–257, 470–487.

17. See also Austin, *op. cit.*

18. For Freud's thinking about variations from pure analytic techniques, see *Lines of Advancement in Psychoanalytic Therapy*, (1919), vol. 17 of *Standard Edition of the Complete Psychological Works of Sigmund Freud* (London: Hogarth Press, 1955), p. 168.

19. A usage followed by Nathan W. Ackerman in "The Training of Caseworkers in Psychotherapy," *American Journal of Orthopsychiatry*, 19 (January 1949), 14–24, and by many others.

    For discussions of the place of casework in psychotherapy see Annette Garrett, "Historical Survey of the Evolution of Casework," *Journal of Social Casework*, 30 (June 1949), 219–229, and Gordon Hamilton, "Psychoanalytically Oriented Casework and Its Relation to Psychotherapy," *American Journal of Orthopsychiatry*, 19 (April 1949), 209–223.

12 | Family Therapy
by Isabel L. Stamm

As a result of extensive experimentation during the last two decades, family therapy has achieved a significant new place in casework theory and practice. In this approach each family member must be viewed within the context of his relationship to all other family members and the entire complex of family transactions viewed within the context of their relationship with the wider community network. Some form of multiple-client interviews during the course of treatment is the hallmark of family therapy.[1]

Depending on the nature of the problem, or extent of need, and upon the caseworker's own theoretical assumptions about what processes will cause change and improvement, various combinations of treatment modalities are used. Some family therapists, such as Bell,[2] confine themselves by plan exclusively to interviews with the entire family group. Others, such as Bowen,[3] may undertake family therapy with one person if the family evaluation process indicates that this is the only way to effect change in the family. While never losing sight of the family as the functional unit of attention, a caseworker may shift selectively from family group interviews to work with a pair (husband-wife, parent-child, parent-grandparent, two siblings), with family triads made up of various combinations of persons, or with an individual family member. The family group interviews may include members of the extended family, friends, and neighbors if they are actively and emotionally involved in family transactions. Focus also may center on the family in its interrelationship with the network of community agencies or institutions. Selection and timing of these shifts in focus rest upon a rigorous process of understanding and assessing the multiple aspects of the family, the meaning of the problem to the family unit and to each family member, and the meaning to the family of the family-worker relationship.

This emphasis on the family rather than on the individual is buttressed by new conceptual tools from developing theoretical frameworks and by experimental approaches in the use of various family treatment strategies. Although one of social casework's long-standing aims has been that of strengthening family life, it was necessarily restricted in its application, since the theoretical framework then available was not systematized and was based primarily on insights about individual dynamics. Practice procedures in many agencies were firmly and exclusively established on a one-to-one basis and were conceptualized in terms of the individual as "the client," "the patient," "the foster child," "the parolee."

At no time, however, were theoretical perspectives of casework practice bound in a completely closed system. As early as 1917, Mary Richmond declared that "the family life has a history of its own" and indicated that it must be understood in terms of family relationships, values, activities, external circumstances, and the nature of the two homes from which the parents came to make a third one. She cautioned that "the worker who ignores these aspects . . . will never win lasting results in social casework."[4] In practice, caseworkers, as well as many other therapists, were led by their clients' needs to try various ideas in response to what they were observing and learning, even though such treatment activity was sporadic and was not reported in terms of treatment principles or related to theoretical formulations about the family. For example, some clients found an exclusive treatment bond with a worker intolerable but seemed to find that interviews along with other family members were shaped to meet their special needs. Other clients located their unhappiness in the family unit, in the interaction between husband and wife or between parent and child. When the client thus concentrated his attention upon another's motivation and responsibility for the problem rather than on the self, treatment, at the outset at least, required a focus upon those interactions on which the couple were so defensively centered. Interviewing clients together in such instances seemed the most insightful way of beginning treatment and of affecting family relationships. Observations, in many cases, also confirmed the relationship between an individual's problem and his social setting—family values, role relationships, and extrafamilial individual and community influences. Such observations and treatment efforts were unavailable to the field and of little influence until family researchers and practitioners from various disciplines began to report their experience and findings about family approaches and dynamics to give a rationale for family group treatment.[5] Opportunities for direct observations of family group interviews and use of films substantially contributed to the widespread use of family therapy and to critical examination of its explicit theoretical assumptions.

EXPANDING THEORY AND CURRENT APPROACHES
IN FAMILY THERAPY

Recent substantial advancements in theories about social structures, culture, somatic processes, and personality now make it possible for each of these theoretical systems to provide a valid base in its own context for selecting, classifying, and conceptualizing family phenomena. Each of these theoretical systems does not stand alone but is open to transactional exchange with these other systems. In addition, concepts from such diverse sources as general systems theory, cybernetics, communication theory, kinesis, games theory, exchange theory, ecology, and various philosophical systems such as existentialism, are emerging to make substantial imprints on family theory and methodology. To encompass the current knowledge explosion, to test the relevance of ideas and concepts for practice outcomes, and then to build an integrated family theory relevant to practice is a massive task that will require decades of practice research and reports from other sources. Meanwhile, the caseworker faces a confusing variety of treatment concepts and models as he asks what will provide the best vantage point from which to understand an entire family and from which to plan his therapeutic interventions.

A variety of family therapy approaches, each characterized by different parameters, are used in the conceptualization of a family and identification of the locus for potential change. The major difference in theoretical formulations about treatment method is the significance that is given to psychodynamics or to general systems theory. In brief, the "systems purists" use a family system orientation, with attention to communication and transactions. They view the family as a complex, interlocking system within a wider ecological field that includes the therapist. Treatment is concerned with the whole interlocking family system and the interlocking community systems with which the family is involved. It is hypothesized that one should not split up the family to work with couples, individual members, or other subgroups. Instead the family system becomes the focus of change, since individual behavior and symptoms are seen as the product of family processes. Attention in treatment is centered on the present and on the dysfunctional aspects of communication and family rules, the games played out between members, the interlocking transactions between family and community institutions. History of the past, in this formulation, is relevant only as it enables the family to experience the present more meaningfully. Improvements occur as the therapist intervenes to reorganize the system, but family members do not necessarily need to understand how and why they relate to each other the way they do. Instead, the family undertakes different action, such as new role behavior or clear communication, based upon the insights of the therapist. The therapist is the powerful new force that upsets the family balance. Family resistance to this upset may be manifested in some maneuvers of absorption or elimination of the therapist. When a stalemate in treatment occurs, measures designed to force change in the family system may be undertaken experimentally. For example, multiple family therapy, which extends the treatment unit to include two or more families, may be used to stimulate crisis reactions by the family, increase participation of all members, and thereby shift transactional processes. Outcome of treatment remains under the family's control and is not specified by the therapist. His responsibility is the process itself and his delineation of the nature of his involvement—or efforts to remain uninvolved—in the family alignments.

Although application of general systems theory has not been made in a systematic way to family therapy, Jackson and other systems purists have elaborated conceptual issues about treatment aims and methods.[6] Use of some central systems theory concepts (such as equifinality or multifinality) calls for a different kind of case data about the family than we get or are trained to understand as yet. Nevertheless, reports from many practice sources show that this approach offers significant insights about family processes and stimulates further examination of therapeutic aims and techniques.

The other major approach has, in this writer's opinion, even greater potential for treatment outcome and theory development. It attempts to integrate concepts from many theoretical sources, including psychodynamics of both individual and family life. It is assumed that linkages among many theories will be found and an integrated conceptual framework will eventually be developed, however segmentalized it is today. Constructs and principles gained from past experience and other treatment modes are not discarded but are added to new concepts. Assessment or differential diagnosis guides the decision about whether family group treatment and/or a variety of other modes of intervention with various family members will be offered separately or in some combination. Assessment is based on direct observation of the family and also on relevant history of individual development and dynamic patterns, of family culture and vicissitudes over the generations, and of family struggle with existing community institutions.

The goals of family therapy vary as does its length. Goals can be specified in terms of change in the total family unit, or in individuals or subgroups of the family, or even in terms of procedural changes in an institution to ensure better service for the family. It is hypothesized, however, that a permanent change in the fixed, dysfunctional ways a family operates will involve an improved sense of self-identity on the part of individual family members as well as improvements in family transactions. Criteria for use of family therapy or its contraindications vary among practitioners, but it is assumed that a systematic set of such criteria will evolve and be validated.[7] The individual's importance for the family and the family's importance for the individual are reinforced in this family treatment orientation. It is significantly broad and carries the responsibility for selecting and offering various treatment measures, as the effectiveness of these are tested. Implicit, then, in this approach is professional accountability for choice of treatment modes having optimum potential and for outcome studies to test the effectiveness of various approaches.

The fact that differences do exist among family therapists might give an initial impression that family therapy is so unstructured as to be irresponsible, with many untested claims for its effectiveness over other forms of treatment. On the contrary, the present status of family therapy is, in the writer's view, a healthy, open-ended, responsible one that permits rich input of theory from a variety of sources and from related practice innovations, with each illuminating the others. Differences in various conceptual frameworks are gradually being delineated, but differences in those techniques used in actual practice are emerging more slowly. Processes in family therapy that actually result in improvement are as yet undifferentiated. Therefore the present unstructured stage of many approaches maintains flexibility and prevents the adoption of hasty doctrinaire statements and a premature orthodoxy.

RATIONALE FOR FAMILY THERAPY

There is a general agreement that the family can best be conceptualized as an open living system. Its functioning is dependent upon both the functioning of its interdependent, interacting family members and upon the functioning of the wider social system of which it is a part. In other words, all members of the family unit—adults as marital couple and as parents, the children, relatives in the extended family, or others, such as friends or lodgers who are involved emotionally in family problems—participate in a complex process of continuous transactions and meaningful reciprocal relationships to make the family what it is. It is hypothesized that the present form and style of a family are determined by processes that have accumulated over at least three generations.

Problems appearing in one family member are to be understood in terms of personal and interpersonal conflict and also as being reflective of a form and process that pervades the entire family. Children may be the victims of their parents' difficulties, but a pathological family system often allows a child's selfish, antisocial behavior to flourish and to be used in the maintenance of the family balance, or homeostasis. In the healthy family, such behaviors are allowed only limited expression and the child's energy is increasingly sublimated into more acceptable activities. A family unit in which a severe problem exists may, for self-preservation, close ranks and lose flexibility in its role relationships or direct communications. If the problem remains unsolved and if the family system becomes locked in this pattern, potential for fruitful growth or responsiveness to new experiences will be lost. Children born into such an impoverished unit will be affected and will in turn place an additional stress upon the malfunctioning family system. This kind of complex spiral, by its very nature, is not readily interrupted. In any family, it takes a certain family system and a certain individual personality makeup to either change or move out of the transactional family system. Members in a disturbed family do not clearly perceive the pattern of their transactions, define their problem, or turn to others outside the family for help. A crisis or threatened change often serves the useful function of bringing them to seek help.

THE CASEWORKER MEETS THE FAMILY

Many workers prefer to begin their work with a family group interview. If this is impractical, the family is asked early in the exploratory period to participate in one or more family meetings either at home or in the worker's office. Observation and involvement of the family at the outset serve to define, or redefine, the presenting problem and help the worker to recognize unmentioned but serious chronic difficulties such as marital conflict, depression of one person, or inadequate parenting practices. This initial family group meeting is the first step in an ongoing mutual process of exploration and discovery carried on throughout family therapy. It is an essential part of the worker's assessment process, which includes direct observation carried on within a relationship with members of the family unit, as well as other exploratory activities for the purpose of enhancing knowledge about, and sensitivity to, family transactions and alignments among members. Moreover, the family group interview can help to develop the worker's understanding of each family member, since each person is defined not only in terms of his individual personality but also in terms of his relationships with other family members. These facts support a broad, multifaceted assessment.[8]

People seldom experience their problems as located in the total family. A family may be worried about the father's job, may have trouble with the landlord, or may be seeking someone to "make that child behave better." Usually, when families arrive to meet the caseworker they are convinced that only one among them needs to do something different. This person may be agreed upon by all family members. In other instances, there is an exchange of blame. The husband accuses his wife, and the wife her husband. Each comes to the interview just to see that the other gets changed. Each has little idea of getting involved in making some changes himself, although he may give lip service to this, if required to do so by the caseworker. No one person in the family can accurately and objectively portray family relationship patterns, characteristic family transactions, and the meaning of the current way in which each one is handling pain or stress. Usually as this unfolds in initial meetings with the worker or therapist, each one in the family group will acknowledge that the problem, or person with the problem, affects him in some way. The worker helps each one to feel the problem as a family problem, in the solution of which each one will have a part.

Omission of family group interviews during initial exploration may be necessary or justified by the nature of the request or significant aspects of the family. For a young person recently emancipated from his family or for a family in which one spouse has persistently remained uninvolved and removed, insistence upon a family interview would be unproductive and demonstrate to the family a rigid, undifferentiated approach. If some individuals are so uninvolved with their family or if family members are so aggressively uncontrolled as to be disruptive, early exploratory sessions may not be possible. Family members may be critically ill or geographically inaccessible. These and similar factors may make family group sessions impractical. Also, should one family member be simultaneously involved in another form of psychotherapy, the relationship of this treatment to his part in family group sessions should be clarified before proceeding. Aside from the qualifications, however, experience indicates a family that can use individual help can profit by some form of family therapy including family group sessions initially and at other points throughout treatment.

If it should happen, despite the worker's efforts, that only one family member is seen at the outset, attention should be given to the significance of this beginning in the whole family system. Is this one family member the family "reporter," or the family "problem"? When the worker relates to this person only, does the family infer that the worker will tolerate, or even participate in, their pattern of projecting feelings and responsibilities upon others, of scapegoating, or undermining efforts for change in any part of the system? If only members of a subgroup of the family are seen, the significance of their place in the family system should be examined: Are they the "well members"? the "care-taking members"? the heads of the family? the members in need who think they conceal their problem from other family members? By seeing the worker alone first, they may hope to enlist the worker on their side in a current power struggle within the family system. They may hope to control, or blackmail, other family members by getting the worker's attention first. They may see themselves as properly the dominant ones in alliance with a family therapist. Or, they may hope to protect the family from the intrusion of a stranger.

Whatever the pattern of beginning, it will have significance for the family system as well as for individual members. Its meaning will emerge slowly but the worker, by meeting the whole family in the beginning, communicates his own orientation and creates an opportunity to tune in directly and more quickly with family members and their transactions, the family's underlying motives, and its means of maintaining itself. The worker's decision to see the entire family must make sense to the family as well as the worker and must be expressed in terms of purpose and the value of their work together. Care should be taken that the worker's decision about management of the early exploratory process does not rest on his own bias about family treatment, his countertransference reactions to the family or upon agency procedural directives, but rather is based on sensitivity to the family as individuals and a unit, regardless of the nature of their transactions. Conviction about the value of this approach should be shared with the family.

GOALS OF FAMILY THERAPY

Objectives of any form of family therapy should be clearly, though not rigidly, defined, in order to avoid later confusion for the worker and family. General aims of family therapy include changes in the family system so that it better serves family needs as a unit. Interwoven with changes in the family unit are changes on the part of individual family members in feelings, attitudes, behavior, and performance as a married couple, parents, learners in school, and the like. The individual needs his family to achieve his own sense of a separate self and in turn the family system depends upon the transactions of its members to sustain itself. Additional crises may require changes in the way family members and the family unit handle their wider social situation.

However useful these generalizations may be to conceptualizing the aims of family therapy, in actual practice it may not be easy to determine how the family may be able to change, what the aims of those individual members seeking treatment are, or even what exactly is going on in the welter of verbal and nonverbal exchanges within the family or between the family and the wider community. Also, it is important to keep in mind that a family may be seeking, or be satisfied with, something other than what the worker believes they want, or other than what he wants for them. Hence, treatment goals are properly formulated with care and reviewed periodically from the vantage point of differential assessment and open communication between caseworker and family members. The ongoing selection of approach—whether to work with family group sessions, with a couple, with family triads, with an individual family member, or with some combination of these—will depend on such assessment and on the theoretical orientation of the worker or therapists.

The specific goals of the family may be such that the worker's immediate involvement may be time-limited. If a given family's aim is to manipulate the resources or opportunities in their milieu more effectively, specific goals within the immediate context may be achieved during a limited number of meetings of the whole family or selected members accompanied by concurrent work with community agencies or institutions toward that objective. A different aim may be to help a family return to the status quo of role relationships—the way of getting along that had existed before a crisis upset the family balance. Again, this work may properly be time-limited. A family in crisis may manifest all sorts of "pathology," but if family members are able to allow direct expression in family group sessions, they may so benefit as to achieve their clear and circumscribed goals during a relatively brief period. However modest this achievement may appear to the caseworker who sees all the family pathology or the potential for trouble in later phases of family life, the family has gained what it was seeking in order to restore its comfort. Although the family system, in this instance, is not now open to further involvement, at some future date during another crisis, family members may return with trust and renewed readiness for further work.

Some families may need intermittent family therapy for time-limited periods during all phases of family life. For example, when each member of a couple seeks through marriage to meet inner emotional needs that a deprived background never met, they may run into conflict at the beginning of their marriage, almost before the honeymoon is over. Ideally, effective therapy should be immediately available to work through the underlying repetitive individual and interpersonal conflicts of which the family problems are a symptom. Many such families do not find or use the needed early help and thereafter face cumulative problems in later phases of family life, including a range of acting-out behaviors of family members and periodic separations or breaks in the family unit itself. Such a family in its lack of well-being, its alienation and loneliness, may be able to use the stability represented by the dependable availability of their family therapist and may appear at the agency on an "as needed" basis. At such times, treatment objectives may include assistance with family decisions that are immobilizing family members, restoration of a shaky family communication system, prevention of an unsuitable role assignment for a family member forced on him by nagging and labeling by other anxious family members, or just the reassurance that the family still has ongoing support from its worker during periods of depression and that family members are not forgotten.

Treatment objectives in some families may be conceptualized in terms of changes in role relationships, as in the family that must adjust its boundaries and relationships because one member is leaving for something new such as the Army, a different job, or medical treatment. Separation must be made possible for the one leaving and for those staying in the family circle. Reentry into the family also requires preparation for the fact that the one returning is different from what he was before he left and the family system has changed during, and because of, his absence. A specific case of separation occurs when a child is removed from his own family and placed in a foster family. Preparatory work for the child and the two families must be done if the child's own family is not to close ranks against loss and "forget" him and if his foster family is to extend itself flexibly to include a "stranger" and accommodate to changes in the positions, roles, and reactions of all family members. Family group sessions with each family permit each person to react directly in verbal and nonverbal ways to the change in their family transactions that all will be experiencing, and this open communication may prepare the way for new alignments in which the child has a real place in both family systems.

In some instances a family group is unable to discriminate between temporary separation and permanent loss or between a positive, appropriate move and abandonment with rejection. Such a family cannot differentiate among the range of demands upon its resources so as to discriminate among the various kinds of support needed by its various members. Therapy may enable the various family members to achieve a new discrimination and thus shift their behavior patterns from disturbed, inappropriate reactions to supportive behavior appropriate to the situation. For example, the gentle encouragement needed by the youngster leaving home to enter first grade or go to camp must be distinguished from the active support appropriate to the family member trying a new career or to the daughter starting a new home with her husband and from the emotional demands and taxing grief work required when a dying person and his family must part.

When the treatment objective is change in both current family communication and in the more fundamental, deeply imbedded patterns of which faulty communication is only an expression, it involves long-term work. Such treatment certainly would focus upon the "here and now" aspects of experience within the family group interview and within the current family crisis that brought the family to treatment. The goal might include current changes in behavior to reduce pressure or to shift the family focus from exclusive concern with a "problem member." But attention would also be given to how individuals, as well as the family group, see their total experience, including the past, and how they have integrated this experience to reach their present system. The family caseworkers, or therapists, moving back and forth from family group sessions to couple interviews and to interviews with one person, report that they often find treatment progresses better by working with various parts of the family at given times. As one part of the family group responds, they may change the focus in order to use whatever interview pattern appears to be the most effective. Perhaps the most accessible family member may be helped to change first; or parents may be helped to improve their marital relationship and so change their expectations of their children; or other parts of the family system may alter relationships with relatives or others in the broader community system.

Thus, treatment aims or objectives determine, at least in part, the choice of focus for treatment changes, however one assesses the disordered patterns of family dysfunction. For example, family group sessions appear to have a phase-specific usefulness for the family in which parental-adolescent interaction and relationships are disturbed. The adolescent is becoming able to exercise new abilities to conceptualize external reality, form generalizations, and develop new, more adult perspectives about himself, his family, and society itself. He has new potentialities for separation from his parental family as an individual. Anxious parents, intensely reactive to these changes in their child, may behave in defensive and contradictory ways that upset the entire family and fail to give the adolescent much needed support in some maturational areas such as sexuality, work, or decision-making. In family interviews the impact of these difficulties on the functioning of both the parents and the adolescent are vividly enacted. Here, the meaning of interactions is, clarified and the relationship between characteristic parental responses and the disturbance of the adolescent is observed and discussed. Information is given about the actual basis for phase-specific changes in family relationships. Family sessions become an excellent practice ground for both the adolescent and the parents to try out and respond to new feelings and behaviors. The family therapist, as a communication bridge, helps each family member to listen to others and to express himself more clearly. He helps members correct distortions, work out compromises, and share decision-making in more effective ways. He stimulates and challenges the family so that capacities for change are mobilized within these sessions, supplemented, as indicated, by individual work with the adolescent and sessions with his parents.[9]

By contrast, after a series of family group sessions the parental or marital couple is frequently seen as the functionally significant unit within a malfunctioning family and may therefore be chosen as the focus for treatment. The initial exploratory process with the family unit serves to illuminate ways in which disturbance between parents is expressed in overt and covert ways and reverberates throughout the family during constant struggles over authority, control, sexuality, alignments, or dependency. The locus where constructive change in such a family can be initiated is often found to be with the marital couple, whatever the original presenting problem was. For example, in one family only positive emotion was permitted expression, and this was required from each one in the family. It soon appeared that the mother maintained a stance of "universal altruism" in attitude and behavior that masked a desperate attempt to control and a fear of separation. Her chief claim that she did everything only for the sake of her husband and children left her angry at their lack of gratitude and appreciation. The children became intensely reactive to their mother's mixed messages and, as they grew older, their many minor delinquencies intensified the mother's sweetly reasonable control and precipitated unacceptable outbreaks of aggressive, angry behavior by all. This was usually followed by punishment of the children and overwhelming guilt by the parents over their failure. The parents sought help to correct the children's behavior. Family sessions were an arena for the repetitive expression of the struggle by the mother to maintain her giving, by the children to fight it off, and by the father to support his wife but encourage the children. Awareness of the pattern did not lead to alteration in behavior. This was blocked for the parents by their perception of the reality needs of the children for care and guidance. To reverse the cycle of altruism and crisis, sessions were arranged for the parents as a couple. Between them, the real contradiction of the wife's treatment of her husband as an incompetent child rather than as an adult was repeatedly identified in meaningful ways not possible in the family group. The husband's part in maintaining this pattern, once it was recognized between the couple, led to exposure of their long-standing marital difficulties and to changes in their expectations of each other. The mother's conflict, rooted in her own early development, was worked out to a more manageable level in which suppressed needs were acknowledged and their fulfillment legitimatized. During treatment of the couple, the load was taken off the children and marked improvement in their behavior was reported. General satisfaction in more comfortable family functioning was noted.[10]

STRUCTURE AND MANAGEMENT OF FAMILY THERAPY SESSIONS

Criteria are not yet established for determining when family interviews are appropriate or for selecting which persons in the family system should be included. It is hypothesized, however, that most family systems are accessible and will benefit from family sessions at some point in therapy. Factors such as the nature of the problem, composition and size of family, economic status, or communication skills are not of themselves limiting factors in a family's potential availability for family therapy in its various forms. Limited communication skills of young children may restrict their participation. Social agency structure may be a limiting factor only if procedural adaptations are not worked out, since it is hypothesized that in most fields of practice family involvement promotes a desirable outcome.

From the beginning of family therapy, it is important that the worker be clear himself in making arrangements about the duration and frequency of family meetings, who gets included in meetings, what will be done if one or another member is absent, what other forms of treatment will be permitted and arranged either in home or office, and what happens when vacations occur. It is vital that these and similar considerations be clarified sufficiently so that the family makes some connection between the current behavioral meaning of its problems and these arrangements. Family members must immediately become cued in and involved in open discussion about how family therapy will begin, what is expected of them, and how this meets their own expectations.

The foregoing considerations are difficult to make explicit at the outset without the worker's having a troublesome sense that flexibility may later be lost, since one cannot anticipate everything or flood the family with "unnecessary" explanations. However, such a reaction by the worker may be an expression of his own uncertainty about his management of family treatment. By failure to discuss the "ground rules" and expectations in some detail, he may overlook the family's unspoken assumptions and promote a lack of clarity between him and the family. Later these assumptions may be used by various family members as a means of expressing their resistance to involvement or as a subtle exploitation of the worker. The absence of one member, social conversation, silence, noise, playing one worker against another, or involving the worker unwittingly in family alignments are but a few of the ways families delay their involvement in meaningful treatment. Resistance to a change in pathological patterns is inevitable; but it may be more clearly recognized in the behavior of family members if the structure of sessions and expectations for the family's part have already been delineated. Against this framework, the resistance underlying behavior can be identified and is more open to direct handling.

ROLE OF FAMILY THERAPIST

Some family therapists, including caseworkers, are accustomed to working alone despite the total responsibility they must assume. They prefer this method and report satisfactory results. Others prefer to work with another therapist. Beyond recognition of some hazards and values in either pattern no consensus about when to use either is yet possible.

Whether working alone or with another person, the therapist will be more active in any form of multiple-client sessions than he is in interviews with one person. He must give attention to the whole family with its own history and its unique and particular identity. At the same time he must respond to family members in such a way that each person feels the therapist's genuine interest in him as a valued individual. It is small wonder that during some phases of family treatment, a therapist may choose to work with an individual or a smaller subgroup of the family system.

The greater activity of the family therapist is essential to break into the family's customary, stereotyped ways of dealing with one another and with their concerns. He requires them to substitute different communication lines—such as listening more to one another, involving a silent person, observing how family members make things work for themselves and also the reactions of each one to changed patterns required by the therapist. Thus there will be less reflective discussion by any one person and more shared reflection about the currently experienced interaction among members and its effects on each member. Each person is stimulated to speak for himself, to take responsibility for his own behavior and feeling (rather than attribute everything to the power of others), and to observe the effect of his behavior on others. The therapist identifies the meaning (or challenges the family to identify the meaning) of what is going on here and now. He also assists the family in observing and describing various processes of decision-making or other aspects of daily family life occurring between sessions, as well as during sessions. As the family perceives and claims its patterns of response, family members can be helped to connect these to relevant past attitudes and relationships. Thus, through a focus on changes in individual feelings and behavior and changes in family interaction, attention is given both to improvement in an individual's sense of himself as a person and also in the family's identity as a transactional system.

COUNTERTRANSFERENCE REACTIONS

The family therapist takes on special meaning for the family unit and for each member of the family. A therapist may feel excluded by a family's resistance to his entry into their system, or he may be helplessly caught up in chaotic or intensely hostile interaction that suddenly erupts in the family before he can anticipate it or decide what to do. He may become subtly involved in family alignments or be trapped in a not so subtle power struggle. Faced with the complexity of family transactions that he is more directly involved in than he would be if he were to hear about them later from only one member, the therapist is confronted by a greater intensity of his own feelings in reaction to the powerful family forces he is experiencing. Anger at the weakness of parents, pity for the person being scapegoated, or anxiety in the presence of aggressive rejection may blind a worker to other aspects of the behaviors to which he is reacting. The family may demonstrate its awareness of his attitudes by hostility or resistance.

It is not easy to handle countertransference reactions in the real family experience.[11] The worker may side against parents and their authority in order to rescue a child, or he may fear impulsive behavior or delinquencies by the child, so that he takes over the parents' role to control rather than understand the interaction. Any feelings of impatience with family goals or with his part in helping to achieve them, or his fears that treatment will terminate should be examined in the context of transference and countertransference reactions. To be free to use himself imaginatively as an intervening force for the benefit of the family, the therapist needs the safeguard of his own heightened self-awareness of his own vulnerabilities. Direct experience in family therapy is productive toward this end, especially if tapes and films permit further study of one's reactions after an interview. Supervision, training, and collaboration with another therapist expand awareness and support frank discussion of subjective reactions, reduce an inhibiting sense of helplessness, and promote the essential process of continuous learning about family dimensions.

USE OF TWO THERAPISTS

In some settings it is customary for two therapists to work with a family, usually a man and woman, and often representative of two different disciplines.[12] The use of cotherapists seems particularly well-suited to work with difficult families. Together they may more quickly perceive meaning in complex and disturbed family transactions. They can help each other accept and adapt their behavioral responses more flexibly to a family's way of life, different in style and culture from what they are accustomed to. They can share their understanding of the family and make decisions about their handling of different aspects of treatment. In a relationship of trust and mutual learning they can identify countertransference reactions and help each other to be aware of them and control them.

Such an arrangement, however, is preferable only when the two therapists complement each other in a harmonious working relationship. Initially this stability is demonstrated to the family by the clarity of their explanation to family members about how they will work together. Within family sessions, they may discuss their views of the meaning of family transactions with each other as well as with the family. They may play different roles or may work out their own disagreements in the presence of family members as their model. Family members are enabled to use this experience of a stable alliance between therapists during later family group sessions. As a regular or occasional part of treatment, each therapist may undertake different aspects of treatment by interviews with individual family members or subgroups.

If the therapists are competitive or have relationship problems that prevent open communication or trust, they will be unable to share leadership roles flexibly in response to intense family interactions. They may be vulnerable to family resistance or other maneuvers. The potential gains from cotherapists will not be realized unless the therapists can devote time to building a secure relationship. Only on the basis of this planned effort can they maintain clarity and definitiveness about themselves and their own messages to each other and to the family.

FUTURE DEVELOPMENTS

At this stage in practice, new researches are underway, as well as relentless experimentation with different models, such as multiple family group treatment, network therapy, therapy based upon Auerswald's ecological systems approach, further application of multiple impact therapy and crisis therapy to families in various settings.[13] Practice experiences are being reported in terms of increasingly useful middle-range constructs about treatment techniques in various phases of therapy or with various combinations of family members. Different theoretical approaches are being developed through practice and critical discussion. New insights about the way the family is imbedded in the wider social system are creating a bridge between family therapy and social agency policies and planning, in terms of what benefits a family.

Despite the fact that knowledge is incomplete about the comparative effectiveness of the different approaches to family therapy and about the ways in which they operate, efforts to bridge gaps between family research, theory, and practice will likely increase and become more systematic. Although principles at the everyday practice level await verification and practice decisions and techniques are not generally well related operationally to the emerging conceptual formulations, the potential of family therapy to strengthen family life today is attracting therapists from many disciplines. A recent survey of family therapists conducted by the Group for the Advancement of Psychiatry found that 40 percent of the therapists responding were social caseworkers. Another 40 percent were psychologists or psychiatrists. The remaining 20 percent were clergymen, marriage counselors, doctors, nurses, sociologists, and others.[14] The future development of the family field along the interdisciplinary lines it is now following should have useful reverberations. Social casework will both gain and contribute in the process of useful feedback from family therapy into the practice and research of many disciplines. In turn, lines defining and separating disciplines may be bent to alter and improve their communication and collaboration.

NOTES

1. For an orientation to the rationale and historical development of family therapy see the following: Gerald H. Zuk and David Rubinstein, "A Review of Concepts in the Study and Treatment of Families of Schizophrenics," in Ivan Boszormenyi-Nagy and James L. Framo, eds., *Intensive Family Therapy* (New York: Harper & Row, 1965), pp. 1–25. A number of studies about pathologic family interaction in families with a schizophrenic member appeared in the 1940s and 1950s. In these studies, emphasis was on dynamic relationships. Unsuccessful efforts were made to relate specific abnormal traits in parents to their children's abnormal traits or specific type of family to type of symptoms. Finally the central object of attention became the pathological family system. Don D. Jackson and Virginia Satir, "A Review of Psychiatric Developments in Family Diagnosis and Therapy," in Nathan W. Ackerman, Frances L. Beatman, and Sanford N. Sherman, eds., *Exploring the Base for Family Therapy* (New York: Family Service Association of America, 1961), pp. 29–49; Elizabeth H. Couch, *Joint and Family Interviews in the Treatment of Marital Problems* (New York: Family Service Association of America, 1969); Christian C. Beels and A. S. Ferber, "Family Therapy: A View," *Family Process*, 8 (1969), 280–318; Nathan W. Ackerman, "Family Psychotherapy Today," *Family Process*, 9 (1970), 123–126; David H. Olson, "Marital and Family Therapy: Integrative Review and Critique," *Journal of Marriage and the Family*, 32 (1970), 501–538.

2. John E. Bell, *Family Group Therapy,* Public Health Monograph No. 64 (Washington, D.C.: Government Printing Office, 1961).

3. Murray Bowen, "The Use of Family Therapy in Clinical Practice," *Comprehensive Psychiatry,* 7 (1966), 345–374; reprinted in Jay Haley, ed., *Changing Families: A Family Therapy Reader* (New York: Grune & Stratton, 1971), pp. 159–192.

4. Mary E. Richmond, *Social Diagnosis* (New York: Russell Sage Foundation, 1917), pp. 138–139.

5. Pioneer researchers in family therapy introduced hypotheses to describe family pathology and whole family interaction. Ackerman made the first substantial contribution to a description of the structure and function of the family group and described his treatment approach to it: Nathan W. Ackerman, *The Psychodynamics of Family Life: Diagnosis and Treatment of Family Relationships* (New York: Basic Books, 1958).

Therapy and research groups focusing on families of schizophrenics at Palo Alto, Yale, and the National Institute of Mental Health (to name only major centers) invented constructs to describe their observations of patterns of family interactions. The double-bind hypothesis, introduced by Bateson, Jackson, and their colleagues, has created considerable clinical interest, and numerous papers have dealt with the concepts: Gregory Bateson, Don D. Jackson, Jay Haley, and John H. Weakland, "Toward a Theory of Schizophrenia," *Behavioral Science,* 1 (1956), 251–264; reprinted in Don D. Jackson, ed., *Communication, Family and Marriage: Human Communication,* vol. 1 (Palo Alto, Calif.: Science and Behavior Books, 1968), pp. 55–62; Paul Watzlawick, "A Review of the Double Bind Theory," *Family Process,* 2 (1963), 132–153; reprinted in Jackson, ed., *op. cit.,* pp. 63–86; David H. Olson, "Empirically Unbinding the Double Bind" (paper delivered at the Annual Meeting of the American Psychological Association, Washington, D.C., 1968); J. S. Kafka and J. W. McDonald, "Ambiguity for Individuation: A Critique and Reformulation of Double Bind Theory," *Archives of General Psychiatry,* in press.

Wynne and associates introduced the concept of pseudomutuality: Lyman C. Wynne, Irving M. Ryckoff, Juliana Day, and Stanley I. Hirsch, "Pseudomutuality in the Family Relationships of Schizophrenics," *Psychiatry,* 21 (1958), 205–220; reprinted in Norman W. Bell and Ezra F. Vogel, eds., *A Modern Introduction to the Family,* rev. ed. (New York: Free Press, 1968), pp. 628–649. Bowen termed such pathological closeness "undifferentiated family ego mass": Murray Bowen, "Family Psychotherapy with Schizophrenia in the Hospital and in Private Practice," in Boszormenyi-Nagy and Framo, eds., *op. cit.,* pp. 213–243. Hess and Handel refer to it as "connectedness": Robert D. Hess and Gerald Handel, "The Family as a Psychosocial Organization," in Gerald Handel, ed., *The Psychosocial Interior of the Family: A Sourcebook for the Study of Whole Families* (Chicago: Aldine Publishing Co., 1967), pp. 10–24. Lidz and his colleagues introduced the concepts of schism and skew to describe marital relationship patterns in disturbed families: Theodore Lidz, Alice R. Cornelison, Stephen Fleck, and Dorothy Terry, "The Intrafamilial Environment of Schizophrenic Patients: II. Marital Schism and Marital Skew," *American Journal of Psychiatry,* 64 (1957), 241–248; reprinted as "Schism and Skew in the Families of Schizophrenics," in Bell and Vogel, eds., *op. cit.,* pp. 650–662.

These terms describing somewhat similar phenomena observed in work with entire families of schizophrenics have, unfortunately, not been related to each other and standardized. They have not been tested when applied to other types of families and have not been operationally related to treatment procedures. However, this pioneer work enlarged the scope of family therapy, both with the family group and other combinations of family members. For further summary of these contributions see: Jay Haley, "Whither Family Therapy," *Family Process,* 1 (1962), 69–100; Alfred S. Friedman, "The Rationale and the Plan of the Treatment Method," in Alfred S. Friedman, John C. Sonne, et al., *Therapy with Families of Sexually Acting-Out Girls* (New York: Springer Publishing Co., 1971), pp. 28–35.

6. Don D. Jackson, "The Question of Family Homeostasis," *Psychiatric Quarterly,* Supplement, 21 (1959), 79–90; Don D. Jackson and John H. Weakland, "Conjoint Family Therapy: Some Considerations on Theory, Technique and Results," *Psychiatry,* 24 (1961), 30–45; Jay Haley, "Family Therapy: A Radical Change," in Haley, ed., *op. cit.,* pp. 227–236; Andrew C. Curry, "The Family Therapy Situation as a System," *Family Process,* 5 (1966), 131–141; Group for the Advancement of Psychiatry, *The Field of Family Therapy,* Group for the Advancement of Psychiatry Report No. 78 (New York: Group for the Advancement of Psychiatry, 1970), pp. 581–593.

7. Arthur L. Leader, "The Role of Intervention in Family Group Treatment," *Social Casework,* 45 (1964), 327–332; Celia B. Mitchell, "Problems and Principles in Family Therapy," in Nathan W. Ackerman, Frances L. Beatman, and Sanford N. Sherman, eds., *Expanding Theory and Practice in Family Therapy* (New York: Family Service Association of America, 1967), pp. 109–124; Lyman C. Wynne, "Some Indications and Contra-Indications for Exploratory Family Therapy" in Boszormenyi-Nagy and Framo, eds., *op. cit.,* pp. 289–322.

8. Frances Scherz, "Theory and Practice in Family Therapy," in Robert W. Roberts and Robert H. Nee, eds., *Theories of Social Casework* (Chicago: University of Chicago Press, 1970), pp. 219–264; Donald R. Bardill and Francis J. Ryan, *Family Group Casework: A Casework Approach to Family Therapy* (Washington, D.C.: Catholic University of America Press, 1964), pp. 26–28; Arthur L. Leader, "Current and Future Issues in Family Therapy," *Social Service Review,* 43 (1969), 1–11.

9. Roger L. Shapiro, "The Origin of Adolescent Disturbances in the Family: Some Considerations in Theory and Implications for Therapy," in Gerald H. Zuk and Ivan Boszormenyi-Nagy, eds., *Family Therapy and Disturbed Families* (Palo Alto, Calif.: Science and Behavior Books, 1967), pp. 221–238.

10. Robert J. Savard, "Couple Treatment" (unpublished manuscript, National Institute of Mental Health, Bethesda, Md., March 1971); Salvador Minuchin and M. Montalvo, "Techniques for Working with Disorganized Low Socioeconomic Families," *American Journal of Orthopsychiatry*, 37 (1967), 880–887.

11. Celia B. Mitchell, "The Therapeutic Field in the Treatment of Families in Conflict: Recurrent Themes in Literature and Clinical Practice," in Bernard F. Reiss, ed., *New Directions in Mental Health* (New York: Grune & Stratton, 1968), pp. 69–99; Shirley M. Ehrenkranz, "A Study of Joint Interviewing in the Treatment of Marital Problems," *Social Casework*, 48 (1967), 498–502 and 570–574; James L. Framo, "Rationale and Techniques of Intensive Family Therapy," in Boszormenyi-Nagy and Framo, eds., *op. cit.*, pp. 143–212; Jerome E. Jungreis, "The Active Role of the Family Therapist," in Alfred S. Friedman, Ivan Boszormenyi-Nagy, et al., *Psychotherapy of the Whole Family: Case Histories, Techniques, and Concepts of Family Therapy of Schizophrenia in the Home and Clinic* (New York: Springer Publishing Co., 1965), pp. 187–196; Jerome E. Jungreis, "The Single Therapist in Family Therapy," in Friedman, Boszormenyi-Nagy, et al., *op. cit.*, pp. 232–238; Jerome E. Jungreis, "Answers to Typical Questions of the Trainee Therapist," in Friedman, Sonne, et al., *op. cit.*, pp. 48–65; Virginia Satir, *Conjoint Family Therapy* (Palo Alto, Calif.: Science and Behavior Books, 1964), pp. 91–189.

12. Donald R. Bardill and Joseph J. Bevilacque, "Family Interviewing by Two Caseworkers," *Social Casework*, 45 (May 1964), 278–282; David Rubinstein and Oscar R. Weiner, "Co-therapy Teamwork Relationships in Family Psychotherapy," in Zuk and Boszormenyi-Nagy, eds., *op. cit.*, pp. 206–220; John C. Sonne and Geraldine Lincoln, "Heterosexual Co-therapy Team Experiences During Family Therapy," *Family Process*, 4 (1965), 117–195; Celia B. Mitchell, "The Uses and Abuses of Co-therapy as a Technique in Family Unit Therapy," *Bulletin, Family Mental Health Clinic, Jewish Family Service*, 1 (1969), 8–10; Alfred S. Friedman, "Co-therapy as Family Therapy Method and as a Training Method," in Friedman, Sonne, et al., *op. cit.*, pp. 36–41.

13. Elsa Leichter and Gerda L. Schulman, "Emerging Phenomena in Multi-Family Group Treatment," *International Journal of Group Psychotherapy*, 18 (1968), 59–69; H. Peter Laqueur, Harry A. LaBurt, and Eugene Morong, "Multiple Family Therapy: Further Developments," *International Journal of Social Psychiatry*, Special Edition, 2 (1964), 70–80; Ross V. Speck and Uri Rueveni, "Network Therapy—A Developing Concept," *Family Process*, 8 (1969), 182–191; Ross V. Speck,

"Family Therapy in the Home," in Ackerman, Beatman, and Sherman, eds., *op. cit.*, pp. 39–46; A. M. Ritchie, "Multiple Impact Therapy: An Experiment," *Social Work*, 5 (1960), 16–21; Robert MacGregor, "Progress in Multiple Impact Therapy," in Ackerman, Beatman, and Sherman, eds., *op. cit.*, pp. 47–58; Edgar H. Auerswald, "Interdisciplinary vs. Ecological Approach," *Family Process*, 7 (1968), 202–215; Donald G. Langsley, Frank S. Pittman III, Pavel Machotka, and Kalman Flomenhaft, "Family Crisis Therapy—Results and Implications," *Family Process*, 7 (1968), 145–158.

14. Group for the Advancement of Psychiatry, *op. cit.*, pp. 536–537.

13 | *The Client-Worker Relationship*

Basic to all casework treatment is the relationship between worker and client. Three aspects of this relationship are of particular significance: it is a means of communication between client and worker; it is a set of attitudes; and it is a set of responses, expressed in behavior. Since attitudes and responses are basic ingredients in communication, these two aspects will be considered first.

REALISTIC ATTITUDES AND RESPONSES

What attitudes and responses exist between worker and client? We customarily think of them as being of two kinds: realistic and unrealistic.[1] Unrealistic attitudes and responses include transference and countertransference. Realistic attitudes, appropriate to the situation, will differ among clients in accordance with variations in the significance the treatment situation has for them. Almost universally, when a person comes for help with interpersonal problems, he experiences some anxiety. This is because he usually has some awareness that the problem lies partly within himself. Even when he has defended himself against recognizing this, it is still present underneath and a realistic cause of anxiety. Characteristically he also experiences discomfort about entering into a dependent relationship. To come for help signifies weakness, despite the fact that the recognition of the need for help and the decision to come for it require strength. One is acknowledging that another person is wiser or stronger and taking the first step in allowing oneself to come under the influence of another unknown or little known person. Such feelings are almost universal, but the intensity with which they are experienced will vary. Anxiety will be greater, for instance, when the client is consulting the worker about matters in which he has a vital interest than when he consults him about peripheral matters; it will also vary with the degree to which the client consciously or unconsciously believes himself to be at fault, and with the intrinsic nature of the matters about which he must talk.

Many other types of client reaction can be realistic responses to varying circumstances. If the client has been either overtly or subtly pressed to apply for treatment, he may feel anger as well as anxiety. The desire to use casework help to bring about change, particularly internal change, will vary greatly, depending not only upon whether or not the client has come for help voluntarily, but also on the nature of the changes that he may anticipate, the degree of satisfaction he has in his present ways, and the fixity of the ways of behaving that he may have to give up.

What the client knows about the agency or casework will also affect his initial attitudes. If he has heard favorable reports about the agency or an individual worker, he will anticipate a sympathetic, skillful reception. A previous bad experience or negative reports by others may lead him to expect the worker to be critical or hostile or dominating. Community, ethnic, and class attitudes toward casework may affect his feeling as to whether coming for help is a respectable or a degrading thing to do and will condition his expectation of what treatment itself will be like. The less well-educated client who has not previously experienced casework help will usually tend to expect advice and a somewhat authoritative approach, whereas the college graduate, who is apt to have at least a speaking acquaintance with modern dynamic psychology, will anticipate a more sympathetic and thought-provoking approach. The latter, however, may have even more doubts concerning the competence of the caseworker than the former, particularly if he is sophisticated about psychoanalysis and comes to casework because he either cannot afford analysis or is not yet ready to commit himself to it. From the client's point of view these are all realistic responses, in the sense that they are either appropriate reactions to the actual situation or else to reality as it is seen by the client's group.[2]

Although it is useful to anticipate a particular client's reaction, one has to be careful not to stereotype. In the present atmosphere of racial tension the client is apt to feel a certain wariness when worker and client are of a different race, but this may or may not be indicative of a high degree of anxiety or of dislike. In some communities groups and organizations that do not understand the true nature of casework indoctrinate their members with notions about casework that inspire fear and resentment rather than trust. Where this has occurred it may take a good deal of painstaking work to convince the client that the worker's intent is not to intrude but rather to assist.

As soon as client meets worker, the latter's physical appearance and manner set new reactions in motion. A young worker may find an older adult distrustful of his skill, particularly if this is not counterbalanced by obvious superiority in education. On the other hand, he may find himself more trusted than an older worker by an adolescent who expects greater understanding from peers and near-peers than from his seniors. Although class differences, including general education, may increase the confidence of the blue-collar worker in the professional ability of the caseworker, they may also make him fearful of being misunderstood and misjudged and may increase feelings of anxiety and resentment concerning a situation in which he feels inferior and dependent. Sex differences also arouse different realistic reactions. A man often finds it initially difficult to turn to a woman for professional help, the extent of this attitude varying with people of different backgrounds. A particularly pretty, handsome, or vital worker may arouse feelings of sexual attraction, even though there is no seductiveness in his or her actual manner. The appearance of the worker's office and experiences in the waiting room will add to the client's reactions. And all these responses take place independently of what the worker actually does!

What the worker says and the way he acts when he says it are obviously the next set of reality factors affecting the client's realistic responses. Before jumping to the conclusion that a client is displaying either transference reactions or subjectively conditioned resistance, it is very important for the worker to make certain that he is not actually saying or doing something that is giving the client a realistic basis for certain responses. Workers *are* sometimes hostile, or at least critical or disinterested. Some workers, out of their own needs, act in a superior, overly impersonal way. Some enjoy a subtle type of domination that puts the client in an unnecessarily dependent or inferior position. Some reveal their desire to be loved or at least admired and appreciated. Some are unconsciously seductive. Some are late for appointments, forgetful about doing things they have promised, and so on. Even the best of caseworkers will exhibit occasional "untherapeutic" reactions. Caseworkers too are affected by mood changes, health, events in work or private life quite outside the particular treatment situation, and other factors. Who of us at some time—on a hot day or when short of sleep or under the influence of an antihistamine—has not caught himself in a yawn that could not be entirely concealed from the client? (It's usually a repetitious client, too.)

This brings us to the realistic aspects of the *worker's* part in the treatment relationship. The worker's responses are not the natural reactions of one man on the street to another. The worker begins with such natural responses, of course, but they are subject to other influences that are the product of his purpose and training. His perception of the client is not that of the average person, his attitudinal response to the perception is different, and his overt behavior is different. A person who is trained as a therapist never sees a client's or patient's behavior as an isolated event. He has become attuned to the reasons for client responses, the kinds of life histories that lie behind different response tendencies, the defenses people use to cope with anxiety. He reacts not simply to the client's overt behavior but to a complex of stimuli that includes possible reasons for the behavior and the knowledge that, even if they are not apparent, reasons do exist, whether in life experience or in constitution. The stimulus, that is, is different for the worker than for the lay person. The worker's perception—or better, apperception—includes many elements that are part of his experience and education but not part of the experience of the ordinary man on the street. To the well-trained worker the cue "anger" under some circumstances may read "defensive hostility" or "anxiety"; the cue "defensive" may sometimes mean "overly severe superego." If the client's response is thus read, the worker's response automatically is different from what it would otherwise be.

A worker's reactions are also modified by the fact that in his training and experience he has been exposed to the observation of a great deal of human suffering. He has lived with his clients through disappointment, sorrow, physical suffering, death, crippling frustration; he has been closely associated with the torture of mental illness; he has read and listened to life history after life history in which the distortions of the adult personality could be traced step by step to misfortunes, deprivations, mistreatment, mishandling, and misunderstandings in childhood. Unless he has remained untouched by these experiences, he cannot but respond with more spontaneous understanding and acceptance than he would have had he not become a caseworker. Herein lies one of the answers to the question often put to therapists: "How can you be so unspontaneous? Don't you get worn out controlling, or concealing, your natural reactions?" The point is that the worker's natural, spontaneous reaction itself is different from that of the untrained person because both perception and judgment have been modified by training and experience. Of course, no worker ever reaches the perfection of understanding and acceptance just implied, but that does not negate the fact that the typical worker has progressed markedly in that direction.

Even when the worker fails to achieve understanding and acceptance and instead feels hostility, aversion, or some other antitherapeutic emotion, he usually tries to keep from translating it into speech or action. He does this for two reasons: because he knows it will hurt the client and this he does not want to do, and because his purpose in being with the client is a therapeutic one and he knows that to show his own feelings will defeat that purpose. The fact that he has been trained to become aware of his reactions makes it easier for him to control their expression than would otherwise be the case.

One sometimes hears the opinion that the worker should never refrain from spontaneous expression of his reactions on the grounds that to refrain introduces insincerity into the relationship. This is a misleading half-truth. To refrain from showing an emotion is not insincerity. If a client senses anger and asks about it the worker should not deny it but rather handle the situation realistically depending upon whether his response was appropriate to the client's behavior or caused by something within himself. There are special circumstances in which it is highly therapeutic to allow a client to become aware of negative reactions as part of the process of helping him to understand the effect he sometimes has on other people. But the timing of this type of intervention is important and must be geared to the client's readiness, not to the worker's need for spontaneity.

Although the responses of the caseworker to the client usually do have a predominantly positive flavor of sympathizing, accepting, liking, and wanting to help, worker responses that are not therapeutically useful even though they may be realistic nevertheless occur in varying degree. There may be irritation at the client who is hostile and attacking, or who is resistive and thwarts the worker's therapeutic intent (or aspirations). Despite training, there may be residues of dislike of the client whose behavior runs counter to the customs or mores of the worker's own class or ethnic group.[3] There may be particular resentment of the client who mistreats another person, child or adult. An especially attractive client may arouse erotic reactions. Very commonly there is realistic anxiety about ability to help: the client may be confronted by almost insoluble problems, and may sometimes be so seriously disturbed that his problem is beyond the worker's skill. Threats of suicide arouse the worker's anxiety. Occasionally a psychotic or near-psychotic person arouses realistic fear of bodily harm. Despite the worker's efforts to prevent these responses from affecting his work with the client, they sometimes do show themselves in one form or another; when they do, they become part of the reality to which the client is reacting and must be taken into account before the worker judges that the client's responses are due to transference.

UNREALISTIC ATTITUDES AND RESPONSES

A client's unrealistic reactions spring from two sources so closely related that it is often impossible to separate them. When we speak of transference reactions, we usually mean that the client displaces onto the worker feelings or attitudes that he originally experienced in early childhood toward a member of his family—most often but not necessarily his father or mother— and responds to the worker as if he were this person. A similar phenomenon can occur with displacement from later important associates. These are clear and specific transference reactions. Less specific is the client's bringing into treatment any distorted way of relating to people that has become a part of his personality, whether or not he identifies the worker in a direct way with early family figures. All these unrealistic reactions can be positive or negative (in the sense of warm or hostile), and they may represent id, ego, or superego aspects of the personality.

The worker is also sometimes unrealistic in his reactions to the client. He, too, may identify the client with an early or later figure in his life, or may bring into the treatment relationship distorted ways of relating to people that are part of his own personality. Although a very important part of the worker's training consists in developing awareness of these tendencies in order to keep them at a minimum, they are never completely overcome and may therefore be part of the reality to which the client is reacting. The term "countertransference" is rather broadly used to cover not only these unrealistic reactions of the worker but also realistic responses, such as those discussed earlier, that are "countertherapeutic."

Problems of Communication Between Client and Worker

The nature of the feelings and attitudes that exist between worker and client profoundly affects communication between them. If the parent of a schizophrenic child is trying to describe the child's unreachableness to a worker who has negative countertransference attitudes to mothers and blames them for all their children's difficulties, the worker may fail to understand the mother's communication, interpret it as rejection of the child, and fail to be alerted to this and other danger signals that point to the child's serious illness.[4]

If the client, on the other hand, has identified the worker with an insincere, manipulating mother, he may construe the worker's efforts to communicate acceptance and encouragement as flattery with an ulterior motive. This type of misinterpretation can sometimes be overcome by repeated demonstration of the worker's sincerity and lack of desire to manipulate, but the process can ordinarily be greatly accelerated by bringing the client's distrust out into the open. Then it can at least be recognized as a factor in the relationship and reacted to by the worker, and perhaps be understood in dynamic or developmental terms.

Another source of distortion in communication is the assignment of different meanings to symbols. All communication, verbal and nonverbal, makes use of symbols, but if the two people trying to communicate do not assign the same meaning to the symbols, the communication will obviously be distorted. The most blatant example of such distortion is the misunderstanding that can easily occur when the client has only a partial understanding of English. More subtle are differences in choice of words, which may be dependent upon class, education, ethnic background, age, region, and other variables. Not only does the worker need to understand the full significance of the client's words, but he must also be able to express his own ideas in words that will accurately communicate his meaning to the client. This does not require, however, that he adopt the client's vernacular as if it were his own: to do so introduces into the relationship an element of falseness that is antitherapeutic. The client whose background differs greatly from the worker's does not expect the worker to be like himself, and might not come to him for help if he were. But there is a middle ground in which, at key points, words can be introduced that particularly express the worker's meaning in the client's language. With most people, simple nontechnical language is the most likely to be clearly understood.[5]

Not only words but actions are symbolic of feelings and attitudes. Facial expression, tone of voice, inflection, posture, gestures all convey meaning, which varies according to different background factors that must be understood by the worker if communication is to be accurate.[6]

THE CLIENT-WORKER RELATIONSHIP IN
THE DYNAMICS OF TREATMENT

Thus far, we have been considering the elements that go into the relationship between client and worker. What part do these elements play in treatment?

We must first distinguish between the basic therapeutic relationship and special uses to which elements in the relationship can be put. On the worker's part, no matter what the form of treatment, the attitude must be a positive one, with concern for the client's well-being, liking, respect, and acceptance of him as an individual, and a wish for him to be happier or at least more comfortable. For himself, the worker needs to have confidence in his skill and in the possibility of its effectiveness in aiding the client. A study by Ripple, Alexander, and Polemis[7] finds an attitude of positive encouragement on the part of the worker the primary factor in both continuance of treatment and outcome. The initial work with those clients who continued in treatment was characterized "by warmly positive affect, efforts to relieve discomfort, assurance that the situation could at least be improved, and a plan to begin work on the problem." On the other hand "a bland, seemingly uninvolved eliciting and appraisal of the client's situation, in which the worker appeared neutral in affect" was strongly associated with discontinuance and with an unfavorable outcome in those clients who did continue despite the worker's lack of encouragement. The more free the worker is of countertherapeutic communications of any sort, the more likely it is that the client will sense that he can allow himself to be influenced by the worker.

The client will need to have enough capacity to perceive the worker in these terms to keep himself coming for treatment, not only physically in the room, but participating in the process. This means that no matter how great are the transference and other unrealistic components of his attitude toward the worker, he must be able at least part of the time to perceive the worker as a person to be trusted. Sometimes in the early weeks of treatment the client is kept coming only by external forces or by his own distrusting desperation. The first task of treatment, then, is to find a way of communicating cues to the real nature of the worker's attitudes so that the client will gain confidence in the worker as a therapist, counselor, or simply "helper." With practically all clients there are periods in treatment when the realistic view of the worker is obscured by unrealistic reactions, but the client is carried over such periods by his previous positive perceptions, of which some part of him continues to be aware.

The worker's good will and warmth toward the client are demonstrated in large part by sustaining procedures. Variation in the use of these techniques with different clients does not depend upon the extent of the worker's actual positive feelings toward his clients but rather reflects the fact that some clients consistently need to have the basic therapeutic attitude demonstrated to them more clearly than other clients do or that a particular client is passing through a period of anxiety in which he especially needs to be aware of the worker's good will. When the client has strong transference feelings toward the worker, sustaining procedures will usually promote the positive side of the transference and will take on added significance to the client, for he will feel as if he is receiving reassurance or love from someone who was important to him in early life. Consistent emphasis on sustaining procedures tends to create a dependent type of parent-child relationship in both its realistic and its transference components.[8]

Techniques of direct influence depend for their effectiveness in considerable part upon the client's confidence in the worker as an expert or, particularly in persuasion and active intervention, as a person of authority. The worker using these techniques must also have this self-image if the client is to take him seriously. One of the troubles young workers encounter in the field of child welfare, where they may have to advise foster mothers who are many years their senior and experienced with children while they themselves may have had mainly book learning, is that they quite rightly lack confidence in the extent of their competence and inadvertently communicate this fact to the foster mothers. Often an emphasis on directive techniques is combined with stress on sustaining procedures. In combination, these techniques encourage and gratify a positive, dependent, relationship of either the real or transference type.

In considering the person-situation type of reflective discussion we turn to the possibility of modifying the relationship by bringing the relationship into discussion. In the types of treatment previously considered, the worker's attitude is really *demonstrated*, even though this takes place through words. It is not in itself discussed. But now the client's reactions to the worker are brought into the open and he is invited to test them against what the worker presents as the reality of the situation between them. In the process the worker becomes better informed about the client's reactions and if they are unrealistic has an opportunity to judge whether they are due to misunderstandings or distortions on the client's part. In either case the worker has an opportunity to straighten the matter out and to establish a therapeutically positive relationship.

The nature of the worker's activities in helping the client think about the person-situation configuration often conveys to the client a picture of what the worker is like; at least, it shows what he is *not* like.[9] The fact that he refrains from advice or condemnation and encourages the client to think for himself may establish him as different from parents who have had a destructive controlling influence on the client. This may encourage strong positive feelings toward the worker based on the reality of the relationship. Sometimes this reflective discussion is buttressed by demonstration of sustaining attitudes and by a mild form of direct influence that encourages pleasurable, psychologically healthy activities discouraged in the past by restrictive or hostile parents. This particular combination of procedures is sometimes known as a "corrective relationship" and is referred to by Austin as "experiential" treatment. Usually the client has at first regarded the worker as a parent substitute, anticipating, because of transference reactions, that the worker will respond to his verbalizations and behavior as his parent would have done. When the worker reacts differently, the effect of the early parental situation is in a measure corrected.[10] The client, responding to the worker as he would to a parent, is now accepted as he was not by his true parent and given, so to speak, a liberal emotional education instead of the restrictive one he originally experienced. While the second experience does not efface the first, it can do much to counteract it.*

* This "corrective relationship" is to be distinguished from the type of

Not infrequently in present-day casework, in which the character disorder is more common than the neurosis, the client's difficulty may spring not so much from oversevere as from overindulgent or inconsistent parents. In such cases the corrective feature in the relationship may be that the worker comes to represent a pattern of more realistic, in the sense of stronger, ego controls than the individual has previously experienced. Sometimes the main therapeutic task is helping the client to refrain from unwise "acting out" behavior that constantly causes him trouble and defeats his own purposes. In this type of corrective relationship it is most important that the client see the therapist as someone who does not stand for an overly restrictive life and is not disapproving, but rather is interested in helping him learn not to defeat his own ends by activities that inevitably boomerang. The work with Jean Emerson discussed in Chapter 3 illustrates this kind of relationship.

An important facet of the corrective relationship is the effect it can have on the client's self-image. We know that children often see themselves as their parents see them. If the client has an unrealistically dismal picture of himself and the worker holds a more optimistic view, he can convey his attitude to the client in many ways. In the context of a transference, the experiencing of such an attitude in the worker can powerfully affect the client's self-image. It can be even further strengthened if through developmental work the client can become aware of the source of some of his self-devaluation and can come to understand the dynamics of how certain experiences have given him an unrealistic picture of himself.

The factor of the client's self-image is affected in a special way by the worker's "therapeutic optimism." This in turn is related to the worker's professional security and optimism. While he can never know in advance the actual outcome of a phase of treatment, the worker does foresee the possibility that as a result

---

corrective emotional experience in which the therapist actually plays a "role" artificially constructed to meet what he judges to be the corrective needs of the patient. It is rather the presentation of a consistently therapeutic attitude toward the client in which the worker is realistic in enlightened terms, represents adult reactions (in the sense of both privileges and responsibilities), and is continuously accepting of the client and his needs.

of treatment the client will be more comfortable or more effective, or both; if there were not some hope of this, there would be no justification for continuing the contact. Such therapeutic optimism can be perceived by the client and for him has the meaning that someone believes in him and his possibilities, sees him as better than he sees himself. Even in the absence of the type of transference and life experience upon which corrective-relationship treatment is based, the worker's optimism affects the client's self-image and is an important therapeutic element in treatment.

Another fairly universal factor in successful treatment springs from the client's tendency to identify with a worker with whom he has a positive relationship. Clients often say, in describing a difficult current happening in their lives, "I tried to think, 'What would Mrs. —— (the worker) do about that?' and then I said ——." And what they then say is often close to what the worker has said to them under similar circumstances. This phenomenon is sometimes described as the worker's "lending the strength of his ego" to the client. It is an imitative sort of learning—similar to a child's learning from imitation of the parent with whom he identifies—that can be incorporated in a lasting way into the client's personality. Such learning depends upon the existence of positive reality feelings toward the worker, feelings often reinforced by a positive transference.

This type of identification is sometimes accelerated by assigning a worker who is of the same sex, a similar age, and sometimes the same race or ethnic background as the client. In this case, however, the worker has to guard against the possibility of overidentifying with the client and overusing the transference. Indigenous workers can sometimes be particularly useful as "role models" but careful supervision by a graduate caseworker is especially important here because of both the possibility of overidentification and the tendency of some technicians and indigenous workers to attempt to impose their own values and goals on the client.

The use of the treatment relationship in increasing dynamic or developmental understanding is an area of casework about which there is not universal agreement. There *is* agreement that casework's handling of the transference is different from that of psychoanalysis, but opinions differ on whether relationship phenomena should be used in casework as a source of self-understanding. These questions have already been discussed at least in part in previous chapters, but they need to be brought together here.

Undoubtedly, the therapist-client relationship, particularly in its transference aspects, is markedly different in casework and in psychoanalysis. In casework, for reasons already outlined, it is certainly less intense. Unconscious relationship components are not brought into consciousness. Since free association is not used, the client is under no compulsion to verbalize all his thoughts about the worker. And, perhaps most important of all, the general way of conducting treatment does not encourage extensive regression in the transference. To put it more concretely: the casework client does not become as deeply immersed as the analysant in the unconscious fantasy that the worker is his parent. Although he reacts to a certain extent as though this were so, the cathexis of the idea is not nearly so strong as it would be in analysis. Likewise, since he is not encouraged to regress—to feel and, within the treatment hour, to behave as a young child or even an infant—the client in his relationship with the worker re-experiences the phenomena of his early childhood in only a very fragmentary way. He is more apt to re-experience the reflections of these earlier reactions as they appeared in his later childhood and adolescent relationship with his parents. As Annette Garrett put it in her excellent paper on the transference in casework, the caseworker does not encourage the transference neurosis.[11]

Some caseworkers, fearful of going too deeply into the transference, have taken the position that transference reactions should not be interpreted for purposes of aiding the client's self-understanding but rather discussed only as necessary for the maintenance—or restoration—of a positive relationship. Such a position arises, perhaps, from our lack of clarity about the various elements in the transference as it appears in casework, particularly about the fact that there are ego-dystonic preconscious elements in the transference just as there are in all other phenomena, and irrational components affected by childhood experiences later than those of infancy and very early life. There is in reality no more "danger" in touching these elements as they appear in the transference than there is in commenting on them in other communications.

Among the procedures used in reflective consideration of pattern-dynamic and developmental content, then, are those that help the client to understand dynamically some of his transference and other unrealistic responses to the worker and the way in which these responses repeat earlier reactions to parents and other closely related people.[12] The client can then put this self-understanding to use in recognizing similar reactions as they occur in his current life outside of treatment. He is then in a position to correct distortions and to respond to people more realistically. We deprive the client of a potent source of help in his struggle toward realistic living if we neglect to use the vivid experiences that occur between him and his caseworker.[13]

NOTES

1. Annette Garrett points out the importance of this distinction in her paper "The Worker-Client Relationship," in Howard J. Parad, ed., *Ego Psychology in Dynamic Casework* (New York: Family Service Association of America, 1958), pp. 53–54, 59–60.

2. Variation among groups, especially among different classes in their attitudes toward and expectations of treatment agencies, has been a subject of interest in recent years and is often touched on in articles on work with poverty groups, blue collar workers and ethnic minorities. For the most part these articles are speculative and impressionistic rather than definitive, but they do serve to alert us to attitudes that may exist. See H. Aronson and B. Overall, "Treatment Expectations of Patients in Two Social Classes," *Social Work*, 11 (January 1966), 35–41; Alejandro Garcia, "The Chicano and Social Work," *Social Casework*, 52 (May 1971), 274–278; Robert Gould, "Dr. Strangeclass: Or How I Stopped Worrying about Theory and Began Treating the Blue-Collar Worker," *American Journal of Orthopsychiatry*, 37 (January 1967), 78–86; Faustina Ramirez Knoll, "Casework Services for Mexican Americans," *Social Casework*, 52 (May 1971), 279–284; Frederick C. Redlich, August B. Hollingshead, and Elizabeth Bellis, "Social Class Differences in Attitudes Toward Psychiatry," *American Journal of Orthopsychiatry*, 25 (January 1955), 60–70; John Spiegel, "Some Cultural Aspects of Transference and Counter-Transference," in Jules Masserman, ed., *Individual and Familial Dynamics* (New York: Grune & Stratton, 1959), pp. 160–182.

3. There are many warnings against this in the literature, going back at least to the twenties if not earlier. Mary Richmond dealt with it briefly in *Social Diagnosis* (New York: Russell Sage Foundation, 1917), pp. 97–98. To what extent recognition of this type of bias has modified it in graduate social workers is not known. The writer is not aware of studies in which such bias in graduate caseworkers has been established as a significantly repetitive factor, though it is often hypothesized. The study by August B. Hollingshead and Frederick C. Redlich, *Social Class and Mental Illness* (New York: John Wiley & Sons, 1958), indicated that the psychiatrists involved in the study not infrequently responded to their patients in terms of their subjective reactions to the patient's social class. This may or may not be equally true of caseworkers.

Scott M. Briar's carefully designed doctoral study, which was reported in his article "Use of Theory in Studying Effects of Client Social Class on Students' Judgments," *Social Work*, 6 (July 1961), 91–97, indicates that the judgments of social work students were influenced by knowledge of the client's class, but Briar did not find a consistent inverse relationship (as had been hypothesized) between the student's own responses versus his predictions of client's responses, and the distance in social class background between worker and client. He did find a slight tendency for students to assume greater similarity between themselves and the client when middle rather than lower class status was attributed to the client. The study did not attempt to evaluate whether the judgments themselves were or were not justified in view of the client's ascribed class status. It is possible that the great emphasis in casework training over the past thirty years on acceptance of differences and on self-determination for the client has acted as a safeguard against at least the grosser forms of class bias entering the treatment process.

Barbara Shannon in "Implications of White Racism for Social Work Practice," *Social Casework*, 51 (May 1970), 270–276, warns against hidden antagonism due "to racism." Charles Grosser's "Local Residents as Mediators Between Middle-Class Professional Workers and Lower-Class Clients," *Social Service Review*, 40 (March 1966), 56–63, deals with the question of bias in indigenous workers. Salvador Minuchin and M. Montalvo in "Techniques for Working with Disorganized Low Socio-Economic Families," *American Journal of Orthopsychiatry*, 37 (October 1967) 880–887, deal with the subject.

4. For a discussion of this in work with foster parents see Robert Nadel, "Interviewing Style and Foster Parents' Verbal Accessibility," *Child Welfare*, 46 (April 1967), 207–213.

5. Camille Jeffers is quite specific about this. See her *Living Poor* (Ann Arbor, Mich.: Ann Arbor Publishers, 1967), p. 122.

6. See note 16 in Chapter 2.

7. Lillian Ripple, Ernestina Alexander, and Bernice Polemis, *Motivation,*

Capacity and Opportunity, Social Service Monographs (Chicago: University of Chicago Press, 1964).

8. For an illustration see Leopold Bellak, "Psychiatric Aspects of Tuberculosis," *Social Casework*, 31 (May 1950), 183–189.

9. John Spiegel puts this in the language of role theory in "The Social Roles of Doctor and Patient in Psychoanalysis and Psychotherapy," *Psychiatry*, 17 (November 1954), 369–376.

10. For discussion of this see Lucille N. Austin, "Trends in Differential Treatment in Social Casework," *Journal of Social Casework*, 29 (June 1948), 203–211, and Otilda Krug, "The Dynamic Use of the Ego Functions in Casework Practice," *Social Casework*, 36 (December 1955), 443–450.

11. Garrett, *op. cit.*, pp. 56–58.

12. For discussion and illustrations see: Gerald Appel, "Some Aspects of Transference and Counter-Transference in Marital Counseling," *Social Casework*, 47 (May 1966), 307–312; Rubin Blanck, "The Case for Individual Treatment," *Social Casework*, 47 (February 1965), 70–74; Andrew Watson, "Reality Testing and Transference in Psychotherapy," *Smith College Studies in Social Work*, 36 (June 1966), 191–209.

13. Additional special aspects of the casework relationship are discussed in the following: Pauline Cohen and Merton Krause, *Casework with Wives of Alcoholics* (New York: Family Service Association of America, 1971), p. 48; Pauline Lide, "Dynamic Mental Representation: An Analysis of the Empathic Process," *Social Casework*, 47 (March 1966), 146–151; Pauline Lide, "An Experimental Study of Empathic Functioning," *Social Service Review*, 41 (March 1967), 23–30; I. E. Molyneux, "A Study of Resistance in the Casework Relationship," *The Social Worker*, 34 (November 1966), 217–223; Allyn Zanger, "A Study of Factors Related to Clinical Empathy," *Smith College Studies in Social Work*, 38 (February 1968), 116–131.

Part Three

DIAGNOSTIC
UNDERSTANDING AND
THE TREATMENT PROCESS

14 | *The Psychosocial Study*

Thus far we have considered the frame of reference concerning the nature of the individual and his situation upon which casework treatment rests (Chapters 2 and 3) and have discussed the various technical means by which the worker endeavors to enable the client to bring improvement in his life (Chapters 4 through 13). We must now turn to the more specific question of how treatment is related to the needs of a particular individual confronted by an adaptational problem.

Treatment planning must rest, first, upon thorough knowledge of the means of treatment—their nature and consequences, and other factors that determine their suitability—and second, upon thorough knowledge of the individual who is seeking treatment, his current situation, interactions within the person-situation system and the variety of factors that have contributed causally to his predicament. In other words, so that the various means of helping may be drawn upon in the most suitable way to meet the needs of a particular person, there must be psychosocial study, followed by a diagnostic formulation leading to the planning of treatment. This planning in turn will include both the goals and the procedures of therapy.

THE NATURE AND PURPOSE OF PSYCHOSOCIAL STUDY

Many factors converge in the making of the series of decisions that determine a plan of treatment. This is by no means a single question that can be settled at the outset of the work. In some instances, especially in rather uncomplicated cases, the major outlines can be planned at the conclusion of an exploratory period, and these actually become the mode of treatment to be followed. More typically, only the early phases of treatment and perhaps some general guides can be foreseen at the outset, with later decisions being made on the basis of new material that emerges during the treatment process. Indeed, the way the client uses treatment in the early phases is one of the most important considerations in later periods. Major trends, to be sure, can usually be outlined further ahead than more detailed steps, but flexibility is an essential ingredient of all skillful treatment, making it sensitive not only to actual changes in the situation but also to new understanding that the worker gains as treatment proceeds. It must also be noted that the worker cannot wait until the end of the psychosocial study and diagnostic process to initiate treatment. In actuality, treatment begins the moment the client meets the worker. But the first couple of interviews usually include a good deal of ventilation and support with only cautious use of other approaches until enough is known for treatment to take more definite direction.

The idea of planning treatment and treatment goals raises serious value questions in the minds of some casework practitioners.[1] If you truly believe in the importance of self-determination for a client, they say, how can you talk about *planning* treatment for him? Isn't this something that is up to him alone? Some solve the dilemma by seeing agencies as offering certain types of services that the client chooses either to use or to reject. This, however, does not really solve the problem, but only circumvents it, for it is the agencies that make the choices, deciding both what services to offer and what constitutes eligibility for them. A client is not given a foster home for a child just because he wants one, nor is he allowed to choose the type of foster home his child is placed in, any more than he can decide to be given financial assistance. He is not likely to know whether his superego needs strengthening or liberalizing, or whether he should be helped to see his children's needs more clearly or should work on the question of why, if he does see them clearly, he cannot put this understanding into constructive action.

The truth that lies at the opposite extreme, however, is that it is not only inadvisable but almost impossible to impose treatment upon a client. Except in certain aspects of protective work, when a worker may be doing something against the client's will

—taking a seriously psychotic woman to a hospital, placing a child who is being badly mistreated, reporting a delinquent's parole violations to the court—the use of treatment always involves the exercise of choice by the client.

There has been considerable misunderstanding about this point in recent years in connection with the offering of casework service to public assistance clients. Very few public assistance agencies are staffed primarily by caseworkers with training or provide adequate in-service training programs. Although some supervisors and workers are doing as good a job as is possible within the limits of inadequate assistance, meager rehabilitative resources, and major bureaucratic obstacles, many others not only lack knowledge of how to give constructive help but also work in a way that is completely contrary to casework principles. This sometimes includes using their power to control assistance as a club to require clients to accept their advice or directives concerning aspects of their personal lives. Unfortunately, these workers sometimes are known as caseworkers because there is as yet very little legal protection of that name. Not only clients but members of other professions and sometimes even social workers who are not caseworkers are confused by this and therefore find it hard to believe that casework has the deep commitment that it does have to the principle of respecting the client's right, if he so desires, to reject casework service as a whole or any particular goal of treatment that the worker may espouse.*

In actual fact, the client can and often does negate the worker's efforts. The worker can offer reassurance with all his heart, but it will not become reassurance to the client until he is willing to accept it—to believe in it. The worker can suggest and advise, but it is the client who chooses whether or not to follow the advice. The worker can try to stimulate the client to think about his situation or himself; only the client can *do* it. Interpretations are futile unless the client is willing to consider their validity. During the course of treatment, methods often have to be changed from one approach to another simply because

* A battle is currently underway on this issue because of recent federal legislation which is being interpreted to mean that assistance can be reduced as a penalty for refusing counseling.

the client is unwilling to make use of the kind of help the worker has first offered or shows that he wants to use something the worker has not yet offered.

The worker does have the responsibility of deciding what treatment to *offer*. Just as he would be wrong to propose a foster home for a child who needs the care of a treatment institution, or to try to induce a mother to go to work who is needed at home to care for her children, so he would be wrong to encourage greater impulsiveness and "self-expression" in a person whose troubles are rooted in an acting-out type of character disorder.

The worker is responsible for what he offers, but the client exercises control over what he accepts. Thus, except for techniques of active intervention, no treatment can be successful if the client lacks *motivation* to use it. Motivation sometimes exists spontaneously in the client. At other times, the creation of motivation is an early task of treatment during the exploratory period.

How, then, does the worker decide what kind of treatment to offer the client? Two preliminary steps are essential: the psychosocial study and the diagnostic process. In this chapter we shall discuss the psychosocial study, and in the next we will consider problems involved in diagnosis.

The term "psychosocial study"—or social study as it is more commonly known—refers to the early period during which observations are gathered upon which treatment is initially based. In long-term treatment this usually takes four to six interviews. If treatment is likely to be limited to eight or ten interviews, less extensive exploration takes place and the initial decisions about treatment may be made after one or two interviews.[2] In crisis treatment or other extremely brief therapy, such decisions tend to be made in the first interview. This early period is not one in which the client is simply studied and receives no help. Certain types of treatment steps can be taken on the basis of immediate knowledge or impressions. Similarly, the initial study by no means completes the worker's understanding of the client. Each interview adds its increment as new aspects of the person and the person-situation gestalt emerge. The worker is dealing with a living, changing process. Feelings change, new events constantly occur, people reveal themselves more fully as trust grows.

It is extremely important to be clear about the difference between psychosocial study and diagnosis. Psychosocial study is a process of observation and classification of the facts observed about a client and his situation, with the purpose of securing as much information as is needed to understand the client and his problem and to guide treatment wisely. Diagnosis, on the other hand, is an opinion—a professional opinion. It represents the *thinking* of the worker *about* the facts and will be strongly influenced by the frame of reference he uses to guide him in understanding their meaning. Mary Richmond once quoted an apt statement from Dr. Richard Cabot: "In social study you open your eyes and look, in diagnosis you close them and think."[3] If these two processes are not kept separate in the worker's mind, he is in great danger of skewing the facts to fit the theory, asking questions in such a way that answers fitting a priori assumptions are bound to emerge. This is not to say that during the study process the worker will not be reaching for diagnostic understanding in his own mind. Indeed, preliminary formulations help him know what areas need further exploration. Nevertheless, if the worker is clear about the difference between the two processes, he will guard against "contamination" of one by the other and will make a clear distinction between his facts and his opinions.

THE SCOPE OF THE STUDY

A diagnosis can be no better than the facts it rests on.[4] The worker needs, then, to secure the information pertinent to treatment as early as possible. In the beginning interviews, however, the worker is also trying to put the client at ease, sometimes to offer at least temporary alleviation of his distress, and always to begin establishing a relationship of trust. The acquiring of information is thus only one of several objectives at the start.

The client is usually ready to talk about his difficulties as he sees them. He also usually spontaneously speaks of, or readily responds to, the worker's inquiries about what he thinks brought his present dilemma into being, what he himself has tried to do about his trouble, and what he hopes can be done about it as a result of his coming to the worker. But in most instances the worker will need to go further. Are there other problems of which the client is not aware or does not speak? What factors beyond those of which he is aware are contributing to the difficulty? What is the client himself like? Are some of his characteristics contributing to the difficulty? What assets are there in his personality and in the total client-situation gestalt that can contribute to lessening of his discomfort or attainment of his goals?

Several questions immediately arise. First, how does the worker know what lines of inquiry to follow and how far to go? Second, how does he go about it? By questions? By following a sort of outline? By just letting the client talk?

People come to a caseworker with a specific problem. "My child is irritable, mopes, and pays no attention to what I say." Or "Since my husband died a year ago everything has gone wrong. Now the rent is going up. I don't want to be a burden to any of the children." Or "We just can't understand each other any more—every time I open my mouth she takes the other side." Always there is an interpersonal or a person-situation gestalt involved. Or to put it another way, certain systems are involved—the husband-wife system, the family system, the parent-child system, health, school, work. A set of interacting forces is at work and what goes on in one system may be affecting what happens in another. The worker listens to the client receptively but not passively. His knowledge of factors that often contribute to different kinds of dilemmas immediately suggests the various systems that may be pertinent. In a marital problem, for instance, the worker is concerned first with the interactions between the partners. Then he needs understanding of the major features of the two personalities. Children are also part of the picture. Since marital problems are so often complicated by interactions with relatives, the worker is alert to references to members of the extended family, either currently or in earlier life, and uses these to inquire about major relationships. Factors in the husband's or wife's employment system are often of significance. Friendships may be important.

A parent-child problem would involve some of these same

systems plus additional ones, especially school. In the case of the older person facing a decision about living arrangements, not only are immediate family relationships important, but also the families of the children (if living with them is at issue), friends and neighbors, the housing situation, the client's health, resources for alternative living arrangements. Each type of problem that emerges in early interviews suggests to the worker avenues that may need to be explored.

The fact-gathering process receives its impetus and direction from two sources: the client's desire to tell about his difficulties and the worker's desire to understand how they came about and what capacities exist for dealing with them. When the problem appears to be one of interpersonal relationships, the current tendency in most casework settings is to follow a fluid form of interviewing that combines these two sets of interests. By encouraging the client to follow trends of thought related to his problem as they come naturally to his mind and by leading him to develop them further, the worker gains access with relative ease to the elaboration of significant matters. At the same time, the worker must fill the inevitable gaps in this type of exploration by directing the interview along lines that the client does not spontaneously introduce. He can do so easily when such matters are "adjacent" to subjects the client is discussing or flow logically from them, or he can explore them when the client has temporarily exhausted his spontaneous productions and is ready to follow the therapist's lead. "You have never told me much about your father." "Set me straight on your schooling—where were you when you finished?" "You haven't said much about your work—what do you do and how do you like it?" The caseworker needs to take a fairly active part in the gathering of information, for he cannot depend on free association to lead to significant material. Clients cannot be expected to know what information is needed, nor can they free themselves, without help, from reluctance to discuss painful material that may be highly relevant to the understanding of their troubles.

In areas in which problems appear, it is important to inquire not only about the details of the problem but also about the client's own participation in the difficulty. It is not enough for the client to say, "My wife is a spendthrift"; the worker needs to follow up with specific questions: "In what way? Could you give me an illustration?" By getting detailed accounts of what happens in the client's household when there is a conflict about money, the worker can evaluate to what extent overspending is actually occurring, what sorts of situations either within the wife or in the interaction between husband and wife touch it off, what purpose it may serve in the marital relationship, the part the husband's response to the overspending may play in its repetition, and so on.

The best way to secure a clear picture of interaction is not to ask direct questions but rather to encourage the client—or if it is a joint or family interview, the clients—to describe things as they have happened. This tends to bring a good deal of ventilation and enables the client to relive the situation with details of what each partner said and did. This style of interviewing does not interrupt the natural flow of the client's thoughts and yet allows the worker to arrive at his own conclusions about the nature of the interplay.

If initial evidence indicates that there is little or no basis for a husband's accusations, the worker must look for the circumstances under which the husband believes it to be true, what within himself or in the marital interaction touches it off, what purpose his unrealistic reaction serves. An important aspect of these explorations is their revelation of how the client tries to cope with whatever difficulty he is experiencing, knowledge that is especially useful in throwing light on the question of his ego functioning.

Throughout the interview the worker is also observing carefully the client's reactions in response to the treatment situation. How much does he demand of the worker and what is the nature of his demands? How sensitive is he to criticism? What defenses does he use? How accurately is he aware of the worker's reactions? To what extent and under what circumstances is he warm, hostile, remote toward the worker? These observations throw light particularly on the nature of the client's demands of the world and on his ego and superego functioning.

An important area of the social study that should not be neglected is the client's physical health. The worker must be alert not only to what the client says about his health but also to other signs that might point in the direction of illness. Appearance, of course, tells a good deal. Other indications of illness that the client may not fully appreciate appear in references to poor appetite, tiredness, or trouble sleeping, as well as to mild symptomatology such as pain, swelling, rashes, indigestion, dizziness, and so on. It is known that certain physical conditions have characteristic effects on personality functioning, and alertness to them will often help account for the client's reactions. Quite aside from these constant effects, any illness is also likely to play a significant part in interpersonal difficulties. It frequently causes pain or anxiety;[5] it often increases narcissistic attitudes and provokes regression to greater dependence; it can be used as an escape from unpleasant responsibilities; it can change the self-image and distort relationships in family life between husband and wife and between siblings. The worker must also be alert to the effect of bodily changes associated with different periods of life—the uneven growth rate and the genital as well as secondary sexual growth changes of adolescence, reactions to the climacteric and to the physical changes of old age. Unusual physical features or disabilities also have direct bearing on social and inner functioning.

When personal adjustment problems are involved it is also well to inquire almost routinely about the use of drugs, especially barbiturates and amphetamines. These are now so widely prescribed by physicians and so easily secured for self-dosage that they are frequent contributors to troublesome moods. "Are you under a doctor's care? What has he prescribed?" Or "Has your doctor given you anything to quiet your nerves?" or "to help you sleep?" or "to give you energy?" To the person who is not seeing a doctor—"Do you sometimes need to take something to keep your nerves quiet?" One does not inquire routinely about such drugs as deliriants, hallucinating agents, and the opiates. But it is most important to be alert to the possibility of their use, especially with younger clients, and to ask about them if there is some likelihood that they are being used. Familiarity with physical changes and behavioral indicators associated with drug addiction is essential. The timing and way in which these inquiries are made are, of course, of crucial importance.[6]

The worker must also be alert for indications of mental or

emotional illness or symptomatology. Clients often refer to these tangentially or even describe them without realizing their significance. Periods of "nervousness," "tiredness," "depression," or extreme boredom should be inquired about. References to periods of hospitalization may mean mental illness or alcoholism as well as physical illness. If reference is made to loss of memory or to periods of "blanking out," further questions about this should be asked. Data that point to depersonalization should be followed up. Affect can be observed. Compulsions usually reveal themselves or are mentioned by the client.

So far we have been considering mainly data from the present or recent past. To what extent is it important to go into earlier history? Certainly the worker wants to learn the client's thoughts about when the present difficulty began. This may be in the recent past, some years earlier, or, in some instances in early life. Usually, however, the client does not see his childhood and adolescence as pertinent to his problem unless the worker in some way makes a connection for him. Exploration of early life should be made only when the worker has specific reason to believe that this will throw light on the problem. Such exploration tends to be thematic rather than wide ranging, pursuing certain relationships or certain time periods that seem to have relevance.

The same careful regard for details must attend the exploration of the client's past that accompanies the exploration of current events. It is not enough for the client to say, "My mother always preferred my older brother." The worker must seek out the details, asking, "In what way?" "What makes you think so?" "Could you tell me more about that?"—and so on.

Thus, starting with what the client sees as his problem, its antecedents, what he has tried to do about it, and his thoughts about how he can be helped to resolve it, the study moves on to analysis of present and sometimes past factors that may be contributing to the current dilemma. Some clients move naturally into talking about significant aspects of their past life. Others need a brief explanation of why this may be important. The order in which these areas are explored varies according to the preference of both client and worker and is less important than the nature of the content.

We see, then, that although the worker does not follow a set pattern for social study interviews, he does have in mind definite ideas concerning the type of information he wants to obtain about the client and his situation. A great deal of ineffectual drifting and failure to formulate suitable treatment approaches results when the caseworker is too passive in seeking specific information, especially in early interviews. What he wants to learn will inevitably be influenced by his frame of reference, that is, the theories he holds about the causation of difficulties in social functioning and about appropriate casework treatment methods.

ADDITIONAL SOURCES OF INFORMATION

In recent years there has been growing emphasis upon the importance of not limiting social study to office interviews with the client only. It is now widely accepted that in cases of marital difficulty, for example, there are great advantages in seeing both spouses—either individually or in joint interviews—for diagnostic purposes at least and, whenever possible, for treatment also. Some therapists refuse treatment altogether unless such interviews can be arranged. Others (of whom the writer is one) would certainly favor interviewing all persons involved in a major way in a problem, but would not insist on it if the client is strongly opposed or if the others concerned are unwilling to participate. If this type of interview is handled as a routine expectation rather than as a major issue the client usually accepts it as a natural procedure, unless there are special reasons for him to regard it with concern. If there are, it is important to understand them, for they are often of great diagnostic significance.

Another procedure of great value in the psychosocial study is the multiple-person interview. This may include husband and wife, parent and child, or even a whole family together. Observing the interaction between people throws a great deal of light on the complementarity, or lack of it, of their behavior, on discrepancies between their individual perceptions and the realities of how they act and how others respond and act, as these appear to a trained outsider.[7]

Without doubt the home visit also can yield important data[8] not only about the client's physical environment, but in the case of the wife and mother about an important area of her functioning. A woman's home points up many personality characteristics. First-hand witnessing of a client's interaction with children in the natural setting of the home provides especially significant diagnostic data. When certain types of situational problems are of importance, or with the "hard-to-reach" family, home visits are essential. In other cases, it is well to grasp any natural opportunity that arises for an interview in the home as a means of widening the scope of the social study. It is not, however, essential or even advisable in all types of cases.

In addition to interviews with the client and his immediate family, it is also sometimes useful to consult, with the client's knowledge and on a very selective basis, other people who may be in a position to add to the worker's understanding of his client. When a child is involved, it may be particularly useful to talk with the teacher or nursery school leader. Often a contact with a doctor yields valuable medical information. Occasionally a clergyman, employer, relative, or friend can add to the understanding of a particular aspect of the client's problem. In seeing collaterals it is always important to gauge the potential effect of the interview on the client himself and on his relationship to the worker. Only under exceptional circumstances, principally of a protective nature, is it wise to seek information at the expense of arousing antitherapeutic reactions in the client. This is not to say that contacts with other people should never be allowed to arouse any anxiety in the client. Anxiety frequently occurs, at least to a mild degree, but discussion with the client beforehand gives an opportunity for helping the client with his anxiety before and after the interview with the collateral.

Obviously, reports of medical or psychiatric diagnosis or treatment, of psychological tests, and of treatment in other social agencies may be pertinent to the social study. These and other types of written material should be secured selectively during the social study period as well as later in the contact.

As the caseworker learns about the client and his life he begins to form opinions about the nature of the client's difficulty. Often in trying to formulate the diagnosis, the worker recognizes gaps in a psychosocial study, areas of information about which he must make further inquiry in order to arrive at a clearer picture of the client and his situation. This is good and necessary, but the worker must guard against allowing speculation to substitute for facts or to predetermine the way in which questions are answered. The best way to obtain a clear and accurate picture is to enable the client to have sufficient confidence in the worker so that he can speak fully and frankly.

NOTES

1. See Kenneth Pray, "A Restatement of the Generic Principles of Social Casework Practice," *Journal of Social Casework*, 28 (October 1947), 283–290, for a statement of this point of view.

2. For discussion and illustrations see: Katherine Baldwin, "Crisis-Focused Casework in a Child Guidance Clinic," *Social Casework*, 49 (January 1968), 28–34; Jeanette Oppenheimer, "Use of Crisis Intervention in Case Work with the Cancer Patient and His Family," *Social Work*, 12 (April 1967), 44–52; Howard J. Parad and Gerald Caplan, "A Framework for Studying Families in Crisis," *Social Work*, 5 (July 1960), 3–15; and Lydia Rapoport, in Robert W. Roberts and Robert H. Nee, *Theories of Social Casework* (Chicago: University of Chicago Press, 1970), pp. 278–286.

3. Mary Richmond, *Social Diagnosis* (New York: Russell Sage Foundation, 1917), p. 347.

4. As background for this chapter, readers should be familiar with chapters 3, 4, and 5 in Richmond, *ibid.*, and with chapters 7 and 8 in Gordon Hamilton, *Theory and Practice of Social Casework*, 2nd ed. (New York: Columbia University Press, 1951).

5. For an interesting discussion of this, see Mark Zborowski, "Cultural Components in Response to Pain," *Journal of Social Issues*, 8 (1952), 16–30.

6. See Howard Steinholz, "Symptoms of Drug Abuse," mimeographed (New York: New York State Community Narcotic Education Center, n.d.).

7. See the following: Emily Faucett, "Multiple-Client Interviewing: A Means of Assessing Family Processes," *Social Casework*, 43 (March 1962), 114–120; Bernard Hall and Winifred Wheeler, "The Patient and His Relatives: Initial Joint Interview," *Social Work*, 2 (January 1957), 75–80; Celia B. Mitchell, "Family Interviewing in Family Diagnosis," *Social Casework*, 40 (July 1959), 381–384; Frances Scherz, in Roberts and Nee, *op. cit.*, pp. 238–243; Viola Weiss, "Multiple-Client Interviewing: An Aid to Diagnosis," *Social Casework*, 43 (March 1962), 111–114.

8. See Marjorie Behrens and Nathan Ackerman, "The Home Visit as an Aid in Family Diagnosis and Therapy," *Social Casework*, 37 (January 1956), 11–19.

15 | *Understanding Through Diagnostic Assessment*

Understanding is central to psychosocial treatment. Much understanding is intuitive.[1] One immediately senses anxiety, anger, grief. Common knowledge of causative factors brings immediate explanations to mind. But intuition and common knowledge alone are notoriously unreliable. They constitute first steps in the process of understanding, actually hypotheses to be checked against reality. Through the psychosocial study the worker seeks to come as close as possible to securing a picture of the client's actual inner and outer situation. In assessment—or diagnosis—he attempts to *understand* that picture in order to answer the question, "How can this person be helped?"

The term diagnosis has been under a shadow in recent years because it has come to symbolize for some social workers what they term the "medical model" of casework. These workers claim that those who use the word diagnosis are placing all the responsibility for difficulty on the client rather than on his situation and are furthermore concentrating on his weaknesses—his "illness," his "pathology"—rather than on his strengths and abilities. Without wasting time arguing about semantics, let it be said that the point of view of this book is that either the client or the situation or both may be making a major contribution to the problem and that the recognition of strengths is of paramount importance to diagnostic assessment.

ASSESSMENT

The total process of assessment consists of trying to understand, first, what the trouble is; second, what seems to be contributing to the trouble; and, third, what can be changed and modified. In each of these questions strengths as well as weaknesses in both person and situation are important considerations. Diagnostic assessment takes place in two different ways. First, as the worker listens in each interview to what the client is saying he constantly tries to answer the three questions just posed, for what he does in the immediate interview will be determined by this understanding. Second, periodically during the total contact, he needs to look back over all that he knows about the person-situation gestalt in order to answer these questions more fully in the light of this total knowledge. When treatment is expected to continue beyond a few interviews the first of these more extensive assessments should occur no later than the fourth to sixth contact. By that time the worker hopes to have a good enough picture of the person and the pertinent systems in which he functions to arrive at a working basis for the major outlines of ongoing treatment, subject to modification by later diagnostic reassessment. In briefer treatment, naturally, this process must be foreshortened.

The Person-Situation Gestalt and Average Expectations

In order to understand what the trouble is, the worker begins by a sort of scanning of the whole "field"—all the known facts in all the pertinent parts of the current person-situation gestalt. Where is the dysfunction? Assessment of the individual and the situation here go hand in hand. One must understand the pressures a person is under before one can have any opinion about the adequacy or inadequacy of his functioning. One can use here the notion of "an average expectable environment," where the term "average expectable" signifies within the range of normally healthy common experience.[2] By this standard an income below the poverty line would constitute an external pressure; so would being subject to race prejudice; so would substandard housing, poor schooling, inadequate medical care, lack of employment opportunity, extremely stressful or unpleasant working conditions, and so on.

In personal relationships, an "average expectable environment" assumes reasonably satisfying family relationships and opportunities for friendships. This does not mean that these relationships are necessarily conflict-free or completely satisfying, any more than in the area of income "average" is equated with great wealth. There is room within the norm in human relationships for considerable tension. These expectations vary, of course, according to ethnic, class, and other variables, and must be viewed from the standpoint of both general expectations and those of the client. An extremely authoritative husband may be "expectable" in Turkish culture, but he may be experienced as a distinct "pressure" by a woman brought up in this country or even by a Turkish woman if she has lived here long enough to partially take on more equalitarian ideas.

If a parent is concerned about his child, whom he sees as a problem, the worker needs to evaluate not only the way the parent is functioning as a parent but also the realities by which he is confronted. What is this son or daughter like to live with at the moment? Has the child withdrawn into himself so that he is hard to reach? Is he provocative in a hostile way, giving ample cause for parental anger? Is his behavior publicly embarrassing to his parents? If he is ill, how much of a strain does caring for him cause? Does it deprive the parents of sleep? Is his mother constantly running up and down stairs, or involved in all sorts of special cookery?

Obviously, in any sort of interpersonal problem, the worker must get as accurate a picture as possible of the pressures, or "presses," to which the client is responding. Moreover, it is the exception rather than the rule to find the pressure in one spot alone; usually there are other people in either the immediate or wider family who are also contributing to the client's difficulty. Otto Pollak[3] has rightly called our attention to the pressures brought by grandparents, aunts and uncles, and by other more distant relatives of either of the parents on the problems of children. Not infrequently these pressures occur in marital problems also.

Even when they are not presented by the client as a major problem, employment, housing, and neighborhood conditions are possible sources of pressure in parent-child and husband-wife conflict. Certainly the realities of the school environment are of great significance for children. Social institutions such as the courts and police have causative as well as remedial impact in problems of nonconformity.

A dimension of assessment that seems to lie midway between the external and internal factors is the individual's physical condition. Here the worker takes account not only of any diagnosed medical condition, but also of the client's complaints and his own observations of physical discomforts. Physical characteristics or disabilities that might be expected in view of the client's age, occupation, or way of life; bodily changes associated with different periods of life; and any unusual features or bodily disabilities all can add to personal distress.

Especially with older people, physical limitations are of paramount importance. Poor hearing and poor eyesight severely limit pleasure in social contacts and in interests such as TV watching, reading, sewing, and some hobbies. Sheer weakness and lack of endurance can interfere with the client's seeking medical and other services that require street travel or long periods of waiting. Some older people are malnourished to the point of severe incapacity simply because they no longer have the strength to cook or to go to the store. The latter is true both in poor neighborhoods, where older people are often found in the cheaper fourth, fifth, and sixth floor walk-up apartments, and in more affluent areas where stores are several blocks away.

It is particularly important to get as accurate a picture as one can of the degree of *functional* disability in any of the more permanent handicaps. A heart specialist, for instance, usually classifies patients according to their capacity for normal life. Varying degrees of legal blindness carry differing functional capacities. There seems to be wide divergence between the amount of brain damage that exists and the extent to which functioning is impaired. Functional disability may well lessen as the client's hope and confidence increase.

The Personality System

In assessment of the personality system it is again helpful to use the concept of "average expectations." Flexible norms exist within every cultural group that set up expectations of how an individual with a "healthy" personality will act. But personality is so complicated that one has to view its functioning in a systematic way in order to understand and to assess its strengths or weaknesses. Here psychoanalytic personality theory can be most useful. Just as one scans the field of the client's milieu, the various systems of the person-situation gestalt, so one can scan the personality of the individual himself. To do so quickly and carefully the worker is helped by having in the back of his mind a picture of the major aspects of personality functioning. These include four major divisions: drive functioning, ego functioning, superego functioning, and symptomatology.

Drives are of two major types—libidinal and aggressive. Essentially the worker will want to know to what extent a person is capable of mature love, friendship, consideration of others, and trust in others. To what extent is he handicapped by an unusual degree of narcissism, or an unusual amount of dependence? Is he relatively free of residuals of infantile stages of development, or does too much orality show itself in such traits as greediness or overtalkativeness? Do too many residuals of the habit training period show in such traits as stinginess, compulsive orderliness, or overcleanliness? Is there overconcentration on qualities normal to the phallic period of the child's development, when he is preoccupied with the wonders of sexual potency but has not yet integrated this with the tenderness and constancy of mature love? Is he relatively consistent in his feelings, or is there an unusual amount of ambivalence? Are there unresolved hostilities or overly intense positive attachments to parents? Is he able to love a person of the opposite sex or is he attracted primarily to his own sex? What about aggression? Is the individual able to stand up for himself and pursue his ends with vigor? Is he able to be angry appropriately and to a realistic degree? Or is his aggression characterized by destructiveness, a desire to hurt, hatred and hostility that are too easily aroused?

Obviously the extent to which these many questions about drives need to be answered depends upon the kind of problem with which the worker is trying to help a client. Sexual adjustment, for instance, may be of primary importance in marital counseling; but when the treatment problem lies in the area of employment, the worker would certainly not inquire about it, unless it was obviously a component in the work problem, as is sometimes the case. On the other hand, the general quality of social relationships with people can be a most important part of work adjustment, as can also the quality of aggressiveness. Residual qualities from the early infantile periods are often indicative of types of work people may like and perform well.

In recent years particular attention has been given to *ego qualities*. We have already referred several times to one of the most important of these—perception. There are, however, many others. Is the individual capable of seeing things as they are or is there some constant distortion of reality? Is he able to test his perceptions and his plans for action against reality before coming to conclusions about them? How sound is his judgment? What about his intelligence—to what extent is his thinking still dominated by primary thought processes? Is his self-image fairly accurate or does he overestimate or underestimate his own abilities? Does he have adequate self-respect, a sense of self-worth? To what extent is he clear about his own identity? What major identifications does he have? Is there anything unusual about his fantasies? Is his impulse control adequate? How able is he as an executant? Are his affects appropriate and is he able to express them adequately? How anxious is he and how does he handle his anxiety? When he feels guilt, is it appropriate and commensurate with its cause? What mechanisms of defense does he chiefly rely upon? Are these in the main helpful or are they dysfunctional in his life situation? In general, what is his level of competence?

Forming an opinion about whether or not a person's functioning is within the "average expectable" range or varies from it sufficiently to be problematic is not an easy task. There is no single model of appropriate responses. What is adequate or normal or appropriate or realistic or healthy (or whatever term is chosen) will be influenced by many variables[4]—sex, age, class, ethnic background, religion, education level, geographic location, social role. A man is expected to respond differently to frustration when he is functioning as a father than when he is at the poker table with the boys from the office. What is normal for a Protestant in certain respects may be abnormal for a Roman Catholic. Behavior indicative of normal virility for a highly

educated man from a highly educated family might label a
stevedore a sissy. Normal aggression for a person of one background is overaggressiveness for one of another. People of
different backgrounds normally emphasize different defenses and
have different norms for sexual expression and for the expression
of aggression. Even the level of psychosexual maturity expected
of men and women may vary in different cultures.[5] Certainly
concepts of appropriate male and female ways of acting are very
differently defined in different parts of the world. In this country
they are clearly in the process of redefinition.

As with the drives, the extent to which the worker needs to
assess ego qualities varies with the predicament about which the
client is seeking or willing to accept help. The majority of ego
qualities are pertinent to most areas of functioning and therefore
important to the question of how an individual can be helped.

The general atmosphere within which an individual is reacting
and particular antecedent events are significant to personality
assessment. In periods of turmoil, such as when students or
black communities are enraged by events like the invasion of
Cambodia or the assassination of Martin Luther King, it would
be a grave error to think that the passions unleashed indicated
abnormal character traits in the participants. Campus and community rioting, it is true, provides a heyday for overly aggressive
individuals with poor impulse control, but many normally well-
controlled individuals also find themselves enraged beyond their
endurance or may even have become convinced that aggressive
action is appropriate.

In evaluating the client's *superego* functioning, the worker must
consider both the general structure of the superego—its relative
strength or weakness in the personality—and the *quality* of its
demands, that is, the level of its demands and the consistency of
the standards it supports. Particularly in this aspect of the personality, assessment must be made in the light of ethnic background, class, education, regional differences, and variations in
age. Aspirations are an important part of the ego ideal, a component of the superego. Clients sometimes have multiple reference groups from which the ego ideal is derived: they are exposed
to the general culture, which upholds one set of aspirations, and
to family and peer cultures, which may each be quite different.
The conflict among the three can be a major source of trouble.

By *symptomatology* is meant the specific signs that are generally recognized as characteristic of known neurotic or psychotic disorders, such as phobias, compulsions, hallucinations, depression. There often is an overlap between such symptomatology and the various ego qualities, but behavior widely recognized as a sign of a specific type of disorder should be noted as such.

How does one go about assessing these complicated personality characteristics? It is a process of applying clinical judgment to knowledge of the ways in which the client interacts with others, including the caseworker, and handles his own affairs. It is impossible to evaluate the personality properly except as it is seen in the context of the individual's situation. For instance, one cannot judge whether a reaction of anger or anxiety is normal or excessive unless one knows the realities behind it. It is one thing to be plagued by the fear of losing a job in normal times when one's performance is adequate, and quite another when there is a recession on or one's performance is marginal. It is one thing for a client to accuse his wife of belittling him when in actuality she does constantly criticize and devalue him, and quite another for him to distort her remarks, projecting on to them his own devaluated self-image. Feelings of depression may be part of a particular physical illness syndrome, a reaction to the loss of a valued friend, or, in the absence of any such provocations in reality, evidence of emotional or mental illness.

This disentangling of reaction from reality is a most complicated task. It is simplest when the worker can observe the externals directly or can look at the situation in terms of his own general knowledge. For instance, the worker often knows what a given neighborhood is like, or how a particular doctor reacts to patients, or the eligibility procedures in the local public assistance agency. General knowledge of this type must, however, be used with caution. Sometimes the doctor, public assistance worker, or school principal has not acted in a specific instance in the way prior knowledge would lead one to expect. Direct observation is more certain. Here lies the great advantage of the worker's having direct contact with the principals in any interpersonal problem, and of the home visit, and of joint and family interviews from which so much can be learned. But even insights thus gained are not infallible and can sometimes give the worker a false sense of certainty.[6] Things that have been "seen with my own eyes" and "heard with my own ears" carry great weight, but they are also subject to misinterpretation by the worker because of his own countertransference and subjective judgments.

Another method of disentangling the objective from the subjective is to evaluate the circumstantial detail that the client himself uses to support his own opinions and reactions. Does the situation he describes bring the worker to the same conclusion? Insofar as the worker's own perceptions and judgment are realistic, he can then evaluate the client's reactions. The importance of self-awareness in a worker's training—so that his biases will be reduced or at least near enough to consciousness that he is alert to possible sources of error in his judgment—can easily be seen.

Repetitiveness provides another useful clue in assessing behavior, for if an individual has a tendency to over- or underreact or to distort, it will not occur in a single instance only but will show itself again and again. If the same type of seemingly unrealistic response arises several times, and particularly if in each instance it occurs in reaction to different people, the chance is very great that an atypical personality factor is involved. This illustrates the special value of knowing the client's past history when the nature of the problem requires particularly careful assessment of the personality. Since much of the personality structure is shaped early in life, repetitive patterns will often show themselves clearly in the life history. Specific symptoms of neurotic or psychotic disorders in the client's past are, of course, of great significance.

The assessment process provides a workable knowledge of the client's strengths and weaknesses—the pressures, gratifications, and potentials of his situation, based on a study of his current life, pertinent aspects of his past life, and his behavior in the casework interviews. Strengths and weaknesses are not viewed separately, but rather are seen in relationship to each other.

THE DYNAMIC-ETIOLOGICAL DIAGNOSIS

The discussion of the diagnostic process now moves from delineating *what* the realities of the client-situation gestalt are to *why* they are. In this step the worker seeks to understand what factors are contributing to the client's dilemma both in terms of current interactions and in sequential terms, that is, in the effect of prior events—recent or remote—on current functioning. He tries to learn to what extent and in what way the causative factors of the client's problem lie within the situation that confronts him and to what extent and in what way they are the product of unusual needs within the client or of poor functioning within his ego or superego.

The process of trying to understand the "why" of the client's difficulty is sometimes called the *dynamic-etiological diagnosis*. This simply refers to the effort to understand the interplay of forces responsible for the problem or problems that exist in the person-situation gestalt. In this process a systems theory approach is again useful. For the problem does not lie simply in a given weakness in the personality or a specific lack or condition in the milieu but rather in the way in which various weaknesses or idiosyncrasies in the total system interplay and affect each other. As we noted earlier, every factor in a system affects every other factor in that system, and when systems overlap by virtue of having common membership, events in one system affect the other. Now the worker scans "the field" again, but this time he looks for interactions.

Suppose that we have noted that Johnnie is retarded in school despite normal intelligence and we know that he and his teacher are in constant conflict. Is the teacher critical of Johnnie because he is impudent, or because he is overgraded, or because his mother criticized her, or because Johnnie comes from a poor neighborhood, has poor clothing, and no privacy for study, or because he is big for his age and looks as though he ought to behave in a more grownup way than he does? Or is she critical because the principal is pressing her about the reading-grade average of her class or because she is embroiled in faculty disagreements about the wisdom of a strike and is irritable with all her students. Only by talking with her can we get hints of what the causes of the strain between her and Johnnie may be. And only as we come to understand this will we know what steps might or might not be helpful.

Pete sees himself as a delinquent and begins acting like one. What part in his trouble is played by his neighborhood, his housing, the lack of decent recreation facilities, his teacher's attitude, the curriculum offered by the school? Was he put in a "general" course because he was not bright enough for vocational high school? Has he come to think of himself as a delinquent because he was taken into court for truancy?

When a client's affect is characterized by high anxiety, we seek to understand possible contributing factors—current provocation, historical factors, and interrelationships within the personality itself. Is it fear of the superego or fear of a breakthrough of the instinctual drives or fear of external reality? Is it a recent development or a long-term pattern? If the latter, what developmental factors account for it? Is health a factor? What in the situation may be provoking the anxiety? What effect does it have on the client's functioning? What responses does it provoke from others toward him?

In problems of interpersonal adjustment, such as marital or parent-child problems, one person is in a sense the other person's situation, and vice versa. The term "transaction" is used to describe the flow of currents between two individuals who are in close personal interaction. It was suggested in an earlier chapter that this interaction or transaction is not a billiard-ball type of direct impact of one force upon another.[7] A better parallel could be drawn to football or lacrosse. When the ball is thrown from one team to the other it is first passed around within the opposing team according to its plan of play, and when it finally reemerges within the reach of the first team, its location, direction, and speed are only remotely related to the way it was originally thrown. In the same way the action of one person upon another takes effect only in the form in which it is perceived by the other. The first person may have used a complaining tone because he was tired, but if the other perceives the tone as anger, he will react to it as such. His response, in turn, may be silence, or martyrlike murmurings, or explosive retaliation, depending upon his own personality, earlier experiences of the day that have set his mood, his perception of the first person, his notion of the requirements of the role in which he is functioning, and a variety of other things. The first speaker's next response is subject to similarly complicated influences.

If one studies a series of such transactions, one finds that characteristic patterns begin to emerge. It is as if the captains of the teams had caught on to the inner workings of the opposing team and each is now manipulating the other. In 1949 the present writer called attention to this factor in the form of complementarity between marriage partners. More recent writings have pointed out similar patterns in interaction characterizing the behavior of whole families.[8] Without question, casework diagnosis in cases of interpersonal conflict must include comprehension of the interaction between the main participants in the conflict. Such comprehension involves understanding of the way in which one person's behavior sets off or provokes certain responses in the other, the extent to which this is consciously or unconsciously purposeful, and the extent to which unrecognized complementary needs are being met in the process. In marriage conflict, certainly, the worker will make serious treatment errors if he is not aware of the factor of complementarity in such combinations as "father-daughter marriages," "mother-son marriages," marriages in which there is some degree of reversal in masculine-feminine patterns, sado-masochistic marriages, certain marriages of alcoholics, and so on. He will often find that serious trouble has emerged in a family where a previously existing complementarity has been disturbed.[9] In such cases serious consideration should be given to the possibility of restoring the previous balance in the family. Marriage is not infrequently the means by which two neurotic or otherwise disturbed individuals are enabled through complementarity to function at a reasonably high level of personal satisfaction and social effectiveness.

The important part played by communication in any social or interpersonal system was noted earlier. Such defenses as repression, suppression, and inhibition may interfere with communication. Attitudes expressed verbally may be contradicted by nonverbal behavior (which is often unconscious or ego-dystonic preconscious). Words, tone of voice, gestures, and bodily behavior may be misinterpreted because of the internal needs or attitudes of the other. Defenses of projection, denial, and turning against the self are particularly likely to distort reception. Even differences in the literal meanings of words exchanged between individuals using the same basic language will cause misunderstanding. Not only different classes and geographical regions but even individual families give special meaning to words.

It was also noted earlier that previous life history sometimes reveals repetitive patterns. These can be immensely valuable in helping the worker to understand causation in the developmental sense of how the person came to be the way he is. Knowledge of early family relationships is particularly helpful in understanding the level of psychosexual development, parental attachments, sexual identification, superego development, and the basis for the anxieties against which the ego is defending itself. Early family history can also give greater understanding of many qualities of the ego. Sharp discrepancies in the way an individual functions at different times in his life provide excellent clues to the ways in which situational factors affect him.

A final note of warning is in order against oversimplifying either the assessment or the dynamic-etiological part of the diagnosis. Some caseworkers use two phrases over and over again in diagnostic discussions—"ego strength" and "oedipal problem." "Ego strength" is an almost meaningless term, despite its use in the best psychotherapeutic circles. The ego is not a composite force to be measured on a single scale of strength; it is rather a series of functions and qualities of many different dimensions. Perception is accurate or inaccurate, judgment is sound or unsound, self-image is appropriate or inappropriate; only controls may be strong or weak. One may say about the ego as a whole that it functions well or poorly, but this description is not useful as a delineation of *which* aspects of the ego function well and which poorly, and when poorly, in what way.

The term "oedipal problem" is likewise almost meaningless. Sometimes this diagnosis is actually wrong, the worker having mistaken a primitive oral attachment to the mother or father for an oedipal one. For the most part the observation will be correct, but it will not be of much value if the worker regards it as the total answer to the problem and is satisfied to stop his diagnostic thinking at that point. It is only as the observation is related to other parts of the dynamic diagnosis that it takes on real meaning. Are the effects of the oedipal tie increased anxiety, sexual inhibitions, hostility to men or to women, reversed identifications? Does it show itself in transference reactions, in defensive hostility? Is perception distorted, self-image awry? Oversimplification is one of the worst traps into which the worker can fall.

The dynamic-etiological part of the diagnosis, then, represents the caseworker's effort to understand the nature of the multiple factors contributing to the client's difficulty. It seeks to discover *why* the situation is as it is. It tries to establish interrelationships among the various factors that combine to create the client's discomfort or poor social functioning. It seeks to comprehend the interaction of internal and external factors, the past sources of the present difficulty insofar as these lie in the past, and the internal dynamics within the personality or among the environmental forces. Together the assessment and the dynamic-etiological diagnosis should define as clearly as possible the key features that treatment must attempt to modify and locate the assets in both person and situation that can facilitate change.

CLASSIFICATION

A third step in diagnosis is classification or categorization—recognizing that a characteristic or set of characteristics belongs to a known grouping about which generalized knowledge exists. Three types of classification or categorization have so far been found to have value for treatment. The first has to do with health—the physician's diagnosis of a medical disorder. The *medical classification* often has implications for personal and social consequences, which are guideposts to casework treatment.

The second type encompasses various *descriptive problem classifications*—terms such as marital conflict, parent-child problem, unmarried mother, family breakdown, delinquency, drug addiction, alcoholism, unemployment, old age problem. These are essentially descriptive categories, centered around the symptomatic behavior resulting from the interaction of the person and the situation. They tell something about the difficulty and can become the focal point for assembling data about the disorder. They also sometimes suggest major dimensions of the treatment steps that will need to be taken. "Out-of-wedlock pregnancy," for instance, immediately indicates that prenatal care may be needed. Arrangements for confinement may have to be made. The worker will need to explore whether or not the mother wants to keep her child. In either case certain steps and alternatives follow. If she is undecided she will need to be helped to come to a decision. Her feelings toward the father will need to be explored, and if marriage is a possibility she may need help in both clarifying her feelings and making plans. Interviews with the father may be indicated. Abortion may also be an issue.

Third, the *clinical diagnosis*—the only well-developed categorical scheme of diagnosis used in casework—is a combination of terms derived from psychoanalysis and psychiatry and used to designate certain major personality configurations. The worker does not always have a sufficiently extensive contact with a client to make a clinical diagnosis with any degree of certainty. In many situations, if there is no indication of psychosis further delineation of the clinical diagnosis is not needed in order to help the client with the particular problem that has brought him to the worker. But when rounded understanding of the personality is desirable, such a diagnosis brings greater clarity to the treatment process.

The system of clinical diagnosis developed by psychoanalysis has progressed considerably further than other categorizations employed in casework in the direction of being a "conditional-genetic" rather than a purely "descriptive" system of classification. These are terms Lewin[10] uses to distinguish between Aristotelian and Galilean methods of classification. In an interesting chapter in his *Dynamic Theory of Personality* Lewin points out that in Aristotelian classification things are grouped together on the basis of external or superficial characteristics, because they look alike or behave alike. This is comparable to our "problem" classifications that categorize people as "unmarried mothers" or "delinquents" or "unemployed" without regard to the dynamics or the etiology of their behavior. In Galilean classification, on the other hand, distinctions are based upon "an essentially functional way of thinking," the conditions under which things occur or the causes of their occurrence.

Before the introduction of Freudian theory, psychiatric classification was largely Aristotelian, descriptive; and in many respects it still is, as for instance in the terms "antisocial reaction" and "emotionally unstable personality." Increasingly, however, psychoanalytic terminology is becoming Galilean or "genotypical" rather than "phenotypical," again to borrow Lewin's terminology. This tendency is best seen in the designations for different neuroses and in the major distinctions between neurosis, psychosis, and behavior disorder. Within the general behavior disorder category itself such classification is just beginning to emerge. Predominantly, these categories rest upon common etiological and dynamic features and thus can be particularly useful in the planning of treatment.

Contrary to a currently popular assumption, casework has not borrowed psychiatric terminology in wholesale fashion but rather uses only those terms that apply to conditions with which caseworkers are recurrently familiar and concerning which they have access to diagnostically discriminating data. The worker first attempts to arrive at the broadest discriminations. Is this client probably psychotic, or does he fall somewhere in the neurotic group? Does there seem to be a character disorder of some type, or is this individual within the broad normal range? If he does not fit clearly into any one of these classifications, between which major categories does his difficulty seem to lie?

The caseworker's right to diagnose psychosis is sometimes questioned on the grounds that such a diagnosis is a medical question. If, however, the caseworker did not arrive at his own opinion that this is, or at least may be, psychosis, how else would he know enough to refer the client to a psychiatrist for a medical diagnosis or to consult the psychiatrist himself for confirmation of his opinion? Should every client in every casework agency be seen routinely by a psychiatrist to determine whether he is psychotic? If in the worker's opinion psychosis may be involved, psychiatric consultation is clearly a necessity.[11] Often the worker can go somewhat further and, subject always to medical confirmation, discriminate in clear-cut cases at least between major categories such as schizophrenia and manic-depressive psychosis. Where any organic factor is involved, the caseworker has very little diagnostic competence, but he should have sufficient knowledge of symptomatology to recognize signs that should be reported to the medical consultant. *Definitive* diagnosis in psychosis cannot be made without knowledge of the psychological manifestations of numerous physical conditions that produce psychotic symptomatology.

The worker is not making a medical diagnosis simply by using the same terms as the psychiatrist. An opinion about the nature of a mental disturbance becomes a medical diagnosis only when it is expressed by a physician. Furthermore, such a diagnosis is designed for use in medical treatment; when the caseworker expresses such an opinion, it is a casework diagnosis and is designed for casework treatment. A most important part of casework treatment when either psychosis or borderline psychosis seems possible is either to refer the client for psychiatric care or to consult a psychiatrist about the advisability of such care and for medical confirmation of the casework diagnosis. If by joint agreement it seems advisable for the caseworker to carry the treatment, the diagnosis of psychosis will indicate that emphasis will be upon reality adjustments and sustainment. When a diagnosis is being transmitted from one agency to another it is essential, if there is any possibility of confusion as to whether a diagnosis is medical or casework, that the professional source of the opinion be made clear.

When psychosis is not indicated but the cause of the problem seems to lie sufficiently within the client to indicate some type of personality disturbance, the next distinction to be made is most frequently between some type of character disorder and psychoneurosis. In most cases in which long-term treatment of interpersonal maladjustment is undertaken it is possible for the experienced caseworker to make finer distinctions, such as those among hysteria, obsessive compulsive neurosis, and neurotic depression. There is less standardized nomenclature for the various character disorders, but it should be possible to distinguish among three major types: (1) oedipal, phallic, or hysterical, closely related terms sometimes used interchangeably; (2) obsessive compulsive; and (3) oral, impulsive, "acting out," or infantile, also more or less interchangeable terms. The terms "neurotic character" and "character neurosis" are also used to designate the hysterical and obsessive compulsive types. It is the exception rather than the rule, of course, to find "pure" types—people who fall exclusively within any given diagnostic category. Clinical terms represent focal points on several different continua, and most individuals show some characteristics of one category and some of another. When this is so, both should be mentioned with indication of where the greater emphasis lies.[12]

When intensive work on interpersonal problems is being undertaken with individuals suffering from any type of personality disturbance, there is great value in psychiatric consultation. The more severe the disorder appears to be, the more important such consultation is. Any sort of physical illness also calls for medical evaluation, even when in the worker's judgment the illness appears to be hysteria. Psychosomatic disorders should be given psychological help only under medical auspices or, if the work is of a supportive nature, in close coordination with medical treatment. If depression is present in any significant degree, psychiatric consultation is of great importance, partly because the border between neurotic and psychotic depression is sometimes hard to distinguish, partly because medication may be indicated, and partly in order to have a medical opinion as to whether the severity of the depression makes medical supervision or even hospitalization advisable. When deviations such as sadism, masochism, voyeurism, and drug addiction come to the caseworker, they also call for immediate psychiatric consultation.

From time to time the value of the clinical diagnosis is questioned, for there is a tendency to feel that the dynamic-etiological diagnosis is sufficient. But the clinical diagnosis has the additional value of designating a cluster of factors characteristically found together. For instance, the term "compulsive neurosis," when correctly used, immediately conveys certain information about a client. It signifies that the individual has reached the oedipal stage of development in his relationship to his parents but has not resolved the conflicts of this period and has regressed in substantial degree to ways of behaving characteristic of the anal or habit training period of development. It indicates that he has a severe superego to which he may be overly submissive on the surface but which he is unconsciously fighting. He usually is very sensitive to criticism and has strong dependency needs, although they may be covered over; he sometimes very much wants to please the worker and other parent figures but at other times is either negative to suggestions or subtly sabotages them. He is often perfectionistic, usually ambivalent, often confused in masculine-feminine identifications. He is apt to make heavy use of such defenses as intellectualization, rationalization, isolation, and reaction formation. He usually has had a strict upbringing by a parent or parents who loved him but imposed rigid training in habits and behavior. He may be strict in bringing up his own children, or ambivalent in training them, or else he may be strict on the surface but unconsciously promote vicarious acting out. Of course not all these characteristics will be true of every compulsive person, but the presence of a few of them in the absence of contrary evidence will alert the worker to the probable diagnosis and to avenues to explore that will either confirm the diagnosis or contraindicate it.

As it takes firm shape the clinical diagnosis becomes a sort of index to many things about the individual that have not yet become clear from what has been observed or said. It often enables the worker to anticipate reactions to contemplated treatment steps and to guide them accordingly. The worker knows in advance, for instance, that a compulsive client will be very sensitive to criticism; the worker therefore will be extremely careful to avoid remarks that could be construed as criticism until the client is sufficiently secure with him to respond constructively. Such foreknowledge can also help greatly in the control of antitherapeutic countertransference reactions. The intellectualism often found in the compulsive, for example, can arouse feelings of frustration and dislike in the worker. If, however, the worker can recognize this trait as a defense against the anxiety created by an oversevere superego and can see that he is really dealing with a scared little boy or girl afraid of a harsh mother, the dislike may well be quickly replaced by the desire to help.

In other words, if one knows enough about some characteristics of a person to designate his clinical diagnosis, one immediately has the key to a great deal of other knowledge that will be useful in the process of helping him. In the psychoneuroses proper, specific symptoms such as phobias, hysterical paralyses, obsessions, compulsive rituals, and evidences of depression are distinctively related to the different categories and quickly alert the worker to the possible diagnosis. Symptoms alone, however, do not establish a clinical diagnosis. There are always several possible explanations of any symptom. It is only when a specific form of behavior can be shown to be part of a larger configuration characteristic of the disorder in question that any certainty can be felt about the diagnosis.

Knowledge of the major outlines of the better established

clinical entities and of their characteristic symptomatology can greatly sharpen the worker's diagnostic thinking. One weakness of the dynamic-etiological diagnosis taken by itself is that it tends to see a little bit of this and a little bit of that in an individual without reaching a definitive delineation. It is when one tries to say whether the difficulty is primarily a character disorder or a neurosis, whether the client is a borderline schizophrenic or a severe hysteric, and so on, that incompleteness in the psychosocial study or lack of clear-cut evaluation of the facts becomes apparent. This assumes, of course, that the clinical diagnosis itself is not a glib designation based on superficial impressions.

There are indeed several dangers involved in the use of diagnostic categories. One is that of stereotyping, assuming that all people in the same category are exactly alike. Each person has many individual qualities that make him quite unlike his fellows, despite the fact that in the rough outlines of a personality disturbance he may have much in common with others suffering from the same disorder. Another danger is that of careless labeling, assuming a person belongs in a given group because of superficial qualities or overlooking other qualities that point in another direction—the old story of Cinderella's sister cutting off her toe to make the shoe fit.

Diagnosis is admittedly a subjective process, despite the fact that it is an effort to increase the objectivity with which one views the client and his treatment needs. As a subjective process that often deals with impressionistic data, it is open to influence by suggestion. One form of suggestion that is prevalent is the currently popular diagnosis. Just as appendicitis was widely overdiagnosed in a recent period of medical history and before that tonsillectomies were far too widely performed, so in psychiatry schizophrenia has sometimes been too easily assumed to exist, and, especially today, character disorder may too often seem the appropriate designation. This type of error must be consciously resisted.

Some diagnoses—particularly that of schizophrenia—are so discouraging that there is danger that they may in effect relegate the person to very superficial treatment or even to no treatment at all. Obviously this should not happen. The diagnosis tells the worker something about what will help and what will not help, but it certainly should not be used as an excuse for not *trying* to help. Realization of the great variation among individuals having the same clinical diagnosis precludes such stereotyping of treatment. Furthermore, the whole person-situation gestalt concept puts the clinical diagnosis in perspective as only one of several aspects of the total diagnostic assessment.

Another danger is that of premature diagnosis, when definitive material is not available to make a clinical diagnosis. It is far better to admit that we have not been able to establish a clinical diagnosis than to affix a label superficially. It is well known that in scientific tests the rate of agreement among diagnosticians in psychiatry and psychology is not high. The same is undoubtedly true of caseworkers. But the fact that no profession has yet developed a high degree of accuracy is no argument against an effort to improve diagnostic skill. It *is* an argument against snap judgments and against *overreliance* on the clinical diagnosis. The greatest safety lies in seeking to arrive at both a clinical and a dynamic-etiological diagnosis, using each to supplement the other.

It is surely apparent that there is no simple one-to-one relationship between diagnosis and choice of treatment. Diagnostic assessment involves a many-faceted but orderly understanding of the client-situation configuration. In treatment planning, all that is known—strengths as well as weaknesses—is reviewed and evaluated for the purpose of learning how best to help.

As the contact progresses, the fund of knowledge grows and the worker repeatedly refers to it in making the decisions that either modify or implement plans made at the outset of treatment. The more orderly the ongoing diagnostic process by which assessment is made and dynamic understanding grows, the more wisely will the worker decide what treatment to offer his client.

NOTES

1. For empathy as a component in understanding, see note 13, Chapter 13, p. 244.
2. Heinz Hartmann, *Ego Psychology and the Problem of Adaptation* (New York: International Universities Press, 1958), p. 23.

3. Otto Pollak, *Social Science and Psychotherapy for Children* (New York: Russell Sage Foundation, 1952).

4. The sources of knowledge concerning these variations are myriad. Many useful references have been included in note 8, Chapter 2, p. 36. The following are also of value:

Charlotte Adland, "The Attitude of Eastern European Jews Toward Mental Disease: A Cultural Interpretation," *Smith College Studies in Social Work*, 8 (December 1937), 85–116.

Celia Benny, et al., "Clinical Complexities in Work Adjustment of Deprived Youth," *Social Casework*, 50 (June 1969), 330–336.

Urie Bronfenbrenner, "Socialization and Social Class Through Time and Space," in E. Maccoby, T. Newcomb, and E. Hartley, eds., *Readings in Social Psychology* (New York: Holt, Rinehart & Winston, 1958).

Shirley Hellenbrand, "Client Value Orientations: Implications for Diagnosis and Treatment," *Social Casework*, 42 (April 1961), 163–169.

Alex Inkeles, "Some Sociological Observations on Culture and Personality Studies," in Clyde Kluckhohn, Henry Murray, and David Schneider, eds., *Personality in Nature, Society, and Culture* (New York: Alfred A. Knopf, 1959).

Sidney Levin and Ralph Kahana, eds., *Psychodynamic Studies on Aging* (New York: International Universities Press, 1967).

Elizabeth Meier, "Social and Cultural Factors in Casework Diagnosis," *Social Work*, 41 (July 1959), 15–26.

S. M. Miller and Elliot Mishler, "Social Class, Mental Illness, and American Psychiatry: An Expository Review," *The Milbank Memorial Fund Quarterly*, 37 (April 1959), 174–199.

Allen Pincus, "Toward a Developmental View of Aging for Social Work," *Social Work*, 12 (July 1967), 33–41.

Beatrice Whiting, ed., *Six Cultures: Studies in Child Rearing* (New York: John Wiley & Sons, 1963).

Carle Zimmerman and Lucius Cervantes, *Successful American Families* (New York: Pageant Press, 1960).

5. See Margaret Mead, *Sex and Temperament in Three Primitive Societies*, (New York: William Morrow & Company, 1935), and *Male and Female: A Study of the Sexes in a Changing World* (New York: William Morrow & Company, 1949).

6. For an excellent discussion of "evidence," see Mary E. Richmond, *Social Diagnosis* (New York: Russell Sage Foundation, 1917) chap. 4.

7. For another discussion of this, see Roy R. Grinker et al., *Psychiatric Social Work: A Transactional Casebook* (New York: Basic Books, 1961), pp. 11–14. The author was amused to find, after using the bil-

liard ball simile, that Grinker had expressed the idea in almost identical terms.

8. See Nathan W. Ackerman, "The Diagnosis of Neurotic Marital Interaction," *Social Casework*, 35 (April 1954), 139–147; Florence Hollis, *Women in Marital Conflict* (New York: Family Service Association of America, 1949), pp. 90, 97, and 209; Carol Meyer, "Complementarity and Marital Conflict: The Development of a Concept and Its Application to the Casework Method" (doctoral dissertation, Columbia University School of Social Work, New York, 1957); and Bela Mittlemann, "Analysis of Reciprocal Neurotic Patterns in Family Relationships," in Victor Einstein, ed., *Neurotic Interaction in Marriage* (New York: Basic Books, 1956), pp. 81–100.

9. See Marjorie Berlatsky, "Some Aspects of the Marital Problems of the Elderly," *Social Casework*, 43 (May 1962), 233–237; Sue Vesper, "Casework Aimed at Supporting Marital Role Reversal," *Social Casework*, 43 (June 1962), 303–307.

10. Kurt Lewin, *A Dynamic Theory of Personality: Selected Papers*, Donald K. Adams and Karl E. Zener, trs. (New York: McGraw-Hill, 1935), p. 11.

11. Many cases involving psychosis or borderline psychosis are now referred to casework agencies. With proper precautions, including psychiatric consultation, considerable help can be given many of these clients by use of sustaining procedures, direct influence and discussion of current person-situation realities.

12. An excellent psychiatric reference as guide to the clinical diagnosis is John C. Nemiah, *Foundations of Psychopathology* (New York: Oxford University Press, 1961). For more detailed understanding, the following add depth: Franz Alexander, "The Neurotic Character," *International Journal of Psychoanalysis*, 11 (1930), 292–311; Franz Alexander and Helen Ross, eds., *Dynamic Psychiatry* (Chicago: University of Chicago Press, 1952); Norma Cameron, *Personality Development and Psychopathology* (Boston: Houghton Mifflin Co., 1963); Helene Deutsch, *Psycho-analysis of the Neurosis* (London: Hogarth Press, 1951); O. Spurgeon English and Gerald H. J. Pearson, *Common Neuroses of Children and Adults* (New York: W. W. Norton and Co., 1937); Otto Fenichel, *The Psychoanalytic Theory of Neurosis* (New York: W. W. Norton and Co., 1945); Arthur Percy Noyes, *Modern Clinical Psychiatry*, 5th ed. (Philadelphia: W. B. Saunders Co., 1959); and Herman Nunberg, *Principles of Psychoanalysis: Their Application to the Neuroses*, Madlyn and Sidney Kahr, trs. (New York: International Universities Press, 1955).

16 | *Understanding and Choice of Treatment Objectives*

We now come to the question of treatment planning—the purpose for which psychosocial study and diagnostic assessment are undertaken. By *planning* is meant the caseworker's formulation of the kind of help he will *offer* the client, the kind of treatment he believes will be of most value to him. As we have noted, treatment in the end depends not on what the caseworker offers but on what the client is willing to accept and participate in. It involves the willing participation of both client and therapist, with the client's response to treatment throughout the contact being a most important indicator of his capacity and motivation.[1] It has also been stressed that treatment is a very fluid affair, changing its direction and emphasis as it proceeds in response to new understanding, which sometimes confirms but at other times modifies the earlier picture.

The knowledge made available by the psychosocial study and the diagnostic assessment is used in two ways. First, it supplies the basis for major decisions concerning the general direction of treatment and for details of its early stages. Second, it provides a fund of information that the worker will continue to draw on in treatment planning and treatment throughout his whole association with the client. Later content enlarges upon earlier content as it is compared with earlier content in the worker's mind. Knowledge attained early gives perspective to what comes later and often is drawn on in helping the client to increase his understanding. Similarly, throughout treatment, diagnostic conclusions remain a backdrop against which necessary decisions about details of procedure can be made.

In thinking about the best way to help a client the worker must first envisage tentative goals of treatment and then assess the technical means by which the client can be helped to reach them. Goals are influenced not only by what types of changes might be desirable but also by whether or not the means for bringing such changes exist, both in the client-situation gestalt and in the casework process. In the present chapter we will consider goals, moving on in the next to examine treatment methodology.

GOALS: INTERMEDIATE AND LONG RANGE

When we speak of goals we really refer to a series of intermediate or subgoals as well as to the overall or ultimate objective of treatment. This ultimate goal is always some type of improvement in the client's personal-social life, that is, in his personal sense of comfort or satisfaction in life and often in his functioning as it affects the people with whom he is associated. These two types of improvement often do go hand in hand, although the client may be primarily concerned with one more than with the other and the causes of his malfunctioning or discomfort may lie primarily in either himself or his social situation.

The long-range goal is, of course, related to the problem that the client is either aware of at the beginning of the contact or comes to recognize as treatment proceeds. Sometimes the client has a broad awareness of the nature of his problem at the outset of treatment. In the very first interview a mother may say, "I know there must be something wrong with the way I am handling Tommie." She does not know all that lies behind the trouble, but she sees that she herself is involved as well as Tommie and at least implicitly recognizes that the goal of treatment includes modification of herself as well as of the child. Very often, however, in interpersonal problems, the client sees the trouble as lying only in the other person—child, husband, wife. This was the case, for example, with Mrs. Ryman, whose treatment was outlined in Chapter 3. An important part of treatment in this case was bringing Mrs. Ryman to recognize her own role in the marital conflict and working through her resistance to trying to understand and modify her own behavior. Sometimes the problem does lie primarily in someone else, but even here interaction is involved and there is need for change in the person seeking help, whether or not other people involved in the situation are also willing to change. Frequently, too, the very location of a problem appears to be in one area of functioning at the outset of treatment but in another after a few interviews. The client may see his problem as difficulty with a child, while the worker, listening to him describe the divergent ways in which he and his wife handle the child, may locate the trouble as being also, or even primarily, in tension between husband and wife.

In some cases where the problem is almost exclusively an external one, the goal is to bring changes in the outer situation either directly or by helping the client to do this. In others of this type the goal includes the client's learning to cope with such situations himself, so that when similar ones occur in the future he will be more able to handle them without outside help. In problems of interpersonal adjustment the ultimate goal from the caseworker's point of view is not solely to find a solution to the immediate problem or dilemma but, whenever possible, to enable the client to achieve a better way of functioning at least in this one area of his life.

Ultimate goals are sometimes quite limited and specific and at other times quite broad. The goal may be to enable an older person to arrange more suitable living arrangements, to work through a patient's reluctance to consent to a necessary operation, or to help a mother decide whether to send a deaf child to a residential school. On the other hand, it may be to bring about a better marriage adjustment or a better parent-child relationship or to help a borderline schizophrenic client to make a better work and social adjustment. The choice of the final goal is influenced first by what the client wants, second by what the worker thinks is both desirable and possible, and third by certain peripheral factors.

The intermediate goals of treatment are always way-stations on the road to the ultimate aim, means by which it is hoped the final goal will be achieved. For guidelines to these subgoals the worker relies upon the insights gained in the diagnostic study. The strengths and weaknesses and the dynamics of the person-situation systems have now been at least partially clarified; there is some measure of understanding of etiology. Again, in effect, the field is scanned—this time to see where modification may be possible. What factors seem to be salient in bringing the difficulty about? Which of these factors can be changed? Which are not likely to change or would do so only with great difficulty? Where are the weaknesses or idiosyncrasies in either the client's personality or in his milieu? What strengths can be brought to bear on the dilemma?

Systems Considerations

Several concepts concerning the nature of systems bear on the question of ascertaining intermediate goals. Since any change in any element in a system has an effect on every other element, it is not necessary to work directly with every aspect of a problem. Improvement in one part may well bring improvement in another. But this is not automatic. Sometimes improvement in one part of a system can affect another part adversely. For instance, in a situation where the presenting problem is a teenage boy's hostility to his mother, if this is accompanied by jealousy between father and son, encouraging a better mother-son relationship may result in greater father-son tension and greater husband-wife tension also. In such a situation other approaches may be both possible and preferable. A better husband-wife relationship may need to precede work on the son's problem. Or it may be best, depending on other factors, to work first with the father, helping him with his fear of displacement by his son. Or it may be better to work with the boy himself, helping him to build greater security outside the family. Or the best approach may be to treat the total family problem in family interviews. Only by looking at all pertinent aspects of the total picture—assets and liabilities, interrelationships, and motivations—can one find guidelines as to which approach is most likely to bring improvement.

In doing this the worker often makes use of another characteristic of systems, the fact that there is usually in each system what is called "a point of maximum reverberation." As we mentioned before, this refers to a spot in the system at which any change will bring about a great amount of modification in other elements. One member of a family may be a "key person." Or in an employment problem the key person may be a shop steward rather than the foreman, or it may even be the wife. In other words, by looking at the interrelationships within and among systems the worker can judge where the point of greatest potential effectiveness lies. The same principle holds for factors within the personality, or personality system, of the individual.

Illustrations of intermediate goals may be useful. We speak of hoping to induce a mother to send her child to camp, or a husband to share his thoughts and feelings more fully with his wife. Or we say that we will endeavor to reduce the severity of the superego, or to strengthen the client's ability to assert his own needs or to modify his tendency to project. These objectives are sought only because they are seen as necessary for the achievement of an ultimate goal of improved personal-social functioning. They are closely related to the procedures of treatment and are often articulated in combination with them. A worker will say that he intends to "try to reduce anxiety by acceptance and reassurance and by getting the sister-in-law who lives nearby to visit daily," "try to reduce hostility to child by ventilation of mother's anger," "endeavor to get father to see he is displacing hostility to John from his own brother," "help mother to see that her failure to control Sidney is increasing his anxiety," "use corrective relationship to help Mrs. George reduce her tensions about sex," "try to get Mr. Brown to recognize his underlying hostility to his father" "confront Mrs. Field with the consequences of her impulsiveness in an effort to get her to control it." None of these objectives is an end in itself, but rather a way-station on the road to better personal-social functioning. Each rests directly upon some aspects of the diagnostic assessment.

Problem Considerations

Some valuable work has recently been done on "crises" as one form of dilemma or predicament a person may face. Going back to Erich Lindemann's work on the Coconut Grove fire and the effects of this catastrophe on its victims,[2] Howard Parad and Gerald Caplan,[3] and more recently David Kaplan,[4] have pointed out the value of studying the exact nature of the crises by which individuals or families are confronted in order to understand the tasks they must undertake in order to surmount them. For instance, David Kaplan and Edward Mason, in their analysis of the crisis of premature birth,[5] point out that four distinct psychological tasks confront the mother of a premature child. Beginning with her expression of "anticipatory grief" in preparation for the possible loss of the child, she must then face her feelings about her inability to deliver a normal full-term baby. If the infant survives, he may be kept in the hospital for as long as eight to ten weeks. The mother is thus confronted by the task of establishing her relationship with the child long after this would have grown through natural maternal tasks and the child's response to her care. Finally, she has the task of understanding how a premature baby differs from a normal baby in its special needs and growth patterns. The accomplishment of each of these psychological tasks actually constitutes an intermediate goal of treatment.

Similar analyses could be made of many other situations that confront clients, whether or not they can be called "acute situational disorders." In the previous chapter the case of the woman who is pregnant out of wedlock was used to illustrate the significance of the problem classification for treatment. The points listed in that case were actually intermediate goals. Similarly, in the situation of Mrs. Kord, a sixty-five year old woman whose husband's mental and physical deterioration following several strokes appeared to require his permanent hospitalization, a worker could delineate a number of such subgoals: (1) to learn through a medical appraisal whether he was right in believing that hospitalization was the best plan; (2) to help Mrs. Kord to realize the need for this step; (3) to prepare Mr. Kord for this change insofar as this was possible; (4) to help Mrs. Kord work through her feelings of guilt over no longer being able to care for her husband; (5) to help Mrs. Kord work out the actual plans for hospitalization; (6) to deal with close relatives who were concerned about Mr. Kord and unrealistically brought pressure to bear on Mrs. Kord to continue to keep him at home; (7) to help Mrs. Kord work through her guilt over the placement itself and her grief over losing her husband; (8) to help Mrs. Kord resume former interests and pleasures. The nature of the problem itself, that is, is an important determinant of both long-range and intermediate goals.

GOALS AND MOTIVATION

Another factor that is as important as the nature of the problem in determining both ultimate and intermediate treatment goals is the client's motivation.[6] Motivation involves, first, the client's own degree of discomfort with things as they are. Has he come in of his own volition or has he been urged or even coerced into seeking help? In the latter instance much will depend on the therapist's skill in enabling him to recognize that he himself may gain from participating in treatment. He may need to ventilate a good deal of feeling about the situation that precipitated the opening of the contact and the person responsible for his coming. More important, he will need to gain some preliminary understanding of the nature of the treatment situation. Above all, he will need to be convinced of the worker's acceptance of him and interest in understanding and helping him for his own sake rather than to please others who are dissatisfied with him. And, except in certain protective situations, he will also need to know that the worker does not intend to impose help or change upon him but rather is there as an enabler, and only with his consent.[7]

In sociological terminology we can say that the client gradually becomes "acculturated to the role of a client," that is, he adapts himself to the treatment process, learning how to be a patient or client.[8] A first step in this "acculturation," and a crucial one for developing and maintaining motivation, is that of coming to appreciate the intent of the therapist and his basic attitude toward his client. The client must also learn what kind of participation is appropriate in interviews. This too begins in the first interview, which is in itself a sample of what treatment will be like and thereby makes its own contribution to the client's motivation to continue in the undertaking.

Another major component of motivation rests upon the client's values. Only if the parent believes that a child should do well in school will he become interested in improving his child's school adjustment. Only if he believes that a child should be happy and spontaneous will he be disturbed by his child's excessive anxiety and inhibitions. Only if a wife believes in the ideal of an equalitarian marriage will she complain if her husband is dominating. Clearly, class and ethnic factors, as well as more individualized family and personal norms, enter into these values.

In general the client's aspirations for himself are likely to be in terms of the norms of his own culture unless he is trying to identify himself with a group other than that of his family of orientation.[9] The fact that a certain way of functioning is the "mode" for a particular ethnic group or class is not in itself, however, sufficient to assure that it is the most useful way of functioning either for the client's associates or for himself. We are well aware of the fallacy in a worker's trying to impose on the client his own way of doing things. It is equally fallacious to give blind allegiance to cultural pluralism.[10] Cultures can be sick too. The worker must steer carefully between these twin errors, neither introducing culturally foreign goals because of personal preference for them nor feeling inhibited from trying to motivate the client to changes in culturally conditioned ways of behaving when his social functioning and personal well-being will be improved by such change. In considering this question the worker should also weigh in the balance the expectations, interpretations, and reactions of the client's associates as these are influenced by ethnic or class factors.

In recent years there has been a healthy reemphasis on the long-recognized fact that the worker's personal values, including those of his own class and ethnic background, enter into his judgments concerning treatment goals and that attention must be paid to the question of whether these are realistic in the client's terms. Certainly the worker's *personal* values must not be translated into goals for the client. His *professional* norms and values, on the other hand, inevitably and quite appropriately become a factor in treatment objectives. When a mother complains about an adolescent's behavior, the worker compares her description with his own conception of the range of adolescent behavior that can be tolerated without bringing harm to the child or his associates, and of the relationship of the type of behavior shown by the child to later adult adjustment. The worker's evaluation should include, as well, considerations of class and ethnic background that influence role expectations and constitute part of any evaluation of norms. The objective of treatment then becomes an effort to narrow the gap between the initial situation and the worker's professional conception of socially and personally "healthy" functioning. It might take the form of helping the mother to see that her child was only showing normal adolescent growing pains, or else of helping her in various specific ways to respond more appropriately to real disturbance in the child. This type of evaluation is a constant part of the setting of treatment objectives.

It has long been recognized by caseworkers, and has recently been emphasized in role analyses, that the client initially comes to treatment with a good deal of trepidation and often with underlying resentment at having to take what is essentially a dependent position. This is true even when he comes of his own volition, with favorable knowledge of the agency and of the nature of the treatment. In a culture that values independence as much as ours, it is not easy to admit that one cannot handle one's own problems. Fear of criticism and fear of the changes to which treatment may lead are often present too. But it must also be recognized that anxiety and discomfort are important components in motivation.

We are accustomed to think of anxiety as something to be gotten rid of. Without it, however, motivation may lag. With too much, on the other hand, there may be immobilization. The ideal therapeutic situation is one in which the client is anxious enough to want help and to keep coming for it, but not so afraid that fear interferes with his ability to use help.

Motivation is also affected by the client's appreciation of his problem and its ramifications. Most individuals tend in one way or another to minimize or to blind themselves to their difficulties. A husband remembers that he was grouchy last night but does not appreciate the fact that last night was only one of many and that he is slowly becoming disgusted with his marriage, while his wife is becoming withdrawn and despondent. His motivation for treatment may be very low unless in the first few interviews he can come to realize that his marriage is really breaking up and that his wife, despite her defensive appearance of disinterest, is deeply hurt because she still has a great deal of love for him. Not infrequently, when in joint interviews one partner's caring for the other comes to light during the exploratory period, the other will exclaim, "But I didn't know you cared any more—why didn't you tell me?" or "How could I have been so blind!" Following such realizations motivation may come to life. Their occurrence at any stage of treatment may mark the turning point from resistance to full participation and may make possible intermediate treatment goals quite different from those thought feasible before.

Motivation is also affected by hope. It is always easier to pursue a goal if one has hope of achieving it. Hope is partly controlled by the dilemma itself, which may be either a stubbornly intransigent one or one that can be remedied with relative ease. Most troubles, however, fall between these extremes. The worker's attitude, both expressed and unexpressed, can then have considerable influence upon the degree of hope felt by the client. It often helps if the worker puts into words his belief that the client can achieve greater comfort or satisfaction through treatment, when the worker is confident that this is so.[11]

GOALS AND ETIOLOGICAL FACTORS

Obviously, intermediate goals are related to the worker's view of what is *causing* the difficulty—its *etiology*. But one hesitates to use the word "cause" for it tends to suggest a definite entity that one can put a finger on and say "*this* is the cause." The term "contributing factors" perhaps conveys the actuality more accurately. Many factors interrelate in the shaping of any human problem. So when one talks of causation, or etiology, one is not referring to single entities but rather to the many factors that taken together and interacting within a common system or among related systems comprise the problematic condition.

It is not enough, however, simply to locate what appear to be the salient contributing factors. A second question then arises —which of these numerous factors lend themselves to modification?

Modifiability of Contributing Factors

Not infrequently the most important etiological factor is not the one most likely to yield to treatment. The most direct cause of disturbance in a family may be the presence of a severely retarded child who, for the benefit of the rest of the children as well as the mother, should be institutionalized. Sometimes early work shows that it is impossible at this time to enable the mother to agree to place the child or even that there is no suitable place to send the child. The objective then becomes improvement in the mother's household management and in her relationships with the rest of her family. Household or other help may free more of her time for them, and her perception of their requirements may be heightened so that she responds more adequately to their needs. Later, work with the other children's problems may lead to intrapsychic shifts that make it possible to return to the question of placement of the retarded child. Poor housing may be another factor that cannot be improved by treatment: a family's low income and crowded conditions in the city may make it impossible to do anything about their housing. Attention may be focused instead on the children's peer relationships and opportunities to build these up in the local community center, and on health care and income management. Sometimes a marital and parent-child problem arises because of mental disturbance in one parent, which is not so serious as to require hospitalization but does make substantial modification of the marital relationship impossible. Although this major cause of the family's problem cannot be remedied, as an alternative it may be possible for the healthier parent to work on the problems of the children.

Sometimes the unmodifiable contributing factor lies within the personality of the client himself. It may, for instance, be clear that a woman is overly dependent and that an excessive need to be cared for in a childish fashion leads her to involve herself in unwise relationships with men who give the appearance of strength but always have character defects that eventually cause her unhappiness and suffering. Her dependence may be so strong and deep-seated that it is impossible to reduce it, but the caseworker may be able to help her recognize her pattern and the consequences of her haste to satisfy her needs, and may endeavor to strengthen her perception and judgment to the point that she can find a more stable person to lean on. Or a mother may be overly protective of her child because she is thus attempting to control or compensate for unconscious wishes to destroy him, but her guilt and anxiety may be so great that it would be unwise to bring any of her hostility into the open. The underlying cause of the overprotectiveness may not be modifiable by casework methods, but other treatment goals may be set up, seeking either to protect the child from the mother or to enable the mother to modify her behavior toward the child through helping her to understand his needs better.

Indeed, there is one whole group of contributing factors that can never in themselves be changed—harmful developmental experiences. The individual's *reactions* to these experiences can be modified, but not the experiences themselves. Sometimes the client can reevaluate them in the light of more mature judgment, or can see that he has actually distorted the early picture. This was true, for example, of the woman who blamed her parents for not letting her go to college when, as she later came to see, she had never let them know that college interested her (see Chapter 8). At other times, however, even the reactions cannot be modified, but some control can be gained over them as the client becomes aware of them and of their effects in his current life.

It must be abundantly clear from the examples given that when we speak of the influence on treatment aims of etiology or of modifiability we actually mean the worker's thinking about these factors. How he views them rests not only on his individual perception and judgment but also on the body of theory that influences his conclusions. A second worker viewing a client and his situation from the vantage point of a different theory might well come to different conclusions about causation and modifiability and therefore envisage different treatment aims. Theory of causation, or etiology, and treatment goals are closely related. It follows that insofar as one theory is either more or less adequate than another theory, treatment will correspondingly be either more or less effective.

Thus far we have been discussing treatment goals from a client-centered perspective. A number of other factors must of necessity enter into the emergence of both intermediate and long-range goals.

Needs of Other Family Members

It is the exception rather than the rule that the worker can be concerned with the welfare of only the client. The caseworker always has an overall responsibility to the people with whom the client is interacting and sometimes, as when he is dealing directly with several members of the same family, a very direct responsibility. This constitutes another variable intervening between motivation, etiology, and treatment. The worker must take into consideration the effect on others in the family of changes sought in the individual who for the moment is the focus of attention. This does not mean that he sacrifices the interests of one individual to those of another, but rather that it is his responsibility to bring into the treatment planning in both his own and the client's mind pertinent interrelationships between the client and other members of his family. Nor is this an intrusion into the integrity of the treatment process, for neither worker nor client can move wisely without giving full consideration to the interactions among family members.[12] Complementarity exists in family relationships. A change in one part of the equilibrium not only brings changes in other parts but also results in "feedback," counterreactions that in turn affect the person with whom the change originated.

Increasingly in interpersonal adjustment problems, work is conducted with two or more people in a family at the same time. Sometimes they are seen separately and sometimes together. Whichever mode of treatment is used, goals can never be formulated in isolation. The ultimate goals are often, though not always, the same for the several people involved. Intermediate objectives usually vary. The needs and ways of functioning of family members interlock, and certainly interact in a transactional way, but each member of the family is nevertheless an individual in his own right. Neither his goals nor his actions are solely the result of interaction; they are firmly rooted also in the individual personalities.

Treatment, whether in individual, joint, or family interviews, must make substantial use of interactions, mutual provocations, and misunderstandings among family members, but for full effectiveness it must be guided by diagnostic understanding of each individual as well as by knowledge of family interrelationships. Otherwise, it will lack sufficient direction and specificity and may even be seriously misdirected. It is change in the individual after all—in his perceptions, his judgments, his understanding, his motivation, his controls—that enables him to contribute his part to change in any social system of which he is a member.

Peripheral Factors

Before going on to an examination of the choice of treatment procedures in the next chapter, we must consider additional variables—somewhat peripheral but nevertheless important—that intervene between treatment and the ideal objective of modifying or removing the causal factors in the client's difficulty.

An obvious one is time. If experience indicates that a certain type of change is likely to require a number of months of work and the client will be available for only a few interviews, it certainly makes no sense to embark upon a line of treatment that will have to be interrupted midway. A decision on this factor will be influenced not only by the special function of the agency—as in Travelers' Aid, where contact is almost always limited to a short time span—but also by circumstances affecting the client. The matter about which he is coming for help may have to be settled within a few days or a few weeks. Even in long-term treatment the time factor may unexpectedly become important. After six or nine months of treatment a client may have to move to another city. Themes may be emerging at this point about which treatment decisions must be made. If they cannot be developed profitably within the time available, they should be circumvented rather than opened up and dealt with inadequately.

Another variable affecting the nature of treatment may be the way in which the agency function is defined. The course of a case in which there are both parent-child and marital problems is apt to be very different, depending upon whether the client applies to a child guidance clinic or to a family service agency. A woman who is deciding whether to separate from her ill but very difficult husband may be offered very different treatment, depending upon whether she goes to the social service department of the hospital for the mentally ill where her husband is being treated or to a mental hygiene clinic in her own community.

An agency's view of priorities in its function will often translate itself into other variables affecting treatment: offices that do or do not provide privacy or protection from interruption during interviews; caseloads that permit forty-five to sixty minute interviews per week for each client who needs the time, or caseloads that are too large to permit interviews of this length or frequency; and so on. Casework that has as its objective a substantial change in individual functioning usually requires uninterrupted and regular interviewing time. Exceptions to this occur in crisis treatment, but this requires a special set of circumstances.

The availability of dynamically oriented psychiatric consultation is another variable that may influence choice of treatment aim and procedure. Work with types of intrapsychic problems in which considerable anxiety may be stirred up is usually not undertaken without consultation with an analytically trained consultant.

The caseworker's skill is an intervening factor of great importance.[13] Different themes, aims, and procedures require different kinds of skill. It is essential that the worker define treatment aims and employ procedures that lie within his range of competence and, within these limits, treat with skill rather than

venture in a clumsy fashion into forms of treatment he is un-
sure of. This requirement, however, must not be taken to mean
that treatment skill is static and cannot be further developed in
workers, but rather that development is achieved by gradual
reaching just beyond the border of one's present ability and not
by luring the client into deep and troubled waters to sink or
swim along with the worker.

Ideally, of course, the client's need should be met by whatever
form of treatment will bring him the greatest relief from his
discomfort. This means either that the agency function should
be sufficiently flexible to adapt to varying needs or that when
possible transfers should be made to other agencies that offer the
required treatment. It also means that within agencies clients
should be referred to workers whose skill is adequate to meet
their particular needs. These are objectives toward which the
worker should and does work. Meanwhile, however, the variables mentioned here are realistic factors that must be taken into
consideration in setting treatment objectives and planning treatment strategy that will result in greater comfort for the client
and improvement in his functioning.

Treatment goals, then, are arrived at jointly by client and
worker, whether the process is implicit or explicit. It is often
of great value for the goals to be explicit, for the client will
more surely move toward his objectives when he is conscious
of what they are. Goals are finally implemented only when they
are shared by both client and worker. The objectives of treatment must be thought of as fluid, changing with changes in the
client's understanding of his own needs and in his motivation
and as the worker's understanding of the client's needs and
capacities develops. The response to treatment itself is a major
component in these reformulations. Although the ultimate goal
is often seen at the beginning of treatment, intermediate and
short-range goals are set as new phases of treatment emerge and
may exist even within single interviews.

To have goals in mind is of the greatest importance in treatment. They not only enable the worker to avoid drifting along
in a kindly, noneffective way, but also make it possible to avoid
blind alleys. Conscious treatment planning serves the purpose

of trial action. It compels the therapist to think through the possibilities and consequences of a line of treatment before undertaking it. Many pitfalls can be foreseen without the client's having to participate in the worker's trial and error. Well-focused and consciously planned therapy is more apt to be effective therapy.

NOTES

1. See Helen P. Taussig, "Treatment as an Aid to Diagnosis," *The Family* 19 (January 1939), 289–294.

2. Erich Lindemann, "Symptomatology and Management of Acute Grief," *American Journal of Psychiatry*, 101 (1944), 141–148.

3. Howard J. Parad and Gerald Caplan, "A Framework for Studying Families in Crisis," *Social Work*, 5 (July 1960), 3–15.

4. David M. Kaplan, "A Concept of Acute Situational Disorders," *Social Work*, 7 (April 1962), 15–23.

5. David M. Kaplan and Edward A. Mason, "Maternal Reactions to Premature Birth Viewed as an Acute Emotional Disorder," *American Journal of Orthopsychiatry*, 30 (July 1960), 539–547.

6. The subject of motivation is often discussed under the name of its opposite—that is, resistance. In many ways these are two sides of the same coin: to "reduce resistance" is to "increase motivation." For discussion of resistance in early interviews, see Gordon Hamilton, *Theory and Practice of Social Casework*, 2nd ed. (New York: Columbia University Press, 1951), pp. 52, 56–57, 80, and 210. A useful discussion of resistance per se can be found in William H. Wilsnack, "Handling Resistance in Social Casework," *American Journal of Orthopsychiatry*, 16 (April 1946), 297–311. See also Beatrice Werble, "Motivation for Using Casework Services. I. Current Research in Motivation," *Social Casework*, 39 (February–March 1958), 124–130.

7. In recent years the term "contract" has come into use to describe the explicit common understanding of conditions and goals of treatment arrived at by client and worker. For the general subject of client and worker goal setting see: Werner Gottlieb and Joe Stanley, "Mutual Goals and Goal Setting in Casework," *Social Casework*, 48 (October 1967), 471–481; Sylvia McMillan, "Aspirations of Low-income Mothers," *Journal of Marriage and the Family*, 29 (May 1967), 282–287; Genevieve Oxley, "The Caseworker's Expectations and Client Motivation," *Social Casework*, 47 (July 1966), 432–437.

8. See Helen H. Perlman, "Intake and Some Role Considerations," *Social Casework*, 41 (December 1960), 171–177, and "The Role Concept and

Social Casework: Some Explorations. I. The 'Social' in Social Case-work," *Social Service Review*, 35 (December 1961), 370–381. See also letters to the editor appearing in subsequent issues following each of these articles and the article by Aaron Rosenblatt, "The Application of Role Concepts to the Intake Process," *Social Casework*, 43 (January 1962), 8–14. Also of interest is John Spiegel, "The Social Roles of Doctor and Patient in Psychoanalysis and Psychotherapy," *Psychiatry*, 17 (December 1954) 369–376.

9. See especially, Mirra Komarovsky, *Blue-Collar Marriage* (New York: Random House, 1964); Hylan Lewis, *Culture, Class and Poverty*, (Washington, D.C.: Cross Tell, 1967), pp. 5 and 37; Sylvia McMillan, "Aspirations of Low-income Mothers," *Journal of Marriage and the Family*, 29 (May 1967), 282–287.

10. For an excellent statement of this, see Louis Lehrman, "Science, Art and Social Casework," mimeographed (Pittsburgh, Pa.: University of Pittsburgh Graduate School of Social Work, 1957).

11. Lillian Ripple, Ernestina Alexander, and Bernice Polemis, *Motivation, Capacity and Opportunity*, Social Service Monographs (Chicago: University of Chicago Press, 1964), deal extensively with the fore-going in their study of the importance of the "discomfort-hope" balance in the client's use of treatment. For their conclusions see pp. 198–206; Jerome Frank also stresses the importance of hope in "The Role of Hope in Psychotherapy," *International Journal of Psychiatry*, 5 (May 1968).

12. See Dorothy Aiken, "A Project on Family Diagnosis and Treatment," National Conference of Social Work, *Social Work Practice* (New York: Columbia University Press, 1963), pp. 4–18; Edna Wasser, "Family Casework Focus on the Older Person," *Social Casework*, 47 (July 1966), 423–431.

13. Mullen's and Reid and Shyne's findings concerning worker differences amply demonstrate variations in worker approach. Edward J. Mullen, "Differences in Worker Style in Casework," *Social Casework*, 50 (June 1969), 347–353; William Reid and Ann Shyne, *Brief and Extended Casework* (New York: Columbia University Press, 1969), pp. 76 and 84. Ripple, *op. cit.*, demonstrates the effect of differences in worker warmth and encouragement. Frank, *op. cit.*, sees this aspect as one of primary importance.

17 | *Understanding and Choice of Treatment Procedures*

When we turn to the choice of treatment procedures by which we hope to move toward long-range and intermediate goals, we are again confronted by the necessity to look at the *whole*. No treatment step should be taken without the worker's being attuned not only to goals but also to the personalities of the people with whom he is working, their immediate states of mind and feeling, the quality of the relationship between worker and client or collateral, and the nature of the various ways of helping among which the worker can choose.

The nature and potential uses of the major casework procedures have already been discussed in considerable detail. The overall objectives of casework are major determinants of priorities among these procedures. One of these objectives is *competence* on the part of the client. This requires that emphasis be given to the client's doing things for himself when the task is not beyond his power and that he be encouraged to gain understanding of his milieu, of others, and of himself. The reason for the first requirement is that one learns by doing; the reason for the second rests on the fact that the ego is more able to cope with reality when the individual understands the situation by which he is confronted or the person with whom he is interacting or himself, than it is when he is blindly following suggestions or advice given by the worker.

A second overall objective of casework is to increase or at least maintain the client's sense of *self-worth*, his legitimate respect for himself. This requires that the worker avoid procedures that will threaten the client's sense of his own worth or his own competence and that he communicate an attitude of support, sustainment, and basic respect.

ENVIRONMENTAL CHANGE BY CLIENT OR WORKER

The general casework objectives of enabling the client to increase his competence has direct bearing on the decision of how to deal with problems that either involve environmental etiology or in general depend upon the use of environmental resources for their solution. For the worker is always confronted by the question of whether he should intervene on the client's behalf or encourage him to attempt to tackle the milieu problem himself. By and large, the more he can do for himself the greater the increase in his own competence and his own self-respect. But if this is to be the outcome, the change that is required must be one that he is likely to be able to bring about. Some milieu factors are more responsive to the worker than to the client.

It sometimes happens, for instance, that while a patient could talk to a doctor himself about his condition, the worker's knowledge of both doctor and patient leads him to think that the client would not get the information needed for future planning if he asked for it initially himself. Not infrequently the worker, because of his status and role, can influence the environment in a way that the client cannot. At other times the worker's knowledge or skill in human relations may enable him to effect changes beyond the client's capacity to achieve by his own efforts.[1]

Similarly, agencies have resources to supply the means of making up for environmental deficiencies that could not be overcome in any other way. In two fields in particular—public assistance and the provision of substitute care, such as foster homes, institutionalization, or adoption for children—agencies offer resources for changing the environment that the client could not provide for himself or could obtain only with great difficulty.

Furthermore, factors within the client himself may make him unable or reluctant to act on his own behalf. Depression or great anxiety—the very state of mind that one is attempting to alleviate—may make it impossible for an individual to reach out for the comfort and support of relatives or friends, and this may have to be done for him. Sometimes, too, the expenditure of effort required is out of proportion to the benefit that would come from the client's acting for himself. It doesn't make sense for a man to lose a day's work to get a piece of information from his public assistance worker that the caseworker can get for him over the telephone.

Nevertheless, a very large part of the time it is possible for the client to bring about environmental changes himself. When this is so, direct work with the client to this end is the preferred form of treatment. It is important for the client to learn how to make his needs known to his public assistance worker, important for him to know what his rights are, how to pursue them effectively, and how to enlist the help of others in the community—persons or organizations—in his own behalf. The same is true for other external "instrumental" problems—difficult landlords, problems with the school system, health systems, and so on. The recent increase in community resources for effective citizen and consumer action now provides many opportunities for clients to help themselves, but they need to know about these resources, their purposes and methods, and how to use them. The decision of when and when not to intervene in the environment rests upon the knowledge gained in the diagnostic assessment of both the modifiability of milieu factors and the client's capacity to handle them.

When the decision is to help the client to deal more effectively with his own environment, the worker must decide what blend of sustaining procedures, direct influence, exploration-description-ventilation, or person-situation reflection will be of the greatest benefit. To make this decision, he turns to his diagnostic impression of the client's personality, evaluating his capacity *in relation to the particular task at hand*. Is he intellectually able to deal with the situation? Can he verbalize adequately? Does he have the necessary language ability or does he need an interpreter? Are the client's perception, judgment, control, and directive capacity sufficiently good that, with help in understanding the situation that confronts him, he will be able to handle it himself? Is he immediately ready to do this, or are his feelings so deeply involved in the situation that he first needs to ventilate them as a prelude to clear thinking? When the pressure of underlying emotion is so great that it interferes with wise action or even consideration of action, ventilation may be required. When anxiety is high, or the self-image low, or the defense of turning against the self is crippling the client's self-confidence or causing him to behave in masochistic, self-damaging ways, a large measure of sustaining procedures may need to precede and accompany reflective discussion of his situation and ways in which he can change it.

Note that personality is not being assessed in the abstract here but rather in relation to the task or situation that the individual faces. A person may be capable of rational consideration of one type of dilemma, but not of another; amenable to advice about matters on which the caseworker is regarded as an expert, but not amenable about others; overwhelmed by anxiety under some circumstances, cool and collected in others that to an outsider might seem just as threatening.

Still another factor can enter into the decision to "do for" the client at certain points rather than encourage him to handle an environmental matter himself. This is the question of what effect the use of one mode of treatment or another in dealing with a particular aspect of a problem will have on treatment as a whole. For instance, it has been demonstrated that in order to convince the hard-to-reach client that the worker is really well disposed toward him and interested in helping rather than reforming him for someone else's benefit, it is necessary to do practical things for him from which he can derive benefit and pleasure.[2] With such a client the worker would welcome the opportunity to bring about environmental changes, whether or not the client might eventually learn how to effect the changes himself. Learning to do for himself will come later in the contact; in the early stages of treatment, priority must be given to measures that will build a therapeutically useful relationship.

Occasionally, too, the matter of timing enters into the decision. For the benefit of a child it may be important for a teacher to be seen immediately. Though it would be better for the child's mother to make the contact, it may take some weeks before she can be brought to do so. Under these circumstances, if the mother is willing for the worker to visit the teacher, this would be the advisable course to follow.

Even when the need for direct intervention by the worker in the client's environment is great, treatment also always includes purposeful use of procedures for work with the client himself. At the very least these include exploration, sustainment in the form of courtesy and interest, and the giving of information. The first two forms of person-situation reflection, those that concern the promotion of understanding of situational factors and the weighing of the advisability of one course of action or another, are usually prominent in interviews.

When the casework contact goes beyond one or two interviews, emphasis is usually placed on direct work with the client himself rather than on environmental intervention by the worker in order to enhance the client's ability to deal with his milieu. Only with the client who is severely handicapped in his ability to handle his affairs or extremely distrustful of the worker may the balance need to be adjusted in favor of environmental work, and then usually in early contacts more than in later ones.

WORK WITH COLLATERALS

When the worker does intervene directly in the client's milieu, he is again guided in his methodology by his understanding of the individuals with whom he is working and the systems of which they are a part. There are two vantage points from which to consider the relationship between diagnostic understanding and treatment in work with collaterals. One is the type of communication. The other is the role taken by the worker. We noted earlier that the first four types of communication are used with individuals in the client's milieu, as well as with the client himself. They can be angry. They can be anxious. They can lack information about the client that would modify their attitude toward him. They can be genuinely baffled and uncertain about what to do. While there is no formal psychosocial study of collaterals, the worker does often know a good deal about pertinent aspects of such people from the client and others. In addition, a worker makes a rapid assessment of the person as he talks with him whether it be in person or by telephone. The collateral too may need an opportunity for ventilation before he is willing to listen to what the worker wants to say or to ask. There are times when sustainment is needed to demonstrate that the worker is not coming in a spirit of attack or criticizing. Usually the worker's effort is either essentially exploration to learn about the client or about resources or opportunities that might be made available to him or it is an attempt to change or expand the collateral's understanding of the client. Here, as with the client, the worker has to be attuned to the person's response, including his facial expression and other nonverbal behavior, to assess his receptivity. These observations guide the worker as to whether he goes on and asks further about the other person's thinking. Sometimes discussion of consequences is appropriate and even necessary. Intrareflective procedures on the other hand are rarely a part of work with collaterals.

As with the client, care must be taken to estimate the ability as well as the willingness of the collateral person to participate in reflective discussion about the client or steps that the collateral himself can take either to help him or to lessen the pressures he is under. Language must be adjusted to that of the collateral.

The worker's clarity about the role he is taking in collateral contacts strongly influences the degree of *directiveness* of his communications. He must be clear as to whether he is interpreter, mediator, or active intervener. He can only interpret if there is readiness to listen on the part of the person to whom he is trying to explain the client. Sometimes the worker goes to the teacher or employer with this in mind but soon discovers that it is mediation rather than simple interpretation that is needed. As noted earlier, mediation in an environmental problem is preferable to aggressive intervention. Therefore it is better to apply every means of promoting voluntary acquiescence before turning to strong measures. Here too, as the worker listens, he gains understanding of the attitudes of the person with whom he is dealing and of the total situation that confronts the collateral. Collaterals are usually not free agents. They are part of a system—school, business, court. Many influences in addition to the client and his needs enter into their decisions. The worker must have some comprehension of these either to be persuasive or subsequently to help the client understand his situation better.

Making the decision to turn to active intervention in any form requires assessment in two areas.[3] First, is it necessary? Have other means of achieving the desired environmental change been tried? Is the need sufficiently important that strong measures are warranted? Second, what are the chances of success? Does the worker have a good enough case and sufficient power to force change? If this is uncertain, will anything be lost that would not be lost anyway? Here one has to assess not only the effect on the client but also on future relationships between the person or organization involved and the worker or his agency. In this case it is usually a social system rather than a personality that is being "diagnosed." But personalities cannot be ignored. To use an extreme example, when the collateral is a litigious paranoid personality this becomes, to say the least, a highly pertinent factor in such decisions. Casework has as yet little experience in active intervention. There is still much to be learned about it. Here as elsewhere, the heart must be well advised by the head, if in the long run this client and others like him are to be helped.[4]

INTERPERSONAL RELATIONSHIPS AND INTERNAL CHANGE

When we turn to problems that primarily concern interpersonal relationships and internal change, we find that procedures designed to promote both outwardly directed and inwardly directed understanding move to the fore. Occasionally in such situations a person is so depressed or grief-stricken that treatment at first is very heavily weighted with sustainment, ventilation, and some direct influence. But characteristically there is soon some movement into thought about the details of everyday living and an effort to expand the client's awareness of his own feelings beyond depression and grief per se to other emotions.

As the worker listens to a client discussing interpersonal problems, the question constantly arises: Which thread of his communications should be picked up? Keeping in mind the principles discussed at the beginning of this chapter, we see that we must find a way that will enable the client to gain the under-

standing he needs to deal with his dilemma more competently as
rapidly as he can but without running the risk of overloading
him with more new ways of looking at things than he can comfortably assimilate or is ready to take on. To go too fast may
be to lose him.

A recent study comparing fifteen clients with marital problems who continued in treatment with fifteen who dropped out
after the first or second interview found that the workers were
markedly more inclined to make lengthy interpretations and
explanations in the initial interviews with those who dropped
out. Furthermore, it was found that these communications in
many instances had distinct potential for arousing anxiety. In
contrast, in early interviews with clients who continued, anxiety-
arousing comments had been avoided.[5]

When the sequence in which matters are taken up rests on
the worker's choice in following one lead or another, assessment
of the anxiety-arousing potential of each choice is highly pertinent. In general, except in crisis treatment and planned short-
term treatment the first two interviews are primarily exploratory
and ventilative in a strongly supportive atmosphere. When there
is tension and anger in family relationships it is usually very important to give adequate opportunity for the expression of hurt
and anger before there is much receptivity to interpretations
concerning how the other person feels or why he acts as he
does. Even less readiness may exist for any appreciation of the
way in which the client is hurting the other person or provoking
his reactions. Not only ventilation of the feelings involved but
also acceptance of the hurt and understanding of the desire to
retaliate may be needed to prepare the way for the client's willingness to understand the other's needs or to consider his own
contribution to the troubles.

Factors within the personality of the client will also influence
his readiness to try to understand another. This is well illustrated by two contrasting marital counseling cases carried by
the same worker. In the first case the worker was very active
during early contacts in promoting the wife's reflection concerning her husband. In the second, emphasis was placed instead on the wife's awareness of her own feelings. The reasons
for the difference in treatment lay not in the situations but in

the personalities of the two women. Both women were very afraid of not being loved, both were volatile women of southern European background, both were belittling their husbands and initially putting all the blame for the family unhappiness on their husbands. Both were intelligent and motivated to seek help. The first client, however, had no doubt of her love for her husband and had matured emotionally to the point that she was well related to other people and cared for their welfare as well as for her own. She immediately responded with understanding to the worker's carefully worded questions about how her husband might feel, why he might be acting as he was, and what effect some of her impulsive hostility might be having on him. So it was possible to proceed rapidly with this. The second client was a more dependent person, preoccupied with her own anxieties; she clung to her husband but was less giving of love herself. She had less spontaneous interest in her husband's feelings and reasons for them. She wanted and needed to talk about herself and how he had hurt her. Her understanding of the nature of her own feelings and the way in which this affected her feelings toward her husband had to be given precedence over attempts to develop her understanding of him.

The quality of a person's capacity to love others—referred to in Freudian terminology as the capacity for object relationships —is of primary importance in influencing his readiness for understanding others and the effects of his own ways upon others. When an individual is greatly retarded in this capacity he may lack motivation to look within himself for the cause of his difficulties. He is not sufficiently attuned to others to appreciate their feelings easily or to see the ways in which he provokes and hurts them. He is very unlikely to be able to put to good use treatment that requires much self-examination. He may be introspective, but it is a narcissistic or self-pitying type of introspection. He often can be reached only to the extent that he feels very strongly the worker's interest in helping him for his own sake. Sometimes he can be led to think of the effects of his actions on others in the context of his own self-interests.

The client's capacity for logical thinking, his experience with this thinking, and the extent to which secondary rather than primary processes dominate his thinking also strongly influence the extent to which reflective procedures in general can be used and the direction and pace at which the work can proceed. Can the client make only rather simple connections or is he a sophisticated thinker? Can he be led to reason things through for himself or must the worker explain concretely step by step? Some people know a good deal about psychological mechanisms long before they see the worker. Others are psychologically naive and must have things explained in detail. The former are not necessarily the most ready to change. Greater intellectual knowledge sometimes leads to a superficial acquiescence or to facile denial of the importance of an interpretation, even though it may be an accurate one. And it is extremely important not to mistake lack of education for intellectual handicap. Many clients with very little education are psychologically astute if time is taken to give simple straightforward explanations and concrete illustrations. Often behavior similar to what the worker is trying to help the client to understand is commonplace in children and can first be understood in them. "Look, have you ever noticed how Verne when he's mad at Phil (older brother) starts jumping on Stella (little sister)?" If the client's response shows understanding—"What about that! He sure does, he just takes it out on her"—the client will probably be able to understand the same defense mechanism in her own displacement from husband to son.

For some people, however, this sort of reasoning and the carry-over from one situation to another parallel one are impossible. Yet in some of these situations the interpersonal adjustment problem is acute. If the handicap in thought processes is not accompanied by general emotional immaturity, progress can sometimes be made by suggestion and advice. But this is not likely to be effective unless a strong positive relationship has been established so that the client has confidence in the worker's good will as well as in his good sense.

Some work has been done in both office interviews and home visits using demonstration as a teaching device. That is, in a family or joint interview the worker deals with a child's behavior himself in the way he hopes the parent will learn to do. Sometimes this is combined with talking about what was done and why, thus moving by way of demonstration into reflective discussion. Here again a strong positive relationship is necessary. Special care must also be taken not to undercut the client's self-respect or his place in his own family. No matter how wise the worker, parents do not want to be displaced by him.

In extreme situations, such as those described by Bandler in *The Drifters*,[6] one finds a combination of little conceptual ability and infantile relationship patterns. It is then extremely difficult to be helpful in interpersonal problems. Sometimes, through assisting with practical needs and difficulties, one can build a relationship through which such help can be given. Auxiliary services such as day nurseries can also be used to advantage for children in such families but, as the Drifters experiment so well demonstrated, very immature parents may actually be jealous of the services offered their children. Their own needs may have to be met before they may be ready to make use of opportunities available for their children.

Families who are plagued with severe environmental problems are often so beset by these that relationship problems seem of lesser importance. Their total energy may be consumed by the difficulties of everyday living. Casework should then concentrate on these practical problems. Once these are alleviated perhaps there will be motivation for tackling internal family stresses and strains. Even motivation toward self-understanding can be clouded by severe environmental pressures, for these prevent the client from seeing his personal involvement in his own troubles. There are too many other places to put the blame, and it is very hard for the caseworker to demonstrate the intrapsychic problem to the client convincingly. This is not to say that the presence of severe practical problems entirely precludes work on interpersonal strains. In extreme situations this is so; in others it makes work in this area more difficult but not impossible.[7] There is still much to be learned about how to give effective help under these conditions.

Ethnic factors are extremely diverse in their significance for treatment. Certainly language differences of any major proportion are a deterrent to the kind of communication necessary for intrapsychic reflection. Attitudes of personal reticence, distrust between races, a marked difference in experience and values between client and worker, difficulties in casting the worker in a therapeutic role—all are obstacles to treatment of any type and might be particularly obstructive to the pursuit of inward understanding. The degree to which these handicaps to treatment can be overcome obviously varies in different cases, but they are not to be construed as insurmountable.

The choice of procedures within the various reflective types obviously depends also very strongly upon the dilemma that the client is trying to resolve and the worker's assessment of the factors contributing to the problem. In interpersonal problems, unless contraindicated, treatment themes usually include both outwardly and inwardly directed reflection concerning the current interactional gestalt.

Specifics of what the worker seeks to help the client to become aware of and understand will depend directly upon the ongoing diagnostic assessment of what factors are contributing to the social dysfunctioning, modified constantly by the assessment of how much insight the client can assimilate. Only as the worker himself recognizes dysfunctional responses and sees the factors in personal interactions that touch off such responses can he enable the client also to recognize them.

PATTERN-DYNAMIC AND DEVELOPMENTAL REFLECTION

Whether or not to lead the client to pattern-dynamic or developmental reflection depends on the extent to which such factors are disabling and the readiness with which they can be reached, as well as on the many other considerations already discussed in this chapter. Often ego mechanisms of defense can be recognized easily by the worker but we know that these have the purpose of defending the personality against anxiety. Before calling the client's attention to a defense, one therefore has to consider whether the client can deal with the anxiety that may be aroused by his recognition of it. Under favorable circumstances it may be both helpful and important for him to understand selected defenses.

Ordinarily, however, it is not important for an individual to gain extensive understanding of dynamic and developmental factors if he is able to overcome problems in his social functioning without such insight. In many matters of perception and judgment the client, if his ego in general functions realistically, will respond to help in understanding the current person-situation interplay without the need for further understanding of his own psychological patterns. Where controls are defective or the superego is too lax, the difficulty usually does not lie in an intrapsychic conflict but rather in the relationship of the individual to the external world. Consequently, understanding of the dynamics of these inner interrelationships is usually not called for. It is true that such disturbances are frequently caused developmentally, but they are generally due to lacks in a child's upbringing rather than to influences that can be undone —or at least overcome—by reconsideration in adulthood. Insofar as treatment is possible, it consists of supplying in the present something that was lacking in the past. To accomplish this task, reflective discussion of current realities—often with an educational flavor—is the necessary approach.

On the other hand, if the client's difficulty is rooted in tension or conflict between different facets of his personality, or if the destructive developmental experiences by which he has been influenced can be counteracted by insight concerning them, procedures useful in promoting pattern-dynamic and developmental understanding should be considered. The most usual type of conflict is between the ego and either a generally overly strict superego or one that sets up special prohibitions against aggression or pleasure. The ego then reacts with defense mechanisms that cause tension either between the ego and the unmet needs of the id or within the ego itself when it is torn between realistic responses to internal and external realities and unrealistic or inappropriate defensive responses. Common destructive developmental experiences include overly restrictive or repressive upbringing, parental deprivation or hostilities, which later are displaced on other personal relationships, parental fears and inhibitions passed on to children, unrealistic parental expectations, excessively close parental ties, and emotionally traumatic experiences that are not realistically assimilated and result in anxiety, fear, or guilt against which unhealthy defenses are set up.

Until recently, it was generally held that in some cases "clarification"—or the processes of pattern-dynamic and developmental reflection—became such a major component of treatment that special diagnostic criteria had to be established to ascertain whether it could wisely be used. The subsequent research discussed in Chapter 10 has brought a different perspective to this question. It is now clear that some reflection of this kind occurs in many cases that are primarily concerned with person-situation reflection and that in very few cases is a great deal of time given to such reflection. Reflection of this kind appears rather to be part of a series of reflective types of communication, closely interwoven with general understanding of the person-situation gestalt, rather than something special and apart. In the earlier edition of this book, the writer saw pattern-dynamic and developmental reflection as having greater anxiety-arousing potential than other forms of treatment. It now appears that pattern-dynamic and developmental reflection vary in their anxiety potential in much the same way that other intrareflective procedures do. The same principles for guarding against too much anxiety would seem to apply. That is, the worker must be attuned to the specifics of client vulnerability to anxiety and to the client's ability to cope with it constructively. The same steps can be taken as in other reflective procedures to avoid arousing too much anxiety and to allay it when it does occur. Within these general guidelines, pattern-dynamic and developmental reflection would be encouraged either when such understanding is necessary in order to help the client see how and why he is reacting in unrealistic or dysfunctional ways or when such understanding will strengthen his grasp of his own patterns and contribute to his ability to change them. Here we are talking about *patterns* of intrapsychic behavior, not isolated instances. Opportunities for developing more than isolated bits of understanding do not arise except when the client is motivated toward the development of considerable self-understanding.

One wonders whether the fact that clarification was so long thought of as a sort of specialty has led to its neglect as part of the training of social workers. Mullen[8] in his work as part of the Reid-Shyne research found that some of the caseworkers in that experiment never used dynamic or developmental reflection at all, although the design of the experiment called for them to do so. He quite properly raises the question of whether this means that a substantial number of workers, even among those who are considered well·trained, may lack skill in promoting these forms of reflection. If, as research seems to indicate, clarification is not something apart but is rather appropriate in varying degrees with a large number of clients, it follows that skill in this area should become part of the knowledge of most workers who expect to concentrate on helping clients with interpersonal relationship problems.

ANXIETY AND GUILT

We have commented a number of times in this chapter on the significance of the client's anxiety. Some further points need to be made. Anxiety and guilt may logically be considered together, for guilt is one form of anxiety—in Anna Freud's words,[9] the ego's fear of the superego—and what is said about anxiety in general applies with equal force to guilt.

No single factor in treatment is more important than the worker's keeping his finger on the pulse of the client's anxiety. To begin with, he must be sensitive to the actual existence of anxiety and to the degree to which it is present in the client at any one moment. He must know the extent to which the client chronically carries anxiety around with him or is vulnerable to its arousal. What particular things in the client's present or past provoke his anxiousness? How does his anxiety show itself and how does he handle it? In particular: Does his anxiety impel him to unwise acting out? Does it result in increased neurotic or somatic symptomatology? What defenses does he use against it? Is he immobilized? Will he run away from treatment?

In order to be alert to the presence of anxiety in the client, the worker must have sound knowledge of the ways in which anxiety expresses itself. Occasionally it is shown physically, by trembling of body or voice, body tenseness, sweating or pallor, nervous gestures or excitement, and so on.[10] Sometimes the client reveals it by posture or gesture, sitting on the edge of the chair or at a distance, wrapping his coat tightly or refusing to take it off. More often anxiety shows itself in increased use of the client's characteristic defense mechanisms. The intellectual goes off into theoretical, often contentious discussions; defensive hostility erupts in the challenge that treatment is not helping, with the implication that the worker is incompetent; rationalization, reaction formation, denial—any of the mechanisms of defense—will be brought into play in their characteristic role of attempting to protect the individual from experiencing anxiety. Avoidance may finally result in the client's skipping interviews altogether. If these signs are spotted early enough, they can alert the worker to the cause of the anxiety. He can then allow the client to withdraw from exploration of the anxiety-arousing content if it is not necessary or advisable to pursue it further at that particular point.

If it does seem wise to go on, the worker can proceed in a number of ways. Sometimes it is possible to draw the client's attention to his defensiveness. At other times, and this is often true with compulsive clients, it may be necessary to work first on the personality characteristic that makes the individual respond so strongly—with compulsive clients, the overly severe superego and perfectionism. At other times it is necessary to have a period of relaxation in treatment, the worker saying directly or in effect, "perhaps later you will feel more able to talk about this." And at still other times, when the worker has good reason to think that the client is close to talking about certain experiences but is afraid to do so, he may find ways of framing a question or comment that relieves guilt or anxiety before the frightening content is actually expressed.

One often finds that after a difficult piece of self-understanding, the client, in the next interview, stays on superficial, more or less self-congratulatory material. This relaxation is necessary, and the worker must not become impatient for further immediate progress but must rather seek a balance between relaxing and sustaining measures on the one hand and procedures pressing toward self-understanding on the other.

When anxiety—or guilt—is either chronically very high, or aroused because of the experiences the client is going through when he comes for treatment, a goodly measure of sustaining procedures is of particular value. If the anxiety is immobilizing, the worker may need to rely more than ordinarily on suggestion and advice and to be even more active than usual in leading the client to think about his current dilemma.

Anxiety Aroused by Treatment

As also noted earlier, reflective consideration of intrapsychic content is by no means the only set of treatment procedures by which anxiety is aroused. Merely describing, as part of the application process, life events one is ashamed of may be a very painful, anxiety-arousing experience. Ventilation that involves the expression of emotions or desires of which the client is afraid may bring fear that talking will be a forerunner of acting. Guilt may very easily be aroused in a sensitive person by discussions that make him aware for the first time of the harmful effects of his own actions on others, or even of needs of his child or wife to which he has been blind. The individual with a very severe superego will feel guilt very keenly whenever matters come up in which he believes he is or was even slightly in the wrong. Even when the worker merely listens, such an individual anticipates criticism, often projecting his own self-condemnation onto the worker; he fears loss of love, or the worker's disinterest; he may need to defend himself by projecting blame on others or by outright denial or by defensive hostility or even withdrawal from treatment. Similar sensitivity may exist in the very narcissistic person.

Even in the giving of suggestions and advice the worker must know his client's personality well enough to foresee the possible arousal of anxiety. In one case known to the writer the worker was greatly and rightly concerned about the severity with which an impulsive mother was in the habit of disciplining her seven-year-old son. Early in the contact she advised her against it and was gratified at the change in her client's handling of the child and his immediate improvement. Unfortunately, however, she had not made a careful diagnostic study of the mother nor thought ahead to the probable consequence of her advice. In the first place, the child had never been controlled in any other way. His initial reaction was to be very good, but he soon began to explore the limits of his new freedom and became increasingly defiant of his now disarmed mother. In addition to being impulsive, the mother had a great deal of compulsiveness in her makeup. A good diagnostician could easily have identified the clinical signs of this and would have known that along with her impulsiveness this mother had a very severe conscience and a great need, like a small child, to win the worker's approval. She tried very hard to be a good mother along the lines the worker suggested. In fact, however, after the initial good news of improvement in the child, she found it very hard to let the worker know that things were not going so well. Eventually one day "all hell let loose," and her anger against her son burst forth in a really dangerous way. Then, to justify herself, she had to condemn the child as uncontrollable by any other means and turn completely away from the worker and her advice.

On the whole, the development of understanding of oneself and one's own functioning tends to arouse more anxiety than do other treatment processes. The reasons for this are several. These are types of self-examination. As the client lends himself to such treatment he comes to realize that there is something wrong with his way of functioning, something that requires inward examination. He may not have said it in so many words, but his very willingness to participate in a major way in the pursuit of self-understanding indicates tacit realization of it. He senses that there may be damage to his self-image. Once a person admits that he needs to look to himself for the cause of his troubles, he is laying himself open to criticism. He is likely to find that he had made mistakes, that he is distorting, or blaming others unnecessarily, or is inappropriately hostile, or childishly dependent, or what have you. His emerging picture of himself is almost certain to turn up some flaws of which he was previously unaware. All these realizations cause discomfort and pain, particularly if the client has a severe superego. They also constitute a narcissistic injury. These discomforts, in turn, characteristically stir up anger at the worker—the bearer of evil tidings—which causes the client still further anxiety.

Another source of anxiety is related to the client's capacity to control impulses of which he may become more aware during the course of treatment. Realistically or unrealistically, there is often fear of a breakthrough of forbidden impulses and of translating wishes and desires into action.

Anxiety can be great, too, when treatment involves the client's bringing to consciousness memories and realizations that he has hidden from himself, or has at least refrained from talking about to others. These matters would not be hidden away if they were not in some way painful. It may be the pain of sorrow and frustration. Or the superego may be affronted, for the client may be defying parental standards in producing particular memories or becoming aware of certain feelings and attitudes. This source of anxiety is similar to that experienced by the patient in analysis, who feels it even more strongly in relation to unconscious, repressed material. In analysis it is recognized as a principal source of resistance, and in casework a similar factor is involved. Painful early experiences have sometimes been of such traumatic proportions that extreme anxiety would be involved in reliving them. In such cases there is usually strong resistance to recalling them, and this should serve as a caution signal to the worker. This situation arose with people who suffered the extremes of persecution in the Second World War. Some of the things that happened to them could be assimilated only by very exceptional people and more often could be surmounted only as they could be walled off by suppressions and repressions that it would be unwise to disturb.

On the whole, a past experience that arouses anxiety concerning only the pain of reliving the experience itself is more easily borne than one that arouses guilt. If, for instance, the memory involves actions or even feelings and wishes that the individual thinks are shameful or wrong, his fear of his own and the worker's disapproval may be very strong. Guilt is frequently associated with childhood hostilities toward parents and others in families where such high value was placed on surface amiability that all anger had to be hidden. It is also associated in a great many people in our culture with childhood sexuality, current and past masturbation, and any type of sexual deviation. Both individual and cultural values are strong determinants here. For one person hostile feelings will be taboo; for another, lying; for still another, erotic responsiveness.

A further source of anxiety that may be present in any form of treatment that has as its goal some degree of change in personality functioning is the fear of the change itself. Even though present ways of functioning may cause discomfort, they also have their gratifications. A known discomfort is often not as frightening as the uncertain result of change, for the known at least has been adjusted to and lived with a long time. The direct implication of the discovery of faulty functioning is that it must be modified. Sometimes such modification is immediately gratifying, but more often there have been secondary advantages in the faulty functioning. The new understanding often requires greater self-control, less expression of hostility, less blame of others, more altruistic and less narcissistic behavior. The client may desire change, but he is also uneasy about it and reluctant to give up comfortable self-gratifying ways. But now a new discomfort has entered the picture, because the ego has seen the unreasonableness of the old ways and the superego is no longer comfortable with them.

One might well ask why with all this anxiety involved anyone ever seeks or continues to pursue greater understanding of himself and his functioning. First, let it be said that intrareflection is not universally anxiety-arousing. Certain themes, even when they are dynamically or developmentally explored, may be fairly low in their anxiety potential, and therefore can be safely explored even in "fragile" personalities. A case in the group studied, for example, included a borderline schizophrenic woman who was able to see that her suspicious expectation of hostile attack from a woman in her current life was a displacement from a childhood experience in which she had actually been very badly treated by a harsh grandmother. Discussion of the circumstances not only did not arouse anxiety, but allayed it. Talking about the oppressive grandmother was not frightening, because the worker did not attempt to explore whether the client was partly at fault but rather accepted the situation as an externally caused and regrettable hardship. Recognition of the possibility of displacement also involved no blame for the client; instead it gave her a rational explanation for some of her fears so that she was able to look more realistically at the lack of evidence in the current situation to justify them.

Second, clients sometimes find great relief in talking about painful experiences in the presence of a sympathetic worker who is not overwhelmed by their ventilation. This process may help the ego to assimilate the memories, to be less afraid of them, more able to bear the pain involved, and to express the natural emotions of grief and anger associated with the experiences. Such verbal activity is similar to the play activities of children, in which they repeat painful and frightening experiences in an effort to assimilate them. When the happenings that are being aired are also responsible for some current reaction that is causing the individual trouble, he may in the very same interview also experience a sense of relief from talking about them. For instance, a person who in reality had very critical parents, with consequent feelings of distrust in his own ability, may obtain almost immediate relief from talking about their unjust criticisms of him, and by sensing the confirmation of the worker's agreeing that they were unjust, experience some freeing of himself from his earlier acceptance of his parents' views.

Dealing with Anxiety

There is much that the worker can do to keep the anxiety level low. Of primary importance is the worker's basic attitude of support and acceptance, which softens the impact of his comments. The client must be basically secure with the worker; whatever the exigencies of the moment, there must be a strong underlying conviction that the worker feels positively toward the client, respects him, and is endeavoring to help him. This conviction is inevitably obscured from time to time at difficult moments in treatment by transference elements and by projection of the client's own attitudes. Such distortions can be corrected, however, only if the actual relationship is a positive one and fundamentally perceived as such by the client. To achieve this basic relationship and keep it alive, sustaining procedures are necessary; on the other hand, it is often necessary to refrain from reassuring and comforting remarks in order to keep the client at work pursuing understanding of his difficulties.

To illustrate: a woman who tends to be overly critical of her husband tells the caseworker about an incident in which this tendency was prominent and half apologizes for her disparaging words. The worker may either make a reassuring remark about her annoyance being understandable, or may comment more directly, "You do have a sharp tongue!" The latter procedure will not be very reassuring. It will increase rather than decrease the client's anxiety and, if the worker has correctly gauged her ego and superego qualities, will serve to motivate her to seek understanding of her overreaction. Great care must be exercised in finding the balance by which to give enough warmth and security to nourish progress and protect the client from excessive anxiety, and at the same time to maintain a level of tension conducive to motivation toward self-understanding.

As noted earlier, timing and sequence are important. The worker's diagnostic assessment of the client and his sensitivity to current moods and reactions enables him to avoid observations and insights for which the client is not yet ready.

What might be called the "form" or "style" of worker communications used in promoting reflective thinking also has a direct bearing on the client's potential anxiety. Worker comments can vary, as we have seen, from a direct interpretation or explanation to completely nonsuggestive questions or comments that merely draw the client's attention to something about which the worker would like him to think. An illustration of the latter is the repetition of the last phrase or so of something the client has said. In general, the more open-ended a worker comment is, the less likely it is to arouse anxiety, since it can be ignored—if the client is not ready to follow the worker's lead he can easily respond without any recognition of the matters to which the worker is trying to draw his attention. More direct comments and questions push the client harder, and interpretations, of course, formulate an opinion with which the client must deal. Other things being equal, the more direct the comment the greater the possibility of stirring up anxiety.

Fourth, a skillful worker finds ways of expressing things that support rather than hurt. Understanding and acceptance of attitudes, feelings, or acts that the client finds hard to face can be expressed along with the comment or interpretation that brings them to his attention. Brief sustaining comments often introduce such interpretations or thought-provoking questions and comments. The worker also in effect often "rewards" the client when he has gained a piece of understanding. It is natural for the worker to be pleased. Sometimes this is put into words.

More often facial expression and tone of voice communicate the feeling that the client has taken a step forward.

Furthermore, if treatment is kept close to the realities of life, if person-situation reflection is the central focus, the client who develops more understanding usually experiences improvement in his interpersonal relationships. He receives different responses from others in reaction to changes in his own ways of handling things. Indeed, in situations where this is lacking it is very difficult for the client not to become too discouraged to continue. This is one of the reasons for the importance of seeing both individuals involved in problems of interpersonal adjustment.

If the worker is thoroughly attuned to the client by means of sensitive diagnostic assessment of both his underlying personality pattern and the nuances of his feelings and reactions while interviews are in process, casework treatment is not basically a painful or even unpleasant process. There are, of course, ups and downs from interview to interview. But if efforts to develop understanding of self and others are well paced, the client usually experiences satisfaction in his greater grasp of his dilemma and his increased ability to cope with it. He also experiences a strengthening of his self-esteem, for the relationship in many different ways is a nourishing one.

LENGTH OF CONTACT

There remains the question of length of time for treatment. For many years it was assumed that a contact continued until the needed help was given, or until the client withdrew, or until the worker decided there was nothing more to be done. Many clients withdrew after only a few interviews. Others continued for many months, sometimes for several years. The functional school of social work had long advocated the setting of limits for the length of contact at the beginning. Proponents felt that the client worked best against such limits. This was part of the Rankian conception of growth through the negative will. Largely because of this theoretical underpinning, other caseworkers objected to what seemed to them an arbitrary setting of limits. Then came the Second World War, with an increase in applicants, shortage of workers, and long waiting lists of clients needing service. On the basis of expediency many different devices were tried to bring help more quickly. Among them was briefer service with more limited goals.

At first this was considered only an emergency measure, but workers began to see that it was more possible than they had thought to give a valid service in relatively few interviews. One form of such service was *crisis treatment*. This is a form of brief service considered appropriate when a person has been thrown off balance by some hazardous external event of a time-limited nature, which touches off within his personality reactions with which he is unable to cope. Anxiety is usually very high, so high in fact that it often produces reactions that bring the client to a psychiatric clinic, where much of the crisis treatment has been carried on. It has been found that in a period when the personality system has lost its equilibrium, it is in a state of flux in which rapid change is possible within a short time. In order to know what help is needed in terms of both objectives and procedures, a rapid diagnosis, well-grounded upon theory, must be made. Treatment tends to be quite active. Pertinent interpretations are made quickly. Goals are limited and well defined. A number of interviews may be held within a short time span.

Another type of brief service is *time-limited contacts*. Whereas crisis treatment tends to be self-limiting, since it revolves around a crisis, in time-limited contacts the worker sets up an artificial end. Interest in time-limited contacts grew as it was found that some clients were more willing to work on problems when a period of two or three months was set than when longer work was contemplated. In marital counseling cases, for instance, one study found that husbands are more apt to be willing to participate in time-limited treatment than in open-ended treatment.[11] We do not yet have adequate knowledge of diagnostic indicators as to when time-limited treatment is preferable. Experimentation is widespread. Usually when a limit is set the option is kept open for further treatment to be considered at the end of the specified period. Treatment again is more focused and more active than in open-ended treatment when no time limit is agreed upon.

We are also seeing a willingness to keep an open door for clients to return for repeated brief periods of help as it is needed in emergencies, particularly in lower-income areas where external problems are many and there is little motivation for any planned period of treatment whether long or short. What help can be given is offered immediately, with the understanding that the client is free to return again. The expectation is that some clients will use the service repeatedly and that perhaps from these recurring experiences either some increased ability to cope with pressures will be acquired or trust in the service will develop, which will make more concentrated help possible.

These various forms of shortened treatment take their places along with treatment of long duration. Many cases require nine months to a year of work and some rightly continue for several years. But the valid alternatives now recognized require that longer treatment be a matter of considered choice.

We have been endeavoring in this chapter to delineate the many ways in which the blend of casework treatment procedures that are used to help a client rests upon the worker's differential understanding of a wide range of characteristics of the client and his personal-social situation.[12] Treatment is always an individualized blend of procedures, themes, and goals. The nature of the blend is not a matter of individual worker artistry or intuition, important though these may be. On the contrary, choice and emphasis follow definite principles and rest upon most careful evaluation of the nature of the client's problem, external and internal etiological factors and their modifiability, the client's motivation, and pertinent aspects of his personality. In addition, there must be comprehension of the nature, effects, and demands of the different types of casework procedures and of the criteria by which the worker can match the client's needs and capacities with the particular combination of procedures most likely to be of value in enabling him to overcome, or at least lessen, his difficulties. It should by now be clear that the process of diagnostic assessment is an ongoing one, with the emphasis in treatment varying in harmony with the changing needs and capacities of the client.

NOTES

1. Bernard Neugebore, "Opportunity Centered Social Services," *Social Work*, 15 (April 1970), 47–52, provides sound examples.

2. See especially: Henry Freeman et al., "Can a Family Agency Be Relevant to the Inner Urban Scene?" *Social Casework*, 51 (January 1970), 12–21; Eleanor Pavenstedt, ed., *The Drifters: Children of Disorganized Lower-Class Families* (Boston: Little, Brown & Co., 1967); Arthur Pierson, "Social Work Techniques with the Poor," *Social Casework*, 51 (October 1970), 481–485.

3. See note 5, Chapter 9, p. 163.

4. Carol Meyer in her *Social Work Practice: A Response to the Urban Crisis* (New York: Free Press, 1970), stresses the need for casework intervention at many points in the social systems in which clients are involved. See especially Chapters 4 and 6.

5. Florence Hollis, "Continuance and Discontinuance in Marital Counseling and Some Observations on Joint Interviews," *Social Casework*, 49 (March 1968), 167–174.

6. Reported by Louise S. Bandler, "Family Functioning: A Psychosocial Perspective" and "Casework—A Process of Socialization: Gains, Limitations, Conclusions," in Pavenstedt, ed., *op. cit.*, pp. 225–296.

7. See Pierson, *op. cit.*

8. Edward J. Mullen, "Differences in Worker Style in Casework," *Social Casework*, 50 (June 1969), 347–353.

9. Anna Freud, *The Ego and the Mechanisms of Defense* (New York: International Universities Press, 1946), pp. 58–60.

10. Lottie Marcus, "The Effect of Extralinguistic Phenomena on the Judgment of Anxiety" (doctoral dissertation, Columbia University School of Social Work, New York, 1969).

11. William Reid and Ann Shyne, *Brief and Extended Casework* (New York: Columbia University Press, 1969).

12. In addition to the references already cited in this chapter, readers will find many of those in earlier chapters on treatment procedures and on diagnosis relevant for this chapter also. Note especially: Lucille Austin, "Casework Treatment with Clients Whose Problems of Social Dysfunctioning Are Caused by the Neurosis of Anxiety Hysteria," in Howard J. Parad, ed., *Ego Psychology and Dynamic Casework* (New York: Family Service Association of America, 1958).

    Celia Benny et al., "Clinical Complexities in Work Adjustment of Deprived Youth," *Social Casework*, 50 (June 1969), 330–336.

    Catherine Bittermann, "Marital Adjustment Patterns of Clients with Compulsive Character Disorders: Implications for Treatment," *Social Casework*, 47 (November 1966), 575–582.

Pauline Cohen and Merton Krause, *Casework with Wives of Alcoholics* (New York: Family Service Association of America, 1971).

Margaret Grunebaum, "A Study of Learning Problems of Children: Casework Implications," *Social Casework*, 42 (November 1961), 461–468.

Margaret Heyman, "Some Methods in Direct Casework Treatment of the Schizophrenic," *Journal of Psychiatric Social Work*, 19 (Summer 1949), 18–24.

Sid Hirsohn, "Casework with the Compulsive Mother," *Social Casework*, 32 (June 1951), 254–261.

Beatrice Reiner and Irving Kaufman, *Character Disorders in Parents of Delinquents* (New York: Family Service Association of America, 1959).

Edward Mullen, "The Relation Between Diagnosis and Treatment in Casework," *Social Casework*, 50 (April 1969), 218–226.

Jules Masserman, ed., *Depressions: Theories and Therapies* (New York: Grune & Stratton, 1970).

Herta Mayer and Gerald Schamess, "Long Term Treatment for the Disadvantaged," *Social Casework*, 50 (March 1969), 138–145.

Jeanette Oppenheimer, "Use of Crisis Intervention in Case Work with the Cancer Patient and His Family," *Social Work*, 12 (April 1967), 44–52.

Edmund Payne, "The Physician and His Patient Who is Dying," in Sidney Levin and Ralph J. Kahana, eds., *Psychodynamic Studies on Aging* (New York: International Universities Press, 1967).

Helen Pinkus, "Casework Techniques Related to Selected Characteristics of Clients and Workers" (doctoral dissertation, Columbia University School of Social Work, New York, 1968).

Rosemary Reynolds and Else Siegle, "A Study of Casework with Sado-Masochistic Marriage Partners," *Social Casework*, 40 (December 1959), 545–551.

Frances Scherz, "Treatment of Acting-Out Character Disorders in a Marital Problem," *Casework Papers, 1956* (New York: Family Service Association of America, 1956), pp. 37–52.

Max Siporin, "Social Treatment: A New-Old Helping Method," *Social Work*, 15 (July 1970), 13–25.

Francis J. Turner, ed., *Differential Diagnosis and Treatment in Social Work* (New York: Free Press, 1968). This is an excellent source for articles pertinent to the relationship between diagnostic factors and treatment.

Hank Walzer, "Casework Treatment of the Depressed Parent," *Social Casework*, 42 (December 1961), 505–512.

Edna Wasser, "Family Casework Focus on the Older Person," *Social Casework*, 47 (July 1966), 423–431.

Sue Vesper and Frankie W. Spearman, "Treatment of Marital Conflict Resulting from Severe Personality Disturbance," *Social Casework*, 47 (November 1966), 583–589.

Miriam Weisberg, "Early Treatment of Infidelity in the Neurotic Man," *Social Casework*, 51 (June 1970), 358–367.

Mary Louise Young, "Marital Counseling with Affection-Deprived Spouses," *Social Casework*, 47 (November 1966), 571–574.

Three Variations in Treatment Emphasis

To conclude this discussion of casework methods of psychosocial study, diagnosis, and treatment, we have selected three cases in which the relationship between diagnostic thinking and treatment methods and objectives can be demonstrated. These particular cases have been chosen because despite certain gross similarities among them there was for appropriate reasons considerable variation in treatment emphasis; in addition, almost all the major types of procedure discussed in earlier chapters were used, at one point or another, in each of the cases. In the first, the worker strongly emphasized reflective discussion of current interactions, in combination with sustainment; in the second, the emphasis was even more strongly on sustaining measures, with considerable environmental work, strong use of ventilation, and considerable reflective discussion of current interactions; in the third, the worker placed greater emphasis on consideration of dynamic and developmental factors, along with considerable reflective person-situation discussion and a good measure of sustainment.

A CHARACTER DISORDER: SELF-DEVALUATION AND SOCIAL RELATIONSHIPS

Susan, the first client, was a very attractive young woman recovering from tuberculosis, for which she had been hospitalized for several years. When she first came to the family service agency, she was living with a friend and was allowed to work several days a week. Her clinical diagnosis, arrived at after a period of study, was oral character disorder with some oedipal features and a tendency toward depression. In spite of rigid defenses, Susan had good capacity for inward perception. Because of the danger of further physical breakdown and of depression if the client felt too much emotional pressure, the caseworker refrained from anxiety-arousing treatment activities. Susan's own need to understand herself was so great, however, that she herself sometimes initiated discussion of her own reactions, seeking to understand their dynamics and herself tying them up with developmental experiences.

Susan's mother had died when Susan was born, and she spent her early childhood in an orphanage. During her latency and adolescence she had many different living arrangements, sometimes with relatives, sometimes in boarding homes, and sometimes with her father, who died when she was fifteen. Several subsequent living arrangements broke up because she could not get along with the women in the household and—according to her—because they were jealous of her good relationship with their husbands. She never felt that she could trust women.

Susan's present problems arose from her illness and her personality rather than from external pressures. Her relatives were helping her financially, her living arrangements were adequate, and employment was available as her strength permitted her to undertake it. She was under good medical care. What difficulties there were with relatives and friends appeared to spring more from her own reactions than from unusual behavior on their part.

It was with these reactions that Susan most needed help. Her capacity for accurate perception, judgment, and reality testing was not impaired. Sometimes, however, she functioned poorly in these respects because of her low self-image and her tendency to project, which led her to think that others held her in low esteem. Her subsequent feelings of hostility were also projected so that she thought other people were hostile to her when they actually were not. Indeed, one of her most striking characteristics was the discrepancy between her attractive appearance, her intelligence and responsive personality, and her own deep-seated feeling that she was not lovable.

Both anxiety and guilt were high, although the guilt feelings were at first hidden even from herself. Her considerable sexual promiscuity at first seemed to indicate laxness in this area of the superego; it later developed, however, that a great deal of underlying guilt existed, which she had handled by denial. There was a good deal of impulsive acting out, ambivalence, and hostility, and little ability to bear frustration. The client's chief defenses were denial, projection, and subtle forms of turning against the self.

Narcissism and dependence were also high, with very limited development of object relatedness. She was childishly self-centered, with little concern for others, and her sexual immaturity was evident in her need to have superficial relationships with many men rather than to develop a single stable relationship. It was apparent that she was still caught in a web of hostile feelings toward the mother who had "just died on her" and positive feelings toward her father. These ties seemed, however, to be on an oral dependent level rather than oedipal in nature. The client had no neurotic or psychotic symptoms, although there was a tendency toward mood swings and mild depressions in response to frustration.

Susan's psychological difficulties, in other words, were many. The central problem was her devaluation of herself, combined with her strong dependency needs. The promiscuity with which she tried to solve this latter problem increased her guilt feelings —already intense on the unconscious level because of her feeling of responsibility for her mother's death—and deepened her distrust of her own worth. In addition, her mild depressive tendencies, impulsiveness, fear of criticism, distrust of women, defensive hostility, and the defenses of denial and projection all in one way or another and to varying degrees became treatment themes.

Her social problems were in three areas: employment, medical care, and relationships with other people, particularly men friends. The strong need for independence that she had developed in her effort to overcome her underlying dependence made it difficult for her to handle her medical and work situations realistically. She was constantly tempted to work harder than was medically advisable and to resist following restrictive medical advice. The worker was quite active in this area, whenever possible helping Susan to think her medical and employment plans through realistically, but adding the weight of direct advice when it was needed. At times, with her client's permission, the caseworker talked directly with the doctor and other medical personnel responsible for Susan's care to make sure that the total health situation was accurately understood.

The early interviews gave the worker an opportunity to demonstrate her interest in Susan and her concern for her welfare, her confidence in her ability and her wish for her to be well and to succeed in her work. She was also able to show her understanding of the client's feelings of frustration and resentment at her illness. Although she denied any discomfort about her sexual nonconformity, Susan almost immediately expressed her fear that the worker would disapprove of her because of this. The caseworker's continued warm acceptance began to overcome the barrier of her deep-seated distrust of any woman. Gradually she brought out her shame at having tuberculosis and her fear that no one would want to marry her because of her illness. After talking about these feelings with the worker, she lost the need to conceal her illness from friends and gradually learned from experience that her fears were not realistic.

This is a clear illustration of the way in which the client's direct experience with the worker can have a corrective influence. This experience gave Susan the courage to experiment with entrusting the knowledge of her illness to others. Their response then reinforced the process of fear reduction that first occurred directly with the worker.

Concurrently with these developments, Susan began to bring out her conflicts about her relationships with men, her need to carry on several affairs at once, and her desire to marry for security. Two different treatment dynamics became prominent at this point: reflective discussion of the qualities of the men in whom she was interested and of her ways of relating to them; and a strong sustaining element made possible by the client's constant testing of the worker's acceptance of her and willingness to let her choose her own way of life. Repeatedly Susan brought up aspects of her promiscuity in ways that invited the caseworker to tell her to give it up. Each time, the worker made it clear that she was not interested in giving advice on this point or in talking in terms of right and wrong, but only in helping Susan to think about what would be comfortable for her and how she could best achieve her own objectives. As the caseworker repeatedly refused to condemn her and as she more and more felt the worker's respect for her and interest in her, the client's own self-respect rose to the point where she could begin to face the guilt feelings she had always denied. She never talked about the feelings per se, but she gradually began to curtail her promiscuity, at first offering the explanation that she was trying to live up to the worker's expectations. When the worker pointed out that she had never mentioned any such expectations, the client began to express her own opinion that her multiple relationships were self-defeating and that she felt better about herself when she exercised more control of her sexual impulses. Many times she spontaneously referred to how much the worker's respect and interest meant to her and how in response to them her confidence in herself had increased. Toward the end of treatment she commented with satisfaction that now she had more regard for herself and therefore less need "to sleep around."

In exploring her feelings toward men and her fear that no man she respected would marry her, Susan, without encouragement from the worker, brought out her great fear of abandonment and in association with this told of her strong feelings of anger when her brother said that she was responsible for her mother's death. It was apparent to the caseworker at this point that unconscious guilt about her mother's death and about her resentment of what she considered her mother's abandonment of her lay at the root of her low self-esteem and self-destructive tendencies. In subsequent interviews the possibility of psychoanalytic treatment was discussed. After careful consideration the client decided she did not want to go through the discomfort that analysis would involve. The consulting analyst advised against urging such treatment, partly because, in view of her medical history, it would be unwise to risk the degree of disturbance that might be involved, and partly because she was making such good progress with casework therapy that it might be best to be content with these gains in the face of the client's own resistance. The worker, therefore, accepted Susan's decision as sound and continued to work in a strongly supportive way, constantly promoting the development of understanding of the client's current feelings and of ways of handling her situation. In addition, there was considerable ventilation of the strong emotions—anger and grief—that Susan experienced in response to the frustrations of her life. Because of her unusual capacity for insight the client often spontaneously recognized her own emotional patterns. The worker used these insights to help her look at the effect of her patterns on her daily life rather than to pursue their etiology. At times, without stimulation by the worker, Susan made connections with influences in her childhood. The worker handled these supportively rather than attempting to bring out anxiety-arousing material.

Susan was able to recognize her impulsiveness, her tendency toward depression and mood swings, her defensive hostility, and her projection. The impulsiveness was approached through reflective discussion of numerous specific instances of acting out in her current life. She was able to recognize the trouble she made for herself and to see alternatives that would have been more helpful. Gradually she learned to stop and think before jumping into self-destructive actions. This capacity was reinforced by her growing identification with the caseworker. From time to time she would report: "I said to myself—'Mrs. W. would say . . .'" Later, shortly after her marriage, she came in for occasional interviews in which she would ventilate feelings of frustration. After one of these outbursts about current happenings, she quickly added, "But I didn't *do* anything silly."

Treatment of the depression and mood swings was limited to helping her achieve awareness of these tendencies and of the ways in which they affected her judgment. This reduced her anxiety during periods of depression and enabled her to protect herself against misjudgments made under the influence of her moods. To have gone any further in this area of self-understanding might have involved the client in a greater amount of stress than she could have handled constructively.

The dynamics of the projection, and of the hostility based upon it, were never discussed as such, but individual instances in which they operated were taken up. Once when Susan had misjudged an employer she was helped to see from details of actual events that there was no realistic basis for her feeling that the employer "rejected" her. The intent of this type of handling was to encourage her to look more carefully at the realities of how other people acted toward her before jumping to the conclusion that they were hostile. Again, the emphasis was on current interactions.

Several very effective steps in treatment, involving consideration of the dynamics of her thought processes, were made possible by Susan's reactions to the therapist. At one point, for instance, she thought that the worker, in conversations with the medical social worker, had divulged information she had given her in confidence, and she became very angry. Actually, there had been no breach of confidence, and it was possible for the caseworker to show Susan that she had misjudged her. This incident was used dynamically to demonstrate the client's readiness to distrust even when a good relationship had existed for so long. She was able from this experience to recognize her general pattern of unjustified distrust of other people. Susan herself put into words that this was one of her basic troubles, saying that she did not trust herself and therefore could not trust others. She subsequently commented that she had often broken up good relationships over trivial matters, or had expressed anger so strongly that other people had responded in the same coin and the relationship had ended. Some time later she commented that the caseworker's trust had enabled her to begin to trust other people. Here we see the combined effectiveness of pattern-dynamic understanding and a "corrective relationship" with the therapist.

In this example of treatment, then, the deep-seated source of the client's feeling that she could not be loved, combined with her serious physical disability, her tendency toward depression, her impulsiveness, and the extent of her libidinal immaturity dictated an emphasis on anxiety-reducing treatment. The client's own push toward introspection offered tempting opportunities to pursue other intrapsychic themes, but their potential for arousing anxiety led the worker to prefer a strongly supportive and anxiety-relieving relationship in which the client was helped immediately to use the insights she had already gained in better understanding of her current interpersonal behavior.

A CHARACTER DISORDER: HEALTH AND
PARENT-CHILD DILEMMAS

It is interesting to compare the treatment of Mrs. Park, who was treated in a medical setting, with that of Susan. In gross clinical diagnosis—oral character disorder—the two women were alike. Both suffered from a serious physical difficulty, in Mrs. Park's case, diabetes. There were many similarities, too, in the details of their personalities. Like Susan, Mrs. Park had trouble with her superego because of promiscuity and because of deeply unconscious hostile feelings toward her mother, who had died when she still very much needed her. Mrs. Park too was impulsive and dependent; she too used hostility as a defense against her anxiety. Like Susan, she had good capacity for accurate perception and judgment, although in current functioning it was impaired. She also suffered from periods of depression.

For Mrs. Park, too, it would have been unwise to press toward anxiety-arousing self-understanding because of the danger that such an approach would result in increased physical illness, increased depression, or unwise acting out. The danger was even greater than with Susan, for Mrs. Park had been in diabetic coma, close to death, on a number of occasions. Her diabetic condition was in general a serious problem, aggravated because she tended to disregard her diet and was obese; because of her neglect of her health she had had to have a leg amputated.

The personalities of the two women differed in that Mrs. Park's impulsiveness was greater than Susan's. She would become violent in her rages, and even feared that she might do bodily harm to her husband or child. Her self-image was not so low as Susan's, nor was she as afraid of abandonment. This difference may be attributable to the fact that although Mrs. Park's mother had died when Mrs. Park was fifteen and had been seriously ill for several years prior to that, there had been considerable warmth in their relationship. On the other hand, her guilt over her earlier promiscuity and her illegitimate child was so great that she was not able to express her feelings about it until after two years of treatment.

There were also sociocultural differences between these clients. Mrs. Park had somewhat less education than Susan; she worked in a factory rather than an office; and she was harder pressed financially. Her husband was an unskilled laborer. Realities of periodic unemployment, inadequate housing, and episodic drinking on her husband's part added to her troubles.

Mrs. Park was referred to the caseworker because her general excitability and outbursts of hostility were detrimental both to her own health and to the welfare of her ten-year-old son. She had sought help for John who, she complained, was disobedient, did poorly in school, and had recently been truanting. Mrs. Park blamed his behavior on a head injury, sustained when he was hit by a car while going on an errand for her when he was five years old. His mother felt responsible for this injury, although it was in no way her fault. She also felt great guilt over the fact that John was an illegitimate child and had not been able to tell him that Mr. Park was not his own father, even though during family quarrels remarks had been made that had aroused questions in John's mind on this point.

After her mother's death, Mrs. Park had gone through a period of rebellion, characterized by some drinking and a good deal of promiscuity. The only child born of her later marriage was mentally retarded. A few months before her application for help for John, this second child had been placed in an institution. Earlier, however, Mrs. Park had given her excellent care. After she had placed her daughter—a realistic step for both the child's welfare and her own—she experienced grave doubts about the care she was receiving. Her husband's relatives were also critical of her for having taken this step.

The objectives of treatment in this case included improvement in practical matters, such as employment, finances, housing and health, and the bettering of relationships between Mrs. Park and her husband and son. Psychological goals included reduction of her impulsiveness, defensive hostility, and guilt. Throughout treatment it was extremely important to guard against an increase in anxiety, for in all likelihood this would have led to further neglect of the diabetic condition and to withdrawal of John from psychiatric treatment. Relief from anxiety and guilt was sought through selectivity in the ways in which self-revelations were received and self-understanding was encouraged. Emphasis was placed on sustaining procedures, relief of pressure by environmental means wherever possible, and reflective discussion of Mrs. Park's ways of dealing with the current realities of her life. The caseworker's first task was to establish a therapeutic relationship. Here was a woman with intense hostility who immediately lashed out at the worker because more was not being done for her. Two things were immediately essential: first, obviously, that the worker not retaliate in kind but rather continue to extend good will and readiness to help, and second—a more subtle point—that she not be frightened or intimidated by the client's outbursts. Fear on the worker's part would have served to reinforce Mrs. Park's own anxiety about the destructive power of her impulses and her doubtful ability to control them. The worker, as we have noted earlier, must be seen by the client not only as kindly disposed toward him but also as competent, or able to help. Clients like Mrs. Park are essentially children looking for strong and kind parents. They do not define competence in terms of professional education, but much more primitively; to them it is symbolized by someone who is not afraid of them and cannot be controlled or hurt by their outbursts. They are not aware of this, of course, but intuitively they know that they need someone who can help them to control themselves and who therefore must himself be strong.

During the early phases of the contact the worker, in addition to listening sympathetically to Mrs. Park's many troubles and accepting her during her periods of hostility, showed her concern and her wish to help in many practical ways. When Mrs. Park was worried about the care her daughter was getting in the institution and could not contact the doctors there, the worker took over and eventually worked out a special appointment with a doctor for her. She intervened with the housing authorities to hasten Mrs. Park's acceptance for public housing. She expedited plans for a new prosthesis for the amputated leg. She arranged for camp for John. In almost every interview some small practical service was either arranged for or reported on.

Throughout, the worker's attitude was consistently one of sympathetic understanding, encouragement, and appreciation of the client's efforts. Gradually it became possible to encourage her, very tactfully, to see instance by instance some of her own provocations of other people by her hostile ways, with the result that Mrs. Park finally made a conscious effort to act differently and in time reported that people were nicer to her now that she was nicer to them. In this area of treatment and in discussions of her ways of dealing with John, the work was a combination of the development of understanding of current interactions and the use of direct influence to encourage wiser actions.

The core of treatment, however, was the reduction of Mrs. Park's feelings of guilt, which lay at the root of her defensive hostility. She felt responsible for her son's bad behavior and his physical difficulties and for her daughter's institutionalization. On an unconscious level she probably thought all this was a punishment meted out to the children for the sins of the parent —her earlier promiscuity, unwed motherhood, and the hostility to her mother that underlay the latter. Close examination revealed that her anger arose not only in response to frustration but also burst forth with particular violence whenever she was criticized to the slightest degree or for any reason experienced feelings of guilt. Hence reduction of the trouble-making hostility depended upon lessening the guilt. In fact, if the worker had tried too soon to influence the impulsive hostility directly, she might have heightened the guilt, thereby increasing rather than decreasing the hostility. Here the factor of timing—the sequence of treatment themes—was exceedingly important.

The first and major approach to the problem was therefore a supportive treatment relationship in which the worker, who no doubt represented the good mother, showed continuous liking and respect for the client. Opportunities were taken whenever it was justified to comment on ways in which Mrs. Park had handled her situation well or had been helpful to members of her family. This served simultaneously as reinforcement and as a means of encouraging greater self-esteem. As the client acquired better control of herself, she experienced increasing satisfaction in her family relationships and was able to feel that she was making restitution to her son for the events about which she felt guilty. Among other things, she was able to tell him about his parentage in a way that relieved some of the anxiety he felt about it.

The one spot at which developmental understanding was gained was related to Mrs. Park's guilt about the acting out of her adolescent and young adult years and to some of her feelings concerning the loss of her mother. The opportunity arose in the third year of treatment, when Mrs. Park verbalized, with a great deal of feeling, her intense shame and guilt about her earlier promiscuity and illegitimate pregnancy. She related at the same time that a doctor some years ago had told her to forget all about it and that she had tried but had been unable to do so. The worker encouraged her to talk about this period fully, so that insofar as possible the guilt would be brought into the open. She also agreed with Mrs. Park that it is not possible just to forget, and suggested that instead of forgetting she needed to forgive herself for what she had done.

Note that the caseworker did not try to deny that there was cause for guilt; rather she showed her own feeling that Mrs. Park was essentially a "good" person by advising her to forgive herself. Up to this point the handling was a combination of ventilation and sustainment. The worker went on, however, to talk with Mrs. Park about how what had happened was understandable in the light of the loss of her mother, the client having brought out her great dependence upon her mother and the closeness of their relationship. The worker emphasized that the mother's death had occurred at a period in her life when a mother's love and guidance are especially important. The worker thus relieved Mrs. Park of some of her feelings of guilt by stressing the pressure she was under rather than by pursuing the theme of the anger that was part of her acting out—a sustaining way of encouraging developmental reflection.

The client then spoke of her difficulties with her stepmother after her father's remarriage, of her father's constant suspicions and accusations about her relationships with boys, and of her own feeling that if he was going to accuse her anyway and insult her in front of her friends she might as well give him something to complain about. The worker's acceptance of the realities of the pressures Mrs. Park had been under helped her to reevaluate her earlier life and fostered the process of self-

forgiveness the worker had advised. Indication that this was
occurring came at a later point, when Mrs. Park talked about
her fears that she might still be promiscuous but at the same time
decided this was no longer likely, because she now cared too
much for her husband and son and would be concerned about
the consequences for them. She felt she was very different
from what she "used to be."

At no time did the worker attempt to uncover the hostility
toward the diabetic mother Mrs. Park had had to spend her early
adolescence nursing, although this undoubtedly was an underlying factor in her acting out and subsequent guilt. Developmental understanding, that is, could be sought in this case *only
when it was primarily anxiety-relieving.* The hope was that
with even partial alleviation of her guilt feelings, Mrs. Park
would be less self-destructive and more able to handle her affairs
in ways that would increase her satisfaction with herself and
decrease her self-precipitated frustrations.

After this phase of treatment, Mrs. Park was greatly relieved
and gradually terminated treatment. Her functioning was improved in terms of both her control of her diabetes and her relationship with John, who in turn showed improvement.

In this case the extent of the practical problems called for
much more direct intervention in the environment on the client's
behalf than was true with Susan. Greater emphasis on sustainment, more ventilation, and more direct influence were also
necessary. In consideration of the current person-situation interaction there was greater stress on actions and their results and
less on intrareflection. The worker deliberately avoided drawing
into the open feelings of which the client found it difficult to
speak or think, until a strong sustaining relationship had been
created. The subsequent discussion of developmental content
was extremely helpful, but could only be undertaken after two
years of strongly supportive work and even then, despite the
carefully guarded nature of the discussion, Mrs. Park had a
stormy time, lost her job, and had a recurrence of earlier symptoms. Close coordination with medical treatment was very important here.

It is difficult to judge the extent to which factors associated
with social class influenced treatment in this case. The need for

environmental work was, of course, a function of external presses, which are so much more commonly found in Mrs. Park's class. It is possible that had she had more education she would have pressed, as Susan did, for more self-understanding. It is equally possible, however, that her personality pattern would have precluded this. In either case, in view of her emotional and physical condition, it would have been unwise to pursue any more anxiety-arousing treatment than was actually undertaken.

A CHARACTER NEUROSIS: A DISTORTED MOTHER-DAUGHTER RELATIONSHIP

Like Mrs. Park, Mrs. Fillmore, who came to a child guidance clinic, was concerned about one of her children and felt very uncomfortable about her part in her daughter's adjustment difficulties. For her, however, the self-blame was associated not with a specific accident for which she felt responsible but with the way she handled the child. Like both other clients, Mrs. Fillmore suffered from a serious physical disability—recurring difficulty with a gastric ulcer. This condition did not assume serious proportions during treatment, and the client was under competent medical care; at times of stress, however, she did report gastric discomfort, and her physical condition had to be kept in mind. And like the other two women, Mrs. Fillmore had strong feelings of hostility toward her mother that were causing trouble in her current life; unlike Mrs. Park, she was well aware of them. The underlying cause of her hostility did not lie in the death of her mother at a period when she needed her, but rather in competitive feelings: her mother was socially at ease and outgoing, a cause of envy to Mrs. Fillmore, herself shy and lacking friends. She was very close to her father and critical of what she thought was her mother's insufficient affection for him.

Mrs. Fillmore was a well-educated woman, the family income was good, and her marriage satisfying. The only unusual external pressure she was experiencing—the situation that caused her to ask for help—was the difficult behavior of her thirteen-year-old daughter Joan, who was not working up to capacity at

school, indulged in temper tantrums, was nervous and uncom-
municative, and responded negatively to almost anything her
mother asked her to do. Mrs. Fillmore was at times overprotective of Joan and completely unable to control her, being
afraid to discipline her even by such mild measures as sending her
to her room. Although she felt great anger when Joan mis-
behaved, she was not impulsive and was able to control it. Early
in treatment she admitted with much guilt that there were times
when she hated Joan and felt sure that Joan hated her. Even
though this situation was actually a self-created environmental
pressure, it was nevertheless a real one.

Assessment of Mrs. Fillmore's personality showed that perception, control and execution, and intelligence were on a high level.
Her judgment in general was good, except as it was influenced
by irrational elements in her reactions. Her chief defenses were
inhibition, displacement, and projection. Her self-image was
somewhat distorted in that she undervalued herself as a socially
attractive and likable person and particularly lacked confidence
in her ability to function as a mother. She found it difficult even
to feel like a mother to her daughter and was guilty about her
relationship to her. Behind this guilt was further guilt about her
hostility to her mother, who in reality was a self-centered, unloving person. Her feelings toward her mother had been transferred in many respects to her daughter. Aside from this guilt,
or superego anxiety, there was also an underlying anxiety about
being neither loved nor lovable. This was not, however, so
deep-seated a conviction as in Susan's case. The possibility that
the guilt feeling and other anxiety might create tension that
would aggravate the gastric ulcer had to be kept in mind.

Mrs. Fillmore's superego seemed basically healthy. She felt
realistic guilt over her poor relationship with her daughter,
although she was somewhat too strict with herself about her
hostility to her mother and hence about hostile feelings in general. As far as libidinal and aggressive characteristics were concerned, it could be said that Mrs. Fillmore's narcissism was not
more than average. Her dependency needs were somewhat excessive, but her capacity for true object relationships was fairly
well developed. Ambivalence was not unusually strong. Constructive aggressiveness, however, was definitely inhibited, and

hostility toward her daughter was excessive. Details of her relationship with her husband were not explored, but no sexual problem was known to exist. There were definitely unresolved feelings of hostility to her mother and indications of some excessive positive tie to her father. Finally, definite symptomatology lay in the physical area rather than in neurotic or psychotic manifestations.

In dynamic terms, Mrs. Fillmore's difficulty with Joan could be traced to her unresolved hostility to her own mother. This took two principal forms. First, in her effort to protect Joan from the hostility she displaced upon her, Mrs. Fillmore inhibited her aggressiveness to the point where she could not exercise normal parental controls. Joan was therefore left at too early an age at the mercy of her own hostile aggressiveness because her mother did not help her to control it. And as so often happens in such instances, Joan's anxiety took the form of even greater aggression defensively, which in turn created more anxiety—a typical temper tantrum picture. Second, Mrs. Fillmore believed that there could not be a good relationship between herself and her daughter, that she could not be a good mother to a daughter and love her as she should be loved, and that her daughter in turn could not possibly love her—a combination of displacement and projection onto her daughter of her feelings toward her own mother.

From a clinical viewpoint, we first note the gastric ulcer, which is frequently due in part to anxiety caused by emotional stress, especially hunger for love of an oral dependent or maternal type. We do not see specific psychoneurotic symptoms, but we do note character disturbances of the sort usually found in character neuroses of the oedipal type. Mrs. Fillmore's personality was more heavily accented with oedipal qualities than either Susan's or Mrs. Park's. Her narcissism was much less than Susan's. Although she did have unresolved dependency needs, they were not as great as those of the other two women. Her object relationships appeared to be considerably stronger, as was evidenced by her great concern about what she was doing to her daughter, a concern expressed not only in terms of fear of disapproval of herself but also of solicitude about what was happening to the child for the child's own sake.

The overall objective of treatment in this case was improvement in the parent-child relationship. Intermediate goals derived from Mrs. Fillmore's unresolved hostility to her mother and included modification of several factors: her need to inhibit normal firmness in handling her daughter because she confused it with hostility; her displacement of feelings from her mother to her daughter; her fear of being a bad mother; her fear that her daughter could not love her; and her own feeling of being unlovable, or at least less lovable than she really was.

Earlier we noted Mrs. Fillmore's own awareness of her poor handling of her daughter and of her anger towards her. She did not realize, however, that her failure to exercise more control was a central problem. In the early interviews, her attention was called, as instances occurred, to incidents in which she seemed to feel helpless in the face of her daughter's rage. Such incidents, it was pointed up, constituted a problem that needed to be understood. Here, because of the greater emotional maturity of the client, the worker could be freer in making comments that had a somewhat high anxiety potential, in order to motivate the client to recognize and understand the problem. Mrs. Fillmore was soon able to tie up her reaction of helplessness with her fear that she would be a "bad mother" if she allowed herself to become angry. She expressed the fear that her daughter would not love her, in fact did not love her, because of Mrs. Fillmore's own underlying anger. The worker was then able to point up instances in which Joan's love for her mother did show itself, and suggested that both Joan and Mrs. Fillmore were afraid to give expression to their love for each other because of the fear of each that she would be rejected.

In a subsequent interview, Mrs. Fillmore told of her anger at Joan for borrowing a piece of costume jewelry without permission. Since this had not created any actual difficulty for Mrs. Fillmore, the caseworker commented on her disproportionate reaction. Mrs. Fillmore immediately recognized the exaggeration and remarked that she never could have done anything like that with her own mother. She went on to tell of how ungiving her mother was both to her and to her father and how angry this made her. She was then led to see that somehow she had equated Joan's taking something from her with her mother's depriving her and that she had reacted with the fury she had long harbored toward her mother.

An incident arose soon after in which Joan became so angry in a fight with her much younger brother that there was danger that the younger child would really be harmed. Mrs. Fillmore was unable to intervene and instead trusted to Joan's coming to her senses in time—which she fortunately did. The worker now made use of a combination of a direct form of reflective discussion and direct influence, by pointing out the danger of the situation and definitely advocating that Mrs. Fillmore control Joan if such a situation arose again. She also pointed out Mrs. Fillmore's need to try to understand what was behind her inability to exercise normal parental authority. This technique brought into the open Mrs. Fillmore's confusion of firmness with hostile punishment and her belief that to be firm would mean that she did not love her daughter. Again she expressed her fear that her daughter would not love her if she exercised control of her. Further work on this theme enabled Mrs. Fillmore to see that her fear was excessive and was related to her feeling that her own mother had disliked her: again she was displacing her perception of her mother onto her daughter. It was actually impossible for her to believe that a good relationship could exist between a mother and daughter.

It is also true that part of Mrs. Fillmore's belief that her daughter did not love her was a projection of her own anger onto her daughter, but to have taken up this aspect of the problem would have created even greater anxiety for the client. It was not necessary to do this, for her relationship with her daughter improved as she began to distinguish her from her mother.

It also proved possible for Mrs. Fillmore to begin to differentiate between disapproval of some of the things another person does and dislike or hostility toward him as a person. This developed in the context of the worker-client relationship. At one point Mrs. Fillmore said that she felt uncomfortable with the worker. Exploration of the remark brought out the client's feeling that the worker might be angry at her and was critical of her. A good opportunity was thus provided for the worker to explain that although she might think some of Mrs. Fillmore's ways of handling Joan were unwise, this did not at all mean that she was angry at Mrs. Fillmore or disliked her.

Shortly afterward, further discussion of Mrs. Fillmore's relationship with her mother arose out of current difficulties between them in which Mrs. Fillmore's feelings had again been hurt, and she had concluded that her mother did not love her as much as she loved others in the family. Detailed discussion of how her mother reacted to other people brought out that she was in general an ungiving, hostile person. Mrs. Fillmore was then able to see that her mother's behavior was not directed particularly against her, nor was it evidence of Mrs. Fillmore's being less lovable than other people. Rather it was part of her mother's characteristic way of acting; she was just plain difficult with everyone.

These themes, involving both pattern-dynamic and developmental understanding, were reworked a number of times as different incidents brought them to the fore. At the same time there was constant discussion of the details of current happenings in an effort to help Mrs. Fillmore understand Joan's feelings and reactions better, to think about wise ways of responding to her, and to be more fully aware of the unrealistic nature of some of her own reactions. As Mrs. Fillmore gradually became somewhat more free of the feelings toward her mother that she had displaced onto her relationship with her daughter, she became increasingly able to understand Joan's feelings, often equating them with her own adolescent reactions. She also became more comfortable about exercising necessary controls, and the child's problems became considerably less severe, partly in response to the improved mother-daughter relationship, partly as a result of concurrent treatment of Joan herself.

Although Mrs. Fillmore's clinical diagnosis, like Mrs. Park's and Susan's, fell in the general area of character disturbance, the fact that it was predominantly an oedipal rather than an oral type of character disturbance—that is, one of the character neuroses—made possible the strong emphasis on intrareflection, including pattern-dynamic and developmental understanding, even though it was necessary to watch the anxiety level carefully lest tension affect the gastric ulcer. Mrs. Fillmore was less traumatized in childhood than either of the other two clients, her capacity for object relatedness was the greatest of the three, and her aggression, despite its central importance, was probably of less intensity. There was no problem of impulse control. Mrs. Fillmore was also far more aware of her own responsibility for the problem for which she sought help and therefore initially more motivated toward seeking understanding of her own involvement. All these qualities were consistent with her clinical diagnosis.

Although there was a constant basis of sustainment underlying the work with Mrs. Fillmore, no unusual emphasis on sustaining procedures was needed. Direct influence was used only occasionally when the situation demanded immediate change in behavior. Discussion of current interactions, as always in such work, was interwoven with the pursuit of self-understanding. As with Susan, the client's strong motivation toward self-understanding was a clear factor in the direction treatment took, with the difference that in Mrs. Fillmore's case the worker was free to respond fully to the client's desire for it since special caution was not diagnostically indicated. It should be noted, however, that treatment was centered around the theme of the parent-child relationships and that it was terminated at the end of one year without an effort to move further into Mrs. Fillmore's adjustment than was necessary to bring improvement in the parent-child functioning. No effort was made to reach the psychological factors in the physical illness.

These three cases were necessarily presented in very abbreviated form. Treatment lasted from one to five years, and with Susan and Mrs. Fillmore was based on weekly interviews. These cases are certainly not offered as "proof" either of theories or results, but rather as demonstrations of the relationship among psychosocial study, diagnostic understanding, and treatment presented in the previous chapters. They are among the cases from which the theories developed in this book derive.

19 | *Perspectives and Current Needs*

The essence of psychosocial casework is concern for the individual human being—for his relationships with others, for his well-being in a grossly imperfect society, for his achieving an enhanced sense of his own value and increased competence in dealing with the vicissitudes of living. In a world where distrust is rampant, alliances and loyalties constantly shifting, values in flux, and bureaucracies ever more powerful and remote, the individual must develop strength and skill to meet his needs without surrendering his autonomy, to stand up for himself. He must learn to assess his situation realistically. He must use his capacity for love to build islands of refuge and strength in his family, with friends, and with neighbors, so that he and his children may be nourished and may come to value, respect, and trust themselves and one another. This is what casework is all about. It is an effort to strengthen the individual through helping him to deal with his current dilemmas, to find answers to these dilemmas insofar as possible, and to emerge from periods of stress with increased ability to cope with future pressures with greater self-confidence and with increased self-respect.

To accomplish this, the caseworker must first establish a positive and often warm human relationship so that honest communication can take place and trust can develop. He must also understand the client in his full individuality. This is the purpose of psychosocial study and diagnostic understanding. The extensiveness of such understanding must be sufficient to make possible help geared to the needs and capacities of the person to be served.

Treatment is differential, individualized. Sometimes the worker intervenes to modify the environment; almost always he helps the client to understand and cope with his own situation. Often the client learns to understand others more sensitively, to express himself more fully, to foresee outcomes, make decisions of better quality, gauge the effect of his own activities on others. Often he also comes to understand himself and his responses to others more fully.

It is a mistake, it seems to me, to refer to psychosocial therapy as "a process that follows the medical model," as if that were a derogatory label that carried with it the implication that the client is "sick" or "diseased" and even at fault—thus, the primary source of his own troubles. Occasionally clients *are* emotionally sick in this sense, but more often, as was indicated in the discussion of etiology, the trouble is the result of multiple influences interacting within the person-situation complex. Psychosocial casework is in itself a model. As such it has in common with medicine the important goals of reducing discomfort and suffering and of enhancing strength and functioning. The two disciplines also have a common interest in the prevention of both disorder and suffering. They both draw on scientific methodology in maintaining that treatment or service must be adapted to the individual as his needs are ascertained by individualized study and diagnosis. The psychosocial model also has much in common with education, since casework treatment can appropriately be conceptualized as a highly individualized learning process for the client.

It is an even greater mistake to regard casework as primarily an agent of social control. Our effort is distinctly *not* to bend the client to the social system but rather to increase his ability to deal with the complexities of modern organizations, enhancing rather than diminishing his autonomy. It is often the worker's responsibility to attempt to modify rather than reinforce social institutions, either in the short run for a particular client or in the long run for the good of us all. Even when caseworkers are employed in agencies of social control such as the field of corrections, the contribution of casework has been to try to limit the control aspect to the necessary minimum and to stress instead the effort to develop a decent, honest human relationship within which the probationer or parolee may experience respect for himself and his rights and may gain skill in meeting his needs in less self-defeating ways.

As we have indicated psychosocial casework constitutes a broad and expanding set of concepts and theories concerning the nature of the person-situation gestalt and its dynamics and concerning ways to help individuals function more effectively and more fully meet their own needs. It is an open and developing system of thought, combining knowledge and insights from other disciplines with its own content and perspectives in a unique way. Psychoanalysis has been particularly valuable in enlarging our understanding of the complexities of human personality. The growing understanding of the ego has been of special import ever since Anna Freud's writings began to influence casework in the late 1930s. Subsequently, the writings of Alexander, Hartmann, Kris, Rapaport, Erikson, White, and many others contributed to the greater confidence that now exists in the strength of the ego and its coping abilities. This in turn led to greater optimism about the extent to which people could change and find better ways of handling their lives in response to an interviewing process—or communication process—in which the emphasis was on enhancing the ego's ability to deal with current life pressures. More than any other discipline, psychosocial casework has been explicit about engaging the ego in greater understanding of other people and of the situation as well as of conscious and preconscious aspects of the self. It has directed its attention primarily to the important middle ground between "insight development" (which emphasizes growth through the client's understanding of his own personality) and "directive" or "purely supportive" treatment (in which one tries to prevent regression but little attention is given to developing strength and no stress is placed on any type of reflection). This middle ground stresses the client's growth through understanding, through a meaningful, ego-nourishing relationship, and through encouragement to change and fully use the environment and to try out new ways of functioning in real life, so that he will experience the reinforcement that reality itself can provide. In coordination with this goes intervention in the environment by the worker himself as it is called for on the client's behalf. This is a multifaceted, reality-based approach.

To what extent is psychosocial casework class-bound? In the 1930s we set out to demonstrate that interpersonal and social problems were not a monopoly of the poor and near-poor but rather were experienced by people of all degrees of income and education and that all these groups could and would use casework help. By the 1960s this had been so well established that a hue and cry arose to the effect that casework was a middle-class therapy. Some urged that it readapt itself to work with the poor. Others thought it had nothing to offer the poor. In actuality, casework as a field has never stopped serving the poor. In medical and psychiatric clinics, in child placement agencies, in agencies serving youth few of the affluent have been treated by caseworkers. Even in child guidance clinics and family service agencies many clients—and in some agencies, the majority of clients—were from low-income families.

It is true that it is harder to help people who are beset with the host of problems that accompany lack of income—poor housing, poor schooling, crime-infested neighborhoods, unemployment, poor medical facilities, inadequate and often undignified public assistance, public contempt. These are things that cannot be treated by casework alone. Some progress can be made on an individual basis, but these are total community problems and must be tackled by community and governmental action, which social work must help mobilize. But must these families be deprived of skilled individualized effort to help them secure as decent a life as they can in spite of these handicaps? The poor also have family relationships that sometimes go awry; they also have to cope as best they can with illness and handicap and loss through death. They also have aspirations for themselves and their children.

CURRENT NEEDS AND PRACTICAL PROBLEMS

Casework today has two great needs. One is for the development of greater skill among practitioners in using all that is already well established in casework theory. Any reading of a cross section of case records will show a serious gap between what is known in the profession and what is actually being used by the average practitioner. The other need is for research into problems of casework practice, carried on by investigators who are skilled in research methodology, grounded in casework content, theory, and practice, and thoroughly familiar with the nature of the problems and treatment methods they seek to study. Both new ideas and old must be studied in an effort first to formulate them more clearly and then, if they seem worthy of it,* to establish their validity.

Progress in meeting either of these needs depends upon the quality of *both* schools of social work and casework agencies. Certain current developments in schools and agencies, sound in the main, nevertheless offer hazards to quality that must be guarded against. Schools of social work are broadening the content of their curricula. This in itself is a sound development, but breadth alone is not enough; it must be accompanied by greater depth and greater intellectual rigor, in the casework sequence as well as in other parts of the curriculum.

Much attention is given in casework to attitudes and general knowledge, but rigorous intellectual discipline in the breadth and depth of casework theory is often lacking. Classroom teachers have sometimes been away from casework practice too long, and field instructors are sometimes not well informed about theory or not articulate about it. Teachers of casework theory must be thoroughly grounded not only in the literature of casework but also in its practice. Until recently, most instructors in casework had practiced in agencies for many years before beginning to teach. Now, however, younger practitioners are undertaking doctoral work after only a few years of experience and then going directly from their studies into teaching posts. It is undeniable that, as content has expanded, doctoral work has become more and more essential in the preparation of faculty members. These new instructors are often better prepared than their predecessors in their knowledge of the literature of casework, their sophistication about research, and the breadth of their familiarity with modern social and behavioral science. This in itself is good; but if the art of casework is to be passed on in schools of social work, course content must be the product

---

* "In our first contact wth a set of propositions, *we commence by appreciating their importance.* . . . We do not attempt, in the strict sense, to prove or disprove anything, unless its importance *makes it worthy of that honour.*" (Italics added.) Alfred North Whitehead, *The Aims of Education* (New York: Mentor Books, 1960), p. 15.

also of seasoned, first-hand practice; if new ideas are to be adequately screened for their usefulness, teachers must find ways to continue to engage in casework practice. In other disciplines the teacher does not give up the practice of his profession. Casework has here an administrative problem, but one that can be solved if faculty members and deans become convinced of its importance.

Basic changes in education must also come. Casework education at the present time does not have built into it sufficient practice under expert guidance to assure that knowledge will be translated into firmly established skill. Ideally, in addition to field work during graduate study the first two years after graduation should continue to be a learning period of a residency type. The worker should carry responsibility as a staff member but with a variety of provisions to ensure further learning. This should include work with both tape recordings and process recordings of the resident's own interviews, observation of interviews conducted by more experienced workers, and participation in consultations and group discussions of ongoing work. Regular individual consultation on a range of cases would be an essential ingredient of the work of these two years.

Such a residency may become an integral part of doctoral work if the field moves in the direction of stressing the importance of the more advanced degree for practitioners. It is not likely that the doctoral degree will supplant the master's degree as the basic professional degree in the near future, but the doctorate could well become a very desirable degree for the practitioner who wants to become more highly competent. There is no question but that a great deal of pertinent and valuable content cannot possibly be covered within the time limits of study for the master's degree. The near future must see a growth in the number of practice-oriented doctoral programs and in the proportion of students who elect to work for the higher degree in order to acquire advanced competence.

More and better research is very much needed in casework today. Accepted principles must be tested, new approaches must be demonstrated and analyzed, generalizations about the various phenomena with which we deal must be examined. Study of treatment methods in particular requires more precise and appropriate research instruments than we now have. We are constantly borrowing from psychology and education and sociology tools that are designed by those disciplines to measure the phenomena with which they deal in the light of *their* samples, *their* purposes, and *their* theories. Sometimes these borrowings are appropriate, but many times they match the phenomena they are measuring so poorly that the findings they produce are completely lacking in accuracy. This has been particularly true in applying measurements based on middle-class goals, values, and preferences to the measurement of change in poverty-level families.

There has also been a failure to measure "input" and failure to establish goals against which change could be measured. It is a well-known principle of research that if one is trying to examine the effect of a given procedure or treatment step one must first ascertain that the given procedure or set of procedures has actually been employed in the cases being studied. But we are still at the stage of generalized catchall studies in which only a small proportion of the individuals studied along a given dimension have in fact been offered treatment of the type under study. Researchers still fail to design their studies in a way that requires the caseworker to articulate specific goals against which progress can be measured. They also fail to ascertain that the goals they themselves set up to study are of a type that theory would lead them to expect were attainable under the given conditions. These are technical problems to which we must give high priority in the immediate future.

Other problems in research exist. Findings have sometimes been grossly overgeneralized. The reliability and appropriateness of statistical manipulations have often been insufficiently examined. All these problems are the growing pains of a young profession that is just beginning to examine itself with rigor. We must continue to systematically examine practice, and especially we must develop more suitable research designs and research tools. Meanwhile, however, we must examine very carefully the research methodology in every study, be alert to the possibility of spurious findings, and guard against overgeneralization.

Casework education must prepare practitioners to carry responsibility in a demanding discipline. Like other humanistic professions casework requires constant alertness and concentrated attention to the needs of others. It is impossible to know ahead of time the moment at which a client may be ready to talk about carefully guarded thoughts or, behind a passive or "it-couldn't-matter-less" facade, may be watching intently the worker's every reaction for indications of either condemnation or acceptance.

Because so little is known with a high degree of certainty about people and how they can change, the caseworker is constantly confronted by uncertainty. Again and again decisions about treatment have to be made without knowing for sure what is best. *This* is *probably* better than *that*, so we do *this*. The worker therefore must have sufficient personal and professional security to act on his own best judgment, without undue anxiety. He must also be flexible, alert to indications that some other course might be better, ready to modify his approach in the light of new understanding.

No blueprint of treatment can ever be given, any more than a skier can know each twist and turn he will have to take on a steep, unknown course. Like the skier, the worker knows his general direction, but he can see only a little way ahead and must quickly adapt his technique to the terrain. To do this he must be a skilled practitioner; he must know what to do to accomplish what, and when a given procedure is necessary.

Since new ideas are constantly coming to the practitioner's attention, usually without much more to recommend them than the opinions of their proponents and their inherent persuasiveness, the worker must not only find ways of keeping in touch with the experience and opinions of his colleagues but also be both open-minded and hard-headed. This means he must read and exchange ideas and above all, *think!*

As a profession, all of us—practitioners, supervisors, consultants, teachers, and executives—carry responsibility for thoroughly assimilating what is already known about casework treatment, for pushing the borders of knowledge ahead by research, for evaluating new findings as they become available, and for integrating those that prove sound into the main body of theory and practice.

Bibliography

ABRAMS, RUTH D., and BESS S. DANA. "Social Work in the Process of Rehabilitation." *Social Work*, 2 (October 1957), 10–15.

ACKERMAN, NATHAN W. "The Diagnosis of Neurotic Marital Interaction." *Social Casework*, 35 (April 1954), 139–147.

———. "Family Psychotherapy Today." *Family Process*, 9 (1970), 123–126.

———. *The Psychodynamics of Family Life: Diagnosis and Treatment of Family Relationships.* New York: Basic Books, 1958.

———. "The Training of Caseworkers in Psychotherapy." *American Journal of Orthopsychiatry*, 19 (January 1949), 14–24.

ADLAND, CHARLOTTE. "The Attitude of Eastern European Jews Toward Mental Disease: A Cultural Interpretation." *Smith College Studies in Social Work*, 8 (December 1937), 85–116.

AIKEN, DOROTHY. "A Project on Family Diagnosis and Treatment." In National Conference of Social Work. *Social Work Practice.* New York: Columbia University Press, 1963, pp. 4–18.

AINSWORTH, MARY D. "The Effects of Maternal Deprivation: A Review of Findings and Controversy in the Context of Research Strategy." In *Deprivation of Maternal Care: A Reassessment of Its Effects.* Geneva: World Health Organization, 1962.

ALEXANDER, FRANZ. "The Neurotic Character." *International Journal of Psychoanalysis*, 11 (1930), 292–311.

———, and THOMAS M. FRENCH. *Psychoanalytic Therapy.* New York: Ronald Press, 1946.

———, and HELEN ROSS, eds. *Dynamic Psychiatry.* Chicago: University of Chicago Press, 1952.

ALLPORT, GORDON W. "The Open System in Personality Theory." *Journal of Abnormal and Social Psychology*, 61 (November 1960), 301–310.

APPEL, GERALD. "Some Aspects of Transference and Counter-Transference in Marital Counseling." *Social Casework*, 47 (May 1966), 307–312.

ARLOW, JACOB A., and CHARLES BRENNER. *Psychoanalytic Concepts and the Structural Theory.* New York: International Universities Press, 1964.

ARONSON, H., and B. OVERALL. "Treatment Expectations of Patients in Two Social Classes." *Social Work*, 11 (January 1966), 35–41.

AUERSWALD, EDGAR H. "Interdisciplinary vs. Ecological Approach." *Family Process,* 7 (1968), 202–215.

AUSTIN, LUCILLE N. "Diagnosis and Treatment of the Client with Anxiety Hysteria." In Howard J. Parad, ed. *Ego Psychology and Dynamic Casework.* New York: Family Service Association of America, 1958.

————. "Qualifications for Psychotherapists, Social Caseworkers." *American Journal of Orthopsychiatry,* 26 (1956), 47–57.

————. "Trends in Differential Treatment in Social Casework." *Journal of Social Casework,* 29 (June 1948), 203–211.

BALDWIN, KATHERINE A. "Crisis-Focused Casework in a Child Guidance Clinic." *Social Casework,* 49 (January 1968), 28–34.

BALLWEG, JOHN A. "Resolution of Conjugal Role Adjustment After Retirement." *Journal of Marriage and the Family,* 29 (May 1967), 277–281.

BARDILL, DONALD R., and JOSEPH J. BEVILACQUE. "Family Interviewing by Two Caseworkers." *Social Casework,* 45 (May 1964), 278–282.

————, and FRANCIS J. RYAN. *Family Group Casework: A Casework Approach to Family Therapy.* Washington, D.C.: Catholic University of America Press, 1964.

BARTLETT, HARRIETT M. *The Common Base of Social Work Practice.* New York: National Association of Social Workers, 1970.

BATESON, GREGORY, DON D. JACKSON, JAY HALEY, and JOHN H. WEAKLAND. "Toward a Theory of Schizophrenia." *Behavioral Science,* 1 (1956), 251–264. Reprinted in Don D. Jackson, ed. *Communication, Family and Marriage: Human Communication,* vol. 1. Palo Alto, Calif.: Science and Behavior Books, 1968.

BEATMAN, FRANCES LEVINSON. "Family Interaction: Its Significance for Diagnosis and Treatment." *Social Casework,* 38 (March 1957), 111–118.

BEELS, CHRISTIAN C., and A. S. FERBER. "Family Therapy: A View." *Family Process,* 8 (1969), 280–318.

BEHRENS, MARJORIE L., and NATHAN W. ACKERMAN. "The Home Visit as an Aid in Family Diagnosis and Therapy." *Social Casework,* 37 (January 1956), 11–19.

BELL, JOHN E. *Family Group Therapy.* Public Health Monograph No. 64. Washington, D.C.: Government Printing Office, 1961.

BENNY, CELIA. "Casework and the Sheltered Workshop in Rehabilitation of the Mentally Ill." *Social Casework,* 41 (November 1960), 465–472.

———, et al. "Clinical Complexities in Work Adjustment of Deprived Youth." *Social Casework*, 50 (June 1969), 330–336.

BERKOWITZ, SIDNEY. "Some Specific Techniques of Psychosocial Diagnosis and Treatment in Family Casework." *Social Casework*, 36 (November 1955), 399–406.

BERLATSKY, MARJORIE. "Some Aspects of the Marital Problems of the Elderly." *Social Casework*, 43 (May 1962), 233–237.

BERNARD, JESSIE. *Marriage and Family Among Negroes.* Englewood Cliffs, N.J.: Prentice-Hall, 1966.

BERTALANFFY, LUDWIG VON. *General Systems Theory: Foundations, Development, Application.* New York: George Braziller, 1968.

———. "General System Theory and Psychiatry." In Silvano Arieti, ed. *American Handbook of Psychiatry*, vol. 3. New York: Basic Books, 1966, pp. 705–772.

BETZ, JACQUELINE, PHYLLIS HARTMANN, ARLENE JAROSLAW, SHEILA LEVINE, DENA SCHEIN, GORDON SMITH, and BARBARA ZEISS. "A Study of the Usefulness and Reliability of the Hollis Treatment Classification Scheme: A Continuation of Previous Research in This Area." Master's thesis, Columbia University School of Social Work, New York, 1961.

BIBRING, GRETE L. "Psychiatric Principles in Casework." In Cora Kasius, ed. *Principles and Techniques in Social Casework.* New York: Family Service Association of America, 1950, pp. 370–379.

———. "Psychiatry and Social Work." *Journal of Social Casework*, 28 (June 1947), 203–211.

BILLINGSLEY, ANDREW. *Black Families in White America.* Englewood Cliffs, N.J.: Prentice-Hall, 1968.

BISNO, HERBERT. *The Philosophy of Social Work*, Washington, D.C.: Public Affairs Press, 1952.

BITTERMANN, CATHERINE M. "Marital Adjustment Patterns of Clients with Compulsive Character Disorders: Implications for Treatment." *Social Casework*, 47 (November 1966), 575–582.

———. "The Multimarriage Family." *Social Casework*, 49 (April 1968), 218–221.

BLANCK, RUBIN. "The Case for Individual Treatment." *Social Casework*, 47 (February 1965), 70–74.

BOWEN, MURRAY. "Family Psychotherapy with Schizophrenia in the Hospital and in Private Practice." In Ivan Boszormenyi-Nagy and James L. Framo, eds. *Intensive Family Therapy.* New York: Harper & Row, 1965, pp. 213–243.

———. "The Use of Family Therapy in Clinical Practice." *Comprehensive Psychiatry*, 7 (1966), 345–374. Reprinted in Jay Haley, ed. *Changing Families: A Family Therapy Reader.* New York: Grune & Stratton, 1971, pp. 159–192.

BOWLBY, JOHN. "Grief and Mourning in Infancy and Early Childhood." In Ruth S. Eissler et al., eds. *The Psychoanalytic Study of the Child,* vol. 15. New York: International Universities Press, 1961.

———. *Maternal Care and Mental Health,* 2nd ed. World Health Organization Monograph Series No. 2. Geneva: World Health Organization, 1952.

BRENNAN, WILLIAM C., and SHANTI KHINDUKA. "Role Discrepancies and Professional Socialization: The Case of the Juvenile Probation Officer." *Social Work,* 15 (April 1970), 87–94.

BRENNER, CHARLES. *An Elementary Textbook of Psychoanalysis.* Garden City, N.Y.: Doubleday, Anchor Books, 1955.

BRIAR, SCOTT M. "Use of Theory in Studying Effects of Client Social Class on Students' Judgments." *Social Work,* 6 (July 1961), 91–97.

BRITTON, CLARE. "Casework Techniques in Child Care Services." *Social Casework,* 36 (January 1955), 3–13.

BRONFENBRENNER, URIE. "Socialization and Social Class Through Time and Space." In E. Maccoby, T. Newcomb, and E. Hartley, eds. *Readings in Social Psychology.* New York: Holt, Rinehart & Winston, 1958.

CAMERON, NORMAN. *Personality Development and Psychopathology.* Boston: Houghton Mifflin, 1963.

Casework Notebook. St. Paul, Minn.: Family Centered Project, Greater St. Paul Community Chests and Councils, 1957.

CHAMBERLAIN, EDNA. "Testing with a Treatment Typology." *Australian Journal of Social Work,* 22 (December 1969), 3–8.

COHEN, JEROME. "Social Work and the Culture of Poverty." *Social Work,* 9 (January 1964), 3–11.

COHEN, PAULINE E., and MERTON S. KRAUSE. *Casework with Wives of Alcoholics.* New York: Family Service Association of America, 1971.

COUCH, ELIZABETH H. *Joint and Family Interviews in the Treatment of Marital Problems.* (New York: Family Service Association of America, 1969).

CURRY, ANDREW C. "The Family Therapy Situation as a System." *Family Process,* 5 (1966), 131–141.

DAVIS, ALLISON. *Social Class Influences Upon Learning.* Cambridge, Mass.: Harvard University Press, 1962.

DEUTSCH, HELENE. *Psycho-analysis of the Neurosis.* London: Hogarth Press, 1951.

———. *Psychology of Women.* New York: Grune & Stratton, 1944.

DOHRENWEND, BRUCE, and BARBARA DOHRENWEND. *Social Status and Psychological Disorder.* New York: John Wiley & Sons, 1969.

DOLLARD, JOHN, and NEAL E. MILLER. *Personality and Psychotherapy.* New York: McGraw-Hill, 1950.

DOMANSKI, TERESA P., MARION M. JOHNS, and MARGARET A. G. MANLY. "An Investigation of a Scheme for the Classification of Casework Treatment Activities." Master's thesis, Smith College School for Social Work, Northampton, Mass., 1960.

DUNCAN, STARKEY. "Non-verbal Communication." *Psychological Bulletin,* 72 (1969), 118–137.

EHRENKRANZ, SHIRLEY M. "A Study of Joint Interviewing in the Treatment of Marital Problems." *Social Casework,* 48 (October and November 1967), 498–502 and 570–574.

———. "A Study of the Techniques and Procedures Used in Joint Interviewing in the Treatment of Marital Problems." Doctoral dissertation, Columbia University School of Social Work, New York, 1967.

EISENSTEIN, VICTOR W., ed. *Neurotic Interaction in Marriage.* New York: Basic Books, 1956.

EISSLER, KURT R. "The Chicago Institute of Psychoanalysis and the Sixth Period of Development of Psychoanalytic Technique." *Journal of General Psychology,* 42 (1950), 103–157.

ENGLISH, O. SPURGEON. "The Psychological Role of the Father in the Family." *Social Casework,* 35 (October 1954), 323–329.

———, and GERALD H. J. PEARSON. *Common Neuroses of Children and Adults.* New York: W. W. Norton and Co., 1937.

EPSTEIN, IRVIN. "Social Workers and Social Action: Attitudes toward Social Action Strategies." *Social Work,* 13 (April 1968), 101–108.

ERIKSON, ERIK H. *Childhood and Society.* New York: W. W. Norton and Co., 1950.

———. *Identity and the Life Cycle.* New York: International Universities Press, 1959.

———. *Identity, Youth and Crisis.* New York: W. W. Norton and Co., 1968.

FANTL, BERTA. "Casework in Lower Class Districts." *Mental Hygiene,* 45 (July 1961), 425–438.

———. "Preventive Intervention." *Social Work,* 7 (July 1962), 41–47.

FARBER, LAURA. "Casework Treatment of Ambulatory Schizophrenics." *Social Casework*, 39 (January 1958), 9–17.

FAUCETT, EMILY C. "Multiple-Client Interviewing: A Means of Assessing Family Processes." *Social Casework*, 43 (March 1962), 114–120.

FEDERN, PAUL. *Ego Psychology and the Psychoses.* New York: Basic Books, 1952.

——. "Principles of Psychotherapy in Latent Schizophrenia." *American Journal of Orthopsychiatry*, 17 (April 1947). 129–144.

——. "Psychoanalysis of Psychoses." *Psychiatric Quarterly*, 17 (1943), 3–19, 246–257, 470–487.

FELDMAN, YONATA. "A Casework Approach Toward Understanding Parents of Emotionally Disturbed Children." *Social Work*, 3 (July 1958), 23–29.

FENICHEL, OTTO. *The Psychoanalytic Theory of Neurosis.* New York: W. W. Norton and Co., 1945.

FERMAN, LOUIS A., ed. *Poverty in America*, rev. ed. Ann Arbor: University of Michigan Press, 1968.

FLAVELL, JOHN. *The Developmental Psychology of Jean Piaget.* Princeton, N.J.: Van Nostrand, 1963.

FOREN, ROBERT, and BAILEY ROYSTON. *Authority in Social Casework.* New York: Pergamon Press, 1968.

FRAIBERG, SELMA H. *The Magic Years.* New York: Charles Scribner's Sons, 1959.

——. *Psychoanalytic Principles in Casework with Children.* New York: Family Service Association of America, 1954.

——. "Some Aspects of Casework with Children." *Social Casework*, 33 (November and December, 1952), 374–381 and 429–435.

——, and JEANETTE REGENSBURG. *Direct Casework with Children.* New York: Family Service Association of America, 1957.

FRAMO, JAMES L. "Rationale and Techniques of Intensive Family Therapy." In Ivan Boszormenyi-Nagy and James L. Framo, eds. *Intensive Family Therapy.* New York: Harper & Row, 1965, pp. 143–212.

FRANK, JEROME. "The Role of Hope in Psychotherapy." *International Journal of Psychiatry*, 5 (May 1968).

FREEMAN, HENRY, et al. "Can a Family Agency Be Relevant to the Inner Urban Scene?" *Social Casework*, 51 (January 1970), 12–21.

FREUD, ANNA. *The Ego and the Mechanisms of Defense.* New York: International Universities Press, 1946.

FREUD, SIGMUND. *Lines of Advancement in Psychoanalytic Therapy*, vol. 17 of *Standard Edition of the Complete Psychological Works of Sigmund Freud.* London: Hogarth Press and the Institute of Psychoanalysis, 1955.

———. *An Outline of Psychoanalysis.* Authorized translation by James Strachey. New York: W. W. Norton & Co., 1949.

———. "The Unconscious" (1915). In *Collected Papers,* vol. 4. London: Hogarth Press, 1949, pp. 98–136.

FRIEDMAN, ALFRED S. "Co-therapy as Family Therapy Method and as a Training Method." In Alfred S. Friedman, John C. Sonne, et al. *Therapy with Families of Sexually Acting-Out Girls.* New York: Springer Publishing Co., 1971, pp. 36–41.

———. "The Rationale and the Plan of the Treatment Method." In Alfred S. Friedman, John C. Sonne, et al. *Therapy with Families of Sexually Acting-Out Girls.* New York: Springer Publishing Co., 1971, pp. 28–35.

GARCIA, ALEJANDRO. "The Chicano and Social Work." *Social Casework,* 52 (May 1971), 274–278.

GARRETT, ANNETTE. *Case Work Treatment of a Child.* New York: Family Welfare Association of America, 1942.

———. "Historical Survey of the Evolution of Casework." *Journal of Social Casework,* 30 (June 1949), 219–229.

———. *Interviewing: Its Principles and Methods.* New York: Family Service Association of America, 1942.

———. "Modern Casework: The Contributions of Ego Psychology." In Howard J. Parad, ed. *Ego Psychology and Dynamic Casework.* New York: Family Service Association of America, 1958, pp. 38–52.

———. "The Worker-Client Relationship." In Howard J. Parad, ed. *Ego Psychology and Dynamic Casework.* New York: Family Service Association of America, 1958, pp. 53–72.

GEIST, JOANNE, and NORMAN M. GERBER. "Joint Interviewing: A Treatment Technique with Marital Partners." *Social Casework,* 41 (February 1960), 76–83.

GLASSER, PAUL H., and LOIS N. GLASSER, eds. *Families in Crisis.* New York: Harper & Row, 1970.

GOMBERG, ROBERT M. "Family Oriented Treatment of Marital Problems." *Social Casework,* 37 (January 1956), 3–10.

GORDON, WILLIAM. "Basic Constructs for an Integrative and Generative Conception of Social Work." In Gordon Hearn, ed. *The General Systems Approach: Contributions toward a Holistic Conception of Social Work.* New York: Council on Social Work Education, 1969.

———. "Knowledge and Value: Their Distinction and Relationship in Clarifying Social Work Practice." *Social Work,* 10 (July 1965), 32–35.

GOTTLIEB, WERNER, and JOE STANLEY. "Mutual Goals and Goal Setting in Casework." *Social Casework,* 48, (October 1967), 471–481.

GOULD, ROBERT E. "Dr. Strangeclass: Or How I Stopped Worrying about Theory and Began Treating the Blue-Collar Worker." *American Journal of Orthopsychiatry,* 37 (January 1967), 73–86.

GRAY, WILLIAM, FREDERICK J. DUHL, and NICHOLAS D. RIZZO, eds. *General Systems Theory and Psychiatry.* Boston: Little, Brown & Co., 1969.

GREEN, SIDNEY L. "Psychoanalytic Contributions to Casework Treatment of Marital Problems." *Social Casework,* 35 (December 1954), 419–423.

GREENACRE, PHYLLIS, ed. *Affective Disorders: A Psychoanalytic Contribution to Their Study.* New York: International Universities Press, 1953.

GRINKER, ROY R., et al. *Psychiatric Social Work: A Transactional Casebook.* New York: Basic Books, 1961.

GROSS, NEAL, WARD S. MASON, and ALEXANDER McEACHERN. *Explorations in Role Analysis: Studies of the School Superintendency Role.* New York: John Wiley & Sons, 1958.

GROSSER, CHARLES F. "Local Residents as Mediators Between Middle-Class Professional Workers and Lower-Class Clients." *Social Service Review,* 40 (March 1966), 56–63.

Group for the Advancement of Psychiatry. *The Field of Family Therapy.* Group for the Advancement of Psychiatry Report No. 78. New York: Group for the Advancement of Psychiatry, 1970.

GRUNEBAUM, MARGARET GALSTON. "A Study of Learning Problems of Children: Casework Implications." *Social Casework,* 42 (November 1961), 461–468.

HAAS, WALTER. "Reaching Out—A Dynamic Concept in Casework." *Social Work,* 4 (July 1959), 41–45.

HALEY, JAY. "Family Therapy: A Radical Change." In Jay Haley, ed. *Changing Families: A Family Therapy Reader.* New York: Grune & Stratton, 1971, pp. 227–236.

——— "Whither Family Therapy." *Family Process,* 1 (1962), 69–100.

HALL, BERNARD H., and WINIFRED WHEELER. "The Patient and His Relatives: Initial Joint Interview." *Social Work,* 2 (January 1957), 75–80.

HAMILTON, GORDON. "Basic Concepts in Social Casework." *The Family*, 18 (July 1937), 147–156.

———. "Psychoanalytically Oriented Casework and Its Relation to Psychotherapy." *American Journal of Orthopsychiatry*, 19 (April 1949), 209–223.

———. *Psychotherapy in Child Guidance*. New York: Columbia University Press, 1947.

———. "The Role of Social Casework in Social Policy." *Social Casework*, 33 (October 1952), 315–324.

———. "A Theory of Personality: Freud's Contribution to Social Work." In Howard J. Parad, ed. *Ego Psychology and Dynamic Casework*. New York: Family Service Association of America, 1958, pp. 11–37.

———. *Theory and Practice of Social Case Work*, 2nd ed. New York: Columbia University Press, 1951.

———. "The Underlying Philosophy of Social Casework." *Family*, 23 (July 1941), 139–148.

HAMMER, EMANUEL, ed. *Use of Interpretation in Treatment: Technique and Art*. New York: Grune & Stratton, 1968.

HARDMAN, DALE E. "The Matter of Trust." *Crime and Delinquency*, 15 (April 1969), 203–218.

HARTMAN, ANN. "To Think about the Unthinkable." *Social Casework*, 51 (October 1970), 467–474.

HARTMANN, HEINZ. *Ego Psychology and the Problem of Adaptation*. New York: International Universities Press, 1958.

———, ERNST KRIS, and R. LOEWENSTEIN. "Comments on the Formation of Psychic Structure." In Ruth S. Eissler et al., eds. *The Psychoanalytic Study of the Child*, vol. 2. New York: International Universities Press, 1946, pp. 11–38.

HEARN, GORDON, ed. *The General Systems Approach: Contributions toward a Holistic Conception of Social Work*. New York: Council on Social Work Education, 1969.

HELLENBRAND, SHIRLEY. "Client Value Orientations: Implications for Diagnosis and Treatment." *Social Casework*, 42 (April 1961), 163–169.

HENRY, CHARLOTTE. "Motivation in Non-voluntary Clients." *Social Casework*, 39 (February–March 1958), 130–136.

HERZOZ, ELIZABETH. "Is there a Breakdown of the Negro Family?" *Social Work*, 11 (January 1966), 3–10.

HESS, ROBERT D., and GERALD HANDEL. "The Family as a Psychosocial Organization." In Gerald Handel, ed. *The Psychosocial*

Interior of the Family: A Sourcebook for the Study of Whole Families. Chicago: Aldine Publishing Co., 1967, pp. 10–24.

HEYMAN, MARGARET M. "Some Methods in Direct Casework Treatment of the Schizophrenic." *Journal of Psychiatric Social Work,* 19 (Summer 1949), 18–24.

HIRSOHN, SID. "Casework with the Compulsive Mother." *Social Casework,* 32 (June 1951), 254–261.

HOFFMAN, LYNN, and LORENCE LONG. "A Systems Dilemma." *Family Process,* 8 (September 1969), 211–234.

HOLLINGSHEAD, AUGUST B., and FREDERICK C. REDLICH. *Social Class and Mental Illness.* New York: John Wiley & Sons, 1958.

HOLLIS, FLORENCE. *Casework in Marital Disharmony.* Doctoral dissertation, Bryn Mawr College, Bryn Mawr, Pa., 1947. Microfilmed. Ann Arbor, Mich.: University Microfilms, 1951.

————. "Casework and Social Class." *Social Casework,* 46 (October 1965), 463–471.

————. "Personality Diagnosis in Casework." In Howard J. Parad, ed. *Ego Psychology and Dynamic Casework.* New York: Family Service Association of America, 1958, pp. 83–96.

————. "Principles and Assumptions Underlying Casework Practice." *Social Work* (London), 12 (1955), 41–55.

————. "The Techniques of Casework." *Journal of Social Casework,* 30 (June 1949), 235–244.

————. *A Typology of Casework Treatment.* New York: Family Service Association of America, 1968.

————. *Women in Marital Conflict.* New York: Family Service Association of America, 1949.

HUNTER, DAVID R. "Social Action to Influence Institutional Change." *Social Casework,* 51 (April 1970), 225–231.

INKELES, ALEX. "Personality and Social Structure." In Robert K. Merton, ed. *Sociology Today.* New York: Basic Books, 1959, pp. 249–276.

————. "Some Sociological Observations on Culture and Personality Studies." In Clyde Kluckhohn, Henry A. Murray, and David M. Schneider, eds. *Personality in Nature, Society, and Culture.* New York: Alfred A. Knopf, 1959.

ISAACS, SUSAN. *Social Development in Young Children.* New York: Harcourt, Brace & Co., 1937.

JACKSON, DON D. "The Question of Family Homeostasis." *Psychiatric Quarterly,* Supplement, 21 (1959), 79–90.

————, and VIRGINIA SATIR. "A Review of Psychiatric Developments in Family Diagnosis and Therapy." In Nathan W. Ackerman,

Frances L. Beatman, and Sanford N. Sherman, eds. *Exploring the Base for Family Therapy.* New York: Family Service Association of America, 1961, pp. 29–49.

———, and JOHN H. WEAKLAND. "Conjoint Family Therapy: Some Considerations on Theory, Technique and Results." *Psychiatry,* 24 (1961), 30–45.

JEFFERS, CAMILLE. *Living Poor.* Ann Arbor, Mich.: Ann Arbor Publishers, 1967.

JOHNSON, ADELAIDE M. "Sanctions for Superego Lacunae of Adolescents." In Kurt R. Eissler, ed. *Searchlights on Delinquency.* New York: International Universities Press, 1949, pp. 225–244.

JOLESCH, MIRIAM. "Casework Treatment of Young Married Couples." *Social Casework,* 43 (May 1962), 245–251.

JOSSELYN, IRENE M. *The Adolescent and His World.* New York: Family Service Association of America, 1952.

———. *Psychosocial Development of Children.* New York: Family Service Association of America, 1948.

JUNGREIS, JEROME E. "The Active Role of the Family Therapist." In Alfred S. Friedman, Ivan Boszormenyi-Nagy, et al. *Psychotherapy of the Whole Family: Case Histories, Techniques, and Concepts of Family Therapy of Schizophrenia in the Home and Clinic.* New York: Springer Publishing Co., 1965, pp. 187–196.

———. "Answers to Typical Questions of the Trainee Therapist." In Alfred S. Friedman, John C. Sonne, et al. *Therapy with Families of Sexually Acting-Out Girls.* New York: Springer Publishing Co., 1971, pp. 48–65.

———. "The Single Therapist in Family Therapy." In Alfred S. Friedman, Ivan Boszormenyi-Nagy, et al. *Psychotherapy of the Whole Family: Case Histories, Techniques, and Concepts of Family Therapy of Schizophrenia in the Home and Clinic.* New York: Springer Publishing Co., 1965, pp. 232–238.

KAFKA, J. S., and J. W. McDONALD. "Ambiguity for Individuation: A Critique and Reformulation of Double Bind Theory." *Archives of General Psychiatry,* in press.

KAPLAN, DAVID M. "A Concept of Acute Situational Disorders." *Social Work,* 7 (April 1962), 15–23.

———, and EDWARD A. MASON. "Maternal Reactions to Premature Birth Viewed as an Acute Emotional Disorder." *American Journal of Orthopsychiatry,* 30 (July 1960), 539–547.

KAPLAN, LILLIAN, and JEAN B. LIVERMORE. "Treatment of Two Patients with Punishing Super-Egos." *Journal of Social Casework,* 29 (October 1948), 310–316.

KENDALL, KATHERINE A., ed. *Social Work Values in an Age of Discontent.* New York: Council on Social Work Education, 1970.

KING, CHARLES H. "Family Therapy with the Deprived Family." *Social Casework,* 48 (April 1967), 203–208.

KLEIN, EMANUEL. "The Reluctance to Go to School." In Ruth S. Eissler et al., eds. *The Psychoanalytic Study of the Child,* vol 1. New York: International Universities Press, 1945, pp. 263–279.

KLUCKHOHN, FLORENCE. "Variations in the Basic Values of Family Systems." *Social Casework,* 39 (February–March 1958), 63–72.

———, and JOHN P. SPIEGEL. *Integration and Conflict in Family Behavior.* Group for the Advancement of Psychiatry Report No. 27. New York: Group for the Advancement of Psychiatry, 1954.

KNIGHT, DANIEL. "New Directions for Public Welfare Caseworkers." *Public Welfare,* 27 (1969), 92–94.

KNOLL, FAUSTINA RAMIREZ. "Casework Services for Mexican Americans." *Social Casework,* 52 (May 1971), 279–284.

KOEHLER, RUTH T. "The Use of Advice in Casework." *Smith College Studies in Social Work,* 23 (February 1953), 151–165.

KOMAROVSKY, MIRRA, with JANE PHILLIPS. *Blue-Collar Marriage.* New York: Random House, 1964.

KOUNIN, JACOB, NORMAN POLANSKY, et al. "Experimental Studies of Clients' Reactions to Initial Interviews." *Human Relations,* 9 (1956), 265–293.

KOZIER, ADA. "Casework With Parents of Blind Children." *Social Casework,* 43 (January 1962), 15–22.

KRIS, ERNST. "Notes on the Development and on Some Current Problems of Psychoanalytic Child Psychology." In Ruth S. Eissler et al., eds. *The Psychoanalytic Study of the Child,* vol. 5. New York: International Universities Press, 1950, pp. 24–46.

———. "On Preconscious Mental Processes." *Psychoanalytic Quarterly,* 19 (1950), 542.

KRUG, OTILDA. "The Dynamic Use of the Ego Functions in Casework Practice." *Social Casework,* 36 (December 1955), 443–450.

KUBIE, LAWRENCE S. "The Fundamental Nature of the Distinction Between Normality and Neurosis." *Psychoanalytic Quarterly,* 23 (April 1954), 167–204.

———. "Problems and Techniques of Psychoanalytic Validation and Progress." In E. Pumpian-Mindlin, ed. *Psychoanalysis as Science.* New York: Basic Books, 1952, p. 91.

LaBarre, Maurine. "The Strengths of the Self-Supporting Poor." *Social Casework,* 49 (October 1968), 459–466.

Laing, L. P. "The Use of Reassurance in Psychotherapy." *Smith College Studies in Social Work,* 22 (February 1952), 75–90.

Lance, Evelyn A. "Intensive Work with a Deprived Family." *Social Casework,* 50 (December 1969), 454–460.

Landes, Ruth, and Mark Zborowski. "Hypotheses Concerning the Eastern European Jewish Family." In Herman D. Stein and Richard A. Cloward, eds. *Social Perspectives on Behavior.* Glencoe, Ill.: Free Press, 1958, pp. 58–75.

Langsley, Donald G., Frank S. Pittman III, Pavel Machotka, and Kalman Flomenhaft. "Family Crisis Therapy—Results and Implications." *Family Process,* 7 (1968), 145–158.

Laqueur, H. Peter, Harry A. LaBurt, and Eugene Morong. "Multiple Family Therapy: Further Developments." *International Journal of Social Psychiatry,* Special Edition, 2 (1964), 70–80.

Leader, Arthur L. "Current and Future Issues in Family Therapy." *Social Service Review,* 43 (1969), 1–11.

———. "The Role of Intervention in Family Group Treatment." *Social Casework,* 45 (1964), 327–332.

Lehrman, Louis. "Science, Art, and Social Casework." Mimeographed. Pittsburgh, Pa.: University of Pittsburgh Graduate School of Social Work, 1957.

Leichter, Elsa, and Gerda L. Schulman. "Emerging Phenomena in Multi-Family Group Treatment." *International Journal of Group Psychotherapy,* 18 (1968), 59–69.

Levin, Sidney, and Ralph Kahana, eds. *Psychodynamic Studies on Aging.* New York: International Universities Press, 1967.

Lewin, Kurt. *A Dynamic Theory of Personality: Selected Papers.* Donald K. Adams and Karl E. Zener, trs. New York: McGraw-Hill, 1935.

Lewis, Hylan. "Child Rearing Among Low-Income Families." In Louis A. Ferman, ed. *Poverty in America.* Ann Arbor: University of Michigan Press, 1965, pp. 342–353.

———. *Culture, Class and Poverty.* Washington, D.C.: Cross Tell, 1967.

Lide, Pauline. "Dynamic Mental Representation: An Analysis of the Empathic Process." *Social Casework,* 47 (March 1966), 146–151.

———. "An Experimental Study of Empathic Functioning." *Social Service Review,* 41 (March 1967), 23–30.

Lidz, Theodore, Alice R. Cornelison, Stephen Fleck, and Dorothy

TERRY. "The Intrafamilial Environment of Schizophrenic Patients: II. Marital Schism and Marital Skew." *American Journal of Psychiatry*, 64 (1957), 241–248. Reprinted as "Schism and Skew in the Families of Schizophrenics." In Norman W. Bell and Ezra F. Vogel, eds. *A Modern Introduction to the Family*, rev. ed. New York: Free Press, 1968, pp. 650–662.

LIEBOW, ELLIOT. *Tally's Corner*. Boston: Little, Brown & Co., 1967.

LINDEMANN, ERICH. "Symptomatology and Management of Acute Grief." *American Journal of Psychiatry*, 101 (1944), 141–148.

LITTNER, NER. "The Impact of the Client's Unconscious on the Caseworker's Reactions." In Howard J. Parad, ed. *Ego Psychology and Dynamic Casework*. New York: Family Service Association of America, 1958, pp. 73–87.

LONG, LYNN, and LORENCE LONG. "A Systems Dilemma." *Family Process*, 8 (September 1969), 211–234.

LOWRY, FERN. "Objectives in Social Case Work." *The Family*, 18 (December 1937), 263–268.

LUTZ, WERNER A. *Concepts and Principles Underlying Social Casework Practice*. Washington, D.C.: National Association of Social Workers, Medical Social Work Section, 1956.

McCOLLUM, AUDREY T. "Mothers' Preparation for their Children's Hospitalization." *Social Casework*, 48 (July 1967), 407–415.

MacGREGOR, ROBERT. "Progress in Multiple Impact Therapy." In Nathan W. Ackerman, Frances L. Beatman, and Sanford N. Sherman, eds. *Exploring the Base for Family Therapy*. New York: Family Service Association of America, 1961, pp. 47–58.

McMAHAN, ARTHUR W., and PAUL J. RHUDICK. "Reminiscing in the Aged: An Adaptational Response." In Sidney Levin and Ralph Kahana, eds. *Psychodynamic Studies on Aging*. New York: International Universities Press, 1967.

McMILLAN, SYLVIA R. "Aspirations of Low-income Mothers." *Journal of Marriage and the Family*, 29 (May 1967), 282–287.

MacRAE, ROBERT H. "Social Work and Social Action." *Social Service Review*, 40 (March 1966), 1–7.

MAEDER, LEROY M. A. "Diagnostic Criteria—The Concept of Normal and Abnormal." *The Family*, 23 (October 1941), 171–179.

MARCUS, LOTTIE. "The Effect of Extralinguistic Phenomena on the Judgment of Anxiety." Doctoral dissertation, Columbia University School of Social Work, New York, 1969.

MASSERMAN, JULES H., ed. *Depressions: Theories and Therapies*. New York: Grune & Stratton, 1970.

———, ed. *Psychoanalysis and Social Process.* New York: Grune & Stratton, 1961.

MAYER, HERTA, and GERALD SCHAMESS. "Long Term Treatment for the Disadvantaged." *Social Casework,* 50 (March 1969), 138–145.

MEAD, MARGARET. *Male and Female: A Study of the Sexes in a Changing World.* New York: William Morrow & Co., 1949.

———. *Sex and Temperament in Three Primitive Societies.* New York: William Morrow & Co., 1935.

MEIER, ELIZABETH G. "Social and Cultural Factors in Casework Diagnosis." *Social Work,* 41 (July 1959), 15–26.

Method and Process in Social Casework, Report of a Staff Committee, Community Service Society of New York. New York: Family Service Association of America, 1958.

MEYER, CAROL H. *Complementarity and Marital Conflict: The Development of a Concept and Its Application to the Casework Method.* Doctoral dissertation, Columbia University School of Social Work, New York, 1957.

———. *Social Work Practice: A Response to the Urban Crisis.* New York: Free Press, 1970.

MICHAELS, J. "Character Structure and Character Disorders." In Silvano Arieti, ed. *American Handbook of Psychiatry,* vol. 1. New York: Basic Books, 1959.

MILLER, S. M. "The American Lower Class: A Typological Approach." *Social Research,* 31 (1964), 1–22.

———, and ELLIOT G. MISHLER. "Social Class, Mental Illness, and American Psychiatry: An Expository Review." *The Milbank Memorial Fund Quarterly,* 37 (April 1959), 174–199.

MILLOY, MARGARET. "Casework with the Older Person and His Family." *Social Casework,* 45 (October 1964), 450–456.

MINUCHIN, SALVADOR. *Families of the Slums.* New York: Basic Books, 1967.

———, and M. MONTALVO. "Technique for Working with Disorganized Low Socio-Economic Families." *American Journal of Orthopsychiatry,* 37 (October 1967), 880–887.

MITCHELL, CELIA B. "Family Interviewing in Family Diagnosis." *Social Casework,* 40 (July 1959), 381–384.

———. "Problems and Principles in Family Therapy." In Nathan W. Ackerman, Frances L. Beatman, and Sanford N. Sherman, eds. *Expanding Theory and Practice in Family Therapy.* New York: Family Service Association of America, 1967, pp. 109–124.

———. "The Therapeutic Field in the Treatment of Families in Conflict: Recurrent Themes in Literature and Clinical Practice."

In Bernard F. Reiss, ed. *New Directions in Mental Health.* New York: Grune & Stratton, 1968, pp. 69–99.

———. "The Uses and Abuses of Co-therapy as a Technique in Family Unit Therapy." *Bulletin, Family Mental Health Clinic, Jewish Family Service,* 1 (1969), 8–10.

MITTLEMANN, BELA M. "Analysis of Reciprocal Neurotic Patterns in Family Relationships." In Victor W. Eisenstein, ed. *Neurotic Interaction in Marriage.* New York: Basic Books, 1956, pp. 81–100.

MOLYNEUX, I. E. "A Study of Resistance in the Casework Relationship." *The Social Worker,* 34 (November 1966), 217–223.

MULLEN, EDWARD J. "Casework Communication." *Social Casework,* 49 (November 1968), 546–551.

———. "Casework Treatment Procedures as a Function of Client Diagnostic Variables." Doctoral dissertation, Columbia University School of Social Work, New York, 1968.

———. "Differences in Worker Style in Casework." *Social Casework,* 50 (June 1969), 347–353.

———. "The Relation Between Diagnosis and Treatment in Casework." *Social Casework,* 50 (April 1969), 218–226.

MURRAY, HENRY A. *Explorations in Personality.* New York: Oxford University Press, 1938, pp. 38–39.

NADEL, ROBERT M. "Interviewing Style and Foster Parents' Verbal Accessibility." *Child Welfare,* 46 (April 1967), 207–213.

National Association of Social Workers, *Ad hoc* Committee on Advocacy. "Champion of Social Victims." *Social Work,* 14 (April 1969), 16–22.

NEMIAH, JOHN C. *Foundations of Psychopathology.* New York: Oxford University Press, 1961.

NESER, WILLIAM B., and EUGENE E. TILLOCK. "Special Problems Encountered in the Rehabilitation of Quadriplegic Patients." *Social Casework,* 43 (March 1962), 125–129.

NEUGEBORE, BERNARD. "Opportunity Centered Social Services." *Social Work,* 15 (April 1970), 47–52.

NICHOLLS, GRACE K. "The Science and the Art of the Casework Relationship." *Smith College Studies in Social Work,* 36 (February 1966), 109–126.

———. "Treatment of a Disturbed Mother-Child Relationship: A Case Presentation." In Howard J. Parad, ed. *Ego Psychology and Dynamic Casework.* New York: Family Service Association of America, 1958, pp. 117–125.

Noyes, Arthur Percy. *Modern Clinical Psychiatry*, 5th ed. Philadelphia: W. B. Saunders Co., 1959.

Nunberg, Herman. *Principles of Psychoanalysis: Their Application to the Neuroses*. Madlyn and Sydney Kahr, trs. New York: International Universities Press, 1955.

Olsen, Katherine M., and Marvin E. Olsen. "Role Expectations and Perceptions for Social Workers in Medical Settings." *Social Work*, 12 (July 1967), 70–78.

Olson, David H. "Empirically Unbinding the Double Bind." Paper delivered at the Annual Meeting of the American Psychological Association, Washington, D.C., 1968.

———. "Marital and Family Therapy: Integrative Review and Critique." *Journal of Marriage and the Family*, 32 (1970), 501–538.

Oppenheimer, Jeanette R. "Use of Crisis Intervention in Casework with the Cancer Patient and his Family." *Social Work*, 12 (April 1967), 44–52.

Ormsby, Ralph. "Interpretations in Casework Therapy." *Journal of Social Casework*, 29 (April 1948), 135–141.

Overton, Alice. "Serving Families Who Don't Want Help." *Social Casework*, 34 (July 1953), 304–309.

Oxley, Genevieve B. "The Caseworker's Expectations and Client Motivation." *Social Casework*, 47 (July 1966), 432–437.

Panter, Ethel J. "Ego-Building Procedures that Foster Social Functioning." *Social Casework*, 48 (March 1967), 139–145.

Parad, Howard J., ed. *Crisis Intervention: Selected Readings*. New York: Family Service Association of America, 1965.

———, ed. *Ego Psychology and Dynamic Casework*. New York: Family Service Association of America, 1958.

———, and Gerald Caplan. "A Framework for Studying Families in Crisis." *Social Work*, 5 (July 1960), 3–15.

———, and R. Miller, eds. *Ego-Oriented Casework: Problems and Perspectives*. New York: Family Service Association of America, 1963.

———, and Libbie G. Parad. "A Study of Crisis-Oriented Planned Short-term Treatment." *Social Casework*, 49 (June and July 1968), 346–355 and 418–426.

Parsons, Talcott. "Illness and the Role of the Physician." *American Journal of Orthopsychiatry*, 21 (July 1951), 452–460.

———. "Psychoanalysis and the Social Structure." In *Essays in Sociological Theory*. Glencoe, Ill.: Free Press, 1954.

PAULEY, RUTH M. "The Public Welfare Agency of the Future." *Social Casework*, 47 (May 1966), 286–292.

PAVENSTEDT, ELEANOR, ed. *The Drifters: Children of Disorganized Lower-Class Families*. Boston: Little, Brown & Co., 1967.

PAYNE, EDMUND C. "The Physician and His Patient Who is Dying." In Sidney Levin and Ralph Kahana, eds. *Psychodynamic Studies on Aging*. New York: International Universities Press, 1967.

PERLMAN, HELEN H., ed. *Helping: Charlotte Towle on Social Work and Social Casework*. Chicago: University of Chicago Press, 1969.

————. "Intake and Some Role Considerations." *Social Casework*, 41 (December 1960), 171–177.

————. *Persona: Social Role and Personality*. Chicago: University of Chicago Press, 1968.

————. "The Role Concept and Social Casework: Some Explorations. I. The 'Social' in Social Casework." *Social Service Review*, 35 (December 1961), 370–381. II. "What is Social Diagnosis," *ibid.*, 36 (March 1962), 17–31.

————. *Social Casework: A Problem Solving Process*. Chicago: University of Chicago Press, 1957.

PIAGET, JEAN. *The Child's Conception of the World*. New York: Harcourt, Brace & Co., 1929.

PIERSON, ARTHUR. "Social Work Techniques with the Poor." *Social Casework*, 51 (October 1970), 481–485.

PINCUS, ALLEN. "Toward a Developmental View of Aging for Social Work." *Social Work*, 12 (July 1967), 33–41.

PINKUS, HELEN. "Casework Techniques Related to Selected Characteristics of Clients and Workers." Doctoral dissertation, Columbia University School of Social Work, New York, 1968.

POLANSKY, NORMAN A. *Ego Psychology and Communication*. New York: Atherton Press, 1971.

————. "Powerlessness among Rural Appalachian Youth." *Rural Sociology*, 34 (June 1969), 219–222.

————, and JACOB KOUNIN. "Clients' Reactions to Initial Interviews: A Field Study." *Human Relations*, 9 (1956), 237–264.

POLLAK, OTTO. "Design of a Model of Healthy Family Relationships as a Base for Evaluative Research." *Social Service Review*, 31 (December 1957), 369–376.

————. *Integrating Sociological and Psychoanalytic Concepts*. New York: Russell Sage Foundation, 1956.

————. *Social Science and Psychotherapy for Children*. New York: Russell Sage Foundation, 1952.

————, HAZEL M. YOUNG and HELEN LEACH. "Differential Diagnosis and Treatment of Character Disturbances." *Social Casework,* 41 (December 1960), 512–517.

PRAY, KENNETH. "A Restatement of the Generic Principles of Social Casework Practice." *Journal of Social Casework,* 28 (October 1947), 283–290.

PUMPIAN-MINDLIN, E. "The Position of Psychoanalysis in Relation to the Biological and Social Sciences." In E. Pumpian-Mindlin, ed. *Psychoanalysis as Science.* New York: Basic Books, 1952.

RAPAPORT, DAVID. *Organization and Pathology of Thought.* New York: Columbia University Press, 1951.

———. "The Theory of Ego Autonomy: A Generalization." *Menninger Clinic Bulletin,* 22 (January 1958), 13–35.

RAPOPORT, LYDIA. "Social Casework: An Appraisal and an Affirmation." *Smith College Studies in Social Work,* 39 (June 1969), 213–235.

———, and KATE S. DORST. "Teamwork in a Rehabilitation Setting: A Case Illustration." *Social Casework,* 41 (June 1960), 291–297.

REDLICH, F. C., A. B. HOLLINGSHEAD, and ELIZABETH BELLIS. "Social Class Differences in Attitudes Toward Psychiatry." *American Journal of Orthopsychiatry,* 25 (January 1955), 60–70.

REGENSBURG, JEANETTE. "Application of Psychoanalytic Concepts to Casework Treatment of Marital Problems." *Social Casework,* 35 (December 1954), 424–432.

———, and SELMA FRAIBERG. *Direct Casework with Children.* New York: Family Service Association of America, 1957.

REID, WILLIAM J., and ANN W. SHYNE. *Brief and Extended Casework.* New York: Columbia University Press, 1969.

REINER, BEATRICE SIMCOX, and IRVING KAUFMAN. *Character Disorders in Parents of Delinquents.* New York: Family Service Association of America, 1959.

REYNOLDS, ROSEMARY, and ELSE SIEGLE. "A Study of Casework with Sado-Masochistic Marriage Partners." *Social Casework,* 40 (December 1959), 545–551.

RICHMOND, MARY E. *Social Diagnosis.* New York: Russell Sage Foundation, 1917.

———. *What is Social Casework? An Introductory Description.* New York: Russell Sage Foundation, 1922.

RIESSMAN, FRANK, JEROME COHEN, and ARTHUR PEARL, eds. *Mental Health of the Poor.* New York: Free Press, 1964.

RIPPLE, LILLIAN, ERNESTINA ALEXANDER, and BERNICE POLEMIS. *Motivation, Capacity and.Opportunity.* Social Service Monographs. Chicago: University of Chicago Press, 1964.

RITCHIE, A. M. " Multiple Impact Therapy: An Experiment." *Social Work*, 5 (1960), 16–21.

ROBERTS, ROBERT W., and ROBERT H. NEE, eds. *Theories of Social Casework*. Chicago: University of Chicago Press, 1970.

ROBINSON, VIRGINIA P. "An Analysis of Processes in the Records of Family Case Working Agencies." *The Family*, 2 (July 1921), 101–106.

RODMAN, HYMAN. "The Lower-Class Value Stretch." In Louis A. Ferman, ed. *Poverty in America*. Ann Arbor: University of Michigan Press, 1968.

ROHEIM, GEZA. *Psychoanalysis and Anthropology: Culture, Personality and the Unconscious*. New York: International Universities Press, 1950.

ROSENBLATT, AARON. "The Application of Role Concepts to the Intake Process." *Social Casework*, 43 (January 1962), 8–14.

RUBINSTEIN, DAVID, and OSCAR R. WEINER. "Co-therapy Teamwork Relationships in Family Psychotherapy." In Gerald H. Zuk and Ivan Boszormenyi-Nagy, eds. *Family Therapy and Disturbed Families*. Palo Alto, Calif.: Science and Behavior Books, 1967, pp. 206–220.

RUE, ALICE W. "The Casework Approach to Protective Work." *The Family*, 18 (December 1937), 277–282.

RUESCH, JURGEN. *Disturbed Communication, The Clinical Assessment of Normal and Pathological Communicative Behavior*. New York: W. W. Norton & Co., 1957.

SALOMON, ELIZABETH L. "Humanistic Values and Social Casework." *Social Casework*, 48 (January 1967), 26–39.

SATIR, VIRGINIA. *Conjoint Family Therapy*. Palo Alto, Calif.: Science and Behavior Books, 1964.

SAVARD, ROBERT J. "Couple Treatment." Unpublished manuscript, National Institute of Mental Health, Bethesda, Md., March 1971.

SCHERZ, FRANCES H. "Theory and Practice in Family Therapy." In Robert W. Roberts and Robert H. Nee, eds. *Theories of Social Casework*. Chicago: University of Chicago Press, 1970, pp. 219–264.

———. "Treatment of Acting-out Character Disorders in a Marital Problem." In *Casework Papers, 1956*. New York: Family Service Association of America, 1956.

SCHLESINGER, BEN, ed. *The Multiproblem Family*. Toronto: University of Toronto Press, 1963.

SCHORR, ALVIN S. "Editorial Page." *Social Work*, 11 (July 1966), 2.

SCHWARTZ, WILLIAM. "Private Troubles and Public Issues: One Social Work Job or Two?" In National Conference of Social Welfare. *Social Welfare Forum.* New York: Columbia University Press, 1969, pp. 22–43.

Scope and Methods of the Family Service Agency, Report of the Committee on Methods and Scope. New York: Family Service Association of America, 1953.

SEABURY, BRETT A. "The Arrangement of Space in Social Work Settings: A New Perspective in Practice." *Social Work,* 16 (October 1971), 43–49.

SHANNON, BARBARA E. "Implications of White Racism for Social Work Practice." *Social Casework,* 51 (May 1970), 270–276.

SHAPIRO, ROGER L. "The Origin of Adolescent Disturbances in the Family: Some Considerations in Theory and Implications for Therapy." In Gerald H. Zuk and Ivan Boszormenyi-Nagy, eds. *Family Therapy and Disturbed Families.* Palo Alto, Calif.: Science and Behavior Books, 1967, pp. 221–238.

SHATTUCK, GERALD M., and JOHN M. MARTIN. "New Professional Work Roles and Their Integration into a Social Agency Structure." *Social Work,* 14 (July 1969), 13–20.

SHEA, MARGENE M. "Establishing Initial Relationships with Schizophrenic Patients." *Social Casework,* 37 (January 1956), 25–29.

SHERMAN, SANFORD N. "Joint Interviews in Casework Practice." *Social Work,* 4 (April 1959), 20–28.

SIPORIN, MAX. "Social Treatment: A New-Old Helping Method." *Social Work,* 15 (July 1970), 13–25.

SMITH, RUSSELL E. "In Defence of Public Welfare." *Social Work,* 11 (October 1966), 90–97.

SMITH, VEON, and DEAN HEPWORTH. "Marriage Counseling with One Partner: Rationale and Clinical Implications." *Social Casework,* 48 (June 1967), 352–359.

SOBEY, FRANCINE. *The Non-professional Revolution in Mental Health.* New York: Columbia University Press, 1970.

Social Casework, 51 (May 1970). (The entire issue on black experience by black authors.)

Social Casework, Generic and Specific: An Outline. A Report of the Milford Conference, New York: American Association of Social Workers, 1929.

SONNE, JOHN C., and GERALDINE LINCOLN. "Heterosexual Co-therapy Team Experiences During Family Therapy." *Family Process,* 4 (1965), 117–195.

SPECK, ROSS V. "Family Therapy in the Home." In Nathan W.

Ackerman, Frances L. Beatman, and Sanford N. Sherman, eds. *Exploring the Base for Family Therapy.* New York: Family Service Association of America, 1961, pp. 39–46.

———, and Uri Rueveni. "Network Therapy—A Developing Concept." *Family Process,* 8 (1969), 182–191.

Spiegel, John. "Resolution of Role Conflict Within the Family." *Psychiatry,* 20 (1957), 1–6.

———. "The Social Roles of Doctor and Patient in Psychoanalysis and Psychotherapy." *Psychiatry,* 17 (November 1954), 369–376.

———. "Some Cultural Aspects of Transference and Counter-Transference." In Jules H. Masserman, ed. *Individual and Familial Dynamics.* New York: Grune & Stratton, 1959, pp. 160–182.

Spitz, Rene A. "Discussion of Dr. Bowlby's Paper." In Ruth S. Eissler et al., eds. *The Psychoanalytic Study of the Child,* vol. 15. New York: International Universities Press, 1960.

Stamm, Isabel L. "Ego Psychology in the Emerging Theoretical Base of Casework." In Alfred J. Kahn, ed. *Issues in American Social Work.* New York: Columbia University Press, 1959, pp. 80–109.

Steinholz, Howard. "Symptoms of Drug Abuse." Mimeographed. New York: New York State Community Narcotic Education Center (180 Avenue B, New York, N.Y. 10009), n.d.

Studt, Elliot. "An Outline for Study of Social Authority Factors in Casework." *Social Casework,* 35 (June 1954), 231–238.

Sunley, Robert. "Family Advocacy from Case to Cause." *Social Casework,* 51 (June 1970), 347–357.

Taussig, Helen P. "Treatment as an Aid to Diagnosis." *The Family,* 19 (January 1939), 289–294.

Taylor, Alexander B. "Role Perception, Empathy and Marriage Adjustment." *Sociology and Social Research,* 52 (October 1967), 22–34.

Thomas, Edwin J., ed. *Behavioral Science for Social Workers.* New York: Free Press, 1967.

———. "Selected Sociobehavioral Techniques and Principles: An Approach to Interpersonal Helping." *Social Work,* 13 (January 1968), 12–26.

———, ed. *The Sociobehavioral Approach and Application to Social Work.* New York: Council on Social Work Education, 1967.

———, and Bruce J. Biddle. *Role Theory: Concepts and Research.* New York: John Wiley & Sons, 1966.

Thompson, Jane K., and Donald P. Riley. "Use of Professionals in Public Welfare." *Social Work,* 11 (January 1966), 22–27.

Towle, Charlotte. "Factors in Treatment." In *Proceedings of the National Conference of Social Work, 1936.* Chicago: University of Chicago Press, 1936, pp. 179–191.

———. "Social Casework in Modern Society," and "Social Work: Cause and Function." In Helen H. Perlman, ed. *Helping: Charlotte Towle on Social Work and Social Casework.* Chicago: University of Chicago Press, 1969.

Travis, Georgia, and Del M. Neely. "Grappling with the Concept of Self-Determination." *Social Casework,* 48 (October 1967), 503–508.

Turner, Francis J. "A Comparison of Procedures in the Treatment of Clients with Two Different Value Orientations." *Social Casework,* 45 (May 1964), 273–277.

———, ed. *Differential Diagnosis and Treatment in Social Work.* New York: Free Press, 1968.

———. "Ethnic Difference and Client Performance." *Social Service Review,* 44 (March 1970), 1–10.

———. "Social Work Treatment and Value Differences." Doctoral dissertation, Columbia University School of Social Work, New York, 1963.

Varley, Barbara K. "The Use of Role Theory in the Treatment of Disturbed Adolescents." *Social Casework,* 49 (June 1968), 362–366.

Vesper, Sue. "Casework Aimed at Supporting Marital Role Reversal." *Social Casework,* 43 (June 1962), 303–307.

———, and Frankie W. Spearman. "Treatment of Marital Conflict Resulting from Severe Personality Disturbance." *Social Casework,* 47 (November 1966), 583–589.

Walzer, Hank. "Casework Treatment of the Depressed Parent." *Social Casework,* 42 (December 1961), 505–512.

Wasser, Edna. "Family Casework Focus on the Older Person." *Social Casework,* 47 (July 1966), 423–431.

Wasserman, Harry A. "The Moral Posture of the Social Worker in a Public Agency." *Public Welfare,* 25 (1967), 38–44.

Watson, Andrew. "Reality Testing and Transference in Psychotherapy." *Smith College Studies in Social Work,* 36 (June 1966), 191–209.

Watzlawick, Paul. "A Review of the Double Bind Theory." *Family Process,* 2 (1963), 132–153. Reprinted in Don D. Jackson, ed. *Communication, Family and Marriage: Human Communication,* vol. 1. Palo Alto, Calif.: Science and Behavior Books, 1968, pp. 63–86.

WEISBERG, MIRIAM T. "Early Treatment of Infidelity in the Neurotic Man." *Social Casework*, 51 (June 1970), 358–367.

WEISBERGER, ELEANOR B. "The Current Usefulness of Psychoanalytic Theory to Casework." *Smith College Studies in Social Work*, 37 (February 1967), 106–118.

WEISMAN, IRVING. "Offender Status, Role Behavior, and Treatment Considerations." *Social Casework*, 48 (July 1967), 422–425.

WEISS, VIOLA W. "Multiple-Client Interviewing: An Aid to Diagnosis." *Social Casework*, 43 (March 1962), 111–114.

WERBLE, BEATRICE. "The Implications of Role Theory for Casework Research." In L. Kogan, ed. *Social Science Theory and Social Work Research*. New York: National Association of Social Workers, 1960.

———, CHARLOTTE S. HENRY, and MARGARET W. MILLAR. "Motivation for Using Casework Services." *Social Casework*, 39 (February–March 1958), 124–137.

WHITE, ROBERT W. *Ego and Reality in Psychoanalytic Theory*. New York: International Universities Press, 1963.

WHITING, BEATRICE B., ed. *Six Cultures: Studies in Child Rearing*. New York: John Wiley & Sons, 1963.

WILSNACK, WILLIAM H. "Handling Resistance in Social Casework." *American Journal of Orthopsychiatry*, 16 (April 1946), 297–311.

WYMAN, MARIAN. "What is Basic in Case Work Practice?" In *Proceedings of the National Conference of Social Work, 1938*. Chicago: University of Chicago Press, 1939, pp. 179–191.

WYNNE, LYMAN C. "Some Indications and Contra-Indications for Exploratory Family Therapy." In Ivan Boszormenyi-Nagy and James L. Framo, eds. *Intensive Family Therapy*. New York: Harper & Row, 1965, pp. 289–322.

———, IRVING M. RYCKOFF, JULIANA DAY, and STANLEY I. HIRSCH. "Pseudomutuality in the Family Relationships of Schizophrenics." *Psychiatry*, 21 (1958), 205–220. Reprinted in Norman W. Bell and Ezra F. Vogel, eds. *A Modern Introduction to the Family*, rev. ed. New York: Free Press, 1968, pp. 628–649.

YOUNG, MARY LOUISE. "Marital Counseling with Affection-Deprived Spouses." *Social Casework*, 47 (November 1966), 571–574.

YOUNGHUSBAND, EILEEN. "Intercultural Aspects of Social Work." *Journal of Education for Social Work*, 2 (Spring 1966), 59–65.

ZANGER, ALLYN. "A Study of Factors Related to Clinical Empathy." *Smith College Studies in Social Work*, 38 (February 1968), 116–131.

ZBOROWSKI, MARK. "Cultural Components in Response to Pain." *Journal of Social Issues*, 8 (1952), 16–30.

ZIMMERMAN, CARLE C., and LUCIUS F. CERVANTES. *Successful American Families*. New York: Pageant Press, 1960.

ZUK, GERALD H., and DAVID RUBINSTEIN. "A Review of Concepts in the Study and Treatment of Families of Schizophrenics." In Ivan Boszormenyi-Nagy and James L. Framo, eds. *Intensive Family Therapy*. New York: Harper & Row, 1965, pp. 1–25.

Index

Family treatment (*continued*)
combining with other treatment forms, 215–216
diagnostic assessment, 207, 209
in exploratory period, 209–212, 217
goals in, 207–208, 212–217
problems frequently dealt with, 214–216
time factor, 213–215
two therapists in, 221–222
variations in approach, 203
variations in theory, 206–208
psychodynamic theory, 207
systems theory, 206–209
Father figure. *See* Parent figure
Father-son relationship. *See* Relationship
Fillmore case, 342–348
Foster care, 26–27, 82, 143–144
Free association, nature of, 196–197
not used in casework, 192
and unconscious material, 189–192, 351
Freud, Anna, 17, 347, 351
Freud, Sigmund, 13, 17, 29, 188
Freudian theory, analysts trained in, 198
contribution to casework, 17–19
on derivatives from the unconscious, 54, 188–193
on ego-adaptive patterns; *see* Defense mechanisms
oedipal factors; *see* Oedipal conflict
Fuller case, 52–56

Garrett, Annette, 74, 241
Goals. *See* Treatment objectives
Graham case, 65
Group treatment, 7
See also Family treatment
Guilt, allaying or reducing, 79, 104, 117–118, 315–321
in character-disorder case, 336–342
in compulsive personality, 317–318
as key factor in choice of treatment, 315–321
sense of, 89–92, 343
about sex, 43, 90
unconscious feeling of, 56, 186
worker's attitude toward, 104
See also Anxiety

Hamilton, Gordon, 6, 59
Hard-to-reach clients, 22, 94, 121–123, 258
Hartmann, Heinz, 18, 190
Health, 79, 92, 110, 114, 254–255, 261, 263, 331, 336–343
Hidden material, 116–117, 134–135, 188, 191–192
Hope, 292
Hollis, Florence, 60, 106
Home visit, its importance in diagnosis, 257, 267
as sustaining technique, 94
Horney, Karen, 198
Hostility, development of, 18, 20, 23
dynamic understanding of, 104, 116–117, 129, 135
impulsive, illustration of, 336–342
infantile, 186–187
as a realistic response, 91, 230–231
reducing, 28, 31, 34, 46–47, 135

Identification, 13, 51, 240, 334
Impulsive hostility, case illustration of, 336–341
developing understanding in, 130, 339
Indirect treatment. *See* Environmental treatment
Infantile thought processes, distortions of, 20–21, 29, 31, 132, 186, 192
See also Primary thought process; Preconscious; Unconscious
Influence, direct. *See* Direct influence
Ingersoll case, 66
Insight development, 59–62, 109, 193–197
Instincts, in Freudian theory, 18
See also Drives
Interaction, in casework theory, 19
between client and worker, 119–122, 228, 242
between environment and individual, 10, 17–23, 114, 270–271
between family members, 18–19, 44–47, 110–115, 117–118, 258, 295–296
in Freudian theory, 17–19
See also Relationship
Interpersonal adjustment, and casework treatment, 9–13

About the Author

Florence Hollis is Professor of Social Work at the Columbia University School of Social Work. A graduate of Wellesley College, she holds the M.S.S. from the Smith College School for Social Work, the Ph.D. from Bryn Mawr, and the honorary Doctor of Humane Letters from Smith College. She has been a caseworker and later district director in family agencies in Philadelphia and Cleveland, has taught at the School of Applied Social Sciences of Western Reserve University, and given courses at the Smith College School. For a number of years she directed publications at the Family Service Association of America and was editor of *Social Casework*. In addition to many institutes and seminars in this country and Canada, she has given papers and led institutes on social casework held under the auspices of the United Nations and other organizations in England and on the Continent. Her other publications include two books, *Social Casework in Practice: Six Case Studies* and *Women in Marital Conflict*, several monographs, and numerous articles and reviews. Her books and articles are widely read by social work practitioners in England and in other countries (including France, Japan, the Netherlands, Switzerland, and West Germany), where they are available in translation.

In recent years Professor Hollis has developed a typology of casework communications currently in use in both teaching and research. She also has a special interest in the development of the psychosocial approach to casework as an open system of practice theory capable of assimilating or adapting to emerging concepts and findings as these demonstrate their viability and potential value.

About the Author

Florence Hollis is Professor of Social Work at the Columbia University School of Social Work. A graduate of Wellesley College, she holds the M.S.S. from the Smith College School for Social Work, the Ph.D. from Bryn Mawr, and the honorary Doctor of Humane Letters from Smith College. She has been a caseworker and later district director in family agencies in Philadelphia and Cleveland, has taught at the School of Applied Social Sciences of Western Reserve University, and given courses at the Smith College School. For a number of years she directed publications at the Family Service Association of America and was editor of *Social Casework*. In addition to many institutes and seminars in this country and Canada, she has given papers and led institutes on social casework held under the auspices of the United Nations and other organizations in England and on the Continent. Her other publications include two books, *Social Casework in Practice: Six Case Studies* and *Women in Marital Conflict*, several monographs, and numerous articles and reviews. Her books and articles are widely read by social work practitioners in England and in other countries (including France, Japan, the Netherlands, Switzerland, and West Germany), where they are available in translation.

In recent years Professor Hollis has developed a typology of casework communications currently in use in both teaching and research. She also has a special interest in the development of the psychosocial approach to casework as an open system of practice theory capable of assimilating or adapting to emerging concepts and findings as these demonstrate their viability and potential value.